UNANSWERED
LETTERS

P. ARDEN CORBIN

Unanswered Letters
Copyright 2014 by Philip Arden Corbin

Back Cover Author Photo by LifeTouch
Cover Design by Gordon A Kessler

ISBN-13: 978-1499707632
ISBN-10: 1499707630

Also available in eBook

DEDICATED TO

THE READERS OF THIS BOOK. WHO WILL
LEARN WHAT THEY DID WRONG IN THEIR
OWN LIVES.

FORWARD

For the reader of this book, let me suppose that you were confronted with the same situations the main character of this book initially was confronted with. What would you do? Would you continue to fight against any member of your immediate family, or would you run away from home, where you would most likely have to fight even harder to just remain alive?

Would you say So long to your first, second and fourth wives, or would you do as the main character did, which was to continually forgive all of her transgressions. No matter how long it may take.

Would you go out into this world with the tenacity that this main character has done, or would you give it all up and move to some foreign country where life could be much easier to live.

And when after almost thirteen years of very unhappy marriage to a psychologically warped minded woman, this character finally did find a woman whom he had met some twenty years before, of whom he had actually fallen in love with, but did not tell her at that time, but now since they have found each other once again. What would you do in this case?

Would you Divorce your present wife, who is in a Coma in a Hospital? Will this make this character any less of a good person? What a decision he had to make.

It is easy to see that the main character of this Book really did live what has been written about him in this book, but what a life he had to lead, with all of it's disappointments and unforgiving persons, but also with some persons who are forgiving and even giving out encouragements so as to inspire the character to do even better.

But the one thing that hit me in the very beginning of this book is, the tenacity of this character who kept Journals all of his life, from the early age of 3 years of age until this book was finished and still even beyond that time.

When anyone writes a Journal, most often it is the absolute truth about that record of their life, which is something only most persons acquire when they reach a more advanced age.

I am amazed at how this writer has continued to explain with much detail a lot of the many things this character did during his life

So the likelihood of these events of actually taking place and doing what he has written about as actually happening, I think must have happened, because only someone who has lived this kind of life, could actually write about it with such Anger and Love and Tenacity, and Kindness, that such emotions could cause this person to know what and how any person feels deep down in their hearts.

If any person does not read this book, you are missing one of the best-written Novels I have read in a very long time. And seeing where this writer went with all of his stories, was an education unto itself.

Please do not miss reading this book, because it will transform your world into a better world for the reader and your life, and will cause you to stop and think when you are confronted with similar situations in your own lives.

John RB Corbin

Adopted Son of P. Arden Corbin

PART ZERO

PREFACE

The letters in Part One are from a young man, written to his Parents, of which they never answer.

You see when he was two months old, it was stated by the family Doctor, that Clement might have the dreaded Polio Disease. And when he was six months old, it was confirmed that he did have Polio.

Polio is not a disease whereof it can cause anyone to die, but it can cause anyone with a bad case of it, to become crippled, where that person might have to wear leg braces for the rest of their lives, and may also have to use crutches, until they become adults.

Because there is no medicines to fight this disease. And because the Royal family had other children, whereof some of them were old enough to know and understand the disease that Clement has, and after considerable discussion by his Parents, decided that Clement would be taken to the Mayo Hospital in Rochester, Minnesota, where he would be taken care of by Catholic Nuns, who worked in that Hospital.

The Royal family are poor dirt farmers, and this is during the Dust Bowl years during the Great Depression (The 1930's). A club that was located in the County Seat of this part of South Dakota, agreed to pay for a Train Ticket for Clements Mother, so she could take him to Rochester, Minnesota.

Once Clement is settled into the Mayo Clinic Hospital, then

his Mother returns back to the farm in South Dakota. In the beginning when Clement first arrived at the Mayo Hospital, he cried so very much, but when a Nurse comes into where he is located, he becomes quiet and seems to be fairly happy. But who is to know, because he is only a little over six months old at this time.

Clement actually became better with this dreaded disease. And over time he actually learned to walk, even though he was wearing Leg Braces on both of his legs, and he also had to use Crutches while he walked all around this Hospital.

There are other children in this Hospital and Clement got to know all of them. Then after being in this hospital for 2 ½ years, Clement contracted another disease, which is called Scarlet Fever, because his physical being had been so weakened, that his immune system was almost nonexistent.

But again Clement fought with all of whatever is in him to ward off this new disease. And remember he still has Polio, so this is a very difficult period for him.

All of the Hospital Staff always wore protective clothing and gloves and always covered their faces when they came in physical contact with Clement and all of the other children in this Hospital. And again Clement continued to improve in health. Even though he had to fight two different diseases at the same time. I would say that this young man has some additional help from a Higher Authority (GOD).

And something else is discovered about Clement around this time. Which is that he can talk to other Creatures. The Nun who personally took care of Clement noticed that when Clement is allowed to go outside on warm winter days, that he would go and sit on the edge of a Fish Pond, and talk to every creature that came close to him, and they even sat on his lap and shoulders and head and would even bring him various kinds of Nuts, that Clement would eat after they had been broken open by a Squirrel. And Birds came and sat on his shoulders and would sing to him and all of the other creatures.

And then one day an Orange Cat came to where he is sitting, and all of the wild creatures ran or flew away, but because this Cat apparently told Clement that she would not hurt any of them, they then returned to him and they just all sat and talked to each other.

It was at this time that Clement really began to get better much faster than at any other time from all of the Drugs he was being given.

It's interesting how much any physical contact with other creatures can have on helping to cause a human person to get better and even get completely well, after struggling with various diseases.

Because after spending almost five years at the Mayo Hospital, Clement has gotten well enough, so he could be sent back to his real Parents.

Of course Clement did not know what it was like having real parents, because they never came to visit him for all of the time he has been in this place.

So after considerable discussion among the Doctors, it was decided that Sister Maryann would accompany Clement back to his real Parents home in South Dakota.

And Sister Maryann had also decided to take a year off, because she told the Staff at this Hospital that she was burned out, and she needed some time to think about the rest of her future with them.

That maybe she would spend some additional time in a Convent, Praying for all of the children in this Hospital and for Clement especially, because he now has a very difficult time to go through with his real Parents, because they have not even come to see him, so they probably have completely erased him from their memories, and they probably will not even consider him to be their real child any longer.

And for a child to have to confront this kind of situation will be very difficult for him. And if they totally reject him, then he should probably be put up for adoption. So he can have a happier life with Parents who will really Love him and care for him.

But because he still has braces on both of his legs, most potential parents would not likely adopt him, so he would probably have to spend several years in an Orphanage, where he would either become aggressive and possibly mean or if he decided to take up a vocation in Religion or even possibly Veterinary Medicine or, he may even become a Priest or a Minister.

You see, sometimes it is very hard for even real Parents to accept their own child who has something wrong with them. Meaning if that child has what Clement has had, they will think that he is not their child any longer and will actually reject him.

Now can Clement withstand something like this, only time will tell that story? Sister Maryann says it will affect Clement for the rest of his life.

Clement is a very smart child, and if the rest of his so called family are just regular normal children, then again he will not fit into this family, because none of the other children of this family are as bright as he is.

Sister Maryann says that when it is time for Clement to start School, he should be put in at least the third grade, because he is that intelligent.

There will come a time when Clement will be advanced much further ahead of where other children his same age are, because of his intelligence.

Clement has a need to learn as much as he can, at a rate that is much faster than any normal child is capable of doing, so he should be allowed to advance at whatever rate that he can.

But if he remains with his real parents, that most probably will never happen. She says she will know more after she spends some time with them and Clement in his home in South Dakota.

PART ONE

June 30th, 1939

Dear Mom and Dad,

When I got to when I could print, I asked Sister Maryann, did my real parents ever come to visit me while I was in this Hospital, and she told me that you never came to see me? I further asked, why did they not do that, and she says she cannot answer that question either.

So because I am writing to you now, can you answer that question? Why did you never come to see me? I will attempt to answer that question for you. Of course I am only almost six years of age now, but I will try anyway.

So now I have finally been returned back to you, and you still treat me like I still do not exist in this family. How can you not have some feelings for me, since I was created in this family around the time the Stock market crashed?

And since I also have older brothers and sisters, they also do not apparently have any feelings for me either. Will I really be able to survive on this farm?

But as Sister Maryann has always told me, I AM A SURVIVOR. And GOD has always protected me from all kinds of sicknesses, and will always protect me from further ills.

And I still do have the sickness that I initially had when I left this farm, which is Polio. Do you all think that I can somehow now pass this sickness on to all of you? What little faith you must have!!

Using a pencil and some blank paper that Sister Maryann gave me, she has encouraged me to write this letter to you. She says she will give it to you, and because I trust her, I believe she will do just as she has told me she will do.

When we arrived at this Farm, Sister Maryann tells me that you two adults are actually my Father and Mother; it was kind of a surprise for me. Even though I have been told for as long as I can remember, that I did have a Mother and a Father, but still actually meeting you does not change my thinking about the two of you, because the only adult that I felt any kind of affection for is Sister Maryann.

And I also have Brothers and Sisters too. The only brothers and sisters I ever knew were all of the other children at the Mayo Hospital. But because I walk using Crutches and Leg Braces, all of my so called brothers and sisters treat me like I am some kind of Bug.

And you two never think of me as your natural child either. Is my condition so bad that I have to be treated like I am not here? And I cannot sleep with any of my other Brothers, because you have relegated me to sleep out in the hall, near a door that I fear that there is some kind of Monster behind it. And I have Nightmares whenever I sleep on that Cot, just outside of that door.

And whenever you decided to take all of the other children on an outing, I am always left at home, to fend for myself, and you only remember me when it is time for all of you to return back home and then someone says, where is Clement.

I would suppose that because Sister Maryann is still staying at the farm, could have been the reason that you left me at home, but I think your real reason is that I am still not considered to be a member of this family. And you all still feel embarrassed around Sister Maryann, because she is a Catholic Nun, and you are not even all that religious.

But do you really look for me at any other time? I don't think you really do. I feel like I am not a member of this family, and I never will be considered to be related to any of you by you or your other children.

So because I do not feel any kind of affection from any of you, I just go off by myself and make friends with all of the other creatures that I encounter.

And all of you think and really believe there is something else wrong with me. That there might be something wrong with me in my head?

And I hear the two of you talking during the late night hours, as to whether you should send me away to a place called a Sanatorium.

I asked Sister Maryann what kind of place that is and she tells me it is a place where they send Crazy persons. But I tell her that I am not Crazy, but am just a Crippled child, and then I cry while being close to her, because I know I cannot go to either one of you for my loneliness and grief.

And I worry that I will be sent away once again, like my parents are again treating me like a Bug. What am I to do?

Sister Maryann says that she will stay a while longer, until I feel better about myself. And she will try to get you to sign an agreement, guaranteeing that I will never be sent away to a Sanatorium.

So I wipe my tears away and go outside and play by myself, and go and talk to the sheep and all of the wild ducks and other creatures that I meet when I am down by the water in the Sloughs, where I actually take off my leg braces and I crawl out into the water and I exercise my legs, and I even rub mud all over my legs and let it dry for a few hours, as I lay on the ground and watch all of the Clouds in the sky, and I imagine that some of the clouds that I see are in reality my real parents, and when I finally go back into the water, where I wash off all of this dried Mud, and my legs feel better somehow.

I try walking without the braces and I am getting better at doing that also, and I know that one day I will not have to wear these braces any longer.

While I am out in the water exercising my legs, I have also learned how to swim, because one day when I was in the water and I tried to touch the bottom of this Slough, but it was not where I expected it to be, I almost panicked, but I then realized that I had actually swam out so far that I was now in deeper water, so I just swam back towards shore, until I figured I could touch the bottom and I did, so I did learn a lot that day.

After that I began to mentally mark the shore line where I could no longer touch the bottom of this Slough, and I knew that knowledge would come in handy for me one day, when I would be swimming with any of my so called brothers and sisters, and since I had no intention of ever telling any of them that I could really swim, they would be greatly surprised when they discovered that I can actually swim, and swim very good.

Because when I first began to swim, and because I could not use my legs, I instead used my wrists, moving them like a fish would use its fins, and I discovered that I can swim real fast whether I was near the surface of the water or under the water. That too will surprise my so-called brothers and sisters.

When I go back to the house I am again wearing those leg braces and am also using my crutches, but one day those too will disappear. Never to be used again.

Clement

August 31st 1939

To my Parents;

It is now the end of this summer and I have completely quit using my Crutches, only you do not yet know that I do not use them anymore. And I am getting real close to not using my leg braces either. Because I have been doing all of my exercises secretly, in a week I will come back to the house carrying everything, and I will tell you that I do not intend to use them ever again. What can you do?

Back in late June when Sister Maryann left this farm and went to live with her younger Sister in Rapid City, who was the only adult person I have ever known and Loved, with the exception of some of the Staff members at the Mayo Clinic that I was very close to also.

I told her what kind of progress I have made regarding my non-use of my leg braces and crutches and she says when I am ready to tell my parents, just walk up to them carrying all of these devices and tell them that you will not be needing them ever again, and put them in the storage place above the Kitchen.

And

Open the door that you are deathly afraid of, and just throw everything in there and then close it, and tell your parents that there is no Boogey Man in that area, because you finally got enough courage to open that door, and this is where you put your leg braces and your crutches. That if they think I need them, then they will have to go and get them. Sister Maryann says she thinks they will not go and get them.

Anyway I cried a lot when my so-called Father took Sister Maryann to Bradley, where she caught the train that would take her to Rapid City, South Dakota.

I also knew at that time that I would never see her again. She told me she would write me letters every so often, but I never got them.

As I got older, I figured that my so-called parents had received them, but they never gave them to me. I wrote her a lot of letters also, and I actually mailed them myself, by meeting the mail carrier at our mailbox, but since I never received any letters from her, I don't know if she ever got them. Yes, I put the proper postage on my letters, which is 2 cents.

It is my understanding that when any letter is ever mailed with the proper postage on it that it would go to whomever it is addressed to. I was not told anything different at that time that this was not true.

Anyway on this day when I came home, I was carrying my leg braces and crutches and no one was home when I got back to the house.

Where everyone had gone, I never did find out. By evening you all came home, because by that time, my so called father had bought a Car, which made it easier for him to take everyone, other than myself wherever they wanted to go.

I actually took my leg braces and crutches off of my legs and I did open that door to the area above the Kitchen and I threw them in there and then I closed that door, and when I went to sleep that night, I did not have any bad dreams. I am not saying that I didn't have bad dreams after that time, but on this day I did not.

Anyway, I just walked into the house without my leg braces on and not using the crutches, and no one seemed to notice that I was even there. I was invisible to all of you. Like I never existed in this family, EVER.

One of you came and sat on the day bed where I was sitting like I was not even there, and when I complained, you did have to sit somewhere else, but you still did not acknowledge that I was even there.

Because you did not say anything to me, but you talked to someone else that was sitting in the Rocking chair across the room. How can you all ignore a known person that is supposed to be part of that family? I will never understand.

Clement

September 6th 1939

Father;

Today you took me to the local Town, where you enrolled me into the first grade. Even though my first grade teacher told you that I had the intelligence of at least a third grade student.

She said she would take it to the School Board, for them to make that decision. And apparently the next meeting was two days later, but due to the fact that you were allowed to vote, you voted me down, meaning that I had to remain in the 1st grade for this first year in school.

But my primary teacher taught me a lot about music, because she told me that I have perfect pitch, when establishing myself as a musician.

And because I read every book that was in that classroom, and even more, because my primary grade teacher went and got me books that were being read by the 6th grade students, and I even totally understood all of those books too.

I knew that in a few years, things would be different. Especially after you were no longer on the School Board.

You are a very stubborn man, and not a very good parent, because you only recognized me as a member of your family because one day, the postmaster in the post office asked you who I was, because I kept tagging along behind you, so you had to recognize me, finally.

Then I told my story to this other man, and he says that I should be written up in the County Newspaper. You whisked me out of that Post Office so fast that I almost fell down on the sidewalk outside, because you pushed me so hard.

But I never appeared in that County Newspaper ever. But now I could not be ignored any longer either. And then you tagged me with the name of Clumsy, which I hated, and I suppose I began to actually hate you also. The reason for this name was because I would fall down occasionally.

Clement

August 25th 1944

Mom,

This has been a hellish summer. Oh I liked going out and farming with brother Myron, mostly because he recognizes me as actually being his real brother, but when sister Paige came out to the farm and said she would keep house for us, I was not certain that I liked that idea.

Because I had heard some persons say that she and my so-called father were doing something that they should not be doing together.

Now for all of these years that I have been writing letters to you and others, and you and others have never answered any of them, makes me wonder what kind of a family this really is.

And then a week after Paige came to the farm, she cornered me one afternoon upstairs by placing a nylon stocking around my neck, and choking me until I could not breathe very well, and then she actually tied me to her bed and she raped me. I had never even thought about sex of any kind, but on that day, I learned what she knew about SEX. It was as if she could not get enough of me. I was forced to do things to her, that I never dreamed possible. Did I enjoy any of this sex, I DID NOT!!!!!

When she finally let me loose, after she had had her way with me for over two hours, it was getting close to when Brother

Myron would be coming home from working in the fields.

And it was time for me to get the Milk cows to come to the barn, and because I had a special way that I called them, and they always came when I called, I hoped that what happened between Paige and me, would never happen again. But I was wrong.

Because for the rest of that Summer, she would catch me unawares every time, and she would always tie me up, using some of her silk stockings or some Rope, and sometimes when I was Herding Sheep or some of the Cattle, and she would come out to where I was; bringing something to eat, and when I was eating that meal, she would attack me and overpower me and then HER FUN would start all over again.

She told me that she knew that I wrote letters to Mom and Dad, because she says she had actually read some of them, and she said that if I wrote any letters to them or to anyone else, about her and I, that she would "GET ME", and do so much harm to me that I would never be able to have sex with another female ever again.

She always threatened me with a knife at those times, and in fact cut my penis on one side from where my testicles are located to where it ended at the head. It bled like the dickens and she just laughed and let it bleed. It finally stopped though, and I wrapped my shorts around my penis so it would not bleed any more. It was three weeks until she attacked me again. She told me that she had to wait for my Penis to heal.

Actually I went down to the slough and put mud on it so it would not get infected, and if any infection had begun, an Indian had told me that this would stop any infection and would actually draw the infection out of any wound. And it did work, because my Penis did heal, and real fast.

When I was asked about that scar, I told that person that I scratched it while jumping a fence, trying to get away from a Black Angus Bull owned by another farmer. Since some of my so-called brothers had done the same thing, they did not question me any further about it.

Clement

September 10th

Mom,

Now school has begun again and apparently you have gotten my letter, because Paige is no longer living at home or is on the Farm with Myron. Wherever you have sent her, is of no interest to me, just as long as she does not come in direct contact with me ever again. I absolutely HATE her. She is an EVIL person and has been taken over by the DEVIL.

So wherever you have sent her, I would warn anyone that she may be taking care of; that she will strike again, and this time I hope she is sent much farther away from here. I have noticed that she is not in school either.

I was then sent to Ortonville, Minnesota to live with a man who says he will treat me as his Adopted Son. He says he has Documents to prove this. I did not know what kind of a deal that my so-called father had made with this man, but I knew that my life would be forever changed.

Clement

June 30th almost two years later in 1947

Mom,

When I eventually returned back to South Dakota after living with my surrogate father in Ortonville, Minnesota for two years, that brother Myron was still farming on the old homestead where most of us were all born.

I had discovered that sister Paige had gotten caught again molesting a couple of young boys that were about my age, and she was now living in California somewhere, most likely in Los Angeles with one of her older sisters.

And this year I had decided that I would get on a horse and following those wagon tracks that went across the land that Myron and I were farming, and try to find out where they would lead.

The horse I was going to ride is named Kernel, of which is a horse that one of Father's brothers brought back from Castroville, California, because even though he had been John Wayne's horse in most of the Movies he had been in up to that time, Kernel had actually gotten hurt and that is why he was brought back to South Dakota, where he would spend the rest of his life with the Royal family.

Actually I had planned this trip for many months. I was much older now, even though I was only 13 years old, but I was old for my age, because I felt like I was closer to being 18 or even older, because I looked it. Meaning I was over six feet tall and I was as strong as a grown man.

When I returned back to the farm, Myron was the only member of this family who treated me like I was an actual member of this family.

When it came time for me to go to school, instead of allowing me to advance into the Senior Class, instead I was only to become a Sophomore, even though I had Catholic School Credits from the school I had been going to with me, but you and my so called father rejected them and they told the School Board that I would be put in the class that was appropriate to my actual age.

Actually the Public School System would not recognize any School Credits from a Catholic School. So again I was completely stuck, within a System that was 50 years behind the times. What a let down, because I was totally bored while in school and I did not do well because of that. I could not even confer with any of the teachers either.

But I did go to see one of my earlier teachers who now lived on her farm, and she says because she is now retired, that she could not do anything for me, and she is no longer a member of the School Board. She says to go see the man who is the Superintendent at this time, and see what he says.

So I did that, but he too could not do anything to change my situation, because he says that the Public School System will not recognize Credits from a Catholic School. So I was stuck again.

For the first time in my life, I became very sad…so I went to school and got average grades, because if I tried to excel, the other students chastised me. And even some of the Teachers.

I am not saying that there were other students that are not smart like I am, and in certain subjects I did excel. In fact when there was a Spelling Bee, I took First Place over the smartest student in my class.

And when I ended up going to the State Spelling Bee in Brookings, she took first place and I got second place. She told me that I was much smarter than she would ever be. On the other hand, her father was very wise and smart and she loved him very much, and I told this other student that I actually hated my so-called father. She says it shows.

This will be my final letter to you or to my father. Because I cannot confide in either of you, for fear that you will hold everything I say against me. You both have been lousy parents.

Other members of your family actually worship your husband, and I wonder why. I have my private thoughts though, but I will not venture them here at this time. Have a good life, if that is possible with him.

When I return from my trip to the Pacific Ocean, I will be living with him and you in the house in Town, and I hope I have no additional problems with you or him.

No I will most likely only call your husband by some other name. I have never bonded with either of you nor with any of my siblings, so for me to be close to anyone of you is almost impossible.

Maybe one day I can be close to one of my sisters, because when she came along, she became Daddy's most favorite girl.

Most of the older members of this family may not have really noticed, but I did, because whenever I was given a lamb to take care of, when it came time to sell the wool from that grown sheep, who got the money from it, you guessed it, dear little sister.

Or when I would take care of a calf and when it was sold, who got the money from it, again dear little sister. Now whether I can actually form any kind of affection for my little sister, is uncertain at this time.

This is the most disjointed family I know of, and we are definitely not close, and most probably never will be. I hope you keep these letters.

Clement

PART TWO

A little prehistory

This is a group of letters written to my first wife Margaret, who I met on a Wednesday, and married her on a Saturday of the same week, by a Judge in Ortonville, Minnesota. We really did not have much of a chance to get to really know each other.

And after we had gotten married, she became a totally different person. Oh, I knew I was in Love with Margaret, and she had told me she was In Love with me, but I wonder did we really Love each other?

I think this goes back to when a different young lady about a year and a half ago, jilted me before this time, and I vowed that I would never get engaged ever again. And after talking to Margaret, a similar thing had happened to her, so we kind of thought in the same way, so we just decided to go and get married, and not be engaged ever. Which is what we did.

Anyway after we had gotten married by a Judge, we ultimately went to Watertown, South Dakota where we spent the next three days, as a short Honeymoon. We had a wonderful time and I introduced my new wife to an Aunt and some other persons, and we got some Presents and quite a bit of Cash. That was not intended to happen, but once my Aunt knew we were newly married, whatever happened, just happened.

And then after we ultimately returned back to the town near where I was born in South Dakota where my folks lived, and different things happened there also, like a Dance on our behalf, where all of the persons who lived in and around this small town came, and brought presents and more Cash.

And while dancing I actually ran into a chair and broke my nose. Because I was beginning to fall down, and this chair stopped me, and someone was sitting in this chair, because it did not move.

It was suggested to the person who was sitting in this chair at that time, on the next day, that we had had some words about my wife and he hauled off and hit me in my nose. Of course this story was just a fabrication of the truth. But we all had a good laugh anyway. We all were pretty drunk at that celebration.

It was after that time, that Margaret began to change a bit. She was not as Loving as she had been previously, and she wanted to go to some other location, other than where we were still living, but I could not because I was teaching school in that town, and I had to find a replacement for myself before I could go anywhere. And that would take some time. Because who would want to come to Northeastern South Dakota to teach High School subjects, where in the winter time, it could get as cold as 20 to 30 degrees below zero. It would take a very adventurous person. Probably a new Teacher who had never taught in any school before.

Actually that was the kind of person I was really looking for, so my search would take some time to locate that person. I ultimately did find such a person, but he could not get to this small town until October 24th of this year, And then I had to get him up to date with all of my classes and all of the other teachers and especially the Superintendent of the school, who actually lived at my parents house, and of which this person that was replacing myself, would also live in my parents house, because it was only about a block from the school.

He did not have to drive anywhere. He would eat two of his meals at my parent's house and my mother would make him a bag lunch, if that were what he wanted to do.

Anyway we finally left this small town on October 29th and drove to St Louis, Missouri, where I would go to work for Margaret's Father, because he was the Manager of a couple of departments with the Wabash Railroad Company.

From this time forward, I will call Margaret, Peggy, because that is the name that was given to her when she was very young. And because Peggy began to not talk with me about much of anything that I felt was important, I instead began writing letters to her, hoping that she would respond either with a letter back to me, or by talking to me. But that never happened in either case. And this is the story about all of those many letters that she never answered.

This is the end of the prehistory of Clement Royal and his new wife and of their marriage.

PART TWO

October 10, 1955

Dearest Peggy;

The first thing I discovered after marrying you was that you do not tell me how you now feel about me. We talk, but actually do not say much of anything regarding how we feel about each other. Oh – I tell you what and how I feel, but you don't tell me what and how you feel about me. And it never occurred to me that this would be the way you would be, after we had gotten married.

Because I really don't know whether you still love me, or are just occupying the space of where a wife should be in anyone's married life.

The other thing that I initially discovered about you was that even though you told me that you had washed your own clothes, I assumed that you would know how to wash my clothes as well. And after we were married, I then discover that you only hand washed your underwear and silk stockings, but to actually use a washing machine, now that was something different.

Also I discovered that the washing machine that your Mother apparently has is an automatic washing machine, but certainly not the kind that my Mother has, of which is an old fashioned Ringer Washing machine.

And when we announced that we were married, then my Mother, I think out of spite or jealousy, or both, says to you; that now that you have married my Son, you can now wash all of his clothes, and you looked like you were going to go into shock, of which I believe you really did, at least for a while.

And when she asked you to do what she always does when she washes clothes, you again looked like you were going to go into some kind of shock.

So since I knew what to actually do, my mother tells me to show you what to do. Another serious shock. And then to see you doing my washing and your own as well, and then another serious shock; when your own Mother and your sister show up at the house while you were in the middle of doing all of this; WOW ... And the look on your face was something that I will never forget, ever for as long as I live.

And when you had to take all of the clothes that you washed and rinsed and then take them outside and hang all of them on a clothesline, especially since the wind was blowing quite well, of which is the perfect day to do any laundry. Especially when the Sun is shining also.

I don't know whether you ever forgave my Mother, to have you do this. I don't believe you ever forgave me either.

I love you anyway

Clement

October 20, 1955

My Dearest Peggy;

Well we have been married for a total of twenty days now, and you still have not tried to talk to me, nor have you answered my first letter to you. I fear that this may continue for a very long time, meaning for me to write letters to you, with no answers back to me from you. What a waste.

I have noticed that you do not spend much time in my parents home, but take your automobile and go somewhere while I am teaching school and also while I am trying to find someone to replace me, by me calling many Colleges around this Country.

It would be very helpful if you would help me in this endeavor, but I fear that you are not interested in being my temporary Secretary. I feel I have been cheated already.

And because of some of the reports that have been getting back to me from some of my many friends in other towns, I feel that you are cheating on me, by getting involved with other men. Why would you do that to me at this early stage in our marriage?

I fear that you have some kind of sickness that tells you that you have to cheat on me, or else something has happened to you, of which I am not to blame, but you are still taking that out on me, because it is a fear or vendetta against some other person or persons, and you do not know how to handle your problem, psychologically.

I am your husband, and you should be able to talk to me, just like I should be able to talk to you also, but every time we begin to talk about personal things in our lives, you clam up and then your mind just shuts down. It's like talking to barn door.

You certainly were not like this in our speedy courtship. Again you came home late last night. Where were you and whom did you see? What ever happened, will eventually get back to me, but I fear that if I tell anyone about this, that nothing will happen.

My parents know that something is happening that should not be happening, but they will not say anything to either of us, because they figure that I will be able to handle whatever problem that arises.

And if I say anything to your parents, you will say that I am trying to break up our marriage. And because I really don't know what is really happening in your life, I think the best thing to do, would be to have this marriage annulled by the Catholic Church, and or I should file for a divorce.

With Love............Clement

October 24, 1955

Dearest Peggy;

Well, now that I have found another Teacher to replace me, we can go to St Louis, Missouri. That Teacher will be here in this town in South Dakota on the 27 of October, and after I get that person up to date with everything that I teach, then we can drive to St Louis. Where I can go to work for the Wabash Railroad, making 1200 dollars per year more than I am making now, teaching school.

And you still have not answered any of my letters, nor have you tried to discuss with me, any of your personal and or psychological problems. I fear that I must talk to your parents about what I should do with our marriage. I really don't want to do that, but if I don't then, I will not solve any of our problems.

As you can see, I am actually taking on some of whatever problems you are having. Why? Because I kind of feel responsible for them, even though I really don't know what your problems really are.

Now if I find out that whatever problems you are having, are not caused by myself, then I will divorce you and have this marriage annulled. You can then get on with your life, and I can get on with mine. With a woman who can satisfy whatever needs I have? It is quite apparent that I cannot satisfy any of your needs, whether they are personal or Sexual. I have never had any problems before in my life regarding sexual things.

In fact, there was a young lady who accused me of actually getting her pregnant, but after some investigation by the local Sheriff, he found out that she was sleeping with as many as ten other young men, and besides when she accused me of sleeping with her, I was actually on a farm some 50 miles away from her, helping 150 female sheep have their lambs.

And you still have not answered any of my letters to you. And talking to you is like talking to a woman that I have never met before. I say something about what I am doing at the Wabash, and you say something about what is happening where you work.

We never seem to ever answer each others questions or queries about anything. It's like we are in different rooms or different towns. This is the most disjointed family I have ever experienced.

Your parents don't talk like we do. They talk about similar things and sometimes even about actual things that are going on in their lives.

They talk about you and I and you seem to be a million miles away on some other planet or in some other city or country. Tomorrow when I am at work, I am going to tell your father what is not going on in our marriage, and inquire as to what is actually going on in your other life. Or what I am supposing is going on in your other life.

I don't feel that I can handle any more in this marriage. If this is what goes on in most marriages, then marriage will not be what I will ever partake of again.

I really can't imagine that most marriages are like this. I am not saying that the marriage between my own parents was a rosy happening.

Because there were times when my father would tell me that when the next morning would arrive, that he was going to catch the next freight train going in whatever direction it was going and would never return, but that never happened.

I suspect that Dad was not getting much sex from Mom and when that happened for long periods of time, he kind of got discouraged with married life, whether there were any of us children at home or not, he intended on leaving and never returning. But it never happened.

I think I understand married life better than most, because of what Dad told me about that kind of life. We had many discussions about married life, and what to do in certain situations, and what not to do in others, so when I met you and decided that I wanted to marry you, I figured that you were the woman of my life that I wanted to spend the rest of my life with.

But you fooled me, big time. Because after we got married, you just clammed up totally. You would not tell me how you felt about me, even though that is what you did when I led a speedy courtship with you, but after we had gotten married, then it was like you never had to tell me everyday that you loved me, even though I told you that I loved you every day that we have been married.

And about having children, you avoided that question for the entire first month we were married. I wanted children as soon as I could produce them, but you refused to have any sex with me after one full month of having sex every day.

Clement

November 14, 1955

Dearest Peggy;

We have now been married for six weeks, and still you do not want to have any more sex with me. I know that I satisfy you, or else you are faking your orgasms with me. I know I am not faking mine with you. I would like to know how you feel about me, but you seemed to have forgotten what talking about Love is all about.

I did talk with your Father about our marriage, and he says to just give it a little more time. He says he does not know anything about sexual things, as he and his wife don't have sex any longer.

He says that sex in any marriage in not all that necessary anyway, especially after two wonderful daughters have been produced. He says that we should not try to have any children for at least three years after we have been married.

I told him that I fear that his oldest daughter is having sex with a lot of other men, but not with her husband any longer, because now that she has her own car, she comes home late at night, and because she has to be at work by 8:00 AM the next morning, she says she cannot have any sex with me, so we do not.

And it is likely that we will not be having much sex in the near future either. I fear that something has happened sometime in her life before she met me, and she is blaming it on me. He says he will have a talk with Peggy's Mother about their oldest daughter, and he will get back to me within a week.

Well that week has gone by, but I have not heard anything from either of Peggy's parents. And I think that Peggy has cautioned her parents that if they say anything to me about whatever happened to her before we met, that she may do something that they are deathly afraid of her doing, like committing suicide, which would send her directly to HELL.

This is a very strict Catholic family, and whatever one of their daughters might say she would do, they fear that because she is strong willed, that she would actually do it. What a terrible thing to hold over any parent's head. Now what will I do? I really don't know

I would like to get this marriage annulled, but I am also afraid that if I do that, that Peggy would do what she has threatened her parents she would do. And they would surely blame me for her untimely death. Maybe I will just continue to LOVE her and let time pass, and maybe things will level off, if I do nothing. Because when I make a big thing out of what she is doing to me, she just smiles but continues doing whatever she is most likely doing.

Actually since I really don't have any real proof that she is sleeping with other men, but I do have reports from many of my Father in laws friends who tell me that they have seen my wife in various Bars with various men at various times, and they wonder why I don't do something about what she is obviously doing in spite of being married to me.

They think that I really don't care enough for her to allow

her to continue doing what she is doing. I say I cannot do anything about what she is doing. And what I could do is against my religion. And I will not go to Jail for her. That usually says it all, and they do not question me any longer, but just walk away shaking their heads, probably thinking that I am a very forgiving person.

Love

CLEMENT

December 24, 1955

My Dearest Peggy;

Well here it is, our first Christmas together, if due to the fact that you are out somewhere with whomever, and I am at home with your parents. Helping your Mother bake a Turkey.

I told your Mother how I have cooked turkeys in my past, and she says we will do it my way this year. And after 5 ½ hours of baking this turkey, I removed it from the oven, and removed the brown paper bag from on top of it, and your Mother says, she would not have believed it, if she had not seen how it really turned out.

And when we cut into it, it was the most tender and juicy turkey she had ever seen and tasted. So while I am in the vicinity of your parent's house and when they serve turkey, I will be the person who will cook that turkey.

And the dressing inside of this turkey, turned out even better than I expected. It was actually a recipe that I had cut out of a magazine somewhere, and I thought I would try it this one time. Your Mother says she had not realized that I was such a great cook.

I tell her that I have been cooking since I was 11 years old. That I first learned from an old Indian Medicine Man near a lake in South Dakota.

But the turkey's we cooked there were done inside of home

made ovens made out of earthen clay that were made by me also. And while these turkeys were inside of this earthen oven, that all of the juice was reflected back onto the turkey by the top of the oven. And because all of this juice fell back inside of the baking pan it was being baked inside of, none of this juice ever caught fire.

So I thought that what if I used something that would reflect it back onto the turkey, and whatever was over this turkey, was also brown like the inside of this oven was. I ran this idea by my friend the Medicine Man, and he at first thought it was a bad idea, but once I began to try different things, and finally decided on a plain brown paper shopping bag, that was coated on the inside of this bag using home made butter, and it worked very well, that old Indian also began cooking all of his turkey's and other fowl in the same way.

I was then engaged to a young lady who jilted me in the end, but while I spent some time with her Grandmother, who also discovered my cooking abilities, and she taught me even more about other kinds of things she cooked, so some very good cooks have educated me.

Now here I am again, working with another accomplished cook, where I will learn even more about more complicated dishes.

Your Mother says you sure know how to get certain information out of her. I say someday it will all come in real handy when I am able to teach my own children how to cook. That is if I ever have any children. I think the only way that Peg and I will ever have children, is by adopting them. But I also fear that she will not make a good mother.

Your Mother says that she has something to tell me, but she fears that if she tells me that I may let it slip in some of my conversations with Peggy. I say then don't tell me. And the subject never came up again for many years between her and myself.

I just thought that you would like to know that your mother never let the cat out of your bag. That you still are safe in your world. I do know this, and that is that you are a vindictive person. And that you have some kind of hold over your parents, that they fear that if you went through with your threat, you would go straight to Hell.

I can think of only one thing, and that is Suicide, which is a mighty SIN. And I will not put you out of your misery by killing you myself, because I won't go to Jail for you or over you. You will have to instigate that yourself.

Love-------------Clement

January 15, 1956

Dear Peg;

Well here it is a couple of weeks past New Years of a new year, and hopefully this year will be more fruitful then the last one. I have decided to remain in the Mail Room at the Wabash Railroad, at least until my transfer comes through, which will take me to California. Whether you will go with me is not certain at this time, because this will only be for about six months.

But your Father thought it might help to elevate me up the ladder of success faster if I went. My only problem is getting there, and since I have not been able to save enough money for me to buy a train ticket so I can get there, and I have not been with the Wabash railroad long enough to get a railroad pass which if that was possible would allow me to get there free of that cost, and that I would only have to have enough money to buy my meals while on that train, but since none of this is possible, then I am inquiring with various car dealerships to see if any of them have any automobiles that they want driven to that area. I will keep you posted about this transfer.

Or else you can talk to your father about it. And since you never seem to find the time to answer any of my many letters to you, then this is the only way that I can keep in touch with you. And since you work on Second shift at your place of employment, and I think you selected that shift so as to avoid seeing me, because when I am getting ready to go to work, you are just getting home from wherever you have been all night. Since your shift ended at around midnight, I always wonder where you stay until I am ready to go to work the next morning. And when I come home, you have already left for work or have gone somewhere else.

Actually I don't even wonder where you keep yourself any longer. All I know is that you are never home where I am located.

Now if you are interested in going to California, then you will have to let me know somehow. And how you do that bit of communicating is up to you. I will not prevent you from going with me, but you will stay with me while we travel, unless you plan on hitchhiking by yourself. And what do we do with the two cats that we now have. Do we take them with us? I for one will take them with me. Even if they have to sit on my lap for the whole trip.

I'm sorry that I had to turn your automobile back in to the Finance company. Since you had not made any payments since you purchased it, they were getting real touchy and they would have soon reclaimed it anyway. I also called your cousin in South St Louis (the lawyer) and told him what I did, and he says to not worry about any of the money that Peggy had not paid them.

I told him that between the two of us, we had actually put 2500 miles on the speedometer, so it would sell as a used car pretty well, and that I had taken good care of it.

Peg had put a dent in the right front fender, and I personally paid to have that fixed, because we did not have any collision insurance on it at the time of the accident. And the other guy was at fault anyway, even though he threatened to take us to Court, but when I told him that the Policeman who witnessed the accident was actually Pegs Uncle, they backed away from that threat. And that was the truth.

So now you are catching a ride with one of your co-workers and I am taking the Bus. It takes me about an hour and a half to get to work. Actually your Dad and I go to work together these days.

He sometimes takes a Cab home and he calls a County Cab, because he calls them and in fact they cannot pick anyone up downtown, unless they are called by the customer personally, and because your Dad likes a specific Driver, who comes and picks us both up with his 1932 Cadillac Limousine. Of which is a great vehicle. If I were to remain in Missouri, I would entertain the idea of purchasing that vehicle.

Maybe when we return back to Missouri after this tour of duty at the offline Agents office in Los Angeles, California when we return in the early part of 1957. I sincerely hope you have saved some of your salary, because we will need whatever finances we can have after we get to California.

Because I will have two weeks to get whatever vehicle I drive out there in, so we should have enough money to rent an apartment. And because I won't have to get this vehicle to the Pomona Auto Auction until three weeks after we leave St Louis, I figure that we can most likely get to California in two days and then we will have the rest of those days to sight see and or find an apartment. And if this apartment is partially furnished, then we won't have to buy much furniture. I would like to have a television though. We can only take our clothes and our cats. No furniture.

Love. ....Clement

June 17, 1956

Dear Peggy;

When I went to pick up the vehicle I was to drive to California, the dealer fooled me. Instead of driving the Chevrolet Station Wagon, we will instead have to drive a 1956 Ford Thunderbird, Hardtop vehicle, which only has a massive motor and a trunk. So we will have to totally unpack all of our clothes, and using newspapers and or some white paper which I will get from your Dad, we will have to lay all of our clothes in that trunk. And the Cats, and Cat John will have to be put under your feet and they can ride in behind us where there is a fair amount of room.

Or the Cat John can be put behind us and their food and water will be under your feet, or maybe both the cat john and the food and water can be put behind us and the cats will ride on our laps or sleep between us. Whichever way we ultimately decide to do this, will be an uncomfortable trip.

Of course you could maybe take the train and I could take the cats and drive there by myself. Or you could remain in St Louis until I return back there in about a year. The choice is yours. No, I did not decide to do this to get back at you.

The look on your face when I drove up to our place in this 1956 Ford Thunderbird, I wished I would have had a camera handy, because I could see the disappointment on your face.

Even though I tried to warn you by telling your Dad, but I guess you don't talk to him either, or your Mother. What a shame. You must live a very lonely life.

We have been married for 9 months now, and during that time, I have had the opportunity to say no more than a hundred words to you, at least face to face. And you won't even talk to me on the telephone. I will say this, and that is, when we get to California there are going to be some major changes made in our life. You will either remain at home like a good wife, because I will actually be making enough money, so you won't have to work any longer, and I am actually having some of it saved automatically, because it will be put in a savings account at whatever bank I select in Los Angeles.

I will also be contacting my Lawyer Moses Lighthouse, to see how much I have in the bank account that he created when he opened that account for some of my Inventions that I have Patents on and Registered.

You wonder why this is the first time I have mentioned my Inventions. Well, since we both have obviously have had trouble saving any money from our salaries, I decided to activate this account, wherein which will allow us to be able to have access to enough money so I can do more than I have been doing.

Figuring that since nothing else has sparked your fancy, that perhaps Money would finally get your full attention. Now you may ask, how much money is there in this special bank account. Actually I really don't know.

But I did call Moses Lighthouse a few days back and told him that I want a hundred thousand dollars available to me when I get to California. Now I can see that I now have your attention. And why haven't I mentioned this before. Well, I am actually trying to save our marriage. And if this does not do it then I will file for a Divorce from you. While you are 1800 miles away from St Louis, Missouri.

You won't actually get this letter until we arrive in California, because I won't actually mail it until we have an address in that state. But you won't get any of this hundred thousand, because all of this money was made long before I ever met you.

You see, only money that is earned after two persons get married, is available to the spouse of any husband in any marriage, and since I selected an account wherein all of the monies were accumulated before we even met, means that you will not have access to any of this money. And you are not on that account either and never will be.

I could open a separate account in your name, but certain things will have to happen first for that to ever happen. If you don't act like a wife is supposed to act, then I will Divorce you and only let you have enough money for you to return back to St Louis or wherever you may want to end up settling down, finally.

LOVE.   Clement

June 19, 1956

Dear Peggy;

I am glad that you finally decided to go with me to California. This is the day we left for that state, and 32 hours later we were driving into Pasadena, California. Some of this trip where we were flying very low and very fast, which caused a lot of Highway Patrolmen to wonder what actually happened to us, because there were times when we deviated from the main road for sometimes as much as a hundred miles, but we did see some interesting Ghost Towns didn't we.

Only once in any persons lifetime should a person travel faster than your Guardian Angel can fly; and a hundred miles per hour in any automobile. I always made every person wonder at all of the stations where we had to check into on our trek to California, that we were as much as fourteen hours ahead of their schedule.

Actually there was no set time when we had to check in at any of our checkpoints, but it sure was interesting to see their responses when we did check with all of them.

Now that we are in the fair city of Los Angeles, I think I will check with my friend Mose Lighthouse to see if he knows of any apartments that may be for rent in the same good neighborhood where he lives. I don't want to live in the same house as he does, but just the same kind of good area.

Mose says there is an apartment near the corner of 6th street and Alexandria streets. Actually on the corner of those streets is a grocery store, which would be real handy for us if we moved into an apartment nearby.

So when we did inquire at the apartment in question, we did find this great apartment, that was actually larger than what I was looking for, but because of what they were asking for it, I immediately gave them what they wanted. Actually before we saw Moses, I stopped by my bank and I drew out five hundred dollars in 50 dollar bills, so we would be able to afford any reasonable place. Thanks to Moses Lighthouse.

And after we got the cats established in our new place, I took you to a Used Furniture Store I knew about, where we bought a television, and some cookware and after we delivered that back to our apartment, we then went shopping at the corner market, and stocked up on a hundred dollars worth of food for us to eat.

All of the time we had been married, I never really knew whether you could cook. But on our days ahead, I would really find out, wouldn't I?

First you burned the fried eggs, and then you let the teakettle boil over, because you put too much water in it anyway. And then when you tried to toast some bread, you burned that also, because you did not know that there are various settings wherein you can toast it to any persons liking.

So being the understanding person that I usually am, I took you in tow, and requested that you watch what and how I did everything. And perhaps while we lived in California, I would really teach you how to cook for yourself when I am not at home, and when I am home, for me. You decided to write everything down in a steno pad, and that was just fine, because years later this would come in handy for you again.

Now what to do with what time we had while I was waiting to take the vehicle to the Pomona Auto Auction. Since I did not have to report to my new job until July 10th, and I did not have to take the vehicle to the Pomona Auto Auction until July 3rd. I asked you what you wanted to see, and you told me the La Brea Tar Pits. So we went there the next day.

I took you to the Brown Derby Restaurant also, where we saw Jimmy Stewart and Barbara Stanwyck. Jimmy Stewart when he saw you, came to our table and he introduced us to his wife, and then he asked Barbara Stanwyck to come to our table and you gave her a second look and she said she knew she had a twin on this earth somewhere, but did not know she was now in Los Angeles also. Because the two of you looked like you were twin sisters. Anyway this relationship would come in handy for both of us in our distant future.

Peg says that she wanted to buy a newspaper and see what the Job market looked like. I told her she would not have to work from now on, but she says remaining at home all day without me being there also, is not what she is looking forward to doing. She says she is seriously going to try to change her ways, and try to make this marriage the real thing. I tell her that I will welcome that, because it has been a long time in coming to this point.

I tell her that whatever has happened in your past, should

remain in your past. And not interrupt our lives from now on. I have tried to understand your problem, but since I really don't know what that problem is, it is difficult to know what to really do, except to do what I have been trying to do, and that is to wait until you come to your senses.

Peg says that something happened in her past, long before she ever met me, and now that she is this far away from where it actually happened, which was in the St Louis area, that maybe she can break the mold.

Initially when she met me, she says she thought that our marriage could finally work, but when I decided to return to St Louis, the old problem began again.

That's all she can tell me at this time. And she says that is more than her parents really know. I asked if I could make a supposition. And she says go ahead. I say that I believe that your problem is Ken Jenkins. And I believe that he actually raped you sometime before you met me, and most likely that is the main reason you left St Louis in the first place.

Peg says for a person who has not asked any questions of her or of anyone else she knows, she says you seem to know an awful lot about her real problem. Peg says that I am absolutely correct in my supposition.

I tell Peg that there are some things that you still do not know about me, and I am not sure that I should tell you. It has nothing to do with anyone else that could be in my life, other than you. Meaning that I have never cheated on you, ever. No, it's a lot more than that. I have a special ability that was given to me by GOD. And because of that ability, I am able to pick things out of your own memories, and put forth various suppositions about specific subjects.

I just have never made this ability known to you nor to many other persons. I can actually tell you a lot about what you have been doing since you and I got married. Actually what you do in your spare time, when you do not come home. Where you go, and whether you go with any other person or persons. How many times you have spent with Ken Jenkins, and how many times you have had sex with him and where. There is not much that you can hide from me, and since you now know that I can read your mind, then I sincerely hope you will cease and desist your activities with other men.

Because if it ever happens again, I will know, and you cannot do anything about preventing me from knowing this.

Peg asks what are you. I say I am just a Gentle Person, who knows when to speak my mind and when not to speak my mind. I ask, haven't you ever wondered about the cats and me? The times when they get into trouble, as far as you think, and when I come on the scene, they do exactly what I tell them to do. And you know this, but you have never questioned me about this talent of mine. You just think it is a coincidence, but it's a lot more than that, because I can also communicate with each of them. Without saying a word to them.

I cannot explain this ability any better than that. I can actually talk to any creature on this earth. Most persons don't believe this about me, but when a time comes wherein my talent is needed to solve a critical problem with some Veterinarian when he or she is having a problem with whomever they are treating, especially at a city Zoo, of which I have done some emergency work at the St Louis Zoo, then my reputation could come forth, but I try to prevent that from ever happening.

I make sure that the Vet gets all of the credit. Now that we have had this conversation, and because I have continued to write a Journal every day, since I have been three years of age, this will eventually become part of a book that I will write when I am much older and most likely retired from whatever field I end up getting into.

Love Clement

July 3rd, 1956

My Dearest Peggy;

Today I returned the vehicle that we drove from St Louis to this area, to the Pomona Auto Auction. I walked around that vast lot for over an hour, and then I decided to hitchhike back to the Los Angeles area, and after walking for two miles, I was picked up by a black man, who ended up being someone who I knew from some of my earlier days when I lived in Los Angeles in 1948. This man is Roger Thornton.

I drove a Cadillac Limousine during part of that time when I was only fourteen years old, and I used to take him home from where he was recording one of his many songs that he wrote and recorded.

He actually remembered me, and I made an appointment on my first day off, to go see him to see if I can get some small movie parts in the many movies being made locally. He told me he would take me around to all of the Movie lots, and it was likely that I would become a bit player in a lot of movies in my future.

I told him that I am married to Barbara Stanwyck's twin sister, and he says she doesn't have a twin sister, and I said, wait until you meet my wife, then lets see what you think. So you are to come along with me on that day.

So as you well know, on July 16th, Roger Thornton came by our apartment to pick us up and when he saw you, he almost fell out of his car. He says he now knows what I mean when I said that I was married to Barbara Stanwyck's twin sister. And as you know when all of the movie producers and some of the Directors met you, really figured that you were related to Barbara Stanwyck. And remember how many parts you were offered in so many movies and I wasn't even offered one part, at least at that time. That would come later.

As far as finding some work, I really thought you might accept some of these parts. But when Roger Thornton told both of us that these parts were not of good quality, and suggested that we would not accept any of them, until he had gotten us our own agent.

So we took his good advice. Now as you know, he turned out to be a very good friend for both of us. The doors he helped open when we needed them to open became a catalyst in our marriage later that summer.

The one problem that I found, was that you were still attracted to so many second rate movie stars, that did not do you any good, and actually did more harm in our marriage. But being the nice guy that I have always been, I forgave you once again for your cheating.

Love..Clement

November 1st, 1956

Dearest Peggy;

Well here it is on the day that my position was abolished at the offline office in Union Station of the Wabash Railroad in Los Angeles, California. What a bummer this day really is. But when Francis Bell decided to Retire, the Wabash railroad decided to close the offline office of the Wabash railroad in this city.

And because you had had some bad experiences with various men in the office where you worked at the Aetna Insurance Company, we decided to leave Los Angeles at this time and go see some of my Air Force buddies, that I had met when I spent some time in that branch of service.

We saw a lot of beautiful country and met some interesting persons also. But when things got to the point where something had to give, I decided to take a position with the Pacific Gas and Electric Company, as a Radio Shop Foreman, fixing two-way radio's that had been installed in all of the vehicles that roamed around San Francisco and Oakland, California. But that was not to last all that long either.

Especially when I took a special job high on a mountain called Donner Pass Summit, where I and three other men installed some additional equipment at this Booster Station, and we almost got snowed in at that elevation, which was around 9,000 feet. It was hard to breathe up that high, until we got used to it. We remained there for three weeks, even though we had finished our job after two weeks, but it had snowed so much and the wind was blowing so hard that the Helicopter they sent to pick us up couldn't land until another week had gone by, and we just barely got off that rock.

Before that mountain was completely socked in again, which is how it remained until the next spring, or about May 15th of 1957, so they told me some months later, via a phone call from Oakland from some of the friends that I made while working with that company.

Anyway when I got back you told me that we needed to get out of Oakland and go somewhere else, and because your Father had been requesting that I return back to the St Louis area, and we caught a ride with this wild couple who really did not live up to the agreement we had made with them while trying to get back to the St Louis area, and who when they left us in St Louis, and while they were traveling in Illinois, they ran head on into an 18 wheeler truck, because he could not talk to anyone including his wife, without looking directly at you.

And both of them were killed. She was also carrying his baby inside of her. What a waste. It's a shame he did not survive that accident, because they could have sent him to the electric chair.

Clement

February 27th 1957

My Dearest Peggy;

We arrived back in St Louis on this day, and because my Father in law had me listed on the Seniority roster as on a Leave of Absence, I went to work again with the Wabash Railroad, but this time as a Clerk in the Mail Room.

But as you know I did not remain long there, but actually bid a different position in the Transportation Department as a Diversion Clerk, and got it. The only drawback was that it was on Second Shift.

We moved into the Grandview Garden Apartments in Florissant, Missouri, and our apartment was on the Second floor, so it seems that the word Second will be most prominent in our lives for a while.

And you got a Job with Emerson Electric on Second Shift, which allowed me to be able to take you to work on my way to my position. And since I had purchased a 1952 Ford sedan, meaning that is was a four door vehicle, and a lot of your co-workers always seemed to need a ride home after Bowling was finished on Wednesday nights, and how many of these persons actually stayed overnight at our place sleeping on our couch or on the floor, depending on how many stayed with us on those nights.

And then on some nights when your days off did not

coincide with my days off, and you begged me to remain home some of these nights, and when I did not, then Ken Jenkins began coming around again, and you and he began having more sex together again.

But on one of these nights, I decided to fool you, and instead I came home when you did not expect me, and I found you and him in bed together and I told him if he did not get out of there that I would kill him, and I pointed a weapon at him and when he grabbed his pants, I instead shot out all of his tires and made him walk away from our apartment.

And he had a tow truck come and pick up his vehicle three days later, and he never returned, and in fact moved out of the state, to somewhere in Illinois.

And I forgave you again, that you actually thanked me for doing what I did do, and why did I not do it some years before. So I told you that you could have told me about all of these times, but you did not, because you were enjoying having sex with him, and that I now question whether he actually initially Raped you or that you really asked him to force himself on you, so you could say that you had been raped.

And why didn't you get checked out when it supposedly happened. And why wasn't he ever arrested for this offensive Action against you. And you told me that you were too embarrassed to say anything at first, but you later told your mother, but never your father, and for all of these years you have been threatening suicide if your mother ever told me or your father about what happened.

I know what actually happened because I also read Kens mind before he left that last time he was here. I knew he was with you even before I returned that night when I found you in bed with him.

You and I will never have sex ever again, because I feel that you are not my wife any longer. But in point of fact, you are just someone who comes and lives with me every so often. Because you are afraid of living by yourself, for fear that you may someday do yourself in, because of the loneliness that always accompanies depression, which you also have a problem with.

Have you ever noticed that with all of the problems that we have had in our marriage, that I am rarely lonely or depressed regarding anything? I am always happy and most often I smile a lot. And I laugh a whole lot too. I even make you laugh when I do this.

No, you will not see me in the same way that you see yourself, ever. You and I are very different persons. I always feel that I have a lot to offer anyone, but you only think about yourself, and no one else.

What a waste of talent. You should have became an Actress, because you could have put all of this talent to work, to make a great salary, instead of wasting it on men who only want sex and never Love.

Clement

March 23rd 1957

Dear Peggy;

Today is your 27th Birthday, and sometimes I go to your parent's home, where I have been putting together a Taffeta Cocktail Gown, which you will wear at the next Wabash Yearly Dance Festival. Luckily your Mother has measurements that are your present size now. She is much impressed with my abilities as a Taylor.

I also purchased a special Cocktail Pin that I will attach to this Gown. Margaret says that when I married her oldest daughter, that she got a man who can do a lot of things that not many women can do. And that is to know how to Sew garments together.

I tell her that I also make all of my own clothes, and so far Peggy does not know this either, so anything I make for myself, I will do it at your house.

I continue writing these letters, I suppose because I have gotten used to doing this, so as to be able to keep my sanity. You still don't talk to me all that much, but you are talking a little more often than you ever did before, and I welcome those conversations. I have totally given up on ever getting any affection from you. Because you never seem to ever want it from me.

But it's always interesting that when we are in mixed

company, including being with your parents, we appear to be a very compatible married couple. You then want to kiss me and feel around on my body, like you cannot get enough of me, but when we are alone; you are as cold as an Ice cube. Showing me no kind of affection at any time. And no conversations regarding sex or Love or getting together with me.

And then when we are with some of your friends, you seem to be always attracted to most of the other men in the party of persons we are with, and some of these men's wives look at me with pity in their eyes and I know they wonder what kind of a wife do I really have.

Because you become a woman who seems to be after every woman's husband or boy friend, but you never flirt with me, and you rarely dance with me. I know you are a great dancer, and I will keep trying to get you to dance with me.

At the Wabash Club yearly Dance, when I sewed together for you, your Taffeta Evening Gown, and purchased that special Cocktail pin that I pinned onto that Gown, you looked very beautiful.

And then the Dance Photographer came and took photos of you and me and everyone at our table, which included all of your former Girlfriends from your School days, and then I asked you to dance, and you accepted.

I think I surprised you considerably when I showed you that I could do a lot of Ballroom steps, and you seemed to come alive at that time, and for the next half hour, we wowed everyone there with all of our Ballroom Dancing.

Because when we began to appear that we needed the entire Ballroom dance floor, everyone went to the sidelines and just watched us dance, and we sure showed them a thing or two, didn't we?

I was so very happy at that time, and I know that your parents were also, because when we finally went back to our table, your father says to me, that he had never seen such wonderful dancing in his entire life, and in fact he did not know that his oldest daughter could dance like you did.

Actually you couldn't, but I sensed you would certainly try since I am a good leader, and you came through for me, big time.

We looked like we were enjoying ourselves, and I know I was and you appeared to be enjoying yourself also. I think you surprised even yourself, with how well you did that night. Because after that time on that dance floor, a lot of the other men at our table wanted to dance with you but you refused all of them, because you wanted to only dance with me, so I agreed with you and, beginning on that night our lives changed incredibly.

You wanted to dance every dance with me, and most of them we did dance together. But after three hours of almost continuous dancing, I finally said, I have to rest for a while. I had only accepted one drink, and had only taken a short sip of it. You on the other hand seemed to need more liquor, and I couldn't get you to stop drinking for the rest of that evening.

And when the midnight hour arrived, you were eight tenths drunk and I finally had to take you outside and to our car, where you finally got sick, and threw up your supper and everything that you had eaten that evening.

I felt so sorry for you at that time that I wanted to take you home immediately. Then you appeared to fall asleep, and in a little while your Dad came to where I was parked, and I told him that I was going to take you home. He thought that something like this had happened, so he told me to go ahead, because his Brother Jim would take him and Margaret home in a little while.

So we went home to our apartment in Florissant. When I got there, you appeared to still be asleep, and I did not want to leave you in the car, so I attempted to get you to wake up, and then you came alive immediately, and you laughed at me.

You told me that you were just acting like you were drunk. I told you that when you threw up, everything you had eaten that evening came out of your stomach.

You told me that you put your finger down your throat, which caused you to throw up, and once that began, you couldn't stop until everything that you had eaten had come out of your stomach.

You told me that you did not expect me to be able to dance the way I had danced that evening. It did in fact surprise you a lot. Peg said that she had never danced like that before, but because I am a good dance leader, that I made it look easy and when she did what I did, that she just let herself go.

You asked me where did I learn how to dance that way, and I told you that I had a lot of professional lessons when I was going to College. Just because this kind of dancing looked like it would be a lot of fun to do. So one of my college professors, who was a woman, taught me all of the steps she knew how to dance, which were about twenty steps.

Now we did not dance all of the steps that I know how to dance, but some day I will go somewhere, and show you what I know. With another professional ballroom dancer, I could probably win many contests.

I was still reasonably happy that evening when we arrived home, even though you laughed at me, because you said that you had fooled me into thinking that you had gotten drunk.

Actually I know that you can handle a lot more booz than I can, and I rarely drink more than one drink of hard liquor at any one function, so I never worry about getting drunk like a lot of other persons do, when they attend such functions.

Even though you have never told me, I believe that your Father is an Alcoholic, because the first thing he does when he gets home is he gets a Beer from the Frig, or he mixes a drink of some kind. He always seems to have a drink of some kind in his hand at any time when he is at home.

When he is at his office, he does not touch the stuff. So I guess he is a Social Alcoholic. You on the other hand, always seem to need a drink when you first arrive home. You always drink Vodka, called Popov Vodka. And you always drink it straight or with a little ice.

I have noticed that you go through a half gallon of Vodka every week. I would say that you too are an Alcoholic. And one day this stuff will kill you.

CLEMENT

April 6th 1957

Dear Peggy;

When I made your Evening Gown, I also made a suit of clothes for me to wear. What I wore to the Wabash Dance, I actually purchased it, because I wanted to copy it. Of which I have done, but using different cloth and much better material. And adding some additional things to it, so it would not look like it had been copied.

In fact it has become a brand new garment. I also made Stockings made out of the same material as what the suit is made from. The Vest I made is made from material from Ireland, which is very expensive, but it will enhance the suit enormously.

And the Cumber bun is made out of material that I gleaned from a garment that your Mother said was actually an old dress of yours.

That dress is one that you grew out of some years before this time that she had packed away in a Cedar chest, that she said she was saving for one of our own children someday. There is still enough material left, for me to be able to make anything that anyone may want it made into.

Anyway, when you get this letter, and I hope you read my letters, you will discover another person in your life, that you never really knew you had, who is I, but now as a Taylor. It's interesting, that persons of centuries back, created names by what they did in life. If for some reason, I need to change my name, I guess I could change it to Taylor. But that is only one of the things I can do in life.

The fact that I can also read peoples minds and especially other creatures minds, what would I call myself in that profession? Maybe Whisperer, because when I do this, I really don't have to say anything, but just superimpose my thoughts into your thoughts and your thoughts become a whisper of my thoughts. I guess you might call me a Creature Whisperer. Or maybe I could change my name to Creature. There are many possibilities.

One thing for sure, and that is, that for you to try to keep any of your thoughts from me, is probably impossible for you, unless you know how to block your thoughts from me. But I believe that only another person who has the same capabilities that I do, could ever block their thoughts from me. Anyway, I am just rambling on about some additional thoughts about what I can actually do, at sometime in my future.

Since the Wabash Dance, you have been talking a little bit more, especially to me. You don't necessarily have to talk about me, but just to me. I think over time, we might learn how to communicate with each other, like we did, before I married you.

Those were wonderful times, and I sincerely wish those times would return to us. But because I did not actually court you, but we just got married after knowing each other for three days, we never had a chance to get to know each other, personally and psychologically. I suppose if I had known that you would treat me how you have been treating me, I would not have asked you to marry me.

And many times since we have been married, I have wondered whether it was such a good idea. When I asked your Dad what I should do about you, back about a year now, he says to just give our marriage a bit more time. How much time should I continue to give this marriage?

The more I delay doing anything about us, the harder it will be to dissolve this marriage. Actually since your father does not know a lot of things about you himself, he could only give me the advice that he did.

I never did ask your Mother what I should do, and now I am afraid I have waited too long to do anything about us. I have not told you personally how I feel about you, but "I do love you and an awful lot". And I hope you Love me also. You don't ever tell me that you do, but since I have put my feelings in writing, maybe that will instill in you to tell me how you feel about me too.

And if you hate me, then I would like to know that also. But how close is hate to love? Can a person hate another person and also be in love with them? Is loving someone the same as being in love with them or is it different. I say that it is different. But trying to explain that difference will cause many eyebrows to rise up.

Clement

April 16th 1957

My Dearest Peggy;

You finally told me how you felt about me. It was not what I was expecting, but you were really communicating with me nonetheless. Like you told me, we have been living together for nineteen months now, and for us to not have any feelings for each other would be something very rare.

And hearing you tell me that you have some feelings of affection for me is a Revelation of facts. I guess I should not have expected anything more than what you really gave me.

I did not tell you before, but I have enrolled into yet another College. Actually I had to take an entrance exam and I have passed it, so I am going after my Doctorate Degree in Veterinary Medicine. It is a four-year course, but I think I can get through it in less than three years. Since we still don't talk all that much, this will have to continue, because of all of the courses that I plan to take on. To get this Degree, I need to complete 50 credits. So figuring that I will take on 20 credits every year, I will be able to get that degree in about 2 ½ years.

Then because I don't figure that we will remain in the St Louis area for the rest of our lives, I also need to get a Doctorate Degree in something else. And since I am the Expert in Creature Communications, I figure I will write a Curriculum for the University that I will get that Degree from, and just give it to them. And this Curriculum will be a battery of tests that any potential student will have to take, who thinks they may have the same abilities that I presently have, wherein they will have to get 77 percent of the answers correct, to even be considered to be further educated in this field. And writing this Curriculum will take me about 1-½ years to accomplish.

So since I am now 23 years old, and I still have a minimum of 4 years ahead of me so as to get those Doctorate degrees, then I will be 27 years old when that happens. Which will put the year sometime in 1961. I have already made arrangements with Management of the Wabash Railroad so I can go full time at Washington University so I can accomplish what I am after. I sincerely hope you totally Understand, because at times I won't be very easy to live with. I suppose you can always seek other affection from other men, but you have been doing that anyway since we have been married. Turn around is fair play.

LOVE..........................Clement

July 4th 1957

Dear Peggy;

Well at this time, I have been going to this other college for almost three months. And I like all of my professors and they seem to like me too. My grades are high, and it sure is a lot of very hard work. And as you have probably noticed, I don't have much to say to you, when we have the opportunity to communicate with each other. I would suppose I am actually doing what you have been doing since you have been married to me, and that is, I don't even try to talk to you any more.

TURN AROUND IS FAIR PLAY. So if you don't like it, then I cannot help you. I may regret doing this, but this will be the only way I can attain what I have planned for myself. I cannot worry about you any longer. You are actually old enough to take care of yourself, since you are actually 4 years and 2 weeks older than I am. Even though you have never actually told me how old you really are. And no, I did not ask your parents, but just picked it out of your own memories. I have noticed that you have been remaining home most nights, and that is good. Though I don't know what you do on your days off, because when I come home you are never here, so I have to cook my own meals. I also noticed that you still don't cook your own meals yet. Because I always find take out containers everywhere in our apartment.

Of course maybe they are just containers that some of your

friends leave at our place. I have noticed some Rubbers in our bed, apparently left there by some of your men friends. But I have not found any extra pairs of under shorts or men's clothes hanging in our closets. And you still have not answered any of my letters either.

All of our Cats seem to be okay also. Actually they tell me who has been to our apartment, so when you have men friends there, they will tell me, and who that person actually is.

Remember they too can read other persons minds just like I can. Even if you lock them in the other bedroom. But also remember that they too have to go to the bathroom and eat some food, so if I find any extra poop or where they have had to pee in the small bedroom, which I use as the office, and where I do all of my studying, then I will also know that fact.

So you will not be able to escape whatever goes on in our apartment at any time. Now if what ever you do, you do at someone else's apartment or house, then I will only be able to find that out by reading your thoughts. In fact it is always interesting that when I know that has actually happened, you always, when you come home when I am there, are always remembering what transpired at those times, so trying to keep from me what you have done and where it was done, is not possible for you to accomplish. So you might as well tell me, but knowing how you think, you will still try to keep all of this from me.

I LOVE YOU – STILL -

PS:

It's funny about Love. And I still feel responsible for you. I don't think that will change for some time, maybe some day, but not now. I am hoping that you would try to help me in my endeavor to attain what I am after in this medical field. But I guess you don't remember anything from your days when you studied to be a pharmacist. That's a shame, because some of what I am now studying would help me, but I guess you don't really want to help me in any of my studies.

LOVE

CLEMENT

September 10th 1957

Dear Peggy;

Well, I am half way through my first year of Medical school. Pretty good, since it has been a few years since I have been in any college. My study habits have not changed, and all of the work that I am doing at the Wabash and the subjects I am presently taking are keeping me very busy.

And because I actually work four hours every day at the Wabash Railroad and I am getting paid for 8 hours, makes going to College much easier. Of course I do have the extra money that I get from a couple of my patented inventions also, so I am not hurting at all.

You are still working at Emerson Electric, even though you never tell me that you still are, but since there are other students who are going to this same college, who also work for Emerson Electric, and who also know you too, that is actually the way I know that you keep good hours, because you go to work every day on second shift.

And since I purchased an automobile for you to drive, makes it easier for you to get to work now. It has been rumored that you have been bringing home, some men, who stay with you on your days off, but leave before I am scheduled to return home. It makes me smile a little, knowing that whatever you allegedly don't get from me, you always get from other men.

It's also very funny that, you never really enjoyed having sex with me, but it is very apparent that you still require it from other men, no matter who they are, just as long as it is not from your husband. I am not complaining though, because I knew that when I began this program, that you would be having some extracurricular activities with other men. But wouldn't it be nice to do something that I would not expect of you. Like maybe file for a Divorce from me.

But I suppose that would be too drastic for you, because you apparently like being married to a man who forgives you every time you cheat on him. As for my forgiving you, that would be an assumption on your part, but not on mine. I will never forgive you again. It is not a matter of principle, but it is a matter of reality. Here you are a married woman, who constantly cheats on her husband, and you expect me to forgive you, ------- NEVER.

When I eventually graduate from this University, you and I will become HISTORY, because if you don't change your ways while I am going to this college, then you and I will not remain married any longer. And be very careful as to how many men you are seeing at the same time, because one of those days or nights, there will come on the scene, another man, who will either kill you or both of you, because if you continue doing what you are doing, then it will eventually get you killed.

But I won't kill you, because I won't go to jail for you. Because I still want to have a life with a woman that will be faithful to me, even when I am not at home with her. And I still want to have a family, even if I have to adopt every child. But I know that you would not be a good mother, so for you and I to adopt children, is a whispering thought from SATAN.

Clement

December 24th 1957

Dear Peggy;

Well, here it is our third Christmas as a married couple, even though we are not really a couple any longer, but you are just a woman who sleeps in the same bed with me sometimes. But you are a total stranger to me. Why did I ever marry you? What was I thinking? I guess I wanted to get away from South Dakota and you were the way to do that.

But being married to you is like being married to a COLD STEEL ROD. Because even a cold steel rod would be better than you are. You don't ever talk to me now, just like a steel rod would do. It's like you don't really have a mouth, except to do with it whatever you do with it with other men.

My cats tell me what you do with other men. But with me, if I ever asked you to do something like that, you would tell me that I am the most dirty person on this earth, but you apparently like doing with other men doing what you do. Well I guess you have been learning some new tricks from other men.

Anyway College is going well, and in another four months, I will have earned enough Credits to advance me into my third year, because I have actually ended up taking a total of 18 courses though out this year. So I have to get 32 more Credits in order to graduate with a Doctorate Degree in Veterinary Medicine.

So I figure that since I can actually take a total of 18 courses every year that I go to college, that in the next two years I can end up with a total of 54 Credits, which if I continue with my grade point average, will get me into any well known college in this nation so I can get my Doctorate in Creature Communications also, and what ever college that may end up being, will end up getting a FULL CURRICULUM IN THAT SUBJECT, for free. Just as long as that University will give me my Doctorate Degree in that field.

Of course because I am the Authority in that field, I will have to teach others how to give these tests and that would most likely take a complete year to do. But after that, then I can buy a small Animal Hospital and begin my private practice wherever that may happen. Thereby avoiding practicing my field with another Veterinarian for two years.

The only way I figure I will be able to start a private practice is to buy that small Veterinary Hospital and after a few years, expand it into something that has never been tried before, and that is to make it a Teaching Hospital, and to become affiliated with a University that is fairly close by my hospital location.

Where potential students will go to this University, where they will take the test of my Curriculum, to see if they have the same abilities that I have, and if some of them do, then at this university they will be taught how to use that talent and gift. And with whom or what creatures are needed to be communicated with.

Now if you want to be part of that life, then change your ways now, because if you do not, then I will not keep you. And besides, you are getting older now, and one day, the kind of life you are leading now, will have to come to a close, and if you never save any money now, then your life will be completely over, so you might just as well commit suicide now, rather than wait.

Because I won't be around to bail you out of any of the troubles you will have gotten yourself into. Because I will have gone somewhere else and left you behind, with all of your problems, that you have created all by yourself.

And your parents will not bail you out either, because you are old enough to take care of yourself that is if you now change your ways. I cannot help you at this time, because if I deviate from my studies, then I won't be able to accomplish what I have in mind to do.

Of course maybe I could back away from some of my studies after I get my Doctorate Degree, but not until that time. But by that time if you have not changed your ways, then I believe it will be too late for you also.

So now is the time to change your ways, and begin being the kind of wife, that you should be for anyone. Not just me, but for yourself. I cannot stress this enough any more than I already have.

CLEMENT

March 23rd 1958

Dear Peg;

You will note that I have not written any letters to you since December 24th of 1957. And I would think that there would be some kind of changes in what you have been doing, but you are still doing what you have been doing ever since that time and date. When will you ever quit? You cannot do this for the rest of your life.

Actually I went down to an area where there are prostitutes and I made some friends with a few of them. No I did not partake of any of their services, because I told them why I needed to find out something about any of them. And that is, when does anyone of them decide to quit doing what they have been doing for some time now.

They all tell me that when any of them reach the age of 35, they will have to quit that kind of work, because a woman's body begins to do things that they do not expect it to do, and that is it begins to sag a lot in places that are not attractive to most men.

Though there are some men that would marry any one of them, just because they have finally decided to stop what they are doing. I have told all of whom I have talked with, what you have been doing ever since we have been married, and they all tell me that I must be a very forgiving man to allow her to continue to do this. I told all of them that, you are really trying to kill yourself, but doing what you are doing is not accomplishing what you want it to do, and now you are hooked on what you have been doing.

So I have made arrangements for six of them to come and pick you up and they will take you along with them, so you can experience the kind of men they deal with everyday. By the time you get this letter, all of what I have arranged with them, will have been accomplished, and by doing this, I am hoping that you will finally change your ways of doing it any longer. And instead finally begin to be the kind of wife I have been seeking since we have been married. By the way, every one of these prostitutes told me that they would marry me in a New York minute, so beware.

Because if you do not change your ways, I will Divorce you, and marry one if not all of them. And go and live where I can have all of these women as my wives. Like maybe Australia or some other country. Or maybe the state of Utah.

CLEMENT

April 6th, 1958

Dear Peg;

This is yet another letter on this date, because I did write you a different letter to you on my Birthday of this year.

Your Birthday came and went, because you were not home, because you were out with the six prostitutes doing what they were doing. I understand that you fully enjoyed every man that you were with, and you actually made an additional thousand dollars in two days. Because you still work on Second shift, you apparently got to go with a lot of different men.

And after doing this for nine days, you finally said that is enough, because after all of these women talked to you, you finally told all of them that doing what they did every day and night, would actually wear her out and would probably get her killed by some man, when she scheduled more than one for the same time and day. She says that what she does on her own, she does not do that, and probably never will, unless she is drunk, but she says she never drinks when she is doing what she is doing on her own. And as far as me divorcing her, she says that will never happen, because he is too gentle a man. And since she was with these six women, she has made an additional five thousand dollars.

And if you think she just gives sex to any man for nothing on her own, no she actually sells it to all of them and she gets a thousand dollars each time she has or does any kind of sex with any of them.

I was advised by these six women to immediately Divorce my wife, because she will never change her ways. She is a whore and she will always be a whore. And that would be your reason for divorcing her. They tell me that any Judge would grant a divorce from any woman with that kind of excuse.

And my Birthday came and went, even though you were home on my birthday, and you obviously completely forgot about it because you did not buy me any presents. I on the other hand gave you a Bracelet that had Diamonds in it that totaled two full karats, and all you said was it sure is pretty, but you also said that you probably would never wear it, because it is too expensive to wear to work everyday, and since we never go anywhere together, there will be no reason to even keep it.

So I grabbed it back from you and I said that I would take it back so I could get my money back. It was at that time, that if looks could have killed, I would have been dead. But it is your own fault for the way you acted, because you still have not learned to control your feelings and your mouth when it comes to me.

CLEMENT

July 29th 1958

Dear Peggy;

I went to the Archdiocese and talked to one of the Secretaries of the Cardinal at the Cathedral, and gave them five hundred dollars so I could get our marriage annulled. And when I told them why, this priest almost fell out of his chair. He asked me how long has this been going on and when I told him, he says the Cardinal needs to talk to you before he will progress any further.

I told this Secretary that the first person you will talk to will be her Father, and when I told him what his name was, he then called the Cardinal in and they conferred for a few minutes, and then the Cardinal told me that he would talk to your Father personally. I told the Cardinal that your father does not know anything about what his oldest daughter does in her spare time, because I have not told him, and neither has his daughter.

But I suggest that you talk to my wife's Mother, because I have told her. Who works at the Terminal Railroad Company? So the Cardinal told me that he would call my wife's mother, after I gave him her telephone number where she works, and also her home phone number.

But he definitely wants to talk to both of my wife's parents, especially since this has been happening ever since we were married in the Catholic Church in Jennings, Missouri in 1956.

The Cardinal asked me, what are my overall intentions, and I told him that I will file for a Divorce from my wife, even though I know I will be Excommunicated from the Catholic church because in 1957 I too became a Catholic.

Fr. Francis Sylvester Murphy in Bridgeton, Missouri, instructed me about the Catholic faith and I had six month of instructions, which he says is more than enough for me, because I was so knowledgeable about what I was actually doing, and my belief was very strong in this faith.

Besides I had gone to Saint Stanisslaus Seminary, otherwise known as Priests Farm, a few years back, even though I was not a Catholic.

The Cardinal told me that Fr. Murphy is no longer a Catholic priest, because he has been excommunicated from the Catholic Church because he fell in Love with a woman and he got married six months back. And he was one of our smartest priests. I tell the Cardinal that it was something that you did not do for him, which was the initial reason why he strayed from the church.

The Cardinal asks how much do I know about the reason as to why he actually strayed, and I told him that I cannot tell you, because I promised that I would not tell you, if I was ever asked by you. And I will not betray that promise. But the Cardinal says you still became a Catholic? Even though you know why Francis strayed from the Catholic Church. Actually he is not a catholic because of what you did to him, not by his own decision to give it all up. But that is all I will say on that subject. I then walked out of his office.

I don't know if the Archdiocese ever called you to come for

an interview. I do know that the Cardinal did talk to your parents, because Margaret told me what was said, even though it was suggested by the Cardinal to not tell me what was discussed in their interview.

I was actually very disappointed by what actually happened, because it was decided that this marriage would not be annulled. That some time in the future my five hundred dollars would be returned back to me, because that annulment had been refused.

That it was obvious to the Cardinal that I was out to destroy another persons life and he would not be part and party to such an act for such a good Catholic person such as my wife. What a hypocrite.

I really think that because of who your father is, is the real reason why this annulment was not granted, because Margaret told the Cardinal that if this marriage was not allowed to continue then any and all contributions would cease immediately, and since I knew that Joe and Margaret gave at least two hundred dollars every month to the Catholic Church, that that was the real reason this annulment was refused.

Of course I could still get a Divorce from Peggy, but it would only mean that I would be excommunicated from the Catholic Church, but not Peggy. She would still remain the so-called good catholic that they wanted her to be, even though they knew she really was not.

Peggy would go to church whenever I took her, even though I sometimes had to work, because on Sundays I never went to college, so I was quite often asked to work at the Wabash. But I would drop you off at St John and James

Catholic Church in Ferguson, Missouri, because that is where your parents were members and went to church, and then I went on to work. And they would have a Cab take you back to our apartment.

But I did not file for a Divorce from you, because I had gotten used to you being home sometimes. And I figured that someday all of what you were doing would eventually cease. When that would be, would be when it actually happened.

CLEMENT

October 1st 1958

Dear Peggy;

Today is our 3rd wedding anniversary and I have gotten you three-dozen roses. One dozen for every year we have been married. These roses are all red, because red tells the receiver that they stand for Love from the giver. In fact there is a card explaining this fact. I know you did not expect such a gift, since the last gift I gave you for your birthday I returned and got my money back.

And I had made Reservations at a well-known restaurant in Florissant, where they served the best Lobster that I have ever eaten along with a half dozen Giant Shrimp. I even invited your sister and her husband to join us there. Of which they did.

Whether you had anything else planned for that evening, I was not concerned with that, because I had also made arrangements to have us picked up with a stretch Limousine, with even a Mariachi Band inside of it, which played soft love songs all the way to the restaurant and even after we arrived there. And then after that stopped, I had made arrangements to have another band play dance music whereby we could dance some Ballroom dances, and it brought you alive again, just as it had done back in 1955, and you were so surprised when I asked you to dance with me that you almost fell out of your chair.

I also told you to remove your shoes, because the heels were too high for ballroom dancing, especially since you had not danced that way for three years. Anyway when we got onto the dance floor, and the Band begin playing all of the tunes I had requested that they play, I actually knew you would not refuse me, and I actually wore you out that night, because during the last two tunes I was actually carrying you all over that dance floor, only no one knew it except me.

But when we went back to our table, I knew I had finally defeated you, and that if you ever tried to do what you had been doing against me since we have been married, I would take you dancing every night of every week until you finally would tell me that you had had enough of what I was doing. That was my intention and you knew I would carry it out, even if I had to quit going to college. Because while we were dancing, this is what I told you that I would do.

And when we finally quit dancing I then asked your sister if she would like to dance, and she says only if she does not have to dance like you and Peg have been dancing for the last three hours. And where do I get all of my energy, because she says she is tired just watching us dance all of that time.

So she and I danced for three tunes, and then she says she cannot dance any longer, so we went back to our table. You in the meantime had recovered a little and then you asked to dance with me, and when we got back onto the dance floor, the regular music stopped and they started playing all of the songs that I had arranged for them to play when the two of us got on the dance floor.

You asked me, can't they play some regular music and I

say you will have to ask them yourself. And that is what you did, but through an interpreter you were told that they did not understand what you wanted them to do. So out of frustration you went back to our table and the music began playing some regular tunes again. When you stood up to go to the ladies room, the ballroom music began to play again, and this continued until we finally left this Restaurant around 2:00 AM. Anyway I asked whether you had a good time and you told me that you really had.

What was also interesting that happened, that when you ordered a Margarita drink, you were told that no alcoholic drinks would be served at this table, with the exception of Beer being served only to your sister's husband?

And if you ordered any kind of drink, that it would be refused. And if you went up to the Bar and ordered a drink, you again would be refused. So I had actually stacked the deck that evening, so you could not even get any kind of drink.

And when our Limousine took us home, the very first thing that you upon entering our apartment was you poured yourself a full glass of Vodka and drank most of it. And then I told you that you are an Alcoholic, and that if you ever gave up drinking completely, then you would probably give up doing whatever you had been doing since we had been married.

Because it is likely that before you have sex with anyone, even though you tell everyone, that you do not drink when you do these acts, that you drink a full glass of Vodka first. So I am going to take you to St Johns Hospital and put you in the Alcoholic Ward, where they will completely dry you out. And if you refuse me in that endeavor, then I will force you to go to a

Sanatorium where you will remain until I say you are cured. The look on your face would have killed me at that very moment if you had that kind of power.

Because you just realized that I was not kidding, and I would do what I intended to do, even if I completely lost you. I decided to sleep on the Day bed in the office, because I Locked that door with the key that only I had.

When I woke up the next morning, you were gone from the apartment, and you had obviously packed as many clothes as you could carry in the two suitcases that you had, and left me.

I had finally gotten to you, in the only way that I could, by threatening you with confinement for however long that it would take to get rid of whatever sickness you really had. I never went and looked for you, because I was really glad you were gone.

I finally had some time to myself and with the cats that we have, and they seemed to be more calmed down also because of your leaving.

CLEMENT

November 26th 1958

Dear Peg;

It has been almost two months since you have been gone. I have had some reports from various persons while I was in college, of some of your whereabouts, and I also know that you are still working at Emerson Electric, but now you are on the Day shift. Where you are living, I do not know and I have not inquired in that endeavor either.

I contacted one of your previous girlfriends (Hazel) and she says she knows where you are now living, but she will not tell me where, but I told her I do not want to know where she lives, but I will have a letter that I will have written that I would like you to give her when you see her, and she says she will do that for me, so I send them to her address, and I hope you will then get them from her.

My studies are still going very well at the University, and my grade point average has gone up. Which would make me to possibly be the smartest student when I eventually graduate with my Doctorate Degree in Veterinary Medicine.

The reason that I have gotten as far as I have, is because as you know, I have been going twelve months of every year, and accumulating two years into one year.

I have had to make special arrangements through the University governing Staff by paying extra money to these staff members so they would be there to teach me and some others also, that learned about these arrangements, thereby taking advantage of that arrangement by me. So 8 Students will graduate with me in August of 1959, with Doctorate Degrees in various fields.

It was suggested by one of those other students, that perhaps I should suggest to you, that if you would like to go back to college, that since I seem to have unlimited finances, that I should pay for you to go back to college. Now if you want to go to another University, that would be okay also, because if you can pass the entrance exams, then you can go back to college and I will pay for everything, even your books.

And if you wanted to live on Campus, that may help you also in so many ways. Of course whatever you have been doing for the last three years, that would have to stop, but you would get some additional education, which might help you in your future.

You can let Hazel know what you think. All of these letters I am now writing are going to her address, because she says she will not tell me where you now live, and I told her I don't want to know where you now live. I elected to not have thanksgiving with your parents, on the off chance that you may want to have a thanksgiving dinner with them, so as to not accidentally run into you, I am having a thanksgiving dinner with some other friends of mine that I met in the red light district.

I think you probably know most of them. I have invited all of them out to have dinner with me and for all of us to go to a movie at the Grand Theatre on Thanksgiving night. Gone with the wind is playing there and they tell me that none of them have ever seen it before,

I was actually invited to someone else's house but I refused that invitation. Not that I would not have liked to go, but I figured that I might run into you there also, since they told me that they had invited you also. I think they are trying to get the two of us back together again. If and when we ever get back together again, it will have to be your choice, but never mine, because I have had it up to the top of my head with all of your antics of cheating on me. Now how long we will be separated is totally up to you, because I will not ask that we ever get back together.

I think when your father gets tired of making up excuses for you, then you may consider trying to get back with me, but not before. No, I don't really know whether you are really living back with your folks or not, and no one has told me whether you are or not, but keep this in mind, and that is that my ability to read your mind, has no boundaries, because communicating with telepathic means has no boundaries. I just thought you would like to know of my full capabilities.

I don't want you to return back to me unless you are completely cured of whatever sickness you now have, because I will no longer put up with how you have treated me since we have been married. If you cannot remain home and keep all of the men that you know out of our apartment, then I don't want you in my life ever again. It has to be my way, or no way at all. Nothing else will ever do for me.

I thought I had married a great woman, but instead I got the DEVIL or most likely, the woman of the DEVIL. So remain where you are, and don't try to come back to me unless you can stop what you are doing. Otherwise we are just only married as far as GOD knows, and as far as the Catholic Church knows, because we will never live together again as long as I know you are still cheating on me. It's funny, because even though I have had many invitations to be with other women, I have never cheated on you and I never will. Sex is no longer important for me.

CLEMENT

January 1st 1959

Dear Peg;

Now, whether you really read any of my letters, I don't really know for sure. I do see your father most every day for short periods of time, but he mostly does not talk to me, because mostly I am on an errand, wherein I have a message to deliver to someone in his department, and sometimes in the telegraph office. So I rarely ever talk to your father any more. And they never invite me to their house any more either, which tells me that you are actually living with your parents again.

I am still in the Transportation Department, which is on the 16th floor of the Railway Exchange Building at 6th and olive streets, in St Louis, Missouri. I noted this more for the Reader, than for any other reason. The Mail Department and the Telegraph Department are both on the 14th floor of this same building.

Everything below the 13th floor is the Famous and Barr Department store. And this building is a block square. And anyone can get into this department store on every side. But to get to any Railroad companies, you can only enter from the South side or the North side of this building.

I mention all of this so the reader will know that the writer of this book really knows what he is talking about, and anyone who has been to St Louis, Missouri will also recognize what I am saying.

I did get a note from your girlfriend in that I was instructed by, who told me that she knew where you now live, that you might be interested in going back to one of the Universities in St Louis sometime in the near future.

So I wrote a note back to her telling her what my address is, but I am mostly in school or at the Wabash Railroad, but I did give her some approximate times that I am usually home in the apartment. What is interesting is, you still have a key to that Apartment. There are still some things of yours that are still in one of the closets, and I have not disturbed any of it.

So if you need some of what you left there, by using the times I provided your girlfriend, you can come and get these things, unless you plan to return back to me someday. But whenever that may be, may be a long time yet. Oh well, what the hell.

I did take in another kitten about a week back. It was actually sitting on my second floor landing, and because it is now wintertime, I took it inside, and because my two other cats have gotten used to it now, I don't want to deprive them of their need to Love this little Creature.

Maybe you found it and brought it to me, but it is likely that since some of my neighbors know that I Love most Cats, that one of them brought it to me. Anyway because it is a female, I have named her Chili, because she loves any food that is laced with chili powder or pepper. She has about four different colors all over her and one of them is a definite red color, and the others are white and black and yellow. So I think I have named her very well. She also sleeps with me whenever I sleep there, which are most nights.

Some nights I study so long, that I only get a couple of hours sleep. And Chili stays with me no matter what I am doing, so I guess I needed her also.

I am running out of things to say to you. I don't want to keep running you down, as that does not seem to do any thing either. And I cannot seem to remember anything good to say about you either.

Actually you did not give me much to remember you by, except your eagerness to want to learn how to dance the ballroom steps that I know how to dance. But how often will we really have to dance these kinds of steps. Not very often and now maybe never. So I guess I will have to learn how to dance some other kinds of dancing methods.

By the way, you are invited to my graduation. I do not know the exact date yet, but when I find out I will try to give you at least a couple of weeks notice.

If you need transportation, I will arrange to have you picked up with a private Limousine. I don't have to know where you live, but because I will also be inviting your parents, all you have to do is be at their place at the appointed time and date, and you will be transported to that University, along with your parents.

I plan to also invite your sister and her husband, and if they need to be taken also, they can also be picked up at your parent's house. And when it is time to come home then you all will be transported back to your parent's house and then it will go back to wherever it came from.

I will be driving myself. There will probably be other persons that I will also invite that will be transported via a limousine also.

Whether you recognize these persons, I don't really know that you will. Some of these persons are just friends of mine from other sources that I have been associating with of late. Some of them may go into some kind of business with me after I graduate.

CLEMENT

March 23rd 1959

Dear Peggy;

Today I am sending along with this letter, an invitation to my graduation this fall on August 25th, at 8:00 PM. Along with this invitation is two hundred dollars, that you are to use in the Dress Shop I will be sending you to, that you will not use to buy your dress, but in whatever way you like, that you will wear to this function.

I have made arrangements with a famous women's wear shop, wherein the address is on one of their business cards that I am also sending along to you. When you get there, just hand them that card and they will do the rest. Because I have already talked with them about you, and they know what you look like and they already know what this dress will be for. So just leave everything up to them.

You will not be disappointed with what they provide to you. I would suggest that you get those two 100 dollar bills changed into smaller denominations, because the actual cost of the dress that they will provide to you will be paid for by me. This money, or at least ten or twenty dollars of it, will be for a tip to whomever helps you, and if it was me I would give that person no less than 20 dollars.

Of course I will probably give that person more than what you will offer her anyway. But that is just who I am when it comes to high fashion. And you will wait for this dress, and while you are doing that, you can look around this store to see if there is anything else you may want me to buy for yourself. Don't be afraid to go for something that is way out of your range, because nothing is out of my range. It will take about an hour for them to get your dress ready for you to wear. Also try it on in the store, and let them help you with that also.

This is a very high fashion store, and how you will select your dress is by watching Live Models display each dress. This will take about an hour and then after you select the dress that you want made up in your sizes, then they will make it for you, so be sure to try it on before you leave that store. After you are satisfied, they will box up everything that you have ordered and tried on and you can then take it with you.

I am sure you have never done this before in your entire life. So get used to doing this. I am not saying that I won't try to copy that same dress, with some variations here and there, because what I can actually create for you would be just as rich and expensive. Remember I am still a Taylor, and I had intended to make all of your clothes for all of your life, so don't rule that out yet.

You can still come to me and have me make all of your clothes, even if you don't live with me. But since I have not had a chance to measure you for anything, that still has to be done by me.

And to do that you will have to take all of your clothes off and stand in front of me totally naked. While I measure every part of your body for everything I will make for you.

Now if you cannot or will not do that, then you will have to have someone else make your clothes or buy them off of the rack. I have never touched on this before, because you seemed to not want anyone, and especially me to ever touch your body anywhere, especially in your delicate places. So because of that I never told you that I am also a Professional Taylor.

Even though I did make that Taffeta Cocktail Gown for you, unless you thought that your Mother made it for you. No she did not, because I made it, and you may remember how well that did fit you. You can ask your Mother yourself if you do not believe me. I also made myself a suit of clothes, even though I have not had a chance to ever wear it yet. I thought I would wear it when I graduate this August. I am still the same size as I was back then.

Well I have to go to bed now, because I have another very long day tomorrow. Or after looking at my clock will be later today. Chili is sitting in my letter tray on my desk all curled up in it. What a wonderful cat she is. One of these days I need to take her to see our Vet and have her fixed, but I think that will have to wait for about another month yet. She is actually still just a kitten. And our other cats really take real good care of her when I am not here. Probably because they really love her also just like I do.

CLEMENT

July 9th 1959

Dear Peg;

Well today I took my final exams and I think I got every answer correct. The scores won't be posted until the 15th of this month. What a terrible six days this will be. Anyway I heard from that High-class women's store I sent you to and they tell me that you bought a real nice dress and a few other things too. And when you tried to pay for those other things, they told you that they were already paid for.

You see I have a charge card account with that store, so anything you bought was automatically paid for, no matter how much it actually cost. I know you have never been treated this way before. But you did not even try to please me when we were living together. Maybe this will make a difference. I am not saying that if you went back to that store that you could charge anything that you want to charge. No it does not work that way.

They would only approve something that I approved of before they approved it. So perish that thought. And since you do not have a charge card with this store and most likely never will have, because it is far beyond your range of prices that you can actually afford.

So this was a one-time thing for you. I thought I made that very clear in my last letter to you, but I guess you misunderstood what I told you. I am usually very specific in my instructions.

How much did you spend? You don't really want to know, or maybe you do, but you will never know, because as you may have noted when you were there, there are no prices on anything. Either you already know what you are buying and how much it approximately costs or some other person, of which will usually be a man, is just treating you.

Famous and Barr is more in your range of prices, so accept it and be satisfied with being that way. Now I can see that you are wondering how did I get so snobbish?

Actually I am not snobbish at all. I just know what different kinds of materials cost, because remember I am a Professional Taylor, and we know a lot of other individuals who deal with other materials as well as what I would use if I was to ever make something for someone, including myself.

This letter is going to be a short one, because I really need to get some well-earned sleep. Since I will not have any more classes this year, and because I have taken six weeks of vacation, and I may ask for 4 weeks more. I am going to sleep for a solid week. I have earned it.

So if you want or need to see me and or want to talk to me, I will be home for quite some time, because I plan to go through all of the closets in this apartment and box up what is not going to be worn by anyone, including all of your stuff, because since you are not living here any longer, I am getting tired of looking at it.

So if you want it, then come and get it. But in any case, I will probably box it up and put it in some kind of storage place. A storage place that is heated and or air-conditioned, depending on the time of year.

I understand there is not anything like this anywhere. I think it will be of the size where there will be no less than 200 units of various sizes. From a 5 X 5 foot to a 10 X10 foot. I will also have about the same number of units outside too. There is a great need for something like this. I will need someone to manage it though, because I will not do it myself. And no, you will not be that person.

CLEMENT

August 20th 1959

Dear Peg;

Well here it is a few days before I actually graduate from the University with a Doctorate Degree in Veterinary Medicine. When I checked my final exams score, I did get every question answered correctly. It has been requested of me, that I give some kind of Speech at my graduation, of which tells me the score that I have gotten, is most likely the highest that anyone has ever gotten from this University.

What I will say, I am not certain at this time. I think I will just adlib it, because I think I can actually do that. I do not feel scared when I am in front of a large group of persons, and I usually can find something to talk about, hopefully something that most anyone will completely understand.

I am not a person who uses big words, because persons who use big words are only trying to impress someone, or they are using these big words because they really don't want to talk to these persons, because most often big words turn most persons completely off. Now in the field of Veterinary Medicine, anyone's clientele will be from all walks of life, and whatever the creature may be, they could care less about using or receiving any big words.

So I just use the English language like it is supposed to be used, in a simple way. This will be my subject of the speech I will give. Of course since you really don't know me all that well, you don't know how long I can go on and on and on about how to properly speak to anyone.

I think everyone will ask, " How was I able to get a Doctorate Degree within two and a half years, if I only talk using simple language. Well in any language, the most important way to be most completely understood is to speak clearly and use words that anyone can completely understand. Because how many persons can really understand Latin, which is most often the language that most Doctors use when writing Prescriptions? But that is not the language that I will use when talking to owners and or caretakers of various creatures. And most creatures don't even understand words of any language. They most often only speak in their own particular language.

But for me to totally understand any creature, I have created a new language for all of them, which is called Picture talk or image language. And the method I use in talking to all of these creatures is called Telepathy. Now I can see that a lot of you don't really believe me. But let me say this, and I am specifically directing this message to one specific person in this audience.

When this person hears what I have to say, then she will totally know that when I say I can really read her mind, she will probably get up suddenly and leave this Auditorium.

No I will not embarrass her, nor will I say bad things about this person. But when she hears what I say to her, then she will do what I have suggested she will do, even though at this moment she is determined that she will not give herself away. And this message is this:

Last evening when she met a certain man in a Bar in Ferguson, she had not seen this man for three years. And the first thing she said to this man was that message I sent to her Telepathically, and that is what they did. This is at the end of my speech.

Actually when everyone got up to clap their hands, Peggy since she was sitting on an Isle seat, (that I had selected for her specifically for this purpose) left the Auditorium, just like I said she would do. Not many persons realized that she had left until after they had all reseated themselves, and then they wondered what message I had sent to her.

Most persons would never forget this night, especially Peggy. Because she knew absolutely, that I knew what she did last night and with whom. And that if she tried to deny it, that I would further tell her what else they did and for how long.

Now you may ask, with whom did you spend the night with, so I will tell you; Ken Jenkins. And since he is now married, he is also cheating on his wife. And they live in a medium sized town in Illinois. And he and his wife now have two children together. So don't be surprised if you do get pregnant also from last nights entanglement.

Actually I am a bit surprised that you have not already gotten pregnant. But while you were having sex with other men in our apartment, you had all of them wear Rubbers, but last evening you did not use a rubber.

So now you will have to find a Doctor who will give you something to help you get rid of this baby while you are carrying it. Or else get an Abortion, which is strictly illegal in the state of Missouri. Of course there are some folks who will most likely do it for you, for a price, but how will it effect you personally.

And if your parents find out, how will that affect your relationship with them. And will GOD ever forgive you, or will you yell again --- RAPE ---- And send Ken Jenkins to Jail, where he should have been for the past 12 years anyway. YOU ARE STUCK AGAIN.

And if I try to get our marriage Annulled again, and since your father will know that you were pregnant, no matter whom the father may have been, what will he now do. Will he still try to stop our marriage from being annulled once again?

I wonder....................

CLEMENT

October 1st 1959

PREGNANCY

Dear Peggy;

As I suspected, Ken Jenkins got you pregnant on August 24th 1959, and here it is about six weeks later, and because you have not actually told your parents that you are pregnant, and you still have not tried to get rid of this baby using any devious methods, yet, that I wonder what you will do if you wait too long. Meaning when your body begins to show that you have this baby inside of you.

It takes thirty six weeks for a baby to become old enough and large enough for it to be born. So consider that each Trimester is twelve weeks long, and if you wait until it is in the last trimester of this baby's life, no one will abort it.

And of course there is always the possibility of me telling your parents that you are pregnant. But not with my baby, but with Ken Jenkins baby.

Knowing you like I do, you will soon be having "morning sickness" bouts and since you are still living with your parents, what will you tell them? Will you tell them that you have a stomach problem or will you tell them the truth about yourself? And what will they say about you becoming pregnant? Knowing that you are no longer married to me? And if you have an abortion, and get rid of that child inside of you, what will your parents say?

Now how will you be able to live with the fact that you will have murdered your potential child? I know you are very strong willed, but killing your own child, would you really do that? I wonder!

What a very cold thing to be able to do something like that. I know that I could kill another person, but only if that person was actually trying to kill me also.

But to coldly kill a baby in your own womb, would that be possible for you to actually do? And you being a Catholic person in good standing. So if you kill this baby, then the likelihood of our marriage being annulled would most likely be a very good probability.

I know you never figured that something like this would ever come about, but it has and now you are confronted with what to do about it. How do I know you are pregnant, well again I have read your mind, and now also your doctor knows too.

Well I guess I will end this dissertation of this lesson in humility. Wow, what a calamitous situation you have gotten yourself in the middle of.

I did not mention anything about our 4th wedding anniversary because I did not think you even remembered anyway.

CLEMENT

December 10th 1959

Dear Peggy;

I guess my last letter must have gotten to you, because now that you are beginning to show this pregnancy, I have had inquiries about it from persons at the Wabash. And they asked if we were back together again because of it. But I tell them it is not from me, but from another man.

Your father is now wondering whether or not allowing our marriage to be annulled was such a good thing to happen. He asked the same question as to whether it was my baby, and I told him it was not, but it was actually from another married man, who did not live in the St Louis area. He asked me if I knew who the father was, I told him that I did know, but I told him that he would have to ask you for that answer.

And he says he does not talk to you, because you never talk to him. I then told him to talk to your wife. He says I don't know if Peggy even talks to her either.

I then tell him that your life must be very lonely with your oldest daughter living with you, and he says she moved out a month back, and I only know about her pregnancy from other persons who have seen her with some of her other friends.

That he does not know where she now lives or with whom, I then tell him that I want to get my marriage with Peggy Annulled, and this time I want it to be fully approved by the Catholic church. This marriage has been a complete flop, and really should never have even happened.

But due to my need of wanting to get out of South Dakota, I actually used Peggy to accomplish that endeavor. Even though in the beginning I thought it was a great idea. But now she will hinder me more than she will help me.

So because I want to get on with the rest of my life, I no longer want to remain married to her. And I cannot produce any natural children with her.

Now if I had known that she had never wanted children, that would have gone over very well with her. But I did not actually know that she had never ever wanted to have any children. And I am still afraid that the baby she is carrying will never be born. Because she fears the pain of childbirth.

I think she will still try to get rid of it by medical means. What those methods are, I don't have a clue, but she will try, and soon. She will blame it on the fact that her spine is crooked and that caused it to abort naturally. Whether that will actually happen, I do not know, but it will happen within the next two weeks. This is just a warning for you and your wife. You see, she has a plan, and living with the two of you, she could not make this happen. But now she can. How she will make it happen I do not know.

CLEMENT

January 5th 1960

NO BABY

Dear Peggy;

As information, I warned your father that you would find a way to abort this baby you are carrying, and you have done it. And when it happened you would tell them it was because of your crooked spine, that you got hurt when being bucked from a horse while riding in one of the Horse Shows that you rode in while in your teens. And I was correct.

Of course you and I know that is not the real method of how you really got rid of this baby. Actually I know how you did it. Now all you have to do is how to prevent me from telling your parents and your sister and all of the Catholic Nuns who have come to visit you in the Hospital. Even though I never did come to see you, even once. Because you did not want me to come to see you. And now everyone says that I am a mean Husband.

So what I am going to do is I am going to go to the local Newspaper and by writing a letter to the Editor of the Social News department, but before I do this I will let your father read this letter that I have written, so he will also know everything about you and us and our disastrous Marriage.

Then using this letter that hopefully your father will also sign, but if he doesn't, I will still take it to the Newspaper and have it published.

In this letter I will tell all of what you have been doing since we have been married especially all that you have been doing since we came to the St Louis area. Actually how many men you have actually slept with and where, and how many of these men were married when you slept with them.

So I think a lot of Divorces will be taking place in the near future around this area. I will wait one week after I send this letter to you for whatever you may want to try to do, before I actually get this letter published.

The contents of the letter to the Newspaper I will not send to you. I only mention it to let you know what to expect in the near future. And the contents of that letter will not be detailed in this book either. What you do to try to stop me is totally up to you.

CLEMENT

January 13th 1960

Dear Peggy;

Well today is the 13th of January, which is one week and one day after I sent my last letter to you, and I still have not heard from you. As to that letter that I took to the Newspaper, before I had it published, I had their Legal department look it over and after they gave me some advice about the wording, they published it. By the time you get this letter, this letter will have been published in local Newspaper.

I have been told, that if what I say in this letter is all truth, then you cannot do anything about me, meaning if you file a Law Suite against me for trying to ruin your so called reputation, it will most likely be thrown out of Court.

Of course you can always do what you think you have to do, but I would hate to see you lose this case, because it would make your reputation to become more notable than it ever has been before, and men would come from all over just to spend some time with you. Now if that is what you want then, so be it.

CLEMENT

April 6th 1960

Dear Peggy;

My Lawyer Moses Lighthouse in Los Angeles says the news service has picked up on my story about all of the truth in your life and my own. And he has also contacted a Lawyer in the St Louis area who will become my lawyer in case he is needed. But does not believe that you will do anything about what I have had published in that Newspaper. That all you have to do is do nothing and it will eventually die after awhile.

Moses tells me to tell you what I just stated, and maybe you will take my good free advice and it will die a natural death. And he also tells me to not write any more letters to you until you answer any that I have already sent to you.So I guess this will be my final letter, until I cannot stand it any longer, especially about what you are doing with your own life. But to actually try to get our marriage Annulled.

Actually since your Father did not sign my letter to the Newspaper, he will probably fight me in my endeavor to get our marriage annulled. So be prepared to fight the Catholic Church about this case.

And if it ever goes all the way to Rome, it will then probably become a reality, but that will take several years to accomplish. Catholic people are strange folk. Moses says he knows personally, because he is also Catholic. But he will help me whenever I need his help, just like he has always done for me ever since he has known me.

There is talk about the Norfolk and Western Railroad merging with the Wabash Railroad. And if that happens, then the likelihood of me being laid off from the Wabash will be very real. But I have been working a part time job with a veterinary Doctor, and my Special ability has come in real handy on a number of occasions, so I will continue to work at that job, no matter what may happen with the Wabash.

As information, I am now a Trainmaster with this railroad and my offices are in Union Station, and I have lunch with your Mom every day. She is a very sad person since you aborted that baby. She actually liked the fact that I did publish that letter in the Newspaper, because it told her in total what has been happening with you but not with me.

She says she would still like for you and I to get together again, but how that will ever happen will have to be a miracle. But Wonders never seem to cease sometimes. I brought some photographs of my five cats, and she especially liked the ones of Chili and of all of the antics that she does for me.

She says what a wonderful thing for me to be able to teach her all of the things that I have taught her. Since I still smoke, when I need a fresh pack of cigarettes, she goes and gets a new pack for me. And then when I finish a pack, and I scrunch it up, and when I throw it she goes and gets it and brings it back to me, and she keeps doing that for a half hour or sometimes more.

I no longer live in the Grandview Garden apartments. I now live in a Split Level Duplex in the city of Pine Lawn. I also purchased a number of Law Library bookcases and I have lined them with Reynolds wrap paper inside of them so the shiniest part of that wrap is reflecting back. Then I went and bought 500 African Violet plants, of all colors and varieties and now I am reproducing them by the dozens. Because I now have about ten thousand of them. It really keeps me busy all of the while I am home. I may have to give up my part time job in order to take care of all of them.

My whole house is full of African Violets of all of the colors of the rainbow and even more. I take them to all of the local grocery markets that sell them. I am supplying fifteen markets with these plants. I have also contacted some local Nurseries and with them they want 12 dozen at a time. I tell all of them how to take care of them and if any of them die, then they will not be replaced by me, because they mistreated them to cause them to die. So far with the markets I have not lost any at all. So I have not signed any contracts with any Nurseries either. These plants do very well only when they are inside.

They are never to be grown outside, because if you get water on top of any of the leaves, then that leaf will most likely just turn brown and die.

Nurseries think they know it all, so I have been keeping away from any of them. When someone ever tells them how to really take care of these plants, then they will kick themselves for not going with me.

And all of the cats love every color. I also have two additional cats, of which are Siamese. They are brother and sister, even though the female is female only internally, because outwardly she is male, because she has a penis. But in every other way she is a girl cat.

The male who is named Tai and the girl is name Tak. What those names mean I can also tell you but not at this time. I got them when they were kittens also. They are very intelligent. I will keep you in my prayers and try to think of you every so often. You will note my address on the envelope so if you are in my vicinity, stop by and maybe we can talk for a while, of which would be a Revelation. But just in case that address is destroyed somehow, here is my new address:

Clement Royal
2714 Darla Court
Pine Lawn, Missouri

Clement

July 4th 1960

Dear Peggy;

Three months has gone by, and again I am writing another letter to you. Whether I actually send it to you is still being debated in my mind.

Actually I do keep a daily Journal of whatever happens with others, and me and I have done this ever since I have been three years of age, so this is more for just keeping up to date with what is really going on in my life, but not yours.

Oh, I know what is going on in your life, and if it seems that I need to write it down, then I will, but more for just it being a matter of Historical reasons. I heard that you had an automotive accident and that your mother says your car was totaled.

So because I have purchased another automobile, actually a brand new vehicle, I am giving mine to you. And since you are now living with your folks again, I have driven mine to their address and left it in front of their house. And I just dropped off the keys with your mother. But I did not go inside of the house. I had a friend of mine pick me up there and he took me home to Darla court.

Now the vehicle that I purchased is a 1959 Isetta, which was actually manufactured in Italy. I only paid eleven hundred dollars for it, even though it was last years model, because apparently they did not sell very well in this country, so I purchased it while it was on sale. There is only one door on it, and that is on the entire front of the vehicle. When the door opens up, the steering wheel is attached to this door, so it has some connecting parts to it that allows it to be taken out of the way when any person gets inside of this vehicle. It is only wide enough for two persons and a child to sit on the only seat of this vehicle. The main gas tank holds only five gallons of gasoline, with a Reserve tank that holds four gallons. The vehicle does have four wheels, with the two rear wheels about sixteen inches apart, and between and above these two wheels is where the engine is where the motor sits. The top speed I am told is about 70 miles per hour, but another friend of mine says he can raise that speed to about 80 miles per hour by resetting the governor on the Carburetor, of which he has already done for me. It starts real good, and so far I have only driven it back and forth to work. It gets about 75 miles per gallon of gas, so lets say if I drive until I have only a gallon of gas left in the reserve tank, I can still drive 600 miles.

I need to take a ride to Paducah, Kentucky, because I plan to sell my African Violet Business. I have made about fifty thousand dollars so far, and have paid off all of my bills connected with that business, so I am getting out of it.

There is a company in that fair city who says they would like to get into that business, so I have to either go see them or what I would like for them to do is to come to St Louis, and bring whatever vehicle that they are going to use to take all of the plants back with them. But they tell me I should come to their fair city first.

One thing and that is, any truck that they bring to pick up

those plants has to be totally enclosed, because if it is not, then they will lose every plant as they travel.

I really don't think they really know what they are talking about. So if the deal is not made then I have one more person to contact, of which I do not want to actually sell to, but I may have to, unless I remain with it for at least another year or two.

There is good money in selling African violets but like some businesses, it is a trendy business, and I want to get out of it before that trend goes limp.

Good news, I have been contacted by a firm in the Chicago area, who are seriously interested in all of my plants. They will be in St Louis in four days to inspect my plants. I feel better about this concern than the one in Paducah. Wish me luck.

Now here it is a week later and the deal with the Chicago company has been signed and sealed, and in fact they have already came and picked up all of the fifty thousand plants.

My Duplex was totally inundated with African Violets when they arrived. And sure enough, they brought a Semi Truck with a 40 foot trailer, with a tailgate that was automatic, so all they had to do was to load up carts that had three tiers on them that they brought with them and then take them outside and load them. Each one was fastened to the wall inside of this trailer, and around each cart they placed some plastic, so no plants could fall off of any of the three tiered carts. The edges of each shelf was raised up on all sides three inches also, so as to keep any of these plants from falling off of any of these carts. They thought ahead when planning this trip. There was room for just one more cart when they got everything loaded. And the carts that they brought with them filled in the blank space.

They told me that where they will be sold would be inside of what they call a Mall type structure. Meaning that every shop is inside of this vast mall. This will be something for the future of how shopping areas will be built from now on.

Actually they told me that in Minneapolis, Minnesota, they already have built one and companies as far away as southern California and Seattle, Washington are examining it. And Walt Disney has been looking at all of them too.

Before I dropped off my car at your mom's house, I had the Oil changed and the car Greased everywhere there was a place to grease it. And I filled up the gas tank also. I don't know what your financial situation really is, so I figured that this was the only thing I could do, in spite of everything else.

The title is in the glove box and I have actually sold it to you for one dollar, which I have paid to myself already, so you do not owe me any money. Take the title to the State motor vehicle place so you can have it registered in your name. I also transferred the license plate to your name too. So the only time you will have to get either a new license plate or new tags is when it comes up once each year on your birthday. Now since your birthday is in March, they may not change it from April.

Because usually they run in increments of two months, so that would mean that March and April would come due within the same month. Now whether that would be in April or March, is totally up to them, but since I have transferred this license plate to your name using my birthday month, then it is likely that the license will come due in April. Actually I would not tell them anything different. But they may ask anyway. I am just trying to make things easy for you.

So far the annulment of our marriage has not been approved. I have talked to the Archdiocese, and since there is a new and different Cardinal there now, it may totally rest on his shoulders.

I suppose it also rests on your father's shoulders, since it is he who has been blocking this annulment anyway. It would be interesting as to what you might think, and I will leave that totally up to you.

I really do not know why you would want to remain married to me, unless you think that you might get some additional money from me.

Actually since we were not living together when I started my African violet business and I have now sold it, you will not realize any money from that business.

The only money you would realize is while we were still living together, but since you actually left me, then the likelihood of you getting anything from me, is almost down to nothing.

So whatever advice you are being given by whomever, is probably not good advice. Because since we have been married and during all of that time, you actually have not lived with me for the past year, then you will not realize anything other than what I have already given you from my own free will.

And because you have also been working at your own job, means that through your health insurance, most of your medical bills have been paid through them and not any of mine.

I am a fair person, and I have always been completely fair

to you, no matter how unfair you have been to me. So if you are being advised to try to get money out of this Turnip, forget it, because it will never happen.

My lifetime Lawyer in California has hired the best Lawyer here in the St Louis area, and you will never win anything from me through a Law suite. Accept that as a hard fact. The only way you will ever get anything from me is if I decide to just give it to you, but in no other method.

Now if this Annulment does not go through, then you should consider changing your ways and try making a go with me once again. Our life together does not have to end here. If you come back to me, of course I will expect certain guarantees from you. And if you violate those guarantees, then that is when I will really divorce you.

Consider this. If I give up being a Catholic, and I Divorce you, then I can marry anyone I want to. Just as long as I never try to become a Catholic again.

Because if I Divorce you without getting an annulment, then I certainly will be excommunicated from the Catholic Church. And since I have been the main person who instigated that Divorce, I am not sure how the Catholic Church would feel about that either. But ask your Uncle Jim, because I think he would know. But in any case, I don't think you would be kicked out of the church.

Of course if you ever tried to get married again, then you would have to get an annulment from your marriage with me. And that will cost you five hundred dollars. And of course they will ask you why you did not ask for an annulment also when I asked for an annulment of this marriage, so after the horse got out of the barn, is really a poor time to shut the door. I think the example I just stated is a perfect one.

All of what I have mentioned here will give you something to think about while you are recovering from all of your injuries. Maybe GOD is trying to tell you something with this accident. Because it sure shows him what kind of a person I really am, especially since I gave you my vehicle, so you will have wheels when you will need them. I don't know what else I can really do for you. I don't think you really deserve everything I am doing for you, but this is the way I am all of the time.

I am what is called a FORGIVING PERSON. This is not something that any other person would do. Another man probably would have taken a gun and shot you dead, so he could get on with his own life, even though he even might have to spend the rest of it in a prison.

Now what kind of prison do you think I have been living in all of this time? Because that is where I have been living. Because I cannot get an annulment from this marriage. I have tried to be a good Catholic, but not any longer. If this annulment does not come through in the next two weeks, I will file for a Civil Divorce from you anyway and give up my membership in this religion.

CLEMENT

August 6th 1961

Dear Peggy;

Well here it is a little over a year later and I have since gotten a Civil Divorce from you. But not an annulment from the Catholic Church. I have given up my membership with that church, and have gone back to being a Lutheran again.

What a weight has been lifted from my shoulders. And I have seen you in some of the grocery stores, and have even spoken to you some of these times. You are looking well, but you are putting on a bit of weight. I told you at those times that I thought you might be eating too much. And you tell me that the vehicle I gave you is still running just fine. I am pleased that you keep it in good working condition. It is a very nice vehicle even though it is only a 1952 Ford.

That Isetta, I no longer have, because I went completely through the windshield of it, when I was ran into by a big Cadillac, about six months back. And I was pushed into the back end of a yellow cab vehicle.

Actually I lost my memory for a week, but I now have most of it back. Even though I don't now remember the accident at all. I had 21 stitches in my head above the hairline but they too are all healed now. The only number I could remember, belonged to your mothers work phone, and the officer who came to the accident scene was your Uncle Jim, and he recognized me so everything with me turned out okay in the end.

I am a very lucky guy, because where I was sitting in this vehicle, the engine now is located. So things of a certain weight moved first, meaning me, and then the motor, and I have been told, that it was not my time to die yet. GOD is still watching out for me, just like he has always done for me.

The vehicle was considered a total loss, so my Insurance paid me eleven hundred dollars for my trouble.

I went out and purchased a 1955 Mercury Monterey, just like the one you had when I first met you in that same year, only this one is grasshopper green. I paid only 800 dollars for it, and it needed some work done on it, but after I had that done, then it runs great.

I never was partial to green before, but this color is just fine now. I guess I am mellowing in my old age some. Luckily when that accident happened, and I did not get home for a week, my neighbors in the next duplex north of mine, who had a set of keys to my place, just in case I could not get home for some reason, came and took care of all of my cats, so they got along just fine without me.

I did that; because sometimes I am required to work double shifts and I figured that I needed someone to take care of my creatures.

Anyway everything is now back to normal, if coming home late at night is normal. Because I normally work only days, but sometimes my relief does not show up for work, so I have to work his shift too.

The reality of the Norfolk and Western railroad actually buying the Wabash is getting real close now. Because it has been rumored that my job will be taken over by a trainmaster from that railroad.

Well, here it is a week later, and I am now working back in the transportation department with the Wabash Railroad, but I won't be here all that long either. This is just a stopping off position until I am completely laid off from this job. I actually bumped some guy who had been working at the Wabash for two days less than I have been in seniority.

Now it is two weeks later and a guy with 37 years seniority bumped me out and I am now on the street, meaning I am completely out and unemployed again. What a run this has been. I almost had a total of six years with the Wabash railroad, and what have I been during all of that time.

Your father has nothing to worry about with his seniority though. He may have to go to Roanoke, Virginia to work if he expects to continue to work for the Norfolk and Western railroad. So this will give him something to think about and also Margaret. I don't think she will move to that state. And I don't think your father will move either. I think he will just retire instead. After all, he does have almost 45 years in the railroad industry, and on his next birthday he will be 60 years old, so he might as well think about retiring when he reaches 65. And what a retirement party that will be. He knows more than 500 persons and probably twice that many that are still alive.

I just heard that there would be some positions that will remain in St Louis for another four or five years yet. And one of them will be your Fathers. He will now be in charge of both the Mail Room Department and the Telegraph department. In fact every office that is located on the fourteenth floor, he will be the

Manager of.

And since the Katy railroad went to Tyler, Texas, most of the personnel who worked there will now work for your father. I also heard that most of these persons had a lot of personal stuff in their desk drawers and since they moved everything over a weekend, that all of this personal stuff got moved right along with everything else.

I also heard that one guy had over a thousand dollars in one of his locked desk drawers. I too have had some good luck and some bad luck.

I and five other guys pooled our money and went to the IBM Company and rented some machines from them and we started a computer programming school. Another company started another computer programming school a block away from us, but we paid our teachers just enough money so that all who worked for that other company eventually came and worked for us. This went on for a little while, and then when I saw the handwriting on the wall as far as competitors, I told my partners, that if they wanted, I would sell out to them.

They asked me did I know something that they did not know, and I say now is the time to get out of this business, because these schools are going to be a dime a dozen soon, because these type of schools are a trendy thing.

So we sold this company for 85 thousand dollars. Now for an initial investment of 200 dollars each, and selling out at the correct time, we made about 14 thousand dollars each. Not a bad investment for two months work.

I talked to your father, and he told me that the Western

Weighing and Inspection Bureau is hiring, so I went down there a couple of days later and secured a position with that company. And they are on the eighteenth floor of the railway exchange building. And the money I am making with them is pretty close to what I made as a clerk with the Wabash. So all is well with my employment at this time. I heard that you too lost your job with Emerson Electric, but you don't believe it was your own fault that it actually happened.

I also know that your extracurricular activities are almost down to nothing. So maybe now is the time to try to get back with me. Since you have hit a dry period. I think someone in a high place is actually trying to tell you something.

I am not saying that I would remarry you, but it all depended on what and how you treated me. Your father even mentioned it to me one day. Apparently you have been discussing with him some of your feelings regarding me. Only you are a bit late in that endeavor, don't' you think? About six years late.

CLEMENT

October 1ˢᵗ 1961

Dear Peggy;

On this date, we would have been married six years. If what we have been through is what is called married life, of which I do not. But of course we are not married civilly, but in the eyes of the Catholic Church we still are. But I am no longer a catholic.

Hazel Leuders called me and has made an appointment between you and I to meet at Hullings restaurant this coming Wednesday evening at 6:00 PM in downtown St Louis. Of which I have agreed to do. She did not say what this meeting would be about. And I did not ask. But I am curious, so I will meet with you at that appointed time and place.

Actually before I walked into that restaurant, I eves dropped on your mind, to see what you were thinking about. Just in case you had something other than what I thought you might be seeking. At that time you were thinking about some of your liaisons with other men, and you were thinking whether I had really changed my mind regarding children and sex. I smiled but I lost that smile when I walked into this restaurant, and asked for you, using your maiden name.

The hostess told me that there was a Margaret Royal waiting for me, so I accepted and followed her to the table you had selected. It was at a corner table, behind some beaded curtains. You did not get up when I arrived but just remained seated, and then I sat down. You asked me if I wanted to order and I told the hostess that I would like some Lobster tails along with all of the trimmings. She smiled and said that is what this lady said you would order, and then you said to make it two orders. You had not changed either in that respect.

The hostess asked if I wanted any kind of drink and I said no, because I want to have a clear head during these discussions. Then she left. You said that I haven't changed much. That you still don't drink while business may be discussed. I then told you " I don't drink alcohol ever ".

I asked you what kind of business are we going to discuss this evening. I tried not to be harsh, but I guess it came across that way. It's a little hard not being harsh with you. You let it pass and I was grateful. I smiled just a little smile, but a smile nonetheless.

I suggested that maybe we should not call this a business discussion. Because it kind of rubs me the wrong way to think of this that way. Then you smiled, just a little smile, but a smile nonetheless. You then said that she knew that she had not been real supportive of me in anything that I ever did, especially from the very beginning of our marriage.

You then told me that you had been in a Sanatorium kind of place, where they dried you out about your alcohol problem, and talked until you were tired of telling them about your Sexual problems.

Of your need to have sex with everyone, except your husband, who was never at fault with that problem in the first place. But yet you said that you blamed me for everything anyway. That you actually spent the last four months in that place, and it cost you your job, and your marriage, and even most of your friends.

Then you asked me if I would be interested in getting back with you again. I told you only if you are completely cured of all of your extracurricular activities.

I will need some kind of documentation regarding your treatments. And is there a possibility that all of your extracurricular activities would ever begin again, especially if we got married again.

But I will not get married again in the Catholic Church, nor will I ever become a catholic again. If we have children, they will be educated in the catholic system. That is all I can promise you. Now what will you do for me.

Because living down what you have done to me and without me is something that will be very hard for you to do. I must demand total obedience from you regarding another marriage with me.

You see, when I took those marriage vows, I believed totally in them, and getting a Divorce from you was the only way I could get rid of what you never did for me. And that was to obey those marriage vows, because you violated them from the very beginning, even before we were married in the Catholic Church.

And after we got married in the church, your extracurricular activities became worse and worse and incredibly worse. Now you want to try again with me. Because you figured that I would totally forgive you for all of your transgressions. How many times must I forgive all of your transgressions? How much do you think I will take from you?

And if all of what has happened, begins again, what will I do with you. Will I eliminate you from this life, and put you out of your misery or will I just let you continue with all of your activities, until some other man ends your life. Because for all of the threats you have made to your parents, you don't really have the guts to do yourself in by yourself. I know this to be fact. I will think about it for a while.

Now that our meal has arrived, I don't think I am hungry enough to eat it, so enjoy yourself and take my portion home with you, because I am now leaving.

I threw a fifty-dollar bill on the table. And I got up and left you by yourself. Wondering what I would really do. I will make you wait for quite a while before I finally give you my answer. I am quite sure you will think about this for a long time.

CLEMENT

December 24, 1961

Dear Peg;

This is my first six months with the Western Weighing and Inspection Bureau and they are giving me two weeks off, because of the Christmas and New Years holidays. And I will get the same pay just as if I was on a vacation.

I like my boss and he likes me. He tells me that he has finally got someone who knows about Transit Rates and totally understands how they are figured.

I tell him that they are not all that complicated, but for some persons they apparently are. But I do like the work and I am very good at what I do.

I also keep the storage records for all of the grains and also for the corn that is stored in all of the Government granaries in and around the St Louis area.

I also have to go and inspect these granaries and take samples and test all of this grain and Corn, to make sure that there is not too much moisture in all of it.

And if there is, then I have to make arrangements to have it taken out of these storage places and dried and then placed in other storage places in and around this area. And I love that job also. My boss says it is nice to have someone who also knows all of the different kinds of grains and I also keep fully informed of all of the prices of these grains, including all of the Future prices of these grains, because "The Farmers" who have taken loans on all of these grains always want to know what the future looks like, so as to be able to make a decisions as to when to sell what they will or will not own.

It is a very fascinating job to take care of all of this. Your father says that I am a whiz at taking care of Government storage.

I am still thinking about what you asked me three months back. So I have finally decided that I will take one more chance with you, only this time you will either tow the line or I will get rid of you with another divorce, but this time I will take you to court and sue you for everything that you might have at that time. And I will win according to my two Lawyers. One who is in St Louis and the other who is in Los Angeles?

And you will not get any monetary finances from me, unless you do as the marriage vows are dictated. This time I will write my own marriage vows. And if you will not go along with what I write, but say your own, then this marriage will not take place because its either my way or no way. So now it is totally up to you. In fact I will write a Pre-nuptial agreement, that you will either sign or I will not marry you again.

MERRY CHRISTMAS...........

CLEMENT

February 28th 1962

MARRIAGE ONCE AGAIN

Dear Peggy;

You have accepted my agreement, and we actually got married again today. We will still live at 2714 Darla Court, at least for a while yet, but I do have plans to move to a downtown Apartment in the not too far distant future, when the Apartment complex is finally finished. It is now being built and these Apartments are west of the down town area near 15th street and Market boulevard, just a couple of blocks form Kiel Auditorium, which is where a lot of things happen. Like Opera's, and other interesting things go on.

The area is not all that great near the Auditorium, but where these new apartments will be, it is well lit and it will be patrolled by Security guards 24 hours of every day and night.

And I understand that there is a Clothing manufacturing company that is going to move into one of the buildings on Washington Street, which is only two blocks north of these new apartment buildings.

I am told that the starting salary will be for a piecework payroll supervisor will be very good. Now since you have had some experience in that kind of payroll, then I think that may be a good place to begin, if you still want to go back to work.

But for now, you will just remain at home and keep house for me and my five cats. Of which two will soon be not with us, as they are quite old now, and are getting sick more often than I am willing to accept.

There is a retirement home for cats who are looking for residents to retire in, so that is where I plan to take them so they will be monitored by retired Veterinarians who are working there part time, but are still knowledgeable regarding just cats.

This home will cost me a thousand dollars per cat, but I think it will be worth it to them to be in a place where they can interact with other cats around the same age and have their own places to eat and sleep, so I am all for Retirement Homes for Senior Cats.

And I will probably support these homes as long as they are in existence in this area. I will keep Chile and Tai and Tak. Chili has been fixed some time back and she is still a very smart cat. Because she still fetches and has actually taught Tak to do the same. Tai is still the boss of his Pride.

As for actually needing to write these letters, it probably will not be required if you live up to your marriage vows and the pre-nuptial agreement. But I have gotten so used to writing them that I will probably continue to write them anyway. So if I have not mentioned something to you, then you may read any of these letters anytime you want to read them. Or even all of them. I am glad that you kept all of them, because it tells me that you read them, and that is encouraging knowledge…

CLEMENT

March 23rd 1962

Dearest Peggy;

Matter of fact, I would hope that you will honor my request and keep all of these letters, even if some of them are not all that favorful for you. I am not always the kind of person that I should be all of the time. No one is, but I do know what my responsibilities are. And I am willing to work with you in whatever problems you may have, but if I am never given the chance to help you then, why or would you blame me for your problems.

Especially if any problem involves only you and me, then it is up to both of us to solve that problem. You asked me about children. Let me answer in this way. I do not want to have children through intercourse with you, ever.

Because I never want to experience you ever losing another baby under any circumstances. But I think Adopting would more than satisfy my longing for a family. And for our first child, I would like to adopt a daughter. Maybe two at a time. About six or seven years of age. Someone whose personality has already been formed.

The reason for this is because with a person like that, we will have to earn their trust, and that will be most difficult. But if both of us can do that, then we can take on any child of any age. And a female child will be very difficult to gain their trust.

Especially one who has been violated by a male parent or maybe even both of her original parents.

I know of what I speak, because of the way I was treated when I returned home from the Mayo clinic, after being away from my real parents for almost five years.

Because during that time, they had completely written me off as being part of their family. So when I did return when I was almost five years old, it was as if I did not exist in their world. This is what I had to get used to or else I would have been put up for adoption or I would have been sent away to an institution like a Sanitarium. Back in those days they called them Nut houses.

Nowadays they are used to take care of persons with alcohol problems or sex problems or both, as you well know yourself. Or when persons have nervous breakdowns.

What do you think about adopting two girls at the same time? Then you told me that you don't think you will make a very good Mother, whether you had the baby yourself or if it was adopted. Wow - what a let down that statement gave me.

Here I thought by us getting married again, that we would now be able to somehow get a family, but now you say you don't think you would make a good parent. Well it's too late, because we will begin a family.

For many years now, you have always thought in the negative field, and I have always thought in the positive field. Why did you not say that before we got married again? What do you think getting married is all about?

Is it just being comfortable with some special person or is it acting like we are a couple, so as to cause your friends to treat us with more respect, if we instead were just two individuals who are just dating.

I think you have finally realized, that being married to a man who is well respected in whatever community he lives in, and is also well respected in whatever he does in his life, and since you have led the kind of life, that has taken you to the underbelly of society, that if you were a married woman whose husband is well liked most everywhere, that it would make it much easier for you to get along in whatever way that you do, just as long as it is not in the same way that it has been for the past 6 ½ years.

Because when two persons get married, they actually take on new duties with each other, that is only done as a couple. Do you expect me to take you dancing a lot, so you can experience that old excitement and notoriety that we once knew?

I don't fully understand why you married me again. You told me that you loved me. And so stated that again when we took our marriage vows in a church. Not a catholic church, but in a church nonetheless.

You are supposedly a Catholic in relatively good standing, so that whatever children we get will be educated in that church. Now what am I to think? Am I to go for the rest of my life, childless?

When by doing this, I was expecting that we would adopt as soon as possible. In fact I was counting on it. So when I make application to adopt a child, I sincerely hope you back me up, because if you do not, then we definitely will be just two persons leading two very different lives.

Now I don't care what kind of a Mother you will be, just as long as you try to be one. I know there are couples on this earth that should never become parents, but even if I have to do this totally alone, then I will.

But I will not divorce you again, or move out of this state, never to return to it, except to bury someone. So get used to me being in charge of this family, because I won't take no for an answer.

I am getting tired of always having to try to convince you to be someone, that if you put your mind to it, you could do it all by yourself. If we cannot appear to be a relatively happily married couple, then we should still try to get along the best as we can.

But if we are to remain married, then we will talk to each other, and sleep in the same bed with each other, and be totally true with each other, and everything else that goes with being a married couple.

Because I won't live the way I have lived for the past 6 ½ years, with a wife constantly cheating on me, with her thinking that she is getting away with murder.

Now if I sound angry, I suppose I am, because you have cheated me out of 6 ½ years of my life. And your father has been responsible for most of that, because he totally refused to support an Annulment of that first Marriage. I guess you never knew that. And if you did, then I don't know if I want to really know that you approved of what he tried to do.

Actually before I left this letter, where you would find it, I actually read it to you, to see what you would say. And since you did not say anything, am I to assume that you agree with all that I have said here?

So again you are treating me just like you have been treating me for the past 6-½ years. Well I won't be treated that way. Either you talk to me now, or this marriage is ALL OVER. I will give you an hour to decide what you will do.

Clement

HAPPY BIRTHDAY

PS: THERE ARE NO PRESENTS BEING GIVEN TO YOU FOR THIS BIRTHDAY. I HAD HOPED YOU WOULD GIVE ME ONE FOR MY LAST BIRTHDAY.

But you did not,

September 19, 1962

Dear Peggy;

Well, this marriage has turned out better than I had expected it to do, which is real great. Because when you began talking, I have not been able to stop you. I'm not complaining, but WOW. There is a lot of anger in you, that if you had been talking to me for the past seven years, almost, maybe we might have a reasonably happy marriage now. But this is a lot better than what has been happening for the past 7 years.

I have a lot of anger in me also, but venting it to you and towards you would not solve any problems. Yes I know I am still writing these letters, but before I give them to you, I read them to you, so you can respond to what I have written, and we do now discuss some of these very important issues.

You see when I can sit and think about things for awhile, I can fully string words together that make a lot more sense, and when you respond to what I have said in these letters, then I too can respond in like kind with an answer to your questions.

I think this is a good way to solve a lot of our problems. Actually I kind of like the way you have turned out now. Because you do have a lot of knowledge in so many areas that I do not, and I really welcome your input.

I also think that perhaps when we were first married, that you thought that I was not all that educated and it scared you, and you thought that I would be a very dull guy to be with, but now you have discovered that I have many facets to my character, and that I can talk on almost any subject, including one of your favorites, which is Politics and the other is Religion.

Now admittedly, I have learned a lot about religion in the past seven years, fighting the Catholic church all of this time. But I have finally decided that I will not continue with that any longer, because just as long as you are a catholic in relatively good standing, that whatever children we eventually get, that they will be educated in that religion, because I think their overall teachings are much better than any public school system, and I speak from personal experience.

Of course, like all possible adoptions, when we applied, it is progressing so very slowly that it is driving me buggy. Their inadequate system of handling different things dealing with obvious things in person's lives is something to be desired.

Meaning they are full of so much prejudice, that it is hard to know what to do or how to respond to all of their very stupid questions.

For example here we are a married couple, who have been married almost seven years, even though we have been married twice to each other and actually three times, when you include when we got married in the church. Now that seems to totally confuse them. Why I don't know.

Then they tell us that they think we should be given a small baby, when that is not agreeable to either of us, because we both work. And then because we would have to hire a baby sitter to take care of that child, while we are at our work places, they then come back and say that we would not make good parents, because we would not be around this child long enough so as to cause its personality to form like we are formed.

So what I have done is I have gone to a higher authority, who are the persons who regulate the original Charters of these Public administrations, and I have gotten around them by having the Rules changed in my favor. And in doing this, all of these individuals that we have been dealing with, have now been fired.

Of course the problem I now have is that we have to start all over again, by making a new application for an older child, which will be a girl of around 6 of 7 years of age, one which has been very difficult to adopt out to anyone, because this child has some serious problems, wherein other potential parents wouldn't think of taking on that kind of child. But of which is exactly what I am looking for. And this time they are hearing us and especially me.

Because they know that I had all of the other personnel fired who used to run this agency, which they are now running. So I am someone to be listened to and reckoned with.

Anyone that has connections like I do will be listened to. So the likelihood of us getting what we are seeking, is mostly probable. It will just take a little longer to accomplish.

Again I read this letter to you, so as to get your thoughts about what I said in it. And you gave me some other things to think about and eventually to write about in a later letter. But we had some great discussions about this letter, and you really got me going for a while there. But I liked that.

LOVE

CLEMENT

January 16th 1963

Dearest Peggy;

Well this adoption is progressing at a much more rapid rate, even though it is still slower than I would like it to be. But I guess they have to do a lot of investigating of the two of us. How deep they go, I really don't know, but according to my Lawyer here in St Louis, he thinks we will probably be able to see the young girl that we will be getting, because they have told him that they want us to arrange to meet this young lady within a week. Which will make it the 23rd of this month. Which will be 4 days after her seventh birthday.

I asked my lawyer if there is anything that we should get this young lady, and he says definitely not. So on the appointed day, we meet with this young lady; whose name is Susan, and it's real amazing, because she looks a lot like you. I can see that you also approve of Susan. Because even though you did not say anything at that time, I could see that you thought the same thing I thought of, that she looks like you do. WOW.

We asked her various questions and you were very impressed with her answers and so was I. But I also asked her how she felt about Cats, and she says she hates all cats. So I asked her why, and she says they are sneaky and dirty and they always hurt people. So I asked her another question, which was; have you ever been around any Cats, and she says only once, and it scratched her and bit her. So I asked why did it do that. She says she kicked it. And again I asked why, and she says because she does not like them, period.

We then left, and I told you that this is not the child I am seeking. This one will have to find another home. You said that maybe we could get rid of the cats, and I say, only in your dreams. My cats are the most gentle of any cats in this world. If we adopted her, the first thing she would do, for no other reason, except because she does not like cats, she would kick all of them, and I will not have a child in my house who is mean to any creature, just because it is that creature. We could never trust her. And trying to educate her as to how to treat a cat who even though that person would kick them every time she saw them, in the proper ways to treat a cat, I will not take on that responsibility. I would rather go totally without any children than to accept a child that would be mean to any one of them, just because it is a Cat.

Now I know that you thought to yourself that if this is how it is going to be, then we may never adopt any child, and you also thought that maybe he is right in his thinking, because you find my cats very comforting also.

Because you have taken them onto your lap and you pet them and love them just like I do. Maybe not as much as I do, but you love them nonetheless. You see, any person who likes Cats cannot be all that bad, no matter whom they are.

I have read about Criminals who have taken in Cats and or Birds, and loved them with as much love as they could give it, and it was treated with total kindness, so any criminal who can love any creature like a cat or a bird or a dog or whatever, cannot be all bad. For example the Birdman of Alcatraz Island, took in dozens of Birds, and eventually wrote a book dealing with hundreds of diseases of Birds. Which is used even today with Bird Breeders.

So we will keep looking. So I called my Lawyer and told him why we rejected this young lady, and he told me he did not know that about her, and he would make sure that any other future potential parents knew that about her from the very beginning. It would probably prevent her from ever being adopted.

LOVE ....CLEMENT

PS:

Again I did discuss this letter with you and we had some very heated conversations about this one. But we made up with each other so as to get on with our lives. It's interesting that there has never been a book ever written about how to solve various problems in any marriage. With or without children.

Clement

February 15th 1963

Dear Peg;

Another month has gone by and we again have made another appointment to see and meet with another young lady, and we hope this one will be more to our liking. Our appointment is on the 22nd of this month and when it arrives we arrive about fifteen minutes early. I did this because I wanted to observe all of the children that are playing in the yard of this Orphanage.

There is snow on the ground and some of them are making a snowman, and it is becoming quite large. When it is time to place the head on this snowman, I step in and pick it up and place it where it is needed. Then some of the children, who are of all age groups from about three years of age to about 16 years of age.

I would have thought that the 16 year old could have lifted the head of the snowman, but he really looks rather weak in strength. He is tall enough, but just not strong enough.

I figured that the head of the snowman weighed about forty pounds, because I know that the last snow was rather wet, which is great for making snowmen. Anyway some of the other children put Coal for eyes and a nose using a piece of wood and a mouth of the same material, and then placed other tree branches in it for arms and finally an old hat, that had seen better days.

I actually had a Camera with me this time, so I took several photographs of this snowman and I told these children that I would make sure they received a couple of them. They were well pleased and I was also.

I looked around for my Lawyer, but he was not there. And then I looked around some more for the caseworker that was handling our Case.

In about five minutes she came outside of the main building, and with her was a young lady who was rather plain looking and really was not pretty at all. I looked at you and you nodded your head in disapproval, and we just turned around and went back to our car, and we left. It was a big letdown this time.

You said that maybe there is no one for us. I say we will wait for six more months before we even look again. I then took you out to see your sister, because that is where you wanted to go. I knew you needed to tell her about this big disappointment. And I could not think of anything to say to the contrary.

I also knew you wanted to discuss with her about her own children and how to teach a child to like something like a Cat. I did not have the answer to that question myself either. And I wondered also if our quest to adopt was still the answer.

I told you then, that I would go see another Doctor, to see if any better drugs had been developed so as to get a person like myself, to get to the point where he could actually create a child with his wife.

I am not saying that I would have Sex with you, because I will not, but if I was able to build up my sperm, I could have it artificially implanted inside of you.

In fact if the researchers were far enough along in being

able to improve that sperm in a test tube, then maybe that would work also. Only time will tell that story.

You listened to my conversation, and you seemed to be especially interested in my words about being artificially implanted with my built up sperm. So I think that is what my main direction that I will follow. Now whatever the Doctor I will see, will say about this, I don't know.

So from work the next day I called a specialist in producing babies, and all of the research regarding that field, and I was referred to a Doctor whose name is Maple Willows, who is a Gynecologist, which is a medical person who handles women most all of the time.

I thought now this is going to be very interesting. But when I put my situation to her, she says she will be able to probably help me in my endeavor to get me to the point where I can either have another person to cause me to have an orgasm, to get some sperm from me or I can actually have sex with a surrogate woman, wherefrom this doctor will take my sperm from her, or I can have sex with my wife, wherefrom she can take my sperm from her.

Now since I had never cheated on you, I was kind of uncertain as to which one to do. You told me that you did not want to have sex with me either, so whatever decision I decided on taking, would be alright with you, just as long as I never told you which one I used.

Now all of this will be done in a room in where this GYN is located. I will not write down which one I selected. But in any case some sperm was secured, wherein Dr. Maple Willows took it and placed it in a test tube, where she says she will upgrade with various drugs and other sperm from some other creature.

That if it was used, this sperm would totally represent what I am in looks and intelligence and whatever other traits I may have. That this will take about two weeks. And then if everything went well, I will then bring my wife to this doctors office, wherein this sperm will be implanted into her, where it would either merge with some of your eggs of your sperm or it would not.

Actually Dr. Willows says it would be great if you could furnish her with the best times of when it would be to implant my sperm into you. And if that can be arranged this first time, then that will be much better. You asked me what kind of a woman this Dr. Willows really is, and I told you that I think you will like her. She is friendly, but not overly friendly.

She is professional, but I think she has done a lot of research in this field also. Actually I did not tell her that I have a Doctorate in Veterinary Medicine, and I did not put it in as any of the information that I filled out. I did not want to influence her in any way. Meaning I will never use my overall education to influence others to favor what I might want them to do.

You said that is the one thing that you do not like about me. That I don't use another field of specialty to influence others in my direction. You say you don't understand that, but it does set you apart from other men, because you don't.

You say that it kind of humbles me to think that I don't use my education to influence others to get a position that others are vying for also. Actually that is the way I am. Because I never flaunt my education with anyone.

I also say that there are some women who are obviously beautiful, because they do wear a lot of make-up to make themselves more beautiful. In fact I have seen some of these women, who don't wear any makeup at all, just because they are beautiful without it. It is what is called Natural beauty. You are really like that.

Because there are times that you don't wear any makeup and still you are quite beautiful. That is one of the things that attracted me to you from the very beginning. And when you wear makeup, it just enhances your overall beauty. So be thankful that this is the way you really are. Men are always attracted to you, because of that Natural beauty. I have always known this.

Then you told me that this is the most wonderful thing that I have ever told you. Then I said, you really never gave me the chance to ever tell you how I really felt about your beauty before. I think I may have told you in the very beginning, but you apparently did not know that about yourself, or you ignored what I said about you. There are so many things I would like to say about you, but we always seem to be at each other's throats, and are angry a lot at each other.

The trouble with two married persons is, that they have to be able to communicate with each other, all of the time, not just some of the time. Now how often do you think we communicate with each other. Some of the time or all of the time. I could tell that you were giving what I just stated a lot of thought. I really did not expect an immediate answer from you and you did not say anything at all after that. Just some food for thought.

LOVE...............CLEMENT

April 6th 1963

Dearest Peggy;

After our last conversation of talk about the two of us, you then after another week that had gone by, gave me some dates that I was to call into Dr. Willows office and give them to her, which represent the best times that you would probably ovulate. They were well accepted, because two weeks later Dr. Willows told me to bring you to her office, wherein she would plant my sperm into you.

And at that time we were told that this might take a few times before it would work. But now we will have to wait for five days and then I was to bring you back, which would actually be on a Saturday, which was great, and Dr. Willows would see if your sperm had accepted my sperm. She would know for sure at that time. But another disappointment ensued, so I would have to give her some more of my sperm and in fact I later told her that I would like to give her at least three more times some sperm.

And maybe she could put them all together, but she told me that she could keep them in a state where when you ovulated at least three times in a given month, that you could be implanted with my sperm all three times. And that seemed agreeable to you. But those three times also failed to produce a child. What a let down.

Then Dr. Willows said that she would begin treatments on me, because my sperm was the bad culprit in this formula. I told Dr. Willows that I knew that was the problem all along, and in fact had told her that was the main problem. But I also knew she wanted to try the other method first.

So now becomes the very hard part. Taking treatments so as to build up my sperm so that I can really produce a child. If this does not work then we will not be able to have a child that is created by both of us. I fear that we will not have any natural children. I have not given up, because I will take treatments as long as there is a chance that we may be able to produce a child between the two of us.

I think things at home have been going along pretty well also. And by this time we have finally moved into the Plaza Apartments, where we have rented a two-bedroom apartment on the seventh floor.

But there has been some bad news also, when Chili got outside one day before we got ourselves completely moved, when the movers opened up the bedroom she was in and she ran outside, and she got hit by a car and was killed instantly.

I buried her in the back yard because that is where she spent a lot of her adult life, inside of a kind of Cage that was 8 feet square. She is buried beside Freddie the Fly. They each have grave markers, because I made a better one for Freddie last October.

They are both buried in the Flower garden where I had planted all kinds of bulbs, which will continue to come up every spring, no matter who lives there. But we had also gotten another Cat whose name is Midnight, because he is all black, and we still have Tai and Tak. Midnight was only a kitten when we got him and he is well loved by the other cats.

Then after we moved into those apartments, one of the other residents who were moving out of this state could or would not take his Parakeet with him, so we ended up with him also. Mostly because he is kind of sickly, because he sometimes has trouble breathing, and because I am a veterinarian I took him in, and I sometimes have to rub Vicks vapor rub all over his cage bars so he can breathe.

And then I cover his cage so as to cause this to happen. Of which keeps the cats away from his cage. That is most of the time, until Midnight knocked his cage over one night and his cage door opened up, and Jackie (the parakeet) flew into our bedroom and sat on one of our pillows, where he knew he would be safe, because I had taught all of the cats to never come into our bedroom no matter what.

So when I woke up the next morning, there was Jackie sitting on my pillow, with all of the cats sitting in the bedroom doorway, watching him. Never a dull moment in this family.

LOVE...................CLEMENT

October 17th 1963

Dearest Peggy;

Actually I am writing fewer letters now, because we are talking a lot to each other now. About most everything. Once we began to talk to each other, we seemed to need to talk to each other as much as we can. So we talk to each other every day, for hours and hours some times. We even snuggle with each other quite often, and I like that also. I think we are getting closer and closer every day. I suppose because we are both home every night together.

One of my brothers came to visit with us, so I cooked Beef livers and onions and fried potatoes and made some Manhattan style gravy, and he went back for 2nd and 3rd and told me that he had never tasted beef liver that was so tender before.

That when Mom would make it, it was always like shoe leather. He asked for my receipt and when I told him, he was flabbergasted. Because I told him that I fried it using port wine and Butter. And I fried it slowly, not rapidly like Mom would always do. I told him that when a good cook prepares a great meal, that it takes a lot of time to do it. He said I had made a believer out of him. He actually stayed the night, sleeping on my six foot six inch couch. When he woke up the next morning, he said that was the best nights sleep he had had in many a moon. When he was getting ready to leave after we all had breakfast together, he says he is driving to South Dakota, where he will take up farming of his land. I asked him what land, and he says the old Marcus Anderson farm.

I told him that I owned that land. That I had paid five thousand dollars for it when I was 15 years old. He says that Dad told him that it belonged to him. So I told him that I would take you to court for it. He then left.

Three months later, his Lawyer contacted my lawyer in St Louis, and we filed a Counter Suite, sending him proof of the Title of this property, which had been registered at the Webster Court house several years before when I was 15 years of age, and the only reason that brothers name was on the Deed to that farm, was because he was still in the Air Force, and any Service man always got special treatment while they remained in that branch of service, so his name was put on the title was because I was under the age of 18 at that time, and I had always carried it with me, because I had always paid the Taxes on this property also for all of the time that I had owned it.

So I sued him for fifty thousand dollars. Which I figured would make him stop and think. But he countered with another suite, saying that I had not farmed it personally since I was 17 years old. This kind of correspondence went on back and forth, many times.

Since I had the Original title of that farm, I put it up for sale in two Newspapers. The person who eventually purchased it, I was unhappy with, but I wanted to now get rid of it, so I sold it to Chet Duerre for twenty thousand dollars, even though he wanted his name kept out of this deal as being the actual person who purchased that farm.

Even though he and others told a different story to my family, but in reality, that is what really happened. Some say that my brother actually won the suite, and gave it to a Church in California which went bankrupt, and that is how Chet Duere got it, and Chet told the same story, because he never liked me, because I actually took his daughter out a few times without his knowledge, and he made up some stories about me wherein he tried to make me to be a liar. But he failed anyway.

I only saw him one other time, which was when the folks had their 50th wedding anniversary in 1969 at the Local Lutheran Church basement. When I told him that I had contacted the two newspapers wherein I advertised my farm in, and gave them the true story of what actually happened to MY FARM, he shut up and walked away from me, and avoided me for the rest of that day and night.

I don't know when he died, but I would be willing to bet he always wondered how I found out that he had purchased my farm. Because he made it known that he wanted his name kept completely out of being the purchaser of that farm. I have my methods of finding out things that other persons always want to keep from me.

But getting back to my story about you and I in our endeavor to be able to produce a child naturally. I took treatments of various kinds of things related to building up any mans Sexual abilities so he could create a child eventually. I took these treatments for six months, and then Dr. Willows says it is time to try again.

So I went through the same process I had done before, only this time I waited for a solid month between giving my sperm to you. Because the first time it did not work. But the second time it did work. And you carried this baby until it had been in your body for four months, and then one morning I heard a harsh scream from the bathroom, and when I rushed in, I saw that baby in the toilet.

You were hysterical and bleeding profusely. I slapped your face several times until you grabbed my hand and told me to never do that ever again. I asked you why you aborted our child, and you asked me how did I know the truth, and I told you that you knew the truth, because I read it from your own mind. Then you began to cry real hard and then I slapped you across the face, and you immediately quit, then laughed hysterically, and then you flushed the toilet and walked away from me.

Things got real cold with me for a while after that. Because I knew that you had purposely killed our child. And I had to think about what you had done, before I could even talk to you again.

I knew one thing and that was that we would never try to produce another baby between us. I also knew that you knew how to abort any child, no matter who the father may be. So from now on things would never be the same in this family.

I also knew that you never wanted children in this family and you would do most anything to prevent that from ever happening. So the one thing I was going to have to get used to is that this marriage was going to be childless. Even if you had to kill every child that even came into this family.

To knowingly be living with a killer is something that would take some time to get used to. That day I moved into the other bedroom, because I knew I would never sleep with you for a very long time, if ever.

And as far as trying to adopt a child that was far beyond being a baby, would only take place if I did it by myself. Because I would never give you the opportunity to put a blemish on my name.

I would remain married to you, but we would not try to get any child in the near future. And probably never. I was in a real sad place this time.

And trusting you would also take some time to formulate in with my overall feelings about you. It would take time and a lot of it to come to grips with my overall feelings for and about you. What I would eventually do, I am uncertain at this time. I really don't know what I will do about us.

This is going to take some time to resolve. And the other thing, do I ever tell your parents what you really did. And if I did, what would it do to them. Or do I keep this all to myself. I surely know that you will never tell your folks about what you did. I don't know how you did it, but it surely is not legal and it probably is very dangerous.

The blood flowed from you for three days, and I wondered if I would have to eventually take you to see Dr. Willows. When I mentioned her name, you threatened me that if I ever told her what you had done, that you would also kill yourself. I told you that threatening me will not prevent me from doing anything that I believe that I should do. If that is what you will do, then go ahead, because I won't stop you from killing yourself. But in reality, I don't think you have to Guts to do yourself in, because if you did, I would have buried you a long time back. I actually laughed at you, and while doing that I got up and walked out of the apartment.

I had to think for a while. But I did not go very far, because I feared for my cats, so in five minutes I returned back to our apartment.

You instead asked me to remain at home with you. That you would not do any harm to my cats. That it was quite apparent that I loved my cats more than I loved her. I then told you that if you had remained married to me and had never cheated on me, that the love I had for you, would have been very prominent.

But you needed to go screw every Tom, Dick and Harry, whenever you needed to and you never really knew how much I really loved you.

Do you think I would have remained with you for all of the time you were doing all of those other men if I did not love you? You cannot see beyond your nose. And you never think about anyone except yourself. How often have you ever thought about my needs and me? You only think about your needs and other men's needs, but never mine.

So go ahead and plead all you want. I will not divorce you so you will never be able to marry any other man either. When I find the woman that I want to spend the rest of my life with, then I will get a Divorce and marry that woman. I get so tired of trying to please you, but you never seem to notice anyway. But how often have you consciously tried to please me. Only this past year has that ever happened. Now you are back to where you were before we got married this last time.

CLEMENT

February 10th 1964

Peggy;

Somehow I cannot call you Dear or dearest any longer, because I don't feel that way any longer. How am I supposed to feel, knowing that my wife definitely murdered my child by causing it to abort and dropping it in the toilet and flushing it down the drain? Was I supposed to fish it out and bury it, and tell the world, or did it abort by itself, and she just took the blame from me anyway. I am not sure what really happened and I don't think anyone does know what really happened, except you. And even though I read your thoughts as they presented themselves at the moment I came into the bathroom, did you plant them there to cause me to think that you really killed our baby? I wonder. There will be sad times ahead of me for a long time.

Will I ever get to the place where I will ever trust you again? I really don't know. I am afraid that if I turned you in to the local Police, that I would either be laughed out of town or you would be placed in a Nut House, because after I would tell them how you laughed after you flushed that baby down the toilet, that you would be taken away in a Straight Jacket. So I am between a Rock and a Hard Place. I have thought about this problem for a very long time now, and I have decided to go see a Catholic Priest, who administers to persons in the local Jail. So I really have to go to the St Louis Police Headquarters and inquire as to where I will find this individual. Luckily that Priest is standing talking to the Desk Sergeant when I walked in to that station. I asked him if he is the Priest who administers Confessions to Prisoners, and he says he is. I ask him if I can talk to him in private, and he agrees to do so. He asks me if I want to tell him in a Confessional, and I say no, because I am not a Catholic any longer because I have been excommunicated from the Catholic Church.

He says he is not certain whether he can talk to me either, because of what I just told him. I asked him if I had not told you this about me, would you have listened to me, and he says that he would have. So I say what is wrong with talking to a former Catholic. He says actually there is no reason at all. I say I will not give you my name, or anyone else's name. I just want some advice about a critical problem. He says okay. So we just go and sit on some benches. And then I tell him that I suspect that my wife killed the baby she was carrying in her womb, by somehow causing it to come out of her, and flushing it down the toilet. I only saw it for a moment, and it was not very well developed, to the point where it looked like a fetus, but since I knew she was definitely four months pregnant, because she was under the care of a GYN Doctor. Whether it was alive, I don't know. I don't know whether it was developed enough to be able to breathe yet on its own. At least I don't think it was. But like I said, I only saw it for about two seconds, and then she flushed it down to the Sewer, and laughed when she did it.

This Priest tells me that I have a real serious problem. About that time, the Chief of Detectives walked in, and came to where I was talking to this priest. He asked if I was all right, and

I told him, I was very sad. He looked at this priest, but did not say anything else. Then he walked away. This priest asked me if I knew who that person is, and I tell him he is the Chief of Detectives of this Police Department.

This priest asks if my wife is related to this man, and I say I will not answer that question, because we are not in a Confessional Booth, because that is the only place where I can answer that question with any clarity. This Priest says he cannot help me, so I get up and leave. Now since I did not tell this priest my name or my wife's name, but I did know personally the Chief of Detectives of the St. Louis Police Department, I figured that this priest would go and talk to him. Only time will tell that story. Or Jim would seek out this priest, for some answers about me.

Actually there was nothing else I could do about this problem, without some more Professional help from a Lawyer. And that is whom I called next. He tells me that he is not that kind of a lawyer, but he will recommend one to me. And he will have that lawyer call me at home or wherever I want him to call me. I say have him call me at my office, so I give my lawyer my office phone number. Then I go back to work at the WWIB.

An hour later this other lawyer calls me and says to not say anything to anyone else, and if anyone asks me anything about this, to not say a word. Why, because you may have already said too much to the wrong persons. You should have called your lawyer first. I say I am sorry that I did not do that, but I was between a Rock and a Hard place, and in reality I still am. He says just don't say another word about it at all. Since you did not or could not do anything about what happened, you still couldn't do anything about it. So if you don't hear from anyone else about this, then forget it. Sometimes this happens in people's lives. Try to get on with your life and just forget it.

So I did. At least until I heard from my wife, when I got home that night. When she asked me if I had seen her Uncle today, and I told her I only saw him briefly when I was near the police station on another errand dealing with the Office, and he asked how I was feeling and I told him I was a little sad, but just fine. That's the only words we had spoken to each other. He then walked away from me and I went to where I was headed. I told you that I sometimes see him when I am out on the streets, when I am going to some government location locally. I see a lot of people that I know in this town. There is nothing unusual about that. So what. What are you seeking from me? Am I under the gun for some reason? I haven't done anything unusual to deserve this kind of treatment after a hard day at the office. I say get off my back. I am not going to talk to you for a while, because I have nothing to say to you yet. When I am ready to talk to you, then you will know it, but not before.

Private thought:

I think Peg is realizing that if I don't talk to her, that she will begin again with all of her extra curricular activities. Usually I can talk about any subject, but today I don't want to talk about anything, especially about anything that she does. TURN AROUND IS FAIR PLAY in my book. For years she never talked to me, and now that I am not talking to her, this will drive her crazy. Being around me can be very exciting sometimes, but at other times I can be very boring. And today I need some time to do some testing of some Grains and Corn samples, and that is what I tell you that I am going to do. This is part of my job and I do get paid for doing this. Even at home.

CLEMENT

May 15th 1964

Peg;

It is said that time heals most everything. And in this case, it sure is helping a lot. Though it is hard to forget some things that happen in some person's lives, time can, if enough of that time goes by may heal that wound. I have come to the conclusion that we will never have any children, by any means or methods.

Dr. Maple Willows called me today at my office and asked me how the baby is coming and I had to tell her that we lost it suddenly in the latter part of February. That's all I told her. She asked me if we were going to try again and I told her definitely not. That I had resigned myself to realize that for us to be able to have any children in our married life is never going to happen ever. She says in a few years, much more progress will have been made in this field that for persons like us to be able to have a baby will become a way of life. I then told her that this will never happen with us; so don't call me again about this, Okay?

You never said a word, because you had just realized that I never wanted to speak about any child ever again. The look on your face, most of the pink colors in your face left you at that time.

But I did not care what you wanted to say, because I did not want to hear any more words about children by anyone, especially by the two of us. You had cured me of ever thinking about having children ever again. So if you go out and get yourself pregnant again, don't come home and show me that pregnancy, because I will kick you out until you get rid of it, in whatever ways that you do.

And I never wanted to hear about any of your pregnancies ever again. You can be sure of one thing, and that is, I will never be the father of any of them ever again. Now if you cannot handle that, then leave me in my misery and grief.

The next day, you went over to the Clothing Manufacturing Company and got yourself a job as the Payroll Supervisor. Over time I met your immediate boss and the Comptroller of that company, including the president and vice president and the Factory foreman, and a host of other persons. You even brought some of the persons who worked for you; home with you occasionally, where they slept on our couch and ate our food, and for a while one of them remained with us for about five months. This woman had gotten fired and you felt sorry for her I guess.

Until I could not stand her messy ways any longer. I told you that you needed to boot her out the door, or I would, and since you did not tell her to leave, I told her to leave when you were at work one day, when I was home, not feeling all that well. I told her that living in this apartment is now over for you, mostly because you don't know how to keep from making a mess while you and I are at work. And because she says she is looking for a job, but she never goes on any interviews. So you will either leave this apartment or I will call the police and have you arrested for stealing. She asked what did she steal, so I did call the police, and when they arrived, I told the detective that handled our case what she has stolen from my wife and me.

I opened up the two suitcases that we had had to give her, because she did not have any of her own, and I explained this to the detective.

And when I opened these two suitcases, they were filled with a lot of your jewelry, and most of our silverware and even some of your dresses that you had bought from that company you work for, because they still had the tags on them.

So the Police took her away, and I never saw her again until her trial. I was notified by an Assistant District Attorney some six months later when her case came to trial, where I testified about all that she had stolen. Showing photographs of everything, wherein which I had taken these photographs myself when this gal was not home in the apartment. Before I even called the police, and I never told the police I even had them.

Of course she was convicted of Grand Theft and she was sent to a State Prison for women for seven to 15 years. I never saw, nor heard of her again after that time.

CLEMENT

December 10th 1964

Dear Peg;

There is some talk about the office where I am working, may be closing within six months, so I have been looking in other cities for another position with this same company, at least for awhile anyway. I was talking to the Comptroller of Country Set one afternoon, and he told me that they are having trouble at various times in ordering too much Material, and when I asked how much money was involved, he says about a million dollars per year. I thought about that for a week and then I went back to him and I told him that I think I know how to find out how to fix your problem, but I need to accumulate some records first. After explaining a little bit more, he asked me when can I begin working, and I tell him as soon as I can arrange to do this on a part time basis. But I need an office and a lot of paper and a few other things. And I need access to all of your records for the past two years, dealing with how much material that was ordered for each season, and how many projected sales were estimated, and how many actual sales really took place, and where and by whom. All of this is going to take me about three months to develop. Then I will be able to estimate how much material you will order for each season. He asked me how close will I come, and I tell him that I will come within ten yards of material in each season. He says he will arrange for my office space.

Two days later at 4:00 PM I began digging out files and the office that was given to me, which was the Conference room, where there was a very large table for me to work on and a number of very good chairs to sit in, and a lot of room where all of these files could be placed. The paper that I ended up using was the wrapping paper that came in rolls of five thousand feet, of which I absconded with one of these rolls of paper from the storeroom. And when I unrolled what I figured I would need, I then began to put all kinds of lines in pencil on all of them. Each piece of paper was 30 inches wide and eight feet long, so I could eventually hang them all up on this Conference rooms walls. I needed ten pieces of this paper in these sizes. Every once in awhile the Comptroller of this company, came into my office, and asked me how it was coming. I told him it was coming slowly, and I was getting closer to where I would make my estimations.

This will take the entire three months to reach the point when I will make my estimations. Everything else will just take time. Now while I was doing this, and was about two months into this study, the Dress Designer from New York City came for a visit, and when she walked into this conference room, she just about had a terrible hemorrhage. She yelled at me, who the hell are you and what are you doing here. I told her I am trying to save this company more than a million dollars a year in excess expenditures about buying too much material to manufacture all of what you make here. Now if you don't want me to accomplish that, then I will leave. The ball is now in your court.

She says that she has never in her entire life been talked to like I have just done. But of course no one has ever told me that any person can save this company a million dollars in any one-year before either. So whoever you are, just ignore me, she says, and keep doing whatever you are doing.

She says, by the way, my name is Eunice Graves and I told her what my name is, and we shook hands and then she begins to study all of my charts.

After a little while, she came to me and asked me what each chart represented, and when I told her, she says, you really have got something here don't you, and I told her that, in a month, I will make my estimations of how much material you will buy for the next season that you will be selling. And as the seasons get closer, I will do the same thing. And like I have told the comptroller, I will come within ten yards of the actual sales of that season in total. Eunice says, this she has to see. I say stick around and you will.

She asked me how many hours do I work at this, and I told her that I work four hours here and two hours at home. Every day of every week, including Sundays. She says this is very important to you isn't it, and I tell her that it is, because this is more important to all of you.

Now if I am as accurate as I claim that I will be, then what else will I be able to do for this company. She says, I don't know, but probably something. Like maybe a full time position with a larger salary? So I just kept on doing what I was doing, and every once in awhile, Eunice would come in and look at the charts I was working on, but she didn't say anything else, and after awhile she just walked out.

Now I found out that her ex-husband and her had been

married, but they are now divorced. He is the President and Eunice's father who is the Vice President who has his office here also. Anyway Eunice decided that she just had to stay in St Louis until I made my estimations. But of course the real picture would not be realized until after the next season had officially closed as far as all of the Sales of everything that had been manufactured.

So Eunice did go back to New York City, but she gave me her private phone number, and told me that when I knew how close I had actually come with my estimation of the season in question, then I was to call her directly at any time. I gave her my home phone and she already had the phone number in the conference room. And I told her she could call me anytime also. Of course she knows that you are my wife, but sometimes relationships within offices can become closer than expected. But she also knew that I was not looking for any favors from her regarding anything. I was just another friend of hers. But I think some of the factory workers thought otherwise, but Eunice says to just ignore them, and that is what I did while I was there.

I never asked you what you thought, and you never inquired about what I was actually doing there. I think the comptroller eventually told you, but he also told you that what I was doing might save this company a million dollars a year, and especially the first year that I was doing this.

So you never said a word. In reality, I went back three years, regarding everything, but I only recorded two years on all of my graphs. I just remembered the third year, by writing it down in my journal. So when the time came for me to make my first estimation, the comptroller asked if the figure that I stated would really be enough.

So I told him, you will either go with my figures or with your own. He says he will go with my figures, even though they seemed to be a bit low. I told him, that is why you have been over buying for all of these years, because you have been over estimating every season.

So six weeks later when the current season ended, and I always kept all of the records on all of my graphs, And when I brought everyone into the conference room to show them how close I came, they were amazed at how close I really came.

Actually I came within six yards, because I estimated that the amount they would need in materials, I over estimated by six yards. Which was so close to my ten-yard estimation that I made believers out of everyone. So using the comptrollers phone in his office, I called Eunice and I put her on the speakerphone, and when I told her, she says you are a Godsend. Sam says we will keep him for the next four seasons even if he has to pay him out of his own pocket. Eunice says she will personally pay him if necessary. I got up and left and left Sam to continue talking to her.

So after another month had gone by, I brought Sam into the Conference room and told him how much to buy for the next four seasons. And do exactly what I have told you to do.

I probably will not be here for the entire year, because actually the hard part is now done. And if you continue to keep these graphs you can continue to estimate with the same accuracy that I have done. Records really never lie, so based on what you see in these graphs, just keep doing what and how I have instructed you to do, and you will become a Miracle worker.

I told Sam that I have to move on. It's not that I don't like what I have done here, but I can only do so much. Actually your factory needs to be rearranged also, and I could do that too, but I don't think your factory foreman would like that. So I won't go there at this time.

Actually I have never done this before, but because of how my mind works, it fit into my overall abilities, and it was easy for me to do this, and it just took time to get it started. Now if you had computers then they would make this much easier. But that will be at a later time I think.

Of course the right programs would have to be written and debugged, but it could be done. Sam says could you write a program that would take care of the Piece goods problem? I say, yes I could, because I understand piece good payrolls. I actually learned from Peg.

She doesn't really know that I know this, but I do. But like what I did with this, it would take time to write what needed writing, and then I would have to debug it and then present it to whoever needs to know about it.

But if I do it, I will do on my own time, and not get paid for it, because if you all deny my proposal, then I can destroy it, because you did not pay me to write these programs.

Actually if you want me to do this, then I need something in writing saying that it is a suggestion from you, but I will not get paid for doing it.

Actually I would like that in writing from everyone with this company. Sam says he would do this, but no one else will, except maybe Eunice. But she is in New York City. So I said I will think about it for now. But I will not do anything about it.

CLEMENT

January 10th 1965

Dear Peggy;

The WWIB office in St Louis will be closing in one month, and there is a position available in Milwaukee, as a Traveling Auditor, but I will have to take a Train to Chicago for the Interview, which I will do next Monday morning. It will pay 28 thousand dollars a year with a 30 thousand dollar draw for expenses, which will be 2500 dollars every month. That is a total of 58 thousand dollars every year. If I get it, will you go with me? That is all I know about this position at this time.

I talked to your Dad and he says to take it. Because he says that is just a little less than what he makes in any given year. So if I get the position I think I will accept it.

You told me that you would like to go with me, because it has been rumored that someone is writing a computer program, which will be able to handle piecework payroll.

I tell you that Sam wanted me to do that for him, and when I did, and presented it to everyone, that I was voted down, so I completely destroyed that program.

You also told me that you wondered what I had been working on for the last two months, and now she knows, but if they still think they will get that program, and yet will not, then they are fooling themselves and others also.

Peg asked, do they know that you completely destroyed

that program, and I told you that they do not? You then asked me if it was okay for you to tell them, and I told you that it is, and when you told Sam, he says he will take me to court.

And then I wrote a letter to him and told him, that because you did not write a written request for me to write that program, that Country Set did not have a leg to stand on in ever getting it. I would hate to see you all laughed out of Court. They then backed away from that threat.

And then they told you that your position was not in any kind of jeopardy, but by that time it was too late, because since I had already gotten the position in Milwaukee, that you had already tendered your resignation to Country Set.

So in the latter part of January of 1965, we moved from St Louis, Missouri to Milwaukee, Wisconsin. Actually we moved to Cudahy, Wisconsin, into some high-rise apartments. Near Lake Michigan.

CLEMENT

January 30th 1965

Peggy;

So after we got everything moved into that apartment, I then had to return the moving trailer back to the U-haul Company, of which I did. Which also gave me a chance to look this town over.

The town of Cudahy is not all that large. Somewhere in the area of thirty thousand population. The main street is about six blocks long with some smaller businesses on some of the side streets all along the main thoroughfare, so it looked like it might be interesting to take a walk sometime in our near future. About six blocks further towards Milwaukee's downtown area, was Kohl's Supermarket Grocery Store. So I did stop and buy a few items that we would need. The one thing that I noticed they did not have, was Yuban Coffee. I sought out the Store Manager, and asked him if he had ever heard of such a brand, and he says he has, but he does not know where to get it.

So I told him, if I can get you forty cases, will you buy it from me, and he says he will, because he has had numerous orders for such a coffee.

So on the next weekend I did drive back to the St Louis area, where I had made arrangements earlier in the week, to buy forty cases of Yuban coffee. I also got the distributors name of where they had gotten it, and took that back to Cudahy,

Wisconsin and ultimately to" Kohls" Market, who purchased these forty cases of Yuban coffee from me for the price that I initially paid for it, and I suggested as to what price this manager should charge for each jar of this coffee, of which he did, and in one week he sold all forty cases of this coffee.

Each case had 48 jars of coffee in it, which means this manager sold 1920 jars of Yuban coffee in one week.

Of course after the first day, this manager ordered a hundred more cases of this coffee, because he suddenly realized that this coffee would be his best seller of this product. Anyway after that when I went into this market, I was always offered free gifts of some kind of product, but I never accepted any of them, because for me it was just a matter of commerce and need by the people. I guess this manager figured that I was seeking some kind of favor, but I told him that because I drank this coffee, and because I did not see it on any of his shelves, I wondered if this product had not been heard of in this state yet. He told me that Wisconsin is kind of slow in getting some products.

Anyway after that, whenever I had been to other parts of the country, I had noted a lot of the good selling products, and I always wrote them down, so when I returned back to Wisconsin, I would always tell whatever merchandiser was needed to know about some of these other products. I think that most of the merchants that I had gotten to know where we now lived, fully appreciated me as a consumer.

Anyway after getting settled in my Job and my office where it was located in the downtown district of this fair city, I then let you use the car most of the time, because you expressed an interest in finding yourself a job. Because I could always take a cab to where I worked, because I now have an expense account.

One thing about expense accounts, if you never use them, you will lose them, so most days when I worked in Milwaukee, I always took a Cab to work.

When I was scheduled to go out of town, depending on where I was going, I always took a Cab while in all of the various cities and towns near where I lived. And sometimes I also went out of town.

Like to Green Bay or other points further north like into the Upper Peninsula of Michigan. I always took the train to get there. Wherever I went outside of Milwaukee, I always took a Train. But first I had to acquire all of the Foreign Railroad Passes I needed to accomplish this, and ultimately I ended up getting 18 Foreign line Railroad Passes.

So for the first month I remained in my office in Milwaukee. Once I had all of my Railroad Passes, then I most often was out of town. In fact I was told that in any one year, I would only spend about five percent of my time in my home territory. This is not what I was told initially when I applied for this position.

But I suppose if this were told to any potential Traveling Auditor, no one would ever apply for these positions. I know I probably would not have, but since I was now on the job, I would see it through for a few years.

I also knew that in time I would try to make many needed changes to how we always traveled. Actually all of my territory consisted of the entire state of Wisconsin, and the entire state of Iowa, and the entire state of Indiana, and the Upper Peninsula of Michigan, and the Northern half of Illinois, but not Chicago proper. It also included East St. Louis, Illinois.

And if I were very good at my job, I would be sent to other areas, depending on what my specialties were. I was also a Weigh master, and in that job, I inspected all Railroad Scales, and made adjustments when necessary. Or made repairs when necessary. I was also a Hazardous Materials Specialist. I was also an expert when it came to Wharfage, which sent me to most every Port city in the United States, depending on when I could actually go there. So my position was not just an Auditors position in total.

Whenever I was sent on special assignments, I got paid extra money, that being 1,000 dollars. And since I am able to use my expense account, most of whatever expenses I accrue are always paid when I return from that assignment, usually within a week of returning to my home office.

I was actually an EXPERT in many fields. Fields that I had never mentioned to you before. I know that after three months had gone by, that you would be living alone a lot. I actually did not think about how you would take this bad news.

I know how I took it, which was I was very disappointed that I would be away from home so much. Because I worried that you might go back to doing what you had done before, when your needs came to the fore. Because I was a fairly handsome guy, I also knew that I would be offered many times the ability to sleep with another woman, but I would never do that. Like I have said before, Sex no longer interests me. Any kind of sex.

I did like my job, and I met a lot of very interesting persons. One of these persons was a man who worked for the Interstate

Commerce Commission, who was named Dick Tracy. Yeah, you are correct, and he told me that he was always kidded about that name all the while he has been on that job.

Another guy I met while doing my job one day was the Auditor who worked for the Association of American Railroads, by the name of Perry Mason. He like Dick was always kidded about his name. And he was also a Lawyer. But a Corporate Lawyer. He says that his organization needs persons like myself, so if I ever got the urge to change positions, that he could get me a position with the organization he works for. And with probably a lot more money and surely a much larger expense account. Because he says his salary is 50 thousand a year with an expense account being the same as his salary.

He says the only difference between my position and his position is, he has the Authority to levy large fines against whoever is violating the many rules of commerce and Railroad Accounting. Also you never have to take a train anywhere. If you are within 150 miles of your home territory, then you can use your own vehicle.

And if you are beyond that mileage, then you can either take a bus or a train or Fly on an Airplane.

Actually since you are on an Expense Account, however you get to where you are going, it shouldn't make any difference in how you really get there. But the WWIB is still behind the times at least 20 years.

So work with them and maybe within a year, approach the main office in Chicago about maybe getting a Motor home or a Travel trailer, thereby your wife can travel with you. She can register with Manpower and or Kelly girl Employment Agencies, and they usually have positions open in most towns and always-larger cities.

He says his wife has traveled with him for the past three years and she has always gotten work everywhere we have ever gone to.

Clement

July 23rd 1965

Peggy;

Peggy found a position with a Spice Company as a Payroll Supervisor. She says the pay is lower than she is used to, but since my Salary is higher than I have been making ever, and I also have a real good Expense account, we will be able to get by real easy. She says she will need the car all of the time.

So I have gotten a used vehicle, which runs real good even though the body needs some work done on it, I can get that done at some later date, when I find someone who can do the work on weekends when I am at home.

This vehicle is a 1958 Ford Van. It has a V-8 motor in it so the gas mileage will probably not be all that great, but in an emergency I can even sleep in it. In fact I have purchased a single bed mattress that I have placed inside of it. It has an extra high top so I can even walk stooped over a bit inside of it. It would be great for camping some time.

For my first assignment, I have to go to Houghton, Michigan, which is north of Wisconsin, and I have to take a train up there. I will take a passenger train to Green Bay, and then I have to take a Freight train and ride in the Caboose. And it will take a day and a half to get there. Then depending on how many places I have to go to will depend on when I will be able to come back home.

It has been suggested that I will be gone two weeks, just in Houghton. And this is the best time to go there because in the winter months, it would be impossible, because of all of the snow that usually falls starting about November 10th of any year.

And since I will be stopping off in Green Bay, I will also Audit all of the Railroad Stations on my way back, which will probably take another two weeks.

So don't expect me for about a month. I would have liked to be able to pick my own areas to go to first, but because of the winter weather in these two areas, that is why I have been ordered to do these two towns first. After that I can then pick my own places where I will go.

One of the things that I am going to do on this trip is I am going to plan where and when I will be going next and thereafter. And depending on how many improprieties I find, will depend on whether I will need any outside protection from the Law.

I ran into the previous Auditor at the office last Friday, who I will not name, and he told me about some stations where I most likely will find some serious improprieties, wherein I will notify the ICC, and their Auditor will do the same thing I have done, and if he finds the same things I have found, then he will be the person who will levy Heavy fines against these persons, meaning not only the Customers, but also the Railroads.

So if I find any serious problems, to not mention any of them to the Station Agent, but only to the ICC Auditor. And he will notify the Auditor of the Association of American Railroads, and they also will Audit that station and if they find the same thing then they too will levy heavy fines against everyone involved. Thereby keeping my name completely out of any disputes.

Sometimes it's hard to keep your mouth shut. He says that was one of his problems of the previous Auditor. That is why he now works in the office in Green Bay, Wisconsin. At least until he finds something else to do in the Auditing field. He says he will be monitoring my abilities. That is one of the things he now does. He says if I find myself in some kind of conflict, then he will spot it by the reports that I send into my home office. Because if your home office spots a problem, then they will notify himself and he will take a closer look at whatever problem I may be having, and if he suggests to the home office that I be yanked out of that city or town, then that is what will be done. Even if they have to send someone to pull me out. And if I am in some kind of danger from outside sources, then the Law will come and escort me out of that city or town.

And depending on how good I am at this kind of work will depend on whether they will send me on some Special Assignments to other person's territories. This former auditor says that what he has heard about me when I worked in the St Louis Office, that not much gets by me, so keeping yourself totally informed is what you do best.

CLEMENT

July 30th 1965

Peggy;

What a long slow trip that was to this fair town of Houghton, Michigan. This is where Copper is mined, and a lot of it. I can actually taste it in the air, and smell it wherever I go. I made the time go by more slowly by studying all of the dates and places that I gathered when I was in my office in Milwaukee, when I first arrived here.

This is one of the first things I wanted to study, so as to be able to know where and when to go to some of these towns and cities, and how many stations I would have to Audit while here. I probably will not be able to keep a tight schedule that I have now prepared, but I will have a guideline in how long it might take while I am in these towns.

Where I will stay is totally up to me, even though the previous auditor suggested some places I should try to stay away from. Because some of these towns still have seedy characters in some of them. Meaning that there are most likely some graft going on here. And some of the Motels and Hotels are places where some of the Local Whores frequent and even might take rooms where they take their clients. But not to worry, because I am not interested in anything connected with sex acts. I will have daily reports to make out, and if I do any relaxing outside of my motel or hotel room, I will always be alone when I do that.

But getting back to Houghton, Michigan. There are three Railroad Stations where I will have to Audit. In the past there have not been any problems, but the previous auditor says that since he has not been to this town for two years, and because this is in reality a very rich community, because of the Copper mines, that for someone like myself, who is rumored to be the best at what he does, I may find some improprieties.

Of course I cannot tell you if I find any problems, but since I will keep a separate Journal, it will be from that, that I would use to contact whomever else I will need to contact. But I will not contact anyone else until I have left this community.

It is now ten days later and I am catching the morning freight train back to Green Bay, which will take one full day to get there. So I will be arriving in that fair city by tomorrow morning. Green Bay has five Railroads that I have to Audit.

Well here it is the 10th of August and when I got off of the caboose this morning, I was kind of tired so I found a Hotel that has been suggested to me by someone, and I went to bed and I slept for ten solid hours. I got up and showered and shaved and then I went downstairs to the dining room and ordered a large meal. But the meals at this hotel are not all that good, because I left most of the food on the plate. I then went outside and hailed a Cab and asked the driver to take me to every Railroad Depot in this fair city. And he did.

I told this Cab driver, that if he did not take me in a round about way, I would make sure he was well rewarded. As you know, I always talk like I have been in every city or town in this country, so he did what he was told to do. While we were leaving one of these Depots, I noticed a fast food place, so I asked him if he was hungry, and he says he is, so we stopped and got a few things and parked near a park and ate our meals, without the meter running.

This driver says no passenger has ever offered to buy him any meal for himself before, so he says his meter will never run while we eat our meals.

Forty minutes later we were again on our way, and he took me to the other two stations, and then I told him that in the morning, I would like to call and request that he drive me to where I will be going first. During our tour of these Train depots I told him why I was in his fair city, and he says normally he is off tomorrow. He also told me that the Hotel where I am staying is not a good place to stay. He recommended a different place, which was a small Motel, and I asked him why this Motel, and he says because he and his wife own and run it.

So I went to my room and packed what clothes I had not unpacked, and then I called the desk and told them that I am checking out of their Hotel, because there are Roaches in my room and the food in your restaurant is lousy. When I got down stairs, my bill was ready. I questioned two items on that bill, because I told them I did not order any friends to come and visit me.

I only paid for what I figured I owed them and then I went outside, and my Cabby drove up and I got in and when I told him what they had tried to charge me and what the charges were for, he told me that this is the worst Hotel in this town to ever live in, because in effect it is also a Whore House.

I discovered right then and there, that whatever the

previous Auditor told me, I will totally ignore, and when I got to my new place, this Cabby checked me in and when I got to my room, the first thing I did was, I called the previous auditor and told him what I thought of his recommendations as far as Hotels are concerned. He tried to talk me out of moving out of that Hotel, but after this I will stay where I think the best place is. That I have already moved out of that Hotel and have gotten myself a different place. He asked me where, but I told him that was none of his business, and then I hung up.

I went to the front desk and told them that if a particular person called looking for me here, to tell them that you don't know me and have never met me. I did not tell him where I was, but how many places are there to stay in this town?

Well, here it is ten days later and I will be returning back to Milwaukee in the morning. The CNW railroad passenger train is a milk run, meaning that it stops at every town between Green Bay and Milwaukee. But the nice thing is that since I left my Van at the CNW train depot, I will have wheels to drive home in. And I will have a few reports to make out when I do get home.

The first thing after I arrived back in our apartment was I called Dick Tracy. I told him what I found in Houghton, Michigan and what I found in Green Bay, Wisconsin and what stations in each city. He told me that he like the WWIB Auditors have not been to Houghton for two years, and even though there were a few things he had questioned, he was told that those problems would be cleared up, but apparently they had not done what he had asked them to do. So he will drive there tomorrow. And spend a few days in that town. And the same for Green Bay, I also told him about the previous Auditor and what he had done to me, and he says to completely ignore this guy about everything, no matter what he may try to tell you. He is all bull Crap, and can get more persons in trouble than any person he has ever known.

He is not a very good Auditor, and the reason he really got in trouble was because he took Union Records to his home, which should never have ever left the Union office. Don't rely on whatever he may say to you. He works in the Green Bay WWIB office, because he cannot find work anywhere else. And soon he won't even be working there either, because they soon will fire him. But keep that to yourself. And I told him that I did not hear that last statement.

Dick says he wants to meet me someday. He thinks we will become good friends. I told him I felt the same way about him. He says keep in touch. And then we hung up our phones.

When I got home, you were not there, and I wondered where you might be. I asked Tai and Tak, and they told me that you have been having men to the apartment, and have even slept with them. I asked, all of them and Tai says all of them. I asked how many and he says one every other day.

Now since I have been gone for 21 days, which means ten men, have slept with you during that time. But except for mentioning it in this letter, I am not going to mention it in any conversations I may have with you when I next see you.

As information also. I know that you slept with your former bosses only Brother and he actually got you pregnant, so I am wondering whether you are now out getting rid of that Baby at this time.

And since we are fairly close to where another of your boy friends lives, (actually about 120 miles) I wonder if he came to see you too. I asked Tai and he says no, not yet, but she has talked to him on the telephone, where she has asked him to come when she calls him to come.

CLEMENT

August 31st 1965

Peggy;

I don't think I will be telling you in the future where I will be going, or when or how long I will be gone, and I will instruct my office to not give out that information either.

That wherever I am, I cannot be reached by anyone in my immediate family. Even if I am somewhere in the Milwaukee area. You don't deserve to know where I am at any time. And if any of my Cats are harmed in any way, then I cannot put any language strong enough to get your attention of what I will do with you when I return home.

So finding something to say to you, other that where I may have been, will most likely not happen much any more. Because what I do, is of no importance to you anyway. Or what I do. So I guess these letters will either be short or much longer, with not much information in them.

CLEMENT

September 30th 1965

Peggy;

It's interesting about all of the places I have really been, even though I will not tell you where these places were. Some of the persons I have met are real nice, and some are real dogs. Probably something like the way you now are, like a dog that is screwing every Tom, Dick and Harry.

By the way your former bosses brother contacted me and wondered if I have seen you lately. And he wondered if he had gotten you pregnant. I actually told him when I saw you that he had gotten you pregnant, but you got rid of it in some way.

I did not tell him that you actually killed that Baby just like you have killed every one when you had gotten pregnant before. Since I am not home very often now, that you are now available to screw all kinds of other men too. You don't know this, but I am keeping count, just in case this subject ever comes up in any Annulment I may levy against the Catholic Church, and your Father.

I am also keeping count of every time you have gotten pregnant and by whom and when you actually killed that baby. Some day the Catholic Church will hear about all of these accidents (as you call them) when I deem it necessary to tell them about them. I also saw your father when I was in St Louis on this last trip south. But only for a brief period of time.

I wanted to see whether the WWIB office was really gone from the 16th floor, and it surely is. There is nothing there now. All of whatever persons who worked in that office got laid off. I moved out of that office just in time. Because a month later it closed completely.

CLEMENT

January 10th 1966

Peg;

I have been to many cities since I last wrote a letter to you, and I have only been home ten days during that length of time. Which is about ninety five percent of the time I have been away from home.

But I understand that you are getting along just fine, because of all of the men who come to see you. From what I have heard and from your own thoughts, I count 56 altogether. I would think that having sex with that many men would get kind of old after awhile, but I guess you are making so much money from all of them that you just cannot give up doing what you are doing.

But I do understand that you keep good hours, because you always shoo them out the door by 10:00 PM. I would hope you are socking most of that money away in the bank, because keeping all that money in the apartment is kind of risky isn't it?

Now what kind of money are we talking about? Well since you most often get 500 dollars every time you do what you do, then that's 28 thousand dollars. WOW. Maybe I should just let you support me and I can just go fishing. And that is just within the last 112 days. If you keep up this pace, by the end of this year, you will have made 91,500 dollars.

CLEMENT

March 23rd 1966

Peg;

Well here it is again, your Birthday, and today you are 36 years old. And I understand that you are having a lot of trouble with your teeth. I wonder why. All of those big Pricks I would think. Or maybe you caught something from one of those men. Like maybe some venereal Disease. You should go and have yourself checked out at the local hospital.

By the way, when I got off of the Santa Fe train in Dearborn Station in Chicago, there was ice on the steps and I slipped and I fell and hurt myself. But I picked up all of my suitcases and caught a Cab which took me to the CNW Station in Chicago, and when I got off of the train in Milwaukee, my left leg was swollen twice the size it normally should have been.

But I still got my suitcases and typewriter case into my Van and I drove to the local Hospital, and after they X-rayed that leg, which was broken in two places below the knee and cracked in three places above the knee. But they did not put a hard cast on it, but instead put a soft cast on it, and then I got into my Van and drove home to the apartment, where I found you in bed with some man, and after I told him to leave, of which he did not want to do, so I told him, do you want to die? Then he put his pants on and left the apartment.

I told him as he was leaving, that if he ever returned to this apartment that I would make sure he never screwed another woman again. You were thinking that it was a good idea that he had paid you in advance for your services, otherwise that would have been lost, because of the way I ordered him out of this apartment. I told you that I am not going to look for a different apartment, but I will continue to sleep by myself in the other bedroom, because I never wanted to sleep in the same bed where you screw all of your men friends. I also told you, that it is a wonder how you can even look me straight in the face and you still are never ashamed of what you are doing.

You say this is a way to make some good money. You tell me that you are going to have to give this all up soon, because all of the nerves of your teeth are either dying or else you have such god awful tooth aches that the only way to deaden the pain is to drink Black Label Bourbon Whiskey. Which is made in Tennessee. I say you no longer drink Vodka, and you tell me that this whiskey is better and more powerful.

I say, well it still falls in line with your being an Alcoholic doesn't it? You tell me that you are going to have to get all of your teeth pulled, but you don't want to have it done in any dentist office here in Milwaukee.

You tell me that you are going to go to St Louis to get it done, where you can check yourself into the St Johns Hospital and have all of them pulled, all at the same time. Just like you did when you needed to get yours all pulled at the same time back in 1961.

I ask how long will you be gone, and you say you are uncertain. Since I have broken this leg, I cannot leave the Milwaukee area for any kind of work, so I will schedule about two months work to be done here. In fact I have at least three months work ahead of me. Now do I need to take you anywhere?

Of course I can come to Chicago with you and then catch the afternoon CNW train back to Milwaukee. You tell me that you would feel better if I would do that. So I get on the phone and call the CNW station in the town where we live and order a half fare ticket for you.

Of course I will travel on my CNW pass. I then call Union Station in Chicago and get the CB&Q ticket agent and order a half fare ticket for you, and I also order a compartment for you on that same train. I get all of the Train Numbers and when they will be leaving every station. Like I have told you before, when the CNW train gets to Chicago, we will have 35 minutes to get to Union station and get you on board of the CB&Q train with all of your luggage. But I will handle all of what has to be done.

I ask if you have any five-dollar bills, and you check and you have only one. So I hand you ten of them. I always have a supply of them in my shoulder bag.

Of course until you get to St Louis, the only tips you will be handing out will be to your porter on the train. Like when you eat in the dining room, leave no less than a five-dollar tip. And when a porter makes up your bed or whatever, tip him five dollars. They don't get paid all that much, so tips is how they really survive. And of course they will all be black.

I never mention a thing about any of your men clients. I figure what would be the point. I ask if there is any cash you want me to deposit into your bank and you say there is, and when you show me, I put all of this money in one of my money belts, and then I tell you I will wear my shirt on the outside of my pants tomorrow.

By the way   HAPPY BIRTHDAY

CLEMENT

March 24th 1966

Peggy;

Well I got you to Chicago okay and got you settled in your compartment and got you familiar with the Porter you would have on this train to St Louis. It would really get to St Louis in 13 hours, which means it will be dark when you pull into Union Station. Tell the Porter in St Louis that you would like a County Cab. He will know what you want. And tip him five dollars. This is the Porter who works in Union Station. He will handle your luggage when you get off of the train. You may have to hail one, but they usually are very nice.

Of course if there are no County cabs there then you may have to take a Yellow Cab. But tell them when you give them your parents address, that you know the St Louis general area like the back of your hand, and in reality you should. Point is, some cabbies take the long way to St Louis County. Make sure they take Natural Bridge to Florissant road and turn right onto that street, which will take you through Cool Valley and ultimately through Ferguson and you should then know exactly where you are.

Of course you can rent a Car after you have been there for a few days, perhaps after you get home from the hospital. But just call a car rental, and show them one of your credit cards, whether you really use it or not.

I like to deal in cash mostly whenever I can. I don't think it is wise to carry a lot of cash on your person. Use a check when necessary. Especially if you are able to get a County Cab. Write them a check. Your father does that all of time. In fact he has a charge account with them, so you might be able to do that also. Most County Drivers still will remember you. Most of them have been driving for more than twenty years.

CLEMENT

June 30th 1966

Peggy;

I had a call from the Spice Company asking when you might be returning back to your job. I told them that you had gone to St Louis, Missouri to have all of your teeth pulled, and I really did not know when you would be returning back to Milwaukee.

Since you have been gone for three months now, I am also concerned myself, because soon I will have to be getting back on the road where I will have to go to some other cities. And I am concerned about who will take care of my Cats.

I have tried to call you several times but you are not taking any calls from me apparently. I then called Hazel and she says you have not been feeling all that well yet. That you are having some problems with your gums, like you had some kind of gum disease and even though all of your teeth have now been pulled, you are still having a lot of problems with those gums. That you will probably have to wait another two months before you can even get impressions made for your new teeth. That when you try to take impressions, you always gag and they just won't do it right now.

That maybe you should get some teeth implanted into your mouth instead of false teeth. They would still be false teeth, but they would be permanently implanted into your jawbones. That too will have to done in the Hospital and it can only be done in stages. And it also will be more painful.

So I have begun to look around in the Newspapers and in the Phonebook, trying to find someone who can watch my cats while I am gone out of town.

I asked the Apartment Manager and she says her daughter will take care of them. I tell her I need to meet your daughter, before I would approve her or not.

So an hour later the Managers daughter comes to my apartment and when I first see this young lady, I know that she is not the person who will watch after my Cats. I call the Manager and tell her that your daughter is not the person who will watch my Cats while I am gone, because she is not even aware where she now is. Because she is stoned, probably by using some kind of drugs. The Manager says she is always that way. I say she will not watch my cats.

The next day You called and tell me that you are returning back to Milwaukee, because you cannot get any impressions taken because you found out that you would most likely Gag if you ever got the chance to wear false teeth, so you will just return home and go back to work at the Spice Company. I asked you if you wanted me to call them and you tell me that you already did do that.

And you will begin work next Monday morning at your regular time. And by the way, because they missed you so much, they are giving you a raise of two dollars more an hour.

CLEMENT

July 2nd 1966

Peggy;

I don't know whether your Mom and Dad mentioned anything about what I did when I was in the St Louis area back about four month ago, but I made an application again to try to adopt once again.

Only this time I alone applied. I never even mentioned that I was married before and since the last time we applied, I do not wear any kind of wedding ring on my left hand ring finger. I do wear a ring on that finger, but it is a turquoise ring that I made myself some years back.

It has been rumored that the State of Missouri has a number of children in the area of six and seven year of age, who are kind of hard to adopt out to potential parents, for various reasons.

Mostly because none of these children fit into the molds of what potential parents are really looking for. Something like the one we had noted who hated Cats.

I did inquire about that and they did say that they had a number of those kinds of children. So I wrote a separate letter to the adoption agency that I am working with, that I do not want any child who is dead set against not liking Cats or any kind of Pet.

I know it will kind of narrow the field of possibilities but it is because I plan to always have at least one Cat in my family for however long I am on this earth.

There is no point of possibly meeting a child who does not like any kind of Pet and especially cats. Thinking back when you were out of town getting your teeth pulled and living with your parents.

Where would you now be without your parents actually having a Dog, which seemed to be a kind of calming effect on your overall demeanor while you lived with them these last three months.

They told me that there were sometimes when you would go outside and talk to that dog for hours, and when you came back into the house, you seemed to be more calmed down.

That whatever you had told that dog, made a lot of difference somehow. Of course they don't know what you told Duke, but whatever it was seemed to make a difference in how you actually responded to what they then asked you.

Which was what are you going to do when you go back to live with Clement. Are you going to continue to do what you were doing before you came to St Louis to get your teeth pulled. And now that you know that you probably won't be able to ever wear any kind of false teeth, which will ultimately take away your natural beauty, what will you now do in all of your so called spare time.

Will you use all of that time to either write stories or even books, or create something? And you told them that you have been thinking about creating Crossword Puzzles.

That you have contacted a number of Magazines and periodicals, like Readers Digest and other Monthly magazines who always have crossword puzzles in them, and especially Dell Crossword Magazine, who say they are always looking for new crossword puzzles. That if any of your puzzles got published, that you would get 5 cents for each puzzle that was published. Now since Readers Digest has a circulation of at least a million customers, that would mean that whenever one of your puzzles got published, that you would get fifty thousand dollars, and this would be for just this one monthly publication.

Your parents tell you that if that happens, then you should also submit all of these in the Names of yourself and your husband, just in case something might happen to you. It would be like an Insurance policy on your very life. So when you came back to Milwaukee, you told me about what you planned to do with your spare time.

And that like your parents suggested, you would submit all of your Crossword Puzzles in both of our names. I then tell you that I also have taken out a Decreasing Term Life Insurance Policy on my own life, in the amount of One million dollars. That if I reached the age of 65 and above, that at that time this insurance policy would be worth one hundred thousand dollars, and at that time I could convert it over to a full life insurance policy, which means I would have to pay whatever premiums, of which would be around sixty five dollars a month, until I reached the age of one hundred, and at that time this policy would be completely paid up. Which means that this policy would never exceed the one hundred thousand dollars, but it would be a completely paid in full policy.

Of course the WWIB has me insured for a half million dollars, and if I remained with them until I retired at age 65, that that policy would be worth another one hundred thousand dollars, which would be completely paid up at age 65.

Now depending on when I died would actually depend on how much you would actually receive. Because with a million dollar policy and a hundred thousand dollar policy, you could possibly get as much as a million or more dollars for my life. It sure gives you something to think about, doesn't it?

Actually I am worth more dead, than I am while I am alive. But I am hoping that you do not look at me in that way, because I would hope that we still have many good years ahead of us yet.

Admittedly our lives have not been all that rosy so far, but I think that now our lives will become better as time goes by. Anyway the Cats have surely missed you, just like I have also. The one thing that I now realize is, is living by yourself while I am away from home, must be very lonesome.

I usually don't get lonely when I am on the road, because I always have reports to make out Daily and phone calls to make, either to my home office, or to persons with the Interstate Commerce Commission or with the Association of American Railroads personnel. And because I always work as long as I can, wherever I am at, I am always very tired, so after I eat supper, and I always shower and shave in the evening hours, because when I get up, I get dressed and go and eat a breakfast and then I take a Cab to the station where I am working for that day.

I have to go back to southern Illinois next week, so I will

probably be gone at least two weeks and maybe longer. I have gone to the store and I also purchased an upright freezer as you can plainly see, and it is fully stocked with all kinds of meat, meaning there is half of a beef in there, and half a hog, and various marked pieces and bacon and pork chops and there is even two chickens and one turkey. There is also two ducks and two pheasants that I had friends of mine bring back from Minnesota when they went hunting a week back. There is also ice cream in there along with some toppings of various flavors. All of the latter are in plastic containers. And lastly there are six Angel Food cakes in there also. Any frosting you will have to make yourself, and for that there is a new Recipe Book laying on top of that freezer. Which has recipe's for all kinds of other things too.

As you can see, I have also organized the Kitchen as to how it is handy for me, and I hope it is handy for you also. Meaning when I cook, I like to sit down, so that is why I also purchased a Wheel Chair, so it is much easier for me to get around in this Kitchen while sitting in this wheelchair. It takes some getting used to, but try it for a while and after it becomes easy for you, you might even thank me for setting it up this way. By the way this wheel chair is extra wide. I am just thinking about our future.

CLEMENT

August 6th 1966

Dear Peg;

Well like I said a couple of weeks back before I left home once again, Returning back to Southern Illinois has become another headache for me, meaning that there are so many improprieties that it is hard to know who to notify first as far as getting various fines levied against the perpetrators.

Apparently it has been two years since anyone has been to these stations and it surely shows, because there are so many bad practices going on everywhere I have been, that it is becoming difficult to keep my cool.

Though it is obvious to the station agents that I am not very pleased with their Accounting practices. But so far I have kept my temper cool.

I have contacted everyone that I know of to come to this general area, and they will have a ball when it comes to levying heavy fines. I have seen so much graft that it really boggles the mind.

So I am heading North tomorrow on the next Illinois Central Train, which will be coming through the town I am now in at 9:00 AM in the morning. And since this train is what is called a milk train, which means that it will stop between where I am and Chicago at every station on the line, so it will actually take me thirty hours to go from southern Illinois to Chicago, so I will not get home until two days from now. This letter will most likely beat me home, because I am sending it out in tonight's post.

I understand that all of the first class mail is sent over to Louisville, Kentucky, where it is put on a Greyhound Bus, of which the station in Chicago is right across the street from the main post office in that fair city.

Next time I will take that same bus from this general area. Because this Greyhound bus arrives in Chicago 12 hours after it leaves Louisville, Kentucky. Which would be about 9 AM tomorrow morning.

The Passenger Train system is something to be desired, because of how everything is run. Actually you can catch a Train in St Louis, Missouri and two days later you are arriving in Los Angeles, California.

But if you catch a train in New Orleans, Louisiana and you want to go to Chicago, it will really take you four days to get there, because the train connections in and from any southern states actually is like putting you on the Moon, because there are not very many connections that are scheduled to coincide with other train schedules going to any other city.

Now on the east coast, you can go from Washington DC to New York City in a matter of hours, because some persons live in Virginia and work in New York City and they do this every day.

Actually five months back, I caught a train in Chicago and arrived in Washington, DC 13 hours later, because it was a through train. The only reason it stopped only once was, because of a changing of the train crews. Which delayed us about thirty minutes. But we arrived on time in DC.

This is when I went to DC to meet some Transportation persons, and to get some additional instructions regarding Hazardous Materials. And my return trip was the same way. Actually the train crew started in New York City and switched crews in the same town where they were switched when going to DC from Chicago.

CLEMENT

September 7th 1966

Dear Peg;

This letter was actually begun on September 2nd, because I wanted to make a note of where I am actually going on this trip. Because of all of the problems I encountered in Southern Illinois train stations; the word has gone out to every train station East of the Mississippi river that I am someone to be reckoned with, because I am a person who rarely misses anything when it comes to Railroad Accounting.

So the head office of the WWIB is sending me on a Special Assignment to Elizabeth, New Jersey, where I will be auditing the books of a well known company.

Now this is really getting in Big time Accounting. First I will have to check in with the WWIB office in New York City, who will hopefully direct me or take me to Elizabeth, New Jersey. Anyway I will just wait and see what happens after I get there.

I stopped at the Main office of the WWIB in Chicago and talked to Jack Perkins, who is the head guy with this organization, and he tells me that I am the first Auditor who has ever totally understood Railroad Accounting, other than most auditors who work in his office. For a guy who has only been on this job for about a year, this is a great compliment to me. Jack says to just keep doing what you have been doing, in the same organized way that you seem to always do things and you will be just fine.

And don't let anyone intimidate you. Jack says that because of my Stature, and the way I talk, I probably most often intimidate those who I always talk to. That he himself was a little intimidated when he first met me. He says it shows that I am an educated person, and that I don't let any persons get to me.

He also told me that how I handled myself in Southern Illinois was great. He says persons down there won't easily forget you.

I tell Jack that I plan to go back there in a year. I always get out of the general area before I call others in to do the same thing that I do. He says you handled it like a professional.

CLEMENT

September 28th 1966

Dear Peg;

Well, here it is three weeks after I arrived in New Jersey. What an operation this is. I took a full day to get familiar with how their accounting system works, but after I did get it figured out, I then began to find all kinds of improprieties that had been going on here since I don't know when.

And since no one has audited these books for about ten years, with the exception of their own internal auditors, and who knows what they really found, I am thinking that I will also bring in the Interstate Commerce Commission Auditors. But I will wait until I am away from this place.

I have placed certain markers whereby those auditors will know where to seek other information. This is something that I have already informed those auditors of. When any other auditor would do the same thing I am now doing, they would not find any indication of what I have done. It's real interesting what I have created.

So after spending three weeks here, I have finally decided that I cannot do anything further to augment what their accounting officers have really done with their books.

I have not given anyone any idea that I have actually found anything, but have actually made some comments, wherein they have done a good thing while keeping these records.

I have gone back into New York City where I have called the Interstate Commerce Commission and talked to Dick Tracy, and told him what I had found, and what to watch for while he is doing his job.

He says, like every place that I have alerted them to and of, I have found the impossible, whereof others have not. Again he says that someday we must meet with each other.

So at that time I made arrangements to meet him and the auditor from the AAR in Peoria, Illinois next year in March. The exact date I will have to inform both of them of later. He says great.

He also tells me to not live in the Royal Hotel there, because it is also a Whore House. Actually most of the whores own their own houses there, and only use that hotel as a place where they take their clients.

There are a number of good Motels in that town, but the best is the Cottonwood Motel, which is on the southeast side of that town. That Motel also has a dining room and on Saturday nights they have live entertainment.

Most of the entertainers who play there come from various areas in other states whereof they play a circuit. So if I am there for a couple of weeks, which I will probably be, see at least two different groups of entertainers.

So I will be returning tomorrow. But I probably won't get to Milwaukee until the next morning. My Van is parked at the CNW depot there, and I will also have to make a run to my home office, so it will most likely be sometime in the afternoon of next Wednesday when I finally get back to the apartment.

CLEMENT

October 8th 1966

Dear Peg;

I have decided to spend some time in my home territory, because this is the time of year when various Cattle Hides are being shipped to the tanning company in South Milwaukee.

I am not looking forward to this time, because I also have to inspect some of these Green Hides. Meaning that these green hides will be inside of open Gondola cars and they will be completely covered with Flies.

I have purchased some disposable coveralls whereof I will always wear climbing up to the top of these cars and looking at these hides. These coveralls also cover my shoes too, and they also come with a Hood, which is attached to these coveralls. In fact this entire outfit is one complete garment, including the gloves. Over my face, there will be a kind of Net. The same kind of net that Bee Keepers wear.

But they tell me that the overall smell is almost unbearable. So I will also be wearing an Oxygen Mask, so I won't have to taste this smell for some time after I leave this place. How persons ever get used to that smell is something I will never understand.

Anyway it is now two days after I have inspected this tanning company and I never want to return to this place ever again, and I have told my home office this fact.

I told the office manager, who is my supervisor, that if that place needs to be inspected, that I suggest he do it himself. I also wrote a letter to Jack Perkins and told him the same thing.

Guy says if I am ordered to that place again, I will either go or be fired. I told him to go ahead and fire me then. I actually laughed in his face. He turned beet red, but he did not fire me. Because I also told him that I sent a personal letter to Jack Perkins in Chicago and told him the same thing. I think I have made another enemy of the office manager. Oh well, what the hell.

In the city of Cudahy I have also looked at a three-bedroom cottage, which is about three miles further north of where we now live.

It too overlooks the Bluffs of Lake Michigan. The porch on the east side of the house will have to be reinforced, because the owner says that for years now, when winter comes and until the lake actually freezes, that because there are Rocks below the bluff near where the cottage is located, that spray comes up and over this bluff and all of that moisture ends up freezing onto the screens of that porch. He wants 58 thousand dollars for this cottage, and I told him that I would like you to see it before I make any kind of commitment. It also has a three-car garage, where one part of that garage can be made into a workshop. And there is also a stove in that garage. It burns either coal or wood, but a stove nonetheless. And the driveway faces the south side of that whole structure.

Actually the garage is separate from the house. There is a walkway that is covered that runs from the west side of the house to the garage that is about fifteen feet long, but I can also enclose that area. The garage doors have automatic openers also. And there are windows on the north side and on the east and west side of that garage. I think it is a great deal for the price. It does not have a basement. Which is a negative, but nothing is ever the way we may always want it to be.

Buying a house means that I am ready to settle down, finally. And I am hoping that you will think the same way when you see this place. It would be a great place to raise a family.

I have also checked out the School system in this area and any schools that our children could go to are north of that house about three blocks. There is one building which has the Primary grades that runs from the first grade to the fourth grade, and then there is another building that houses the fifth, sixth, seventh, and eighth grade students.

Then there is a totally separate building for the High school grades. It has a kind of Campus setting with a lot of trees and there is a fourteen-foot high fence all the way around this entire campus school.

There is also a Cafeteria where all of the students eat at different times. Starting at 11:00AM until 1:30 PM. The first eight grades eat at 11:00 AM and then the High School begins eating at 12:15 PM until 1:30 PM.

I even went there one day and had a meal there and they do have real good meals planned. And they are well planned. And the food is real good. If I ever lost my position with the WWIB, I could even teach there. I did not check out how much the salaries would be, but since I would not be doing any traveling, I am quite sure it would be enough for us to survive on.

Especially if you will be bringing in other money from all of your Crossword puzzles. And when I told you what I had done, you said, that you still don't trust your wife do you? I said, you have not given me any reason to do so yet. Maybe in time, but not yet.

CLEMENT

November 6th 1966

Dear Peg;

This time when I went out of Milwaukee, I went into the state of Indiana. I decided to first go to South Bend and then work my way back. I knew that I would most likely be gone for at least three weeks, but it all depended on how much snow fell while I was out this time. When I got to South Bend, and I checked into a motel, that night it snowed 11 inches.

Getting around that fair city was almost impossible, so I decided to come home, because all the way back to Milwaukee, there was more snow than there had ever fallen in more than thirty years.

It actually took me all day to get back to Milwaukee. And in Cudahy it also had snowed close to fifteen inches, so when I called my office, an operator came on the line and told me that the office was closed and would remain that way until next Monday, and or until the streets have been plowed out sufficiently so everyone could get back to work. So since this was also now Tuesday night, I had another week off.

You had also called your office and they too had closed completely down, so we would be home with each other. What a Revelation this really is.

So I got one of the Ducks out of the freezer and after I thawed it, I then removed all of what was inside of it, and made some stuffing, and put it in the oven, and while it was roasting I made two pumpkin pies and boiled some sweet potatoes and a number of other things, so when the Duck was fully roasted, I then removed it and called you to supper.

You asked why did I do this, and I said that this is a kind of celebration, because I don't really know whether I will be home for thanksgiving, so I figured we would have it early. And I don't know whether I will even be home for Christmas, so I will give you your presents after we finished with our dessert at this meal.

First I have some bad news that you will not like. Your former boss and his wife have been killed in an Automobile accident near Joliet, Illinois, while returning back to their home in Cahokia, because they were visiting with his only brother in Joliet.

And because now their family (which consists of six sons and one daughter) and it has been decreed that I am now the Father of that daughter, who just turned 14 two weeks back. Other persons whom they also knew are adopting her six brothers.

I also have been approved by the Missouri Adoption agency in St Louis, and I have adopted another daughter who is 15 years old whose name is Mary Beth.

Now her last name will be Royal But because Martha was raised in Illinois and Mary Beth in Missouri, I have decided with the approval of your Mother and the Agency that these two girls will live with your parents.

Margaret has decided to take a leave of absence for now, mostly because Joe has retired, and Margaret says if she is not there, he will destroy everything in and outside of that house. So

I have decided that since all of this is totally agreeable with the Adoption Agency in St Louis, that my Lawyer in St Louis, who I gave a limited power of attorney to, just for this transaction, and because we are completely snowed in here, and this was the time that this all happened, so now we have two daughters that I can call my own family.

You told me some time back that you would never make a good mother. Well you won't have to prove that, because these two daughters will go to school at St Thomas Aquinas in Florissant, Missouri. They will take a school bus to that school and return the same way... They will have to share a bedroom with each other until I can decide where I will eventually make my permanent home. And if you are also part of that permanent home, then so be it.

The adoption was final yesterday around 2:00 PM. In six months there will be another hearing to see how well these two girls are getting along with each other, and how often I have visited with them, since you have not even been considered in this adoption.

As far as the Adoption Agency is concerned, I am a potential single parent, and the fact that I happen to know two individuals of great appearances and reputations, and they have actually sponsored me in this endeavor, I think this will work out just fine.

The Adoption agency knows how much money I make, and the fact that I travel a lot doing my job, and because Mary Beth has been very hard to adopt out to anyone else and I agreed to try her in my life as a family member, and because Martha has been decreed to me personally by her former parents in a notarized and Registered document made in the State of Missouri, and not Illinois, that is why I also adopted Martha.

And she fully approves of me also, because as you know we are very close to each other, because I have babysat Martha and her brothers many times when her real parents were still alive.

CLEMENT

November 15th 1966

Dear Peg;

Over the next few months I will have a number of stations that I will have to Audit in central Illinois, so I plan to visit with my two girls as often as I can. Whether you want to do the same is totally up to you.

Since the Adoption Agency thinks that I am a single parent, and if on the day or days that I am visiting with my family, and you show up, then you will not be my wife at those times, but will be the daughter of the two persons that are the caretakers of my two daughters. In effect you will kind of be like an Aunt.

We will not stay with your parents unless I can arrange to create a temporary bedroom in their basement, of which your Mom has wanted me to do anyway. Just in case these two girls don't get along well in the same bedroom, and also for possible visiting relatives.

I want to make a good impression with these girls, so I would appreciate it if you would go along with me in this endeavor. And I also want to make a good impression with this Adoption Agency also.

I don't intend on being a Traveling Auditor for the rest of my life, because my home life has gone to hell in a hand basket. As you well know, I have only been home a limited length of time of this last year, meaning that I have only been home 95 days out of 365 days.

My life is difficult enough, with you having a lot of extracurricular activities going on when I am away from home. But I am hoping that all of that has now stopped. But if it hasn't then you and I will have to live separate lives, and live in separate homes.

I am not saying that I still Love you, because I am questioning that also at this time. Only you can change how I feel about you.

But I would like to have a Mother for my girls, and if you cannot be that person, then I will seek a Mother in a different port. And when I find that woman, it will be at that time that I will divorce you.

CLEMENT

December 1st 1966

Dear Peg;

Just a short letter to let you know that I will be in my home territory for this week. I still have to Audit the South Milwaukee Station which is on the CNW railroad and I have some more Scales to inspect and probably will have to repair them, because my office has had a number of complaints about these scales. Whether they will need to have new parts or just adjusted, I am not certain yet, but nonetheless it has to be done.

And since it snowed 15 inches here also, will make that job more difficult. So I will be home for my evening meals every day this week, that is Monday through Friday. My breakfast and noon meals, I will eat them away from here.

Now because I will be going back to the middle part of Illinois next week, I will be leaving home Sunday afternoon, catching the 4:00 PM CNW train to Chicago, so I can make connections on the Illinois central passenger train at 10:00 PM that same night.

And because that train will stop at most every town going to where I will be going, I won't actually get to that town until about 10:00 AM Monday morning. I will be going to Mt. Carmel, and I will work my way north from there.

I will be renting a car there, because it will be easier than using trains to travel to my next town. And because for most of this time, I will be within driving distance of St Louis, I will most likely spend weekends at your parent's house. And while I am there, I will build that extra bedroom in their basement.

Maybe I can actually teach your Dad how to use a hammer, or at least show him what end is used most often. And I think your mother will appreciate it if I also do that.

It may keep him from destroying things she has done to the inside of that house. But more than likely she will insist that he goes and finds himself another job somewhere else, so she can go back to work at the Terminal Railroad Association.

But it is most likely that your mother will remain home, so when the girls need her, they can depend on the fact that that is where they will always find her. I know I am asking a lot of her, but I also know that she like me wants to make sure that these two girls have a good home to come home to.

She told me that it is like I am giving her another chance to show the world and herself that she does know how to raise two girls, so they will turn out all right in the end. And she also knows that I will spend as much time as my own job will permit me to be there for the two of them.

It's interesting that there are no instruction books in how to actually raise two daughters, which are only a year apart in age. And the hardest part of all of this will be, whether I can teach both of them my morals and how important my Christianity really is to them and me.

I know that they are both Catholic and what they already know about that religion will most likely be real important in how they do things, but just as important, will be to teach them how important responsibility really is to each of them. That is what you never really learned, and if you did, you have totally ignored your responsibility in what you do know.

I don't want you to teach them your ways of accepting responsibility, as you have not done in your life. And if either of them turns out the same way that you now are, then I will know where they got it.

So be very careful as to what you say to them or what you teach them. If you are with these two girls when I am not there, then whatever you teach them, make sure it is the correct way, and make sure it is the same way I believe.

CLEMENT

January 5th 1967

Dear Peggy;

I am real sorry I could not be home for Christmas, but I did spend Christmas with my two daughters. Your Mom asked me why you had not come to St Louis, and I told her that I had not been home for almost a month, so I could not answer that question.

When I left there on December 7th, the company she works for still had not opened their offices for regular business. But was expected to do that in a couple of days.

I know this because I called you and that is what you told me. And because I am not always in a place where I can make personal phone calls, because sometimes I am invited out to someone's farm for a home cooked meal, and they don't always have a phone. I know that sounds rather old fashioned, but there are still places in this country where not everyone has a phone.

And because you never write me any letters, of which I don't know why, because I would eventually get them, because I often meet the Traveling Post Office Van at a Crossroads, so I can get my office mail, but I never get any letters from you. I also send letters in the same way, because they meet other traveling post office vans that are going where most of my mail is headed.

I asked your mother whether you had ever came to St Louis to visit with her or my daughters, and she told me that you had never came since I had adopted them.

What a shame to realize that you are not even trying to get to know either of them. That tells me that you are also not interested in discovering whether I still might love you. SO BE IT

It will still be at least a month before I can really come home again, because I don't really want to quit Auditing all of these many stations, that some of them have not been audited for three or more years.

I wonder what the previous Auditor was doing when he said he had audited all of the stations he was supposed to have audited. Anyway I have reported all of what I have discovered to my home office and especially to Jack Perkins in the Chicago office. There should be HELL to pay when Jack confronts previous auditors about this.

I think he thought that I would white wash all of these small stations just like the previous Auditors did. Well let me tell you, I am not that kind of person and I never will be. I cannot be bought off by anyone. No matter who the person is who is trying to buy me off.

I am glad that I rented a car while auditing this part of Illinois, because if you always took a train, that is why most of these stations never got audited. Because most passenger trains are not stopping at these stations any longer.

So one of the first things I am going to do is to mention about all of these smaller stations that have not been audited, and my suspected reasons why they were always missed.

And that reason is because no trains stop at these stations

any more, not even Freight trains, because most of the products that comes into these areas, are brought into them by TRUCK.

I am quite sure this will wake up my office, and especially the home office, because this letter I will write to my office, will only be a copy of the one I write to the home office, and specifically Jack Perkins.

What a Revelation this will be. In fact I will write that letter this evening while I am at your Moms house, so I can get it sent in tomorrows mail.

I don't think I will be ignored in my request of being able to use my vehicle when I am within any part of my assigned territory. It should have been mentioned a long time back, but I think that the previous auditor knew that he was in a lot of trouble with the Union we Auditors all belong to, and he thought if he rocked the boat with the head office, he would get in deeper trouble. So he never mentioned it.

He instead covered it all up. Well I am not that way. What ever I see that needs changing, I will always voice my opinion, and I will always back it up with a lot of proof as to why it needs changing. I think they will listen to me.

Well, I wrote that letter to the head office in Chicago with a copy to my office in Milwaukee. I let them know where I planned to be in two days, just in case they may want to call me, from either office.

In my home office I told them that I expected to be in Taylorville, and I am there, and I did get a phone call from Jack Perkins in Chicago, and he says he likes my idea about using my vehicle.

He has thought that should have been suggested a long time ago, but he says he can only go by what his auditors tell him. So he is glad that I am the kind of auditor that tells the straight truth.

An hour later I got another call from my home office in Milwaukee, and he tells me that he dislikes my idea, and he fully intends to talk against it.

So I told him what Jack Perkins had said about me, and I also told him that I really don't take my orders from him any longer, but only from Jack Perkins. He told me that I am ordered home.

I told him to call Jack Perkins and tell him the same thing. He hung up, so I called Jack Perkins myself and told him what I told my home office, and he told me to totally ignore my home office, and I told him that I would only take orders from you from now on.

Jack told me that the Manager of my home office will now be fired, or will be demoted probably back to being a clerk. Or else if he has not kept up his Union dues, then he will be totally out of a job with the WWIB.

So it looks like I will be eventually using my own car in the near future. And whether I will find my former Manager in the office when I get back to Milwaukee is yet to be determined.

I still want to work my way to Springfield before I return back to my home office. But I think I will stop and see Jack Perkins when I am in Chicago, which still won't be for another ten days.

I try to audit all of the stations in two separate towns every day. That is the advantage of driving a vehicle. When I get to towns that have more than two stations in them, then I can usually only do one town a day. So I remain in that town until the next morning and then drive to my next destination.

Of course I always know how many stations I have to audit before I even drive into that town. But now these towns are getting much larger, therefore it will take me probably no less than three days to do them.

And when I get to a town like Springfield, Illinois, where there will be 8 stations to audit, then that will take me probably about 12 days, depending on what and if I find any improprieties. But when I get to Springfield, I won't audit it, because that will be my next destination where I will go when I return to this area.

But I still have some smaller towns to audit yet before I get to that city. You see I go all the way to the Indiana border and then I work my way west back across the state. And then I go to the closest town on the west side of the state I am working in, and work my way east. I think this is the simple way of auditing all of these towns and their railroad stations.

Beyond a specific area in a specific state, of which I will not mention here, the EWIB auditors audit whatever stations they are supposed to audit.

And since I only go to certain cities in Indiana, then the EWIB auditors cover any state beyond that. Other than the stations that I also Audit in Indiana.

And then there is the SWIB, which stands for Southwestern Weighing and Inspection Bureau, and then there is the Southeastern Weighing and inspection bureau.

Now the Transcontinental Freight Bureau, otherwise known

as the TCFB, handles any thing west of the Mississippi River. I know you don't need to know this, but I just thought you might find it interesting anyway.

CLEMENT

January 26th 1967

Dear Peg;

I will be home in a couple of days, so this letter will probably get there after I arrive at home. When I stopped in Chicago to talk to Jack Perkins, he told me that he has issued a Directive that states that any Auditor can now use their own Automobile anywhere in their assigned territories.

What a Revelation this is. He said that he did not say why this Directive has now been issued, but if anyone asks, then he will specifically tell them, that if he had more Auditors like Mr. Royal, then this would have happened much sooner.

He also told me that because of my obvious connections within the Railroad Industry, he now knows that Passenger trains as they used to be, will most likely end by 1968.

And at that time a new system of Passenger Service will be coming on line, wherein a newly created Railroad service will go into effect of which will use everybody's railroad lines so it can go anywhere in this country.

So all of what foreign railroad passes that all of the auditors will then have, must be turned back into this office, and a new railroad pass will be issued, wherein any auditor can travel anywhere in this country, just in case they are sent on a Special Assignment, wherein using their own vehicle is too far away for that to be done.

Jack also told me that a different man took over the Managers position in Milwaukee. He is a totally different man, and he will work with you and others. But if he screws up like the former Manager did, he too will lose his job.

He says he does not want to bring someone like myself and install me in that kind of a position. At least not yet. Maybe in a few years, because he says I am too good of an Auditor to let go of yet.

He told me, that if he had ten more just like me, then all of his problems would most likely disappear. So I guess I am well liked in the Main office.

While I was in Union Station in Chicago, I ran into Phil Evans, the Radio Commentator, and Jack Perkins introduced me to him and we hit it off real great.

I found out that Phil is also from a small town in South Dakota, and we sat and talked until he says he has to run and do his program.

He actually broadcasts from Union Station, because of the fact that the station he works in is a fifty thousand watt station and it is located on the ground floor in the Northeast corner of Union Station.

He told me he lives in Aurora, Illinois and he always eats breakfast in Union Station five days a week. He says we will meet again many times.

After Phil left, I asked Jack how long has he known him and he says about thirty years, and he is just like you are. I didn't ask any further questions, because I distinctly knew what he meant.

Anyway every time I am now in Chicago, I always meet

and eat breakfast with Phil Evans. We have discovered many things that we have in common with each other. He likes the same kind of Music I do, and we appear to like similar foods and we have similar sayings and a whole lot more too numerous to mention here.

Its interesting that even though I am now driving my own vehicle, I still come to Union Station to eat breakfast with Phil Evans. He says he will continue to take the train in from Aurora as long as it keeps running.

The train he takes will continue to operate, because it is a commuter train, it will keep running even after this new train service comes on line. And the Illinois Central line will continue to do the same, until they are eventually forced out.

The same for the CNW Commuter train from Milwaukee, Wisconsin. He says he will be putting forth some comments about those three lines in a couple of days.

CLEMENT

February 14th 1967

Dear Peg;

Today I headed for Springfield, Illinois because by the time I return from this trip, I want to have all of Illinois Audited all the way to Chicago proper.

With the exception of East St Louis, Illinois. And that station I will Audit when I go to see my two daughters. This will probably be just before I go on a special Assignment somewhere far away from Illinois.

Then I will go west from Joliet and work my way north to the Wisconsin border. I don't handle any stations in Chicago, unless it is on a special assignment, which Jack Perkins says I might be doing, because he says I am a very good investigator, and I seem to have a nose for finding any problems, wherever I go.

Jack says," there are some stations in Chicago whereat there have been a lot of problems, and every Auditor who has ever done these stations, has never reported any improprieties," but he knows there are many. So I will most likely be sent to these problem areas. But Jack says, "when it gets warmer and closer to spring, that is probably when I will be sent to these stations". Jack says, "It is not just the Station Agents that he is concerned about, it is all of the Industries that this station handles, because he says he knows there have been some large payouts under the table, but no one has ever reported who these industries have been."

He says if I can discover who these industries are, then when I call in the Auditor with the Interstate Commerce Commission and he calls in the Auditor with the Association of American Railroads, then between these two organizations, all of this graft will be either stopped or the industries involved will be put out of business.

And the reason I won't be sent in until spring is because I will most likely need some protection from the local law in the area. Because when I discover the industries that are causing all of these improprieties, the station agent will most likely be calling these industries, to protect him and them.

Jack says he knows that when I find these entities, I will not let on that I have found anything and in fact I have been instructed to just tell the station agent that I have to go home because I received an urgent message from my wife.

Jack and I have set this up between us, because when I sense a problem, on the day I go back to my motel, I will then call Jack and tell him what I suspect, and he will have his secretary call me the next day and just in case my calls will be recorded, she will say she is my wife, and I have to return home as soon as I can get there, and she will only allude to what the problem really is.

When I know what kind of problem Jack and his secretary have conjured up, I will then tell you, just in case someone other than anyone with the WWIB calls you to verify what I will eventually tell this station agent. I know it sounds mysterious, and it is, but it is the only way I can protect myself and you.

And of course once I know that I am in any kind of danger,

then not only will I be shadowed by a Law Officer, but you will also be shadowed.

Now I have not said anything about myself to any of the station agents I have come in contact with, and when any of them ask me where I hail from, I always tell them I come from a small town in northwestern Montana.

That I have been to many places in this country, but when I get the chance to go to where I was born, then I always go to Northwestern Montana, where I can go hunting and fishing.

Now in case anyone ever checks my Van for any kinds of fishing gear, they will find a couple of fishing rods and a tackle box that has all kinds of lures and other stuff inside of it, but I always keep it locked. And I always keep it in the same place in my Van.

One never knows by what methods anyone will ever try to harm me. I don't want you to worry about me, because I have always been a very careful person when it comes to my own safety. I won't go into my safety regarding you and me though.

CLEMENT

March 10th 1967

Dear Peg;

On this trip I will be auditing all of the stations west of Chicago to the Iowa border and north to the Wisconsin border. I will be away from home for three weeks and possibly four. It all depends on what I find.

I am suspecting that I will begin to find some more improprieties at some of these larger stations. The one town I did not go and audit, is Peoria, Illinois because it will take me three weeks just to audit every station in that town. So I am leaving that to another time. As you know I did go there last year, and even though I did suspect there were some improprieties going on there, I reported this to Jack Perkins and he told me to not tell my home office the same thing.

This is the only way I can protect myself, because I also suspected someone in my own office of informing Industries in that town.

But now since the former manager is gone, I think I will have a better chance of finding something, which I could not find before. It is a terrible thing to suspect a member of the same organization that I work for of being in cahoots with certain industries in specific towns.

When it was suggested by my home office manager that I go there, I actually told Jack Perkins and he told me what he suspected of him.

So I played it cool, and did not report any improprieties to my home office, even though I had found some. I only reported these problems to the Chicago office, directly to Jack Perkins. I did not tell anyone else.

Probably next month I will go to Peoria, unless I am sent on a special assignment in Chicago proper or to some other place outside of this area.

Jack Perkins has told me of some specific companies that he suspects of improprieties, and they are very powerful companies, so I will most likely inform the FBI office in that city before I go to my special assignment.

They will not be inside of the station with me unless they are needed to be there with me, but I will have a special device wherein I can contact them, and they will be with me in less than a minute.

It's a kind of a beeper device that alerts my shadow that I may have a problem soon. They will check with me to see if I am in any immediate danger, and if I am, they will remove me from the station premises. And away from that area.

My shadow will always keep an eye on my vehicle, to make sure no one does anything to it while I am inside of a specific station working. I think I should tell you at this time, that I have been carrying a gun, and I do have a Permit to carry it, in every state that my territory covers. Meaning I have a gun permit to carry a concealed weapon.

Actually I have had this gun since 1965, but I always carry it in my vehicle. I even have a gun permit to carry this weapon in

Missouri.

And wherever I will go, it has been suggested that I apply for a license to carry this weapon in whatever state I will be, or have worked in. Actually, I applied for a federal license when I was in Washington, DC a few months back when I was there with some Federal people, and they told me that it would be better to apply for a license to carry when I am working in a particular state and town or city, which means that whatever state and town or city I am working in, I am legal.

So I contacted Dick Tracy with the Interstate Commerce Commission and Perry Mason with the Association of American Railroads, and with their influence, I have been issued a Federal gun license, which allows me to carry this weapon in any state in the Continental United States. I have to go to a Shooting Range every six months to requalify myself, but that is no problem.

I will only use it if someone else fires at me. Will I shoot to kill, no, that is not my intention, but I will use it when necessary. Have I used it yet, and that answer is no, not yet.

Whenever I take whatever tests I am required to take, when my license is up for renewal. I am an expert shot, and have actually fired at targets that were more than 250 feet from me, and have hit the bulls eye every time. Something that my instructor said could not be done with the accuracy that I do it. I have been putting together another weapon, that I invented myself.

I still need to apply for a patent for this weapon, and my Lawyer, Moses Lighthouse in Los Angeles, is handling that. One thing about new weapons is, they all are checked out very carefully, and to make sure no weapon of this kind has ever been invented before by anyone, anywhere in this world. So this will take some time to accomplish. Hopefully within a couple of years.

Well here it is now getting close to the month of April, and soon I will be returning home. Its sometimes interesting that I take this long to write my letters to you, but it is also a way for me to keep myself informed too, regarding my overall thoughts regarding mostly me, but other things connected with me.

I have one more station to audit and that is Harvard Illinois, and that will only take me a couple of hours. And then I will be coming home, so I will be leaving Rockford tomorrow morning and going to Harvard, Illinois.

Rockford has been very difficult because of all of the improprieties I have found there. This town has got a lot of graft in it. I lived here for a while some years back, but it has gotten much worse in some areas. Most of the whorehouses are gone. A few remain, but they are now very concentrated in only one area.

How do I know this, well because one of the stations I audited is right in the middle of where these places are? But they tell me in a couple of years they too will be all gone.

I have called Jack Perkins and he tells me that where I will go next will be on a special assignment, but he will not tell me over the phone. I have to check in with him after I have breakfast with Phil Evans on Monday morning of next week.

I also called Phil and he says he is looking forward with talking to me, especially about what I now do. He says he checked with Jack Perkins, and he says he can ask only certain questions of me.

It is quite apparent that I am becoming a kind of celebrity with Phil Evans. Jack says he too has breakfast most mornings with Phil, so this should be kind of interesting. I think Jack will be there also, so he can caution me when necessary about some of the questions Phil may ask. I think Phil will also record it.

CLEMENT

April 3rd 1967

Dear Peg;

As you know, I decided to drive to Chicago on Sunday afternoon, so I would already be in Chicago on Monday morning. Thereby making my day go much better.

I also know that Jack gets to Union station about 6:30 AM and is always there when Phil Evans arrives about 7 :00 AM. And at that early hour I can also get a better parking spot closer to the station, so I was there when Jack actually arrived.

He was much surprised to see me already there. He says that is one of the things he likes about me. I tell Jack that I know what I can and cannot talk about, so don't worry as to whether I will say too much, because I will not. When Phil arrived he always comes by train, because he lives in Aurora, Illinois.

First Phil asked me what I really did for the WWIB, so I tell him that I am an Auditor and a Weigh master. Now what do I specifically do? I go to every town within my territory and I audit the books of every railroad station in these towns.

You see Railroad accounting is not like any other accounting methods, because it is a reverse kind of accounting that very few auditors really understand.

But since I do totally understand this type of accounting, I am very good at what I do. So beware. Phil says that's the one thing about me that he likes, which is I always know what the next question will be.

Phil says he only asked one question and he has already found out what and why I do what I do. After he finishes his talking, I go on with my conversation, by saying; Now as to what I do as a Weigh Master, I check all railroad scales that are on railroad property, and if they only need adjusting, then I do that also, but if they need to have new parts, then I order them and when they arrive, which could likely be in about three days, I install them and then recheck the scale again and if any adjustments need to be done, I then do them and then I leave.

As info, Jack has on occasion instructed me to also inspect some city scales, and the reason I do that is because I am that good at what I do. And I do the same thing with them if new parts need to be gotten. Phil asks what do I do when I find some improprieties, and I say it depends on how big of a problem it is.

Some things I cannot tell you. It is a matter of my safety and others safety. It would be like if I asked you who are some of you informers, and you would tell me that it is none of my business. Phil says okay. He knows when he is on thin ice.

Phil also asks me how big is my territory, and I say it all depends on how many special assignments I have been sent on. Phil says he is again on thin ice. I smile but do not say anything to that query. So far Jack has never had to caution me about any of Phil's questions.

Phil says this interview is now over. His hand goes to where the recorder is located, but he does not shut it off, he only places this recorder in his shoulder bag.

I then say, Phil, if this interview is over, then I suggest you shut that thing off, or I will get up and get Jack and myself another table. Phil says okay, and he brings that recorder out of his shoulder bag and shuts it off.

I then ask Phil what about that other recorder in you shirt pocket, which has been on even before you sat down at this table. I tell Jack lets get us another table on the other side of this room.

Phil says you got me, but how did you know I had another tape recorder in my shirt pocket, and I tell him, I cannot tell you that either. But Jack smiles anyway.

I say to Phil, how many of the conversations have you recorded between Jack and yourself, and when that figure pops into his mind, I immediately have it in my mind, so I then tell Phil and Jack that he has recorded 22 conversations with you in the past three months. I get some startled looks from Jack Perkins and especially from Phil Evans.

Phil asks me, do I have abilities that very few persons have? I say I will not answer that question either. I tell Jack I will tell you about all of this when we get upstairs. Phil says he thinks he has just lost two great friends. Jack and I get up and leave, and go to another table clear across the dining area.

Jack asks me how do I know what I know about what just happened, and I say because I do have abilities that even you don't know about me. I can even tell you some things about the former office manager of the Milwaukee office that you don't know anything about, but you did have your suspicions.

I can tell specific things about that man that would curl your hair, and about how dirty he really is and was.

It is a good thing that you fired him, because around that time, I would have told you about what he has been doing for a very long time, and how much money he actually made with all of his dirty evil things that he had done since he was elevated to be the Manager of the Milwaukee office.

Apparently this new Manager is not that way. He is an honest man and he is also a good Manager. By the way, you must fire Will Green in Green Bay, because he too is dirty. I will tell you some of things he is into, in Green Bay.

He never reported any improprieties to you because he was personally involved with these improprieties, wherever he went. In fact he was getting very rich from all of the dirty things he was into, especially in Peoria, Illinois and Rockford, and a number of other places.

A report is coming to you via Special Delivery Mail, which you will hopefully get tomorrow morning, which will tell you about every dirty person within the WWIB and even about persons within your own office and mine and Green Bay.

In that report I explain how I was able to acquire all of this information, even though I was not within speaking distance of any of these persons. I don't need to be within speaking distance of any of these persons to gather the information I did gather. My abilities have no barriers. That is all I will say at this time.

Anyway after breakfast, Jack and I go up to his office, where he gave me some documents that I looked over and when I did a little bit of concentrating, I actually picked up some conversations from the persons involved on these documents.

I tell Jack the conversations I am listening to, and they in fact are talking about some other persons they have to give some money to, to cause those persons to not say anything.

I pass on those other names to Jack and he writes them down, and which company they are connected with. Jack asks me have I always had this ability, and I tell him, I have had it all of my life. I don't always read persons minds, but in this job, I have found it to be very valuable. It's interesting because sometimes I apparently make funny faces when I pick up conversations regarding what I am picking up at that time during my auditing hours.

Jack says, you are a very dangerous person, and I say no, not dangerous, just as long as you are not doing anything you are not supposed to be doing. I don't do this every day. It's just when some persons thoughts get kind of intense, do I actually get more acutely involved in what they are thinking.

I am good at what I do, even without this ability, but it sure comes in real handy when I get on the trail of an impropriety. Because then my ability can go out into the community where all of this is happening, and I can always pick up whatever I need, so as to gather everyone that is involved with all of these improprieties.

You should have picked up on this ability long before now, because in all of my reports to you, I have always given you the names of most everyone involved. Do you think that I was able to glean this information from the documents I had been looking at? No, because that information was never listed anywhere on any document that I have ever seen.

Sometimes when a specific customer is being switched to and the switching crew is delayed for awhile because someone with that Industry asked the Boss of that switching crew to come inside of their offices, and it is sometimes alluded to on some of the documents I am reading, Not just railroad personal but those involved with all of the companies involved also.

Now if any of the persons I have named on my special report to you that is on that report that is coming to you by special delivery, then I would suggest that you take that report to the Federal Bureau of Investigations, and tell them about everyone that I mention on that report.

If you are going out of town within the next couple of days, don't, because this will break this organization wide open, because many persons will have to be fired. And replaced.

Of course you will want to make your own investigation of all of these persons, and I welcome that. But in the end, you will discover that I am absolutely correct in my suspicions.

Jack asks, how did I know he might be going out of town soon, and I just smile, but do not say anything further?

Jack asks, how much of what goes on in his office, do I know about, and I say, I only eves drop on conversations that appear to be headed in a direction where they should not be headed. And I could be at home, but I probably am not, but most likely I am probably driving somewhere and these thoughts just come to me.

I don't consciously seek out these thoughts, they just come to me. Like someone else is directing them to me. I suppose a higher authority is helping me.

CLEMENT

April 6th 1967

Dear Peg;

Well, here it is, my birthday, my 33rd birthday, and I have had no mail nor phone calls from you, wishing me a happy birthday. Oh Well, what the hell.

Today I start my special assignment duties, and I am today working in south Chicago, at an unnamed railroad station, where it has been suspected there is much graft going on here.

Jack Perkins and I had many conversations within the past two days regarding my special abilities, because he says I need to hone those abilities to be much keener than they seem to be now.

So by doing some things together I think I now have some additional ways of gleaning out other information from possible suspects.

When I first come to a station, the first thing I do is inspect the scale, if they have one, and then I take a look at all of the documents I will have to go through, so as to get myself familiar with their filing system. Before I just plunged ahead with what was provided to me, and let my thoughts and my special abilities do the rest.

But I think this way will be much better, because this way, I do my own selecting of whatever files I want to inspect. Actually the other way has always been done this way, and by doing it that way, they kind of directed what the auditor really checked. So if there was any graft going on, it was always avoided, because the auditor never had a chance to inspect those other files.

But now, that will not happen. So when I walked into this station, I was looked at with much suspicion. In fact the station agent told me that his files had been audited just four month back and he is concerned as to why I need to audit them again.

I tell him that I am new, and I go where I am told to go. He shrugs his shoulders, and begins to bring me some files, and I say, no I will select my own files.

Well the ice formed immediately when I said that. I worked completely alone, and by the end of this day, I had all kinds of files set aside. I told the agent that all of these files have to be left where they are, until I have looked at them further.

In fact I will lie out a special string wherein it is to be left where it is placed, and when I come back in the morning, if that string has been disturbed in any way, then there will be hell to pay. It was noted by the agent, that I was wearing my shoulder holster, and he could see my gun in it.

So he asked me if that was necessary, and I told him that I sometimes go into some areas where it is necessary, and when I don't wear it, I feel kind of naked. So it will remain with me at all times.

Another iceberg formed between us. The next morning, I brought a shadow with me, and when the agent asked who that was, I told him the truth, that he was a special agent with the FBI. Another iceberg formed between us. He knew at that time that he was in very serious trouble.

In fact this FBI agent did not remain outside like they normally did, but he came inside of the station where the agent was sitting. And when the agent picked up his phone to make a call, the agent wrote down the number he called. And he immediately got on his radio and called that phone number into his supervisor, and when he was informed about to whom it belonged to, he reached out and took the phone out of the station agent's hand and hung it up. The agent said you interrupted an important phone call.

So the FBI agent told this station agent, that he could not make any more phone calls from this station. That if you needed to call anyone, that you will have do it from a public phone, but when you do that then you will most likely be interrupted again by another agent with the FBI.

But if you try to leave this station or try to get in your vehicle to leave, then you will be detained until I say otherwise.

This FBI agent is here to protect me until I am finished with my audit, and if that means that you cannot leave this station until I go home, then so be it. Now if I am allowed to get on with my audit, then by the end of tomorrow, I should be finished here. Whether you still will have your job is totally up to you. I must be able to inspect what I was sent here to inspect.

I began to read several thoughts from the station agents mind, and I got out of my brief case, a tape recorder, and I began talking into it quietly.

When I finished, I could see that the station agent was very nervous, and really wanted to get out of there, but he knew he would never make it. He asked if he could go to the restroom and I said only if you have an escort. He says forget it. I told him to just sit down and relax, and wait and see what happens.

Anyway I totally ignored the station agent. And got back to what I am best at. When that day ended, I again laid out my string, and placed some other special items attached to this string. And then I got in my Van and left, and the FBI waited until I was at least three blocks away from there before they allowed this station agent to even walk out of his station after he locked it up.

I turned down a number of different streets, until I knew I was not followed any longer, because when I left that station, I was followed, but not by any FBI agent, but by a different vehicle.

But after about fifteen minutes of driving around I lost my tail. It was only at that time that I began to relax a little. I also knew that I was in a fair amount of danger. After another half hour of driving around, I finally went to where I was staying in a motel. I made sure I was not followed.

Actually in my motel room, I had a small kitchen, and I had enough supplies to last me for three more days, just in case I had run into problems at this station. I had reports to make out and luckily I had my typewriter with me, because I would really hate to have to hand write all of what I had to report about. I also made another tape of the one I had made at the station, because I wanted to get that off to Jack in the morning. I always made duplications of every report I ever made out, including tape recordings. One more day at this station, and I will accomplish what I came here to do.

My problem I am thinking about, will that station agent show up tomorrow morning, because I don't think he will? So I make some other phone calls, just to make sure I can get into that station in the morning. I am quite sure that this station will either be closed or it will have a complete new crew of persons that will be operating it.

I don't think that the main office of this railroad knows what has been going on here. And it will not continue. But the other thing is, that will some of the companies that are involved with all of this graft that has been going on here, will they cut and run also. Only time will tell that story.

By morning there will also be the Auditor from the ICC, who will help me audit all of the special files I have set aside. And most likely he will contact the auditor with the AAR.

It's always amazing how long something like this can go on, without the knowledge of the Mother Company really knowing about it. Oh, I figure they will deny having any knowledge of any graft going on here, but something of this magnitude cannot go on for any great length of time without someone within that organization actually finding out about it, because of all of the money involved.

Of course all of the money is coming from all of the Industries that this railroad serves, wherein all of this payout money is going to. So it is not just the Station Agent himself, but it is also the persons who work for this station agent too. However many that will really be.

So we get to our job and go through all of the files I have set aside, and we find so much graft, that these two other auditors are livid with anger, when they discover how much money there really is involved with all of the companies that are being serviced by this station and this railroad.

And if those persons are not there then put out the word for them to be arrested, because it is likely that the agent of this station called all of them last evening, and probably all of these persons have left this city by now. But he says we will find them and bring them back.

I asked the ICC Auditor how much money is involved with all of these companies, and he says probably about thirty million dollars, because this has been going on here for more than a decade.

Dick says you really have a nose for trouble, and when you find them, things really happen. He says this is the largest he has ever seen in all of his years as an auditor. He tells me once again, he says if you ever get tired of auditing, then call him and he will get me a job where I will be home every night.

He says he suspects I have abilities that no one else has, and I can even find out about persons like what you have found out here, without even coming to places like this. He says that kind of talent is very valuable to the ICC and the AAR. And we need you.

Clement

April 10th 1967

Dear Peg;

The Station Agent was arrested before he could get out of town, and they also captured 13 of the sixteen persons with the same amount of companies involved, before they could get out of Chicago. And arrest warrants have been issued for the other three. And all of these companies have been completely closed down, until further notice from the ICC and the AAR.

After considerable testimony by myself, I was allowed to report back to Jack Perkins, where I handed him all of my reports regarding all of what I was able to tell him, because he would also get reports directly from the ICC and AAR Auditors.

Now as to my Special report, he says he personally signed for that package, and yes, he is very surprised as to whom I have accused of doing illegal and dirty things while working at the WWIB.

He has opened up his own investigation of all of the persons in his office, and all of these persons have been suspended without pay, until that investigation is finished.

He says it really surprised him to discover that Will Green had actually had many things added on to his home in Green Bay all of the time he lived in that city.

And he had also purchased another home in another town in, Wisconsin, where he has another wife and three children.

And his wife who lives in Green Bay does not know about the other wife.

It's amazing how I found out about this other wife and their children. And what I really know about some of the persons in the Milwaukee office is also amazing stuff.

This new Manager in Milwaukee will head that investigation, and he has suspended every person so named in my report, without pay. Until that investigation is finished.

Jack says he figures most of these persons don't know what hit them, and how did anyone find out about what they were really doing all of this time.

Jack says, if what I have told him is all true, then what should he do with me? I say send me on a special assignment to some distant location, so I can finally get some sleep, where I won't be in any kind of trouble, unless I find it where I am sent to. Jack says wherever I go I will always find trouble. I smile and say you are probably correct.

So my next special assignment will be, Seattle, Washington. I will have to take a train to get there. If I want you to come along then the WWIB will get you a complete foreign pass also.

In fact if you want a complete foreign pass, I can get one for you, so you can go to St Louis whenever you want to go. If you want a compartment when traveling there, you will have to pay for that yourself, but the train ticket will be free.

I have actually sent in a request for you, and when they issue it to you, they will send it to the apartment. So watch for it. I will have to come home for a few days, so I can get some different clothes. I will buy some in Chicago while I am here, because it will be easier that way. I have to leave in one week. I don't really have to go to the office for anything, so I will remain at home during that week. I will be paid for that time at home anyway.

I have to make out my expense account anyway, and only go to the office to get my next advance on my next expense account. When I return, I am taking a few days off, with pay, and I will go to St Louis to see my girls, and to make it legal, I will audit one railroad in the East St Louis, Illinois area.

CLEMENT

April 20th 1967

Dear Peg;

You have decided to accompany me to St Louis on this trip, so I have also made arrangements with an apartment sitting person who is bonded and actually works through an Agency who has done this type of thing for many years now, so my Cats will be totally taken care of.

I did tell the person who came to watch our apartment, that every piece of furniture and every item in this apartment has been photographed, and all of those photographs are in a special Lock box, that can be gotten to within an hours time, so if anything is missing when my wife returns back here, then the local authorities will be notified, and you will be the only person who will be accused of stealing what was in this apartment.

This person, who I will not name at this time, says that I am a very careful person. She says that my Cats and everything that we own is totally safe with her. I smile but do not say anything further.

You and I then leave, and drive to the CNW Station, of which is still operating a commuter train to Chicago. We then take a Cab to Union Station where we catch a passenger train with this new Railroad which is called Amtrack, which will take us to St Louis, where I will rent a vehicle, and of which you will use while you remain there, but you will have it to drive yourself back to Union Station in St Louis to catch the train back to Chicago.

How long you decide to remain in St Louis is totally up to you. I will take a train out of St Louis heading towards Kansas City, where I will catch one of the new passenger trains with the new company who is now operating under the name of Amtrack Passenger Service, which will take me all the way to Seattle, Washington.

On my return trip, I will catch a train, which will take me directly to Chicago. Where I will report directly to Jack Perkins, and give him all of my reports, rather then mail them to him. This way I can also tell him what I found, if anything that may be personal.

How long I will be gone, I do not really know. It all depends on what I find or discover. Anyway the day after we arrive in St Louis, and I rent that vehicle, I use that vehicle and drive to a station in a north east St. Louis railroad, where I Audit their books, and I do not find anything wrong, so after I congratulate the station agent, I then leave and go to where your parents live.

I then make out all of my reports, and put them in a large brown envelope and take it to the Ferguson Depot, where I give it to the station agent, telling him that this must go out on the next train heading to down town St Louis. He says there is a freight train due here in ten minutes, but he will have to flag it down, so they can receive this large envelope, of which he does, because I remain until that train comes to that station.

The engineer says this is the first time he has ever been flagged down so he can take a large brown envelope to St Louis. I tell him this is very important information as you can see, which goes to the General Manager of the WWIB in Chicago.

He says it will get there tomorrow morning about 7:00 AM. I shake hands with this Engineer and he then leaves. I then go back to where your parents live, and about that time my two girls arrive home from school in the school bus they always take.

When Martha sees me she runs to me and hugs me for a long time. Mary Beth just walks past me and goes into the house.

When Mary Beth sees Peg, she does say Hi, but then goes to her bedroom. Martha and I take a walk for about an hour around the neighborhood so we can talk for a while. Martha asks how long will I be here this time, and I tell her I will be here for three days. And then I have to go to Seattle, Washington on a Special Assignment.

She asks if this assignment will be dangerous, and I say anything can happen, but I really don't expect to have any problems, because as you well know, I have special abilities just like you do.

She asks, how long have you known about her special abilities, and I tell her since she was a little girl. She asks me, why have I never mentioned them to her before this time, and I say because you did not understand those special abilities then, but now you are beginning to totally understand how those special abilities have helped you in school.

She says you really don't miss anything do you. I tell her that when you are worried about something, then I pick up those thoughts from your mind, and I send you the answer to your problems.

She says she has always wondered where some of her thoughts really come from, and now that she knows, she will purposely send me questions, and that way she will get answers more quickly.

She tells me, that she never reads other students thoughts; because they are usually the wrong thoughts she is seeking answers to. I say never cheat, because that is very sinful. If you ever have a problem that you cannot seem to solve, then always send me that problem telepathically, and if I can solve that problem, I will not do it directly, but in a round about way, thereby causing you to come up with that answer out of your own mind. All I do is give you a little shove in the correct direction.

She says that is what she likes about her new Father, that even though he may be hundreds of miles away from her, she still can get in touch with me, to help her solve some of her problems. She says she has only one problem, and that is keeping those thoughts from me, away from Mary Beth. She says she will have to explain further.

When I solve a problem for her, she says she quite often says to Mary Beth that she has been in contact with me, and Mary Beth looks at her like she has something wrong with her. Because she does not believe that we can talk to each other, even though we are hundreds of miles apart from each other. This is how you will possibly solve that problem.

Tell Mary Beth what your problem is. And when she cannot come up with a reasonable answer, then tell her to get in touch with me. In whatever ways she can. Now when I send you my answer, write it down on a piece of paper, and give it to

Margaret, and tell her that this is the answer to a problem that she asked Mary Beth as to whether she could come up with the correct answer, even if she had to get in touch with Father in some way. Have Margaret note the date you gave it to her, and then wait. When Mary Beth comes to you with the answer to your question, then tell Mary Beth to go to Margaret and ask her for the piece of paper that you gave her and the actual date you gave her that piece of paper.

Then have Margaret ask Mary Beth for her answer, which Margaret will compare with the answer on that piece of paper you gave her, and when they match, then have Margaret tell Mary Beth when she actually was given that piece of paper. And maybe then Mary Beth will believe that you have been in contact with me, and had gotten your answer from me on a date long before Mary Beth got her answer from me.

It may work or it will not work. Mary Beth is a very stubborn person, because what she does understand, she will always ridicule. This is not a modern way to think about most things, but it is her way. And she doesn't give a damn what you think of her ways.

She also will always believe she is correct, even when she is totally wrong. So just forgive her and let it pass. Because one day it will all catch up with her, and she will wonder why she never realized it before that day.

Two of the days that I was going to be with my girls fell on Saturday and Sunday and even though I am no longer Catholic, the church where Joe and Margaret belong, I always go with them to that church.

And because I did not go to Confession, Mary Beth

questioned me about that. So I told her that I am not a Catholic, and even though I have been in my past, I no longer am because I have been excommunicated from the Catholic Church.

That does not mean that I cannot go to a catholic church and participate in the services, and even sometimes partake of these services, because I like to get up on the alter as a Lector sometimes, and give my version of the Scriptures. I have a particular way of providing what I know about any scriptural verses, mostly because I once studied to be a priest.

And some Pastors like my method of deliverance of these scriptures. And as you saw on this day, a lot of persons came to me and told me they also liked my method of explaining what I was reading. Most of these parishioners know that I am no longer a catholic, but it really does not matter to them, because they also know that I am a very religious person. Now why do you question my abilities as a CHRISTIAN? Are you a very holy person? Do you when you go to Confession, Humble yourself, because I don't believe that you do.

Of course no Priest will tell me either, but they will know that you did not humble yourself, and certainly GOD will know. So what do you accomplish when you question your own Father about what he really believes.

Just because I am no longer Catholic, does not mean that I don't believe in what they teach. Why do you think you go to a Catholic School? I know that before I adopted you and Martha, that you were of the catholic faith. Do you not believe that I am not doing the correct thing by sending you girls to a catholic school?

Because if you are not happy at that catholic school, then I can send you to a public school, where you will definitely fail most of your subjects. Do you know why? Well let me tell you. Because in any public school, all classes are quite large, and in fact no class has less than 60 students in them, and students like you are left behind, because the teachers don't have time to help you individually.

But in a Catholic school, all of the classes mostly consist of no more than 20 students, thereby allowing the teachers to be able to help students like you, who are slower than all of the other students.

You criticize Martha because she is smarter than you are, but if you took her advice and let her help you in the subjects where you are not so smart in, by the time this school year ends, you would be able to progress to the next grade, which is a Senior even though Martha is only a Sophomore this year and will be a Junior next year.

Right now your grades are so bad, that the likelihood of your going on to the next grade level, is almost nonexistent. And from the Records of where you used to go to school, they tell me that you barely passed your final test that was always given to every student, and you were passed to the next grade because all of the teachers felt sorry for you, because of the ways you were treated in your home life, but now that you are living in a great home, and you are treated respectively, as you ought to be, your grades are not up to where they should be. So what the hell is wrong with you?

But Martha is at the top of her class. Now you are only a grade apart, and you are supposed to be a senior next year, but if the reports that I have been getting from your teachers are true, you will not progress to that grade, but will remain as a junior for another year. Now do you want that to happen?

Or are you willing to take some advice from a much smarter Father than you have ever known before, and let me decide how and in what way you will advance to the next grade level. You see, you don't really have any friends, and Martha has a lot of friends, but they don't ever want to come to this house, because you are here also, because none of them trust you.

I have been told by all of your teachers that there are a lot of girls who would like to be your friend, but because when they try to make friends with you, you are always conniving against all of them, because you think they are always talking about you behind your back, and you are always trying to get back at them, when nothing has even happened to make you think there is anything wrong between you and them.

Now as you know, the adoption was final two months back, so you are totally my daughter, so why don't you ever take any advice from me, because if you don't then you will end up being just like Peggy.

Now ask her what she does with all of her extracurricular time. And if she tells you the truth, then I would think that you would change your ways real quickly. Of course she may lie to you and tell you something that is not true.

I know what Peggy does in all of her spare time, but we just don't talk about it, because it is that bad. She will not take any advice from me either, or her parents. But in reality she is very ill. Only she just will not admit it to herself. So don't take any advice from Peggy, because she will just lead you astray. Now I know I am getting away from you in this letter, but I just had to cover some of these areas of concern to me.

The three days passed too fast, and when I had to leave, I actually called a County Cab who took me to Union Station. Mary Beth and I still do not see eye to eye, and I told Martha to just keep doing what she has been doing, and if Mary Beth does not pass on to being a Senior, then hopefully by that time I will be with her more often and also you, because next year we will be going to California on an extended vacation. And maybe I can get her enrolled in a Summer school where she will be taught at home, thereby getting her into being a Senior.

CLEMENT

May 17th 1967

Dear Peggy;

My trip to Seattle, Washington was mostly uneventful, except the scenery was very beautiful in some places. And where this train traveled, high on the side of some of the mountains we traveled through, was very spectacular.

When returning, I will be traveling through other areas, which they tell me will also be very beautiful and exciting. I selected a motel that is called A HOME AWAY FROM HOME. In this letter I will send you a business card, which has the address on it, along with the telephone number, and the number of my room is 33, which is how old I am this year. I did not select that number it was assigned to me. But I think it is rather ironic, don't you think. I wish you had come also.

The neighborhood is nice and clean and there are restaurants everywhere. Actually there is a restaurant just a half of a block from my motel, and I had a meal there on the first day after I got myself settled, and they have real good meals there. And they will make me a Sack lunch every day, just as if I was living at home.

I cannot tell you where I Audited whatever records that I did audit. Of course, once I check on a specific locations books, then the word will get out, that I will be checking another location eventually.

I will have 13 locations to check out. If I find any improprieties, I am not to let on that I have found anything, but I will only make a note of what I have either found definitely or what I may also suspect of that location, and then go on to my next location.

Of course I will send my reports directly to Jack Perkins by various methods. I cannot tell you by what methods I will use in sending these reports. The most obvious is via Railroad, but that is only one such way. And some ways are more suspect than others.

But before I walk into a specific location, I will always check out various ways of getting away from that location, in the easiest way and methods, though by using my own vehicle is most probable.

I am always very careful, because I know that what I am doing could become very dangerous, very quickly. So don't despair, as I will be all right.

Of course since you never tell me what you feel about situations like this, I really don't even know whether you ever despair at all.

CLEMENT

My first location

I cannot give you the actual location, because the actual locations kind of appear to run together. They really don't but defining them would be real difficult, except to say that a specific location ends at a specific street location.

I will not tell you whether I found any improprieties, just in case my letters to you might be censored somehow. But my first day was real interesting.

Second location

In each location, since I spent three days at the first location, now the personnel at this location treat me like I am an Iceberg. I don't get any cooperation from anyone, but that is fine with me, because I know my way around these locations anyway.

I sometimes just watch all of the personnel who walk around where I am located, and sometimes they give themselves away, by avoiding an area, where I figure there are other files, and when I go to that area, and the office manager says he does not have the key to that door, and he does not know where it may be located.

And when these persons go home at night, an FBI agent follows them. What they do, I am not privy to, but I am sure they do prevent them from calling others who are involved in what has been happening at this location. This is when my job gets real interesting and very dangerous. Because if any kind of word has gotten out to the other persons outside of this location, then almost anything could happen. Meaning it may get real rough.

And when I eventually go to my next location, what will happen there? But since I have always worn my weapon, and I always make sure the FBI agents know that I am licensed to carry this weapon, and they do most often check me out, and when they discover that I am legal, then I don't really know what they think, except I am obviously very well informed about several things about this area. Of course when I leave this location, I always have a bodyguard.

And when that FBI agent is replaced with another one, they all seem to know one another, which is great for me. And when I let my bodyguard know that I need to get my daily report sent off to my home office, he or she always says that they will call their office, who will call a bonded messenger, which will be sent to my location, or to wherever I want them sent to.

And when that messenger arrives, I always ask to see some kind of identification, and when they refuse or hesitate, I draw my weapon and place them under a Citizens arrest, until my bodyguard can take him into custody. And all of my bodyguards tell me, that I am a very careful person. And they always ask me how did I know he was not who he or she said they were, and I tell them I cannot tell you that, but I just know.

My third Location

Now things are getting real interesting, because some of my reports have been tried to be waylaid by an outside source, and I have been refused entry to a specific location, but the door was broken down by force, and what I found would curl your hair. When I arrived at this location, I am treated with possible respect. I know they are taking on a different tact, but it just won't work, because I still see through their methods. Because at various times I still watch most of the personnel at that location, and eventually someone thinks of where other books are located, and when I ask about that location, and how did I know of that location, I am then treated like I am an Iceberg once again.

Of course I now always have a Law officer agent with me, and he calls in the enforcer again, and then I gather up everything I have brought with me, including everything I have learned about at this location, and we go to this other location, which is actually located in another building at this location, and again we have to force another door and at this location yet another door is opened, where we find books that have all kinds of dirt on them, so I know they have not been Audited for at least two decades. So I will most likely spend at least ten days at this location.

My fear is that when I eventually get to my final location, I will most likely have to go to some overseas location to locate all of the files that I need to look at. One of my guards makes this comment to me one day, and I tell him, if that is what I have to do, I do have a Passport and I will do just that.

Of course, what no one really knows at this time, is that the

Interstate Commerce Commission and some International agencies will now get very involved with all of this, after I leave this area. Graft is apparently very enticing. It's interesting that I never think about any kind of Graft or illegal dealings with anyone.

I am not a rich man, nor even a well to do man; I am just an honest man. Who fears his GOD and I actually need and or want some companionship? But I don't seek that kind of relations either. And I do always survive somehow.

Clement

Location four

This location is actually closer to Tacoma, Washington, and it is a very small building. It's probably only about 12 feet square. When we walk into this building, I don't see any files anywhere.

I think to myself that they are now getting real cute, but I still walk in and sit down. I actually don't say a word, but I just sit at the desk that has been provided, and then after a half hour goes by, I get up and leave this building and, I walk to another building, that is obviously locked with two padlocks, and after my guard calls the enforcer team, and after they arrive, I take out my weapon and shoot two bullets at each padlock, which shatters them and then we open the doors and there are files stacked all the way to the ceiling of this room we are in, and it is obvious that they were placed there very recently.

My guard looks at me and smiles, but does not say anything but just goes and clears off a desk nearby, and motions for everyone else to find themselves a place to sit down, while I by using some poles that are conveniently handy, bring down some of these file boxes. The first one I open has two dead Rats in it, and the second, has four dead rats in it.

Of course the station agent is standing behind me, chuckling and then when I strike a match, and begin to get real close to the rest of these boxes, he cries out, that what I am looking for are at the back of this entire pile. And what he is not telling me is, that most of the boxes I was getting close to with my match, were actually filled with Bombs or dynamite, that after they were opened, in a couple of minutes, they would explode, thereby getting rid of me and whoever was close to me.

This agent does what I tell him to do, and then this guy, says there is a working phone over here, and he walks to another desk and opens a drawer and takes out the phone that is in that drawer and he dials a number and within three minutes, five other men show up and this manager tells these five men from his office what boxes they will remove and where to put them. After that is done, I then tell this manager to open up this box, and he says he will not, so I say something to my guard, and he leaves and in about twenty minutes he comes back and he brings with him six other men who are carrying an obvious very heavy box, and inside of this box I place every box that I asked the Manager to open.

This heavy box has wheels on it, and when it is half full, I tell them to take it outside, and where to take it, and then I say stand back, because this box I will put on top of it. We get about two hundred feet away from this heavy box and when I fire my weapon, the box on top of this other box explodes and the explosion sets off what is inside of that box, and actually blows the locked down lid off of this box.

Then I go back to this Manager and ask him once again where are the files I am really looking for, because if you don't tell me, then whether you tell me or not, you will be arrested for attempted Murder, using whatever the FBI agents say was used.

While this guy is thinking, I am picking up where the real files are located, and where other files with more explosives are located, and I am making notes in a notebook I always carry with me.

I then say to my guard to just take him away, because he will not tell me verbally any more information. But when his bosses find out that he has been arrested, then make sure no one sees him, not even any Lawyer, because that lawyer will be a hit man, to shut him up, because this man knows a lot more, but I need another day to find the rest of his files.

My guard says, but he did not say anything, and I say he did not have to. And then I just walked away from that area and back to my vehicle.

But before I put my key into the ignition, I got out of that vehicle, and told my guard that there is a bomb wired to go off when I turn the key in the ignition. So he calls a tow truck and it is taken to a holding yard, where it will be examined very carefully, until they find that bomb. I give my car keys to my guard, and I tell him to not use them to try to start that vehicle until you know that every bomb has been removed.

My guard then takes me to his office, where I am assigned a Federal car, which has a radio and other things in it that I can use to call whatever I need, and it also has a siren on it.

My guard asks me if I know what everything is for, and after I show him what I know about most everything, he asks how do I know so much about what it is in a Federal vehicle, and I tell him I cannot tell you how I know. It's a matter of safety, My safety. He gives me a strange look, but does not say anything further.

He gets out of this vehicle and I start it and drive out of their underground garage. He follows. I call him on the radio, and tell him to lie back about three blocks, he says okay, and I see him get further away from me, but I see him still.

After I drive about two miles, another vehicle gets behind me, and when I try to get rid of that vehicle, he stays with me anyway. And then when I am about two blocks from the Federal building where I know there is a dead end street, of which I turn into it, this vehicle tries to not turn into this street, but my guard is right behind this guy, and he is caught like a Rat in a Trap.

With this guy trapped between my vehicle and my guards, what can he do, so he shoots himself, and yes he kills himself? My guard asks me how did I know this street was really here, and I tell him whenever I go to a town or city, I always get to know it very well, and since I knew that this day would eventually arrive, I wanted to see if the persons involved in these operations knew this city as well as I know it.

So when he realized that he was trapped, he could either

give himself up or do what he did do, which was to kill himself. So he would not give anything away to me. Now is anything coming to your own mind, that tells you more about me, than you really knew before.

He says you have an ability to get inside of other peoples minds. I tell him, would you like to know what I know what you are thinking at this moment. And he says yes he would, so I tell him, and he says you are absolutely correct about every thought. He says that he will stay with me wherever I go, even when I go back to where I am living.

I tell him, that they know that I am some kind psychic, so they will be watching everyone who is watching me, so be very careful. I think that me having no less than three guards on me, would be much better, but these other persons will also know that too, and like I said before, be very careful when guarding me. I am not helpless, because I know how to use any kind of weapon, probably even some you don't even know about.

CLEMENT

Still location four

The places I wrote down in my personal journal, I check out the next day. Both locations. I determine the location where some files are located, where there are explosives inside of most of these boxes. I call one of my guards and tell him, and he goes to an outside phone and calls this information in to a private number that he has told me about. I know what that number is but I cannot pass that information on to you for safety reasons.

I then go to the location where all of the files I am looking for are located, and when we all drive up to this office building, we see persons running to many vehicles, trying to get away, but they are all stopped by all of the FBI agents that I brought with me. They are all arrested. My next problem is, because the front door is locked. But with the enforcer device, we got into that office anyway.

Anyway, the Manager locked himself inside of another office, and another agent by using that ten pound sledge hammer just knocked it in, and this guy was a large man, who could probably take me out, but he just threw up his hands, and when I said to be very careful when arresting him, and when two agents tried, this guy got very active with his hands and fists and legs. But they were expecting this, and even though it took another agent they got him down on the floor and handcuffed him, so he could not even run, because they cuffed his ankles also.

When they got him standing, he yelled at me, that I am a dead man. You will not get beyond this building, and it is likely that you will not even leave this location.

Well I took that as a definite threat against my life, so my guard gets on the phone in his vehicle and called the special number and within a half hour there were ten more agents at that location.

I immediately get to work on what I came there to do, and I do find so very much, that I decided to remain until I have Audited every file, no matter how long it takes.

Of course this would give whoever wanted me to not leave this location more time to gather all of their forces at this location. But when I had totally finished with every file, these FBI agents and I had been at this location for sixty hours. And I mean I worked every hour I was here. Yeah, I was real tired but I finished it.

Now getting away from this location. I was told that there were even some Sherman tanks out on some of the streets that surrounded this place, so I had my guard call an army base that was about fifty miles away from this place, and also some helicopters with all kinds of weapons on them, and when every army vehicle arrived, those vehicles that were not army issue were attacked and taken down, and everyone was arrested by federal agents, and removed from this location.

I got into my vehicle and drove to the Federal Building, where I made out all of my reports, and using various kinds of packaging, and a lot of federal messengers, I sent all of my reports to my Chicago office. I actually sent out fifteen reports.

Clement

Location five

Now, since there have been several persons arrested and put away in some undisclosed locations, even I do not know where these locations are. I told my guards that this next location will most likely have a lot of all whom are involved with what is really going on with the organization that I am auditing. So we must be totally prepared for almost anything to happen.

Because it is quite apparent to me that I am making a lot of critical waves, in what I am doing, which is what I was sent here to do.

As this has been going on for many years now, and it has to be stopped, and stopped while I am here. I think if I can get inside of this location, I can break this whole operation wide open. I have saved this location for this time, because I knew that if I took out that last location, then they will probably gather where they think I will go.

Of course I could fool them and go to a much smaller location, but the location I am thinking of doing next, has better offensive places that will help us to get to it quicker and it has less defensive capabilities on these grounds.

I am in the Federal Building in downtown Seattle, and at this time I tell my main guard what I am going to do. After I finish telling him what I have in mind to do, he does what I have asked him to do which is to ask every federal agent who will be going with me to the next location.

In fact my personal guard will ask everyone that he knows that will go to this location, some questions, and if they all give the correct answer, then they will go with me, but if they give an answer that is not correct, then that person will be detained in a jail cell. And since we will go in a specified number of vehicles, then if an additional vehicle gets in line with the specified amount, that vehicle will also be detained. The only person, other than myself, will be my personal guard, who also knows there will be two other carloads of federal agents, who will follow all of the specified vehicles to the location I will be going to.

Actually only I know the actual location where I will be going, so every federal vehicle will have to follow me, and since I will know the number of every federal vehicle that will be with me, then the Helicopter that will also follow me, will know these numbers also. So if another so called federal vehicle slips into this same line of federal vehicles, they will know what that vehicle's number actually is.

So after my personal guard has asked the questions I asked him to ask every agent he personally knew, and then comes back to me, I then tell him who the odd agent is, who is not a federal agent. He compares that information with the notes he has made in his little black book, and then he goes and arrests this so called Federal agent, who has him taken away in handcuffs.

This information is not allowed out of the group of persons who are federal agents, because I don't want that information let out to the public nor any other persons, until I am good and ready to make it known, who this person really is.

We then leave and get into our vehicles. Since I am the

lead vehicle, who knows where I am going, all of the other federal vehicles can only follow me.

Since I have checked out all of the locations where I needed to go when I first rented the vehicle that I did rent when I first arrived in this city, I know of all of the ways to get to whatever location I am going to. So when I am very close to the location I am going to, I actually drive around this location two times, just to make sure that every vehicle that is following me, still keeps following me, and to see if any of them try to make contact with anyone else.

Then as I am going down a particular street, I suddenly turn into what appears to be a driveway to a private residence, but it is instead a back way onto the location where I am actually going. Some of the vehicles have to stop suddenly and back up some fifteen feet, so they can make the turn, and when they finally catch up with me, I am then parked in front of a one story building, that is about 200 feet square.

When the last car in my line of cars is finally parking, I walk up to it and point my gun at the driver and federal agents are also pointing their guns at everyone that is in that vehicle. After everyone is out of that vehicle, and they are all handcuffed, and by that time a large van has come onto that property, who takes all of these persons inside of this van, of which is in reality a Jail Van, because there are individual compartments inside of this van.

But before every suspect is placed in his or her particular compartment, they are individually searched, whether they are male or female. All in all, there are six persons who are handled this way. Then when this van drives off of that lot, I then go to the front door, which I find to be locked.

So again the sledge hammer is used, which breaks in this door, and we find many persons inside with all kinds of weapons, and they begin to fire them, and because all of the agents and myself are wearing Bullet Proof Vests, we begin to fire our weapons also, while we are getting behind something in that room.

Anyway, I get outside and go to my vehicle, where I put together the weapon I have invented myself, and when I am ready, I go back inside and when I fire this weapon, the firing stops almost immediately, because it is obvious that the weapon I am firing has capabilities wherein there is no other anywhere.

At that time I step out in front of everyone else in that room, and I tell everyone who is firing a weapon at everyone else, to lay them on the floor, or you will be killed. Only one person tries to get away and I have to shoot him, but I only wound that person. When he said to me that he thought he would be killed, I said I was only kidding. He was obviously disappointed.

He also knew that he would be the target of someone within his own organization that would try to kill him, so he could not tell the Federal Authorities anything.

I told my personal guard, that I want to question all of these individuals at some later time, and since all of this was set up before we even came here, all of these persons will be put where no one can get to them, not even any Lawyers, because any potential lawyer will probably be a hit person also.

Anyway, after all of the persons who are arrested inside of this building, and when two other Jail Vans arrive, which don't have individual compartments in them, but are just one large Jail van, and all of these persons are herded inside of these vans, then since the person I wounded I detained in that building, because I could sense that he knew more about what actually went on in that building, than any of the others, I had him held to one side, until I could ask him some questions. Now also since all of these persons tried to stop me here, I also figured that this is where all of the files that I needed to look at are located.

Because why would everyone begin firing at all of us, if there was any explosives located anywhere in any of these files. That likelihood of happening is very faint. So when the detainee was bandaged up and handcuffed to a heavy desk and had been frisked abundantly, I finally sat down in front of him, and began to ask him a number of questions.

Of course he did not answer any of them, except to tell me what his name is and how old he is and a few other nonessential things of no importance, but while I was asking this person all kinds of things, that related to what was going on in the all of the Offices, his mind was going a mile a minute, and I was in fact getting a lot of very valuable information from him, even though he really did not know what he was telling me. And since I have a kind of Photographic Memory, everything he told me, I would certainly remember it all.

All of the agents who are still with me, will remain, because even though I did get onto this property, getting off of it will be another matter, because I am certain that someone in this building did call someone outside of this location, so getting away from here, will not be easy.

So since we all brought something to eat and drink, I tell everyone, that if you will please help to get the files that I need to look at, I will greatly appreciate it, and besides this will also keep most of you busy. And I will need someone to help me make specific notes about some of what is really going on here.

So two female agents and three male agents say they will help, and the rest of the agents will keep watch for anything that may happen outside. I tell all of them that it is likely that I will be here about two days and maybe three, so if anyone can contact that Helicopter and have them bring us some Chinese type meals.

I know it is a strange request, and who ever thought that a Helicopter would be a messenger for an Auditor and some of their fellow agents, so as to keep us all alive while we have to do what we have to do while we are here.

My personal bodyguard since he has been with me since the third day that I arrived in this city, he has taken to me, and he says that he knows what I am doing, because before he became an agent, he was an Accountant.

So I tell him that what is different about the accounting here, is that you have to think in a kind of Reverse order of how everything is handled.

Accounting is just a group of numbers that keep specific records of transactions dealing with specific services. In any other capacity, like say banking, when for a customer a Credit becomes an addition for that particular customer, in Railroad Accounting it is the exact opposite. It takes a while to get used to thinking this way, but once you have it in your mind, then it becomes real easy.

And since most persons don't really understand this type of accounting, the companies who adopt this same system believe they are in very good shape. Thinking that it would take a special kind of accountant to Audit their books, and they are correct, because I am just such an Accountant and I am an Auditor who has a special ability that can seek out improprieties in each of their systems.

Now you personally know of my special abilities, so with those abilities, don't you think I make a great Auditor? He says he totally agrees with me. But when did you get involved with weapons, and what was that weapon that you used in here.

I say that is not a legal weapon yet, but I have applied for a patent on it, and I have not heard from them yet. Sometimes it takes a couple of years to get a patent on weapons such as I have invented. But it will be eventually approved, because as you can see, it did stop all of the shooting in this building.

Anyway, I have to dismantle it, and put it back into my briefcase, until it is needed once again. And that is what I do at that time. My guard says it really does not take up that much room in my briefcase does it.

But when someone in the room asks him a question, and when he is temporally distracted, I adjust a false bottom inside of my briefcase, and when he looks back at it, he says it has disappeared.

Now what did I do, and I say I cannot show you what happened to it. He looks all through my briefcase, but he cannot find it. He says maybe I have it on my body, so I say does that mean that you will search me? And he says no, he will not look for it at this time. Maybe at a later time.

So then the detained man is taken outside and the Helicopter picks him up, and at that time the Captain of this

Helicopter is given my order of Chinese food, and then it leaves, with the captain smiling at me and the other members of the FBI.

But he too has other orders, that when he does not agree with what has been asked of him, he then calls that special person, who will tell him to get what is in my note. He won't like it but he will do it.

I then instruct the agents who are going to help me with all of the files I need to look at, and I then get real serious. Two hours go by and I am deep in thought, when one of the women shows me a box that has some kind of device inside of it.

I immediately take it outside to a garbage container that is behind a cement wall, and after I come back inside, I say to everyone, that soon there will be an explosion, but if no walls fall down, we will just ignore it.

Ten minutes later an explosion does take place, but no windows are broken, but only some things fall on the floor. I tell everyone, that there may be more of these boxes in that pile of files, so be very careful when you open each of them up.

Because once they are opened, most often we will have about two to ten minutes to get rid of it, meaning we have to get it outside very soon after it is opened. I am hoping that everyone that we find is this way. If you think a file is too heavy, then tell me and I will get rid of it, even before we open it. I never said this would not become dangerous, so be very careful with all of those files.

You see if there are no files to look at, then there will not be any improprieties to see. So I think from now on, I will select the boxes that I think I will need to look at. This will take a lot longer but I will feel better if I am the one selecting the files I think I can look at. It is not that I don't trust you, but I don't want any of you to get hurt. But everyone who is working with me, tell me they will continue gathering all of the files I will look at. And that is what happens.

After the first day has gone by, some of the other agents found some bare mattresses in another room, along with some clean white sheets, and everyone took turns sleeping while the rest of us worked. Halfway through our second day, the Helicopter came back with all of our Chinese meals, and in fact actually landed that helicopter near where we had all parked.

I asked the Captain who I recognized, whether he had a replacement crewman, and he says he does, I asked him if he really needs him and he says he does not, so I have him arrested and handcuffed, and I asked him some questions, and when I wrote some words on a piece of paper so he could see it, he says how did you know he was a shooter, and was sent here to kill you. I say I cannot tell you at this time, but probably later after all of this is finished.

But after he was aggressively searched, wherein was found on him two more much smaller weapons, of which he would have probably used once the copter was back into the air, even though he would also have killed himself, but he would have accomplished what he was sent here to do, at least partially, and he would have killed everyone who was part of the helicopter crew, he was then taken away from that location in that helicopter after he has been tied with some additional ropes, so he couldn't even move from where he had been tied.

On this person was also found a suicide pill, which he likely could have gotten to, so he would not be taken alive to any other destination.

Now things are getting real tough, and for the rest of us, it will be very difficult to get away from this location. But I don't want to leave yet, because I have not finished with my investigation. I tell everyone, that when we finish here, I will then go back to where my main office is located, because after auditing this location, this organization will be finished, as far as these locations are concerned.

Because the persons we took into custody yesterday, are the main people who have been keeping everyone else in line with what they have been doing throughout this vast city. If any other locations need to be audited, the Interstate Commerce Commission and the Association of American Railroad Auditors will do it.

When I finish Auditing this Location, I will have done what I came here to do. And I could not have done what I have done, without all of your help.

It's interesting, that when I took this position, I did not expect to make war on a particular organization. But it has turned out that way.

When I get back to my regular territory, I will have some special places that I will most likely have to go to, wherein something similar as to what has happened here, will most likely happen back there. But it has been very interesting. But like I have said before, I could not have done it without all of your help.

It took me an additional day and a half to finish with my duties at this location. When I was ready to leave, the Helicopter and the Captain who I knew came to get me, and an Army group of persons came to get the rest of the FBI agents. No one tried to prevent anyone from leaving that location.

I saw more Army tanks and other vehicles all around that location when I flew away from that location, and I hoped that this would never have to happen again while I tried to do my duties.

I was flown back to the Federal Building where after I had made out all of my reports that I wanted to send back to Chicago, and doing it in similar ways as I had done before, and then someone had called me a special Cab, who took me back to my Motel, where I loaded up all of my suitcases and other things that I always carry, and I was taken to a different location out of the Seattle area, where I got on a train, that would take me back to where I had come from.

When I got on this train, the Personal guard that had been with me most of the time I was in the Seattle area, has also been assigned to accompany me back to where I had come from, which is Chicago, Illinois. He says there are a lot of other Agents guarding me on this trip back to where you are going, because we want you to get where you are needed still.

We kind of got some additional education regarding Accounting methods, and we thought we could learn some more as we travel. I felt like a special person. I did not expect that I would have to be protected for the next two days.

But I think it was just a ploy to spend some additional time with me, and to see some beautiful country from this train. I don't suppose I will ever really know the real reason they all accompanied me, but it is very touching to know that I always make some very close friends, wherever I always go.

CLEMENT

July 1st 1967

Dear Peg;

When I got back to Chicago, and I had had a chance to talk with Jack Perkins, and because all of the Agents still had accompanied me, even up to Jack Perkins office, I introduced all of them to Jack, and I told him that this is the main reason I am still walking around on this earth. They tell Jack and me that they are to accompany me back to where I live, but I tell all of them, that will not be necessary, and I insist that they all go.

Parting is very difficult for me, because I had gotten to know all of them personally while we traveled from Washington State to Illinois. But after they had all left Jack's office, I told Jack, that this assignment was very difficult to handle. It was very dangerous, and I hope with all of my reports and all of the other information I have furnished to you, that the ICC and the AAR Auditors will be able to handle all of the other locations in that area.

Jack says I did a great job, and no I will not be ordered back to that area, probably ever again, because what I actually accomplished there was more than sufficient.

Actually the main reason I was ordered to go to that location was because no other Auditor has ever been able to do what you have done, and that is to break that organization wide open.

In your last reports, what you surmised actually happened,

because we have had word that the main office in Washington, DC are real happy with how I handled everything.

I told Jack that I was not certain whether the main office in Washington, DC had been also involved in what they were all doing out in that area. Jack says no to my previous question. DC persons had requested that we send in our best Auditor to see what he or she could do. You are that person.

Losing you will be a great strain on this entire organization. And because you have not taken any vacation time since you were given this position, Jack says he is sending me on a special vacation wherein I can go wherever I want to go, and it will not take away any of your regular vacation time. When you work, no one gets any sleep, not even you, as we have also had reports from the FBI in Seattle, wherein you seem to know things that even they cannot discover, like crewmembers on a Helicopter who were sent to kill you, but you some how knew that person was really there.

He says that Helicopter Captain really admired and respected you by what you did for him. Well I just do what I always do, and that is to use my special ability to find out things that no one else can seem to discover.

I will take this vacation and go and see my daughters and while there I will write a special program, wherein that companies who have a computer system, by feeding this program into their system, I will be able to discover what I would normally discover using the old method.

It might take a little longer to get it debugged, but I will try to get that done on this vacation. And if I ever leave the WWIB, it will belong to this organization. And I will give it to you and no one else. Whom ever you give it to, make sure they too understand what it will do and make sure they are computer literate and tell them that they would only be able to use it once at any location. Computers are the coming things. So I am just trying to get this organization up to par before everyone else knows about them.

As you know I did not ask you to come along with me to St Louis, because I figured that you would want me to take you to some place, when in fact I wanted this time to write that program. So when I left Jacks office, I got on a train and went directly to St Louis.

You didn't even know that I had even left the Seattle, Washington area yet. I knew you would probably be very mad to find out that I had been to Chicago, and did not come back home, but this is something that I cannot do while living at home, because of you and the Cats. I miss you and the Cats, but some things are just more important than going home.

And besides I could actually see and interact with my girls while I was writing this special program. Even though they would not be in school, and would probably be home most of the time, but I really won't find out what they will really be doing until I get there.

When I got out of the County Cab in Ferguson, and I found no one at home, I wondered whether they might be on some kind of vacation also. But since I have a Key to that house, I just went inside, and went downstairs into the basement where that extra bedroom I had previously built, was located. And it was not occupied by anyone in that house, so I just lay down and went to sleep for a little while.

Someone was manhandling me, very shortly, or so it seemed, but in reality it was Martha, and it was now dark outside, so I must have slept longer that I had expected me to sleep. Martha says how am I and I say I feel fine now.

She says you have at least a two day beard on your face, so you must have slept for at least an entire day, because she says, all of us have been gone for an entire day, and the only reasons I came downstairs, is because I felt you were in this house. I say I guess I was more tired than I knew I was. I have been all the way to Seattle, Washington, and that Special assignment was very difficult for me, and because there were some days that I did not get any sleep at all, I guess it finally caught up with me. She says it is now Saturday evening and the date is July 3rd. I say I got here in the morning hours of July 2nd around 9:00 AM and it is now almost 9:30 PM on the 3rd.

I did sleep a very long time, and I am very hungry as of this moment. Martha says to come upstairs and she will fix me a plate of food. Well every one was surprised to see me, but also pleased, even Mary Beth as she came and kissed me on my cheek.

Joe asked me where I have been for the last two months, and I say in Seattle, Washington, for part of that time, and for another part of that time I have been on Special Assignment in Southern Chicago. I tell everyone that these Special Assignments are quite dangerous and I sometimes have to make a quick exit from those areas. This also happened in the Seattle, Washington area, because I actually was flown out of my last location by a Helicopter, and then taken to another city where I caught a train and came under many FBI Guards all the way to Chicago.

I was sent on this Special Vacation so I could rest up, I guess, because the last two months have been very trying for me.

Anyway while I am here I am going to write a Special Computer Program, which can be used in helping me do my work. Computers are the coming things, and I want to be prepared for when they arrive. Some companies already have them, and because Railroads are usually a few years behind regular industry, when they do arrive, I will be ready for them all.

Joe says you were always way ahead of anyone else he had ever worked with. I say I cannot ever be behind anyone; it is what makes me tick.

Because whatever I do, I am always the Best there is. And I am still this way. I could see that Martha was seeing within my mind where I was headed, but I could not describe to Joe or Margaret or Mary Beth how I was going to get there, but I somehow knew that Martha was already where I wanted to be.

Clement

July 10th 1967

Dear Peg;

I asked Martha if she would like to have my Ford Van, and she says yes, so I told her that I am going to buy a new vehicle which will be another ford product, but it will be a 1967 Ford Falcon, Station wagon, and I am going to pick it up tomorrow morning, and would you come with me when I do that. I would like Mary Beth to come also, but she says she has something else to do tomorrow. But I won't be able to bring my old Ford to you until a couple of weeks from now, unless you might want to come to Milwaukee with me and then I can sign it over to you while you are there, and then you can drive it back to St Louis by yourself.

Martha says that sounds real exciting. On your Person and or in that Van I will give you a signed statement that will tell any Peace Officer that may stop you for whatever reasons, that you are a licensed driver and you will have a bill of sale in that van, signed by me, and Notarized and you have my full permission to own and drive your own vehicle.

And when you get back to this location, you will take the Car Title to this location, and I gave her an address, where you will register that Van in your name. You will also probably have to show them everything I have written out for you, because you are not yet 18 years old. If they give you more trouble, I suggest that you take Margaret with you, and you can make her the owner of that vehicle along with yourself, and then when you reach 18 years of age, you can then become the full owner of that vehicle.

You will have to take good care of it, and don't let Mary Beth drive it, because I understand she is a terrible driver. Mary Beth won't like the fact that you own your own vehicle, but she will have to get used to it, until I can buy her, her own vehicle, and that is what you will tell her when she asks you about your vehicle. That I am looking around for a good used vehicle, but not a new one. I will pick it out for her, and she will either like it, or I will sell it to someone else.

Of course I knew that Mary Beth was listening to me talk to Martha, I think Martha knew it also but she did not say anything to me about Mary Beth listening.

Anyway tomorrow morning after I buy this new vehicle I will bring Martha along with me and then we will drive to Milwaukee. I will probably get home about 7:00 PM, and even though this letter will arrive after I do, I want this to be a record of what I have done, and why. The why of this purchase is because next year we all will take an extended vacation of about four months, to California.

And having a fairly new vehicle will make that journey much easier. Of course I am also thinking about doing something else, but I will wait until 1968 before I make my final decision on that idea. I am still sounding out various officials regarding that last idea.

CLEMENT

July 11th 1967

Dear Peg;

I am writing this letter while I have stopped in a Restaurant while I am traveling towards Milwaukee, Wisconsin. Martha is with me and she is writing down various things about this route that I took so she can drive back to Ferguson more easily. Martha really won't have any problems in driving back to the St Louis area.

I have provided her with all of the necessary maps and she has been guiding me on this trip, so I know she totally understands every map. I tell her that when I or anyone else plans any trip, that you kind of memorize all of the roads and highways you will be traveling on, and you actually write on a separate piece of paper that you can tape to the dash panel of whatever vehicle you are driving. So all you have to do is just glance at it when you are uncertain of which highway to take, and if necessary to pull off onto the shoulder of the road or into someone's driveway or into a gas station. So you can take a better look at your road map. Martha has a level head, so she will know what to do if this ever happens. I will not worry all that much.

She says she has been on this highway before when her real parents came to visit with her Uncle Harry who lived in Joliet, Illinois. He was a single man, and has always been favored with the ladies. Probably because he was better looking than Henry was. But that is all in her past, and now she only thinks of her former dad once in awhile, but now instead she only think of me as her real Father, of which I am.

Of course since you went to bed with Harry you probably know him better than Martha does, because he also got you pregnant, but you conveniently lost his baby also.

It is very difficult to not remember all of these uneventful things about you and all of the babies you have conveniently lost. Losing one is a possibility, but more that one, that becomes some purposeful act. Against whom I really don't know. And it always happens after you have carried that baby for about four months. What a shame. And what a terrible sin.

CLEMENT

July 12th 1967

Dear Peg;

I did write that computer Program, but I have not gotten it debugged completely yet. There is a place in Milwaukee where I can go to do that, and because I will be spending the next two weeks in my home territory, I will get that done. And then I will try to use it in a couple of stations I know of in this area, to see how well it really works. These will be stations I have already audited last year, so this will be a great time to use them.

I made sure Martha got off this morning, and I gave her an additional fifty dollars so she could fill up the gas tank on that van. It was about half empty, and since she knows that it holds 22 gallons, I suggested that she fill it completely before she left the Cudahy area, and refill it again after she gets back to Ferguson.

Anyways it is now near 5:00 PM and Martha called me at my office as I had instructed her to do, and she got back to Ferguson without any problems. And of course Mary Beth is livid with jealousy, just like Martha and I figured she would be.

Mary Beth has made all kinds of threats against Martha, but Margaret told Mary Beth, if she ever did whatever she has threatened to do against her sister, then she will end up in Jail, somewhere in St Louis. Or wherever the women's state prison is really located. I really don't know myself.

Anyway Martha told Mary Beth that she is to never use that vehicle. And Father says to tell Mary Beth, that she is a terrible driver anyway. That is why he is having her taught how to drive by a Professional Driving Instructor, wherein Mary Beth will have to pass not only a written test, but also a Drivers test, and passing only one of them will not get her any drivers license. And our great Uncle and or any other relatives have all been instructed to not give her any favors in helping Mary Beth to get her Drivers License. That right now, she cannot drive any persons vehicle unless they are in that vehicle with her, and since Martha will never allow Mary Beth to drive her vehicle at any time, then she would have to steal it if she wanted to drive it anywhere.

Of course if she crashed it, she would then have to pay for all of the repairs on it. And how would she accomplish that? And I don't want you to help her either, by giving her money that you have made.

Because I know that you have sent her money, because you have been trying to get on the good side of her ever since I adopted her.

If you think you can buy her love, forget it, because there is no love in Mary Beth that she would ever part with. She is a very selfish person, because she only thinks about herself. Something like you have always done. I am afraid that she might end up being just like you now are. And that would be a sin and a shame. Maybe one day she will come to her senses when she is totally on her own, and I will welcome that day.

CLEMENT

July 20th 1967

Dear Peg;

You are again on one of your rampages, since I did state some bad things about you in my last letter to you. But as I always say, if the shoe fits, then wear it, and get on with your life.

Oh I can totally understand why you get so angry with me, because I usually lay out the awful truth of things, and don't usually try to cover them up. But look at these things this way, if I only voice them to you and to no others, then what are you getting so mad about.

You always think that I have been letting the world know about all of your nasty things you always have done against me. Actually I never tell anyone else, except the Cats, and they already know all of the nasty things that you do, because they are always home when you bring all of these men to our Apartment.

Like I have always said, you only look at these things from your selfish way. If you ever realize what you have been doing against me, then maybe GOD will find it in his Heart to Forgive you. And don't wait until the last minute to change your ways, because how you are just before you die, will be how you will be for Eternity.

You don't think I read anything regarding religion and

especially Christianity, but remember before I even met you, I studied to be a Minister. And if they would have allowed me to become a Minister, I would have been the youngest preacher anywhere in this world, but because I was only 20 at that time, I was not allowed to apply for a License, which was being a Lutheran. And since I have been kicked out of the Catholic religion, I in reality could now become a Preacher anyway.

CLEMENT

August 19th 1967

Dear Peg;

I wonder whether I will ever tire of writing these letters to you? I don't think so, because even though you have been in reality answering some of them by talking to me, when I am home, I know that I am getting through to you, so in that sense, they have been coming in very handy.

Of course, when I am old and have white hair or maybe no hair at all, I can use these letters to write a book about our lives. So they will come in very handy eventually. And hopefully none of them will ever get destroyed.

When I eventually write that book about our lives, what and where will I be living? And what kind of life will I be leading at that time, when I am almost 80 or even maybe near 85 when I write that book. And will you still be alive, or will you be dead by that time? Only time will tell that story.

And will I have gotten married again after I outlive you, of which I will outlive you. One of your biggest fears is your dying before your Mother does. Since you never tell me, I wonder whether you know that you have some kind of disease or sickness, but you will never tell me about.

Oh I do think you do have some kind of psychological sickness dealing with SEX, and where that actually comes from, I really don't know, but I know your mother knows, but she will never tell me, so you are safe so far. And it is likely that she will never tell me until after you have died, but then it will be too late to actually help you.

Anyway this letter seems to be a kind of rehashing of things that have already happened. I wish I could completely forget all of these bad things, but they just seem to pop to the surface every once in awhile. OH WELL – WHAT THE HELL....

At the Office, I was asked; if I had a favorite saying and when I told them, they told me I would have to come up with a different one.

So I told them that my next favorite saying is, " WHATEVER YOU DO – DO IT WITH EXCELLANCE ". And one more favorite saying is: Remember that the word Anger is one letter away from Danger, so try not to get angry very often. They liked that one, so that is what I will always put on all of my Business Mail Letters.

In fact it was suggested by my Secretary, that every piece of paper that is used for Business purposes, that saying should be on each and every piece. Whether that will be done, I doubt that will ever happen. I told my Secretary that she will have to put that at the end of all of my business letters, as a kind of Post Script. Eventually other individuals would be saying the same thing.

My new Office Manager, seems to be a real good guy, and everyone seems to like him. I like him, and he seems to have a cool head on his shoulders, meaning that it takes a lot to get him excited or even angry, which is real good for an Office Manager.

He reminds me a lot of your former boss at Country Set, even though he is not that high in this organization. But he is

Handsome in a plain sort of way. He dresses to the fashions, and is always neat and clean, but he is not afraid to get his hands dirty either.

As we had a situation wherein some of us had to get our hands dirty when helping to clean up our part of the office, because we had a water line break, and some of the floors became very wet and of course, dirt came from places where who knows where, and some of us men, donned Coveralls, after we removed our suits, because we did not want to get them wet. And we cleaned up our office in an hour's time, and in doing this, we got real dirty.

Our Office Manager said, that he always thought that the Janitor had always swept up all of the offices, but seeing all of the dirt that the water has dislodged, he now wonders what he actually does when he cleans our office. I wonder also.

Whether he will ask this Janitor how he cleans our office, I don't know, but I think he probably will. I would, because I know what kind of dirt and dust can accumulate while there are several persons in an area like our office.

Based on what Dad and I had to do, when cleaning up the floors in the School Building. And in the Gymnasium Especially after a Basketball game or after I had shown a Movie. The thing that people drop on the floor is ridiculous and stupid.

Anyway this is about all I can think of to tell you in this letter. Have a good day yourself. Thinking about things like this kind of clears my mind of some of the stuff that does kind of collect there.

I do have to go out of town next week, so I am collecting some things at my office, thereby making what I will do when I am on this trip, a lot easier.

I have some Scales to Inspect, and I wanted to accumulate some parts for them just in case I found some of them needing these parts. After I once inspect some of these scales, I become familiar with what is needed every so often.

CLEMENT

August 28th 1967

Dear Peg;

On this trip I am going back to the East St Louis area, because I still have about ten more railroad Stations I need to Audit. These are mostly all switching railroads, and since each of these railroads have many clients, Improprieties are most often found, and since none of these stations have been audited for two years, then the likelihood of some bad things having happened is very possible.

It took me six hours to reach the East Saint Louis area and because I am just across the Mississippi river from where your folks live, I have decided I will stay with them again, so I can also be around my daughters when they come home from school.

It cuts my own day a bit short, but since I don't have to punch a time clock as for my own hours that I keep at work, it will just lengthen my stay in this area to an additional week. Depending on whether I find any problems.

And since I cannot actually levy any fines myself, I can only advise each particular railroad agent what they should do, before an Auditor from the ICC or the AAR shows up, and if they find the same problems that I found, then they will levy very heavy fines against not only the railroad agent, but also against each customer involved.

After working for three days, I knew I was onto some shenanigans, and after another day of rechecking more records, I was absolutely sure I have found a very big problem.

When I got home that evening, I immediately called Dick Tracy with the ICC, and told him what I found, and what I suspected was happening and with whom. He told me that since he was at that time in Springfield, Illinois, that he would see me in the morning of the next day. And when I got to that particular station at 6:00 AM that next day, Dick was waiting for me. He says you still keep very early hours, and I then told him, that my two daughters live with their Grandmother in Missouri, so when ever I am near this area, that is within 30 miles, I always get to work very early, like I did this morning.

Dick says he wondered whether I really had any family, and I told him that I do, but my wife is not their mother, nor is she their adopted mother. I adopted these girls as a Single parent. When they come home from school around 4:00 PM, I am there to welcome them. Because I am on the road a lot, I do this as often as I can arrange it. He says he just wondered. But in reality it is none of his business. I told him I don't mind telling him.

It has been something that has been bothering me for some time now, and I am finally glad that I have told you. It is not any kind of secret, except to say that whenever any of the railroad station agents ask about my home life, I always tell them that my family lives back in Montana. But I always go where I am sent, no matter where it may be. Dick says he gathers that my home is not in Montana, and I just smile but do not say anything further on that subject.

But he does say that what I tell other persons is a wise thing to do. I also tell Dick, that no one knows that my daughters live in Missouri, or that I even have any kind of family. He says it must be very difficult for me sometimes, to be away from them so much of the time. I say it is, but in order for me to do what I do, I have to make some choices, some of which I am not happy with at all. He says he knows what I feel, because he too has a similar problem. But now that the station agent has finally arrived, we can now go to work.

Dick says let him do the talking. When we go inside, Dick tells this station agent that he is my boss, and he was so concerned about what Mr. Royal has found, that he decided he would come and see if he could help in any way.

I then show Dick what I had found, and where it appeared to be leading, and by 3:00 PM, we finally found where it was written in black and white, which was really paying out all of the money that was being paid out and to whom.

Then Dick relayed to this station agent who he really is, and at that moment, Dick says that as of this moment, this station will be closed, until this problem is completely solved. Dick also tells this station agent, that the railroad that he works for will be fined one million dollars for every day that this problem continues to go on, and each client that is part and party to these unlawful deals will also be fined one million dollars for every day that this practice continues.

That he will send a letter to everyone involved in these unlawful dealings. The station agent says if this station is closed, then every industry that it services will not get any of their cars, because every day a train crew departs from this station dragging whatever cars need to be switched to all of the industries that we service, and if that cannot be done, then how many persons will really be laid off, and Dick says. You should have thought of that problem, before you partook of all of these unlawful acts you have been doing for the past two years. How you solve your problem is not totally up to him any longer, but is up to his superiors and no one else.

If you do not fully comply, then some personal from the FBI will come to this station and will make sure that no one, not even yourself will be able to enter this station until some kind of deal has been made with his Superiors.

At that time Dick hands this station agent a card, and on this card is his office address, and on the reverse side are more addresses and names. Dick instructs this agent who he should contact to resolve his problem.

Dick and I then leave. We talk briefly near our cars, and then we each leave, and go to wherever we want to go. I actually go back to Missouri because of the time of the day it really is.

Tomorrow I will go and audit another railroad station, whereby it will probably be not very far away from where I was today. So by the time I get to the last railroad that I will audit, my reputation will have preceded me, and how difficult will it be for me to even get into that last railroad station. This has happened before, but not recently.

By the end of this week I have audited every railroad station except one, and that one is the east St Louis office of the a well known railroad in Missouri with its main office being in St Louis, Missouri. But since it also has a station on the east side of the Mississippi river, I am compelled to audit it too.

And like I suspected, when I drive up to this station, many persons meet me, but suspecting what I would find, I also brought with me some two additional auditors, one from the ICC and the other from the AAR. And when they flashed their badges, all of these persons fell by the wayside, and I entered this small station. I suspected that I would be able to audit this station on this day, and that I would not find any improprieties, because this railroad station only has this station here, so as to be able to transfer train crews from one Engine to another Engine when they hand off whatever cars they are bringing to this side of the river, that will be switched by train crews who know the Illinois side much better that a Missouri Crew.

And by the end of this day, my suppositions are absolutely correct, because I did not find any improprieties. I thanked the other two Agents and we both drove off, following each other, and once I was on the Missouri side of the river, I again wave to these agents, and then I drove to where I wanted to go.

CLEMENT

September 21st 1967

Dick Tracy contacted me at my office this morning, telling me that the ESTL incidents have been completely solved, when first the railroad involved did end up paying out four million dollars in fines, and every company involved paid the same amount, with the exception of the company who was actually paying out all of the money under the table to whomever they paid it to.

That the last company filed for chapter 11 bankruptcy, and that in about two years every person who took payout money will finally come to trial. And when that happens, I will most likely be called to come and testify unless someone comes to me and takes a certified statement that will be witnessed by at least two other persons whom I do not know, but will just be witnesses to my statement and my signature.

That if I lived in some other state, and if it would be a hardship for me to have to travel to the state of Illinois, that that statement would likely suffice.

Of course it all depends on the Judge in whatever court all of this will take place in. But since all of these industries are in the state of Illinois, then this will most likely all happen in the State capitol, which is Springfield. It all depends on what the Lawyers decide will happen, since there are several Defendants against the Interstate Commerce Commission, since the WWIB does not have any authority to levy any kind of fines. And the

AAR only got involved in only one railroad where no improprieties were found, it is likely that I will not be necessary to be included in this trial.

Dick says he would have eventually found out what I did find out, because one of his next places he was going to Audit was the East St Louis area, because he like my company had not actually audited these stations within the last two years, so what I did find, I just alerted the ICC a bit sooner, rather than later, but the end result would have been the same.

And whether I will actually have to testify at whatever trials that are held, will be totally up to the Judge who handles each case, or whether only one Judge will handle all of these cases. But since that is still at least two years in the future, will be determined at that time.

CLEMENT

September 28th 1967

Dear Peggy;

I have been pondering a decision, and now that I have finally made that decision, I will tell you what that decision is. I have been looking at some travel trailer homes, and I have decided to buy one. And it will be a 24-foot Zepher trailer. It is actually a 1966 model, so I will only have to pay a total of 5,000 dollars for it.

It has actually been used since it was new, as an office at the dealership wherefrom I will purchase it from. New carpeting is to be installed inside of it before I take possession of it. And a number of other things, so it will be just like new.

I am also having another Air Conditioner and Heater installed on it, so when I am traveling, it will either be heated or Air Conditioned as I am traveling.

Now what I am asking is whether you would like to travel with me, wherever I go, which will either allow you to do something different, as you can Register with the Kelly Girl Employment Agencies and with Manpower Employment Agencies, and because I am also going to purchase a Moped, whereon I can travel to whatever Station I need to go to, from whatever Trailer Park we will be parked in. Or wherever we will park this trailer.

Therefore you can use the Automobile that I am now

driving, which is a new 1967 Ford Falcon Station wagon. It still has to be fitted with the pulling mechanism, which will become part of the vehicle itself. Meaning it will take about one full day to actually install everything on that vehicle wherein it will become a permanent part of that vehicle.

I am also having installed another 12 volt Battery inside of the trailer, so I will have twice the normal energy available to run everything inside of this trailer. I am also having some additional devices built onto this trailer, so it will look like they were installed at the factory. And this will take two more days. So I will not be returning home for another week, until I can have everything that I want installed on this trailer, placed there. You see, next year we will be taking an extended vacation to California for a period of four months.

I have also done some research for you regarding some Magazines wherein you have been approved to submit all of your newly created Crossword puzzles, where they will pay you one cent for every puzzle that is published in these magazines. Meaning for example, if one of your new crossword puzzles is published in a Readers Digest Magazine, and since that magazine has circulation of around two million persons every month, means that you would receive twenty thousand dollars for these two puzzles, for the one month it is published in.

I know that Readers Digest quoted you a figure of five cents for every puzzle they accepted, which would be published. But when I mentioned that deal, the person I talked to told me that whoever told my wife that they would give her a nickel for every puzzle that she submitted and it was published is no longer with this company, because that person did not know what they were doing.

And since your wife did not have a contract with us, that we would not honor that statement. I in fact did have a Contract sent to me, and when I return home, I will present it to you, for you to sign, so at any future time that you send in any of your crossword puzzles to Readers Digest, and they do publish it, you will get the figure I quoted to you in this letter. And as their distribution increases, so will your checks from them increase. They have a reputation to uphold, so with this signed contract, they will not jip you.

I also have a contract from Dell Crossword Magazine, and in that contract they state they will also give you a penny for each crossword puzzle that they publish in their magazine. I am trying to accumulate contracts from as many magazines that I can find, where they do publish a crossword puzzle in each issue that comes out every month.

And since I do not usually try to solve any crossword puzzles, mostly because I really don't have the time, but knowing how many times you have solved so many puzzles, that the fact that you now create puzzles, is what you can probably do best.

And I am supposing that these take a lot of time to create. But I could be wrong in that assumption. I know what you have done with some of your time, but I am trying not to think about any of what has gone before

So you probably would not even have to work outside of this trailer. I am not trying to dictate what you will do for the rest of your life, but it sure beats getting into an automobile in a strange town and going to work for some company who really does not know anything about your working habits or whether you would even like working for them. Or how long you would be working for them.

You always said you would like to write some books, and this will now give you the chance to further that endeavor also. I have also purchased a brand new Typewriter for you along with two-dozen pages of Carbon paper, so you could keep copies of every story you would write. I have also purchased a new tape recorder, just in case you might want to dictate these books onto tape and two dozen new tapes, wherein you can have them transcribed by someone other than myself, who could also be a kind of Editor for you. Maybe someone of your own choosing.

Anyway I want you to think about all of this, and when I do come home, then you can give me your answer. I will be sending this letter to your office and to our apartment via a special courier, so you will have plenty of time to consider everything. I will also be doing some special work for the WWIB in the St Louis area, compliments of Jack Perkins from Chicago, which will keep me busy for the next few days, as my vehicle will be in various shops in St Louis. Whereon what needs to be installed will be installed. So I will be staying at your parent's house, just in case you may want to contact me.

HAPPY ANNIVERSARY

By the end of this day, there will be delivered a special present from me and one from my Daughters, and another one from your parents. I made arrangements to have all of them delivered all at the same time. I hope you fully enjoy what you will be getting. And enjoy your dinner out on this October 1st, with the Escort I arranged for you. He is not the normal run of the mill Escort, but is being well paid by myself. I wish I could be there with you, but things being what they are, makes this night impossible for me to be anywhere but in your parents house.

CLEMENT

October 1st 1967

Dear Peggy;

I have also invented a device that will help me when I try to hook up with this trailer. A travel trailer company has offered to buy the rights to install this device to every vehicle of every owner of any of their travel trailers that they sell. Which will net me an additional twenty dollars every time they install it, so I will most likely be getting some additional monies every year until that contract expires, whether I will extend it, I am not sure at this time.

Moses Lighthouse is handling all of the paperwork regarding this new account. This is another reason I am getting this new one year old trailer for only five thousand dollars, because this company tells me that every time I show this device, will most likely expand their overall sales by fifty times more than what they have been for the past ten years. That until one of their representatives contacted the main company, their sales of travel trailers had fallen off by as much as sixty percent.

But now that they will also be installing this device, that their sales will go up appreciably. I have also contacted many other Travel Trailer Manufacturers who are also interested in installing this device.

The company, who manufactures this device, is not the issue here. But I have informed them that this other Company and some other Travel Trailer companies will be installing some of these devices on vehicles that some of their parties who purchase their trailers, and because it is so needed in this industry, was the reason I even invented it.

During my travels, I often encounter many travel trailers, and the one thing that everyone has trouble doing, is backing up to the trailer hitches, wherein they don't have to keep jockeying many times to get the hitches just perfect, and since this device makes that possible the first time they do this, will make a lot of persons very happy that I ran into all of them.

Even you will be able to accomplish this with your first try. Just as long as you do what the instructions say to do. Anyone can learn to do this, anyone that can drive an Automobile.

The problem we will have is, what will we put in storage, because this trailer has everything installed inside of it. Meaning that we will not have any of our regular furniture inside of it. It has beds and sofas and tables and seating areas, and refrigerators and stoves and showers and a commode, everything that any person needs to go anywhere. And two Air conditioning units, and two heaters.

One air conditioning unit will run while we are traveling, depending on the time of year, or the heater will operate which will keep the temperature at a constant 78 degrees, and if a day becomes cloudy or full of sunshine, what ever is necessary will take over, because these units will be operated by electricity only. This electricity will be furnished by the extra batteries I have had installed inside of this trailer.

In the beginning I had decided to install only one extra battery, but the Mechanic who was doing the work actually installed two extra batteries, and now I am glad he misunderstood the work order. It did not cost me any extra money. Sometimes things that happen, happen for good reasons.

The hookup is real neat also, because when the vehicle is hooked to the trailer, it is considered one complete unit. It was displayed to me that way, and to prove their point, they removed both rear tires from my vehicle, and the wheels never did touch the ground.

So if a person had a vehicle, which had front wheel drive, one could travel this way. But of course this has not been invented yet. I guess I will have to invent that also.

Anyway, I hope you had a good time this evening, and since I have not, nor have you called your parents home, I guess the Escort that I hired to take you to many places this evening, saw that you had a great time. I hope you enjoyed the Dinner Theatres I sent you to.

And lastly I hope you enjoyed your new dress that I made for you, but I had it delivered to our apartment by special messenger, an hour before your escort was to show up. Of course I do not know whether you had another of your special dates lined up, and just in case you had a date, you will have noticed that he did not arrive at your door. Because I had that person escorted off to the local Jail.

Telling the Officer that arrested this man, that he was there to have sex with a married woman who was actually pregnant again. And if this man took my wife out on a date, he would probably end up raping her.

Now whether this had to be done, I am not certain this really happened, but that is what would have happened if that were to take place. At any rate, I made sure that no man would take you anywhere, except the person I arranged to have you taken to all of the places you were taken to.

And now that today is almost over, meaning it is near midnight, and you have not called your parents house yet, you are either too angry or are too happy to do anything, so I guess I will just go to bed in my downstairs bedroom, where I will finish writing this letter.

I have decided that I will finish this letter tomorrow morning, so good night my love, and have pleasant dreams.

CLEMENT

October 2nd 1967

Margaret told me that you did call at 2:00 AM, only I did not hear the phone ring, because of my sleeping in the basement bedroom, and because I actually unplugged the telephone that is down in that basement. And because I actually put earplugs in my ears, so as to not hear the phone in the hall upstairs.

Margaret tells me that you did have a great time, and you did like the dress I made for you and you also liked all of the presents you received. And that the evening was perfect, except for one thing and that was I was not there to enjoy it with you. Margaret says to tell me that your wife loves you very much, and she needs to tell you more of that Love.

I have not heard you say anything about Loving me for so long, it is hard to believe whether you really mean what you say or maybe you are just tired of living totally alone by yourself, except for the Cats.

Margaret tells me that I need to now go back to Cudahy, to be with my wife. That my girls will be just fine remaining here in the St Louis area, living with her and Joe. Besides they have all of their friends here, and leaving them at this time would not be a good idea.

Mary Beth will not be needing a vehicle yet, because she needs Martha to always be in the vehicle when she does drive any car, and since Martha will never let Mary Beth drive her vehicle, she will just have to get by, until I can buy her, her own vehicle.

And besides Mary Beth is still taking her driving lessons and whether she will even graduate from that driving school is still questionable. Because she still wants to drive the way she wants to drive, and the instructor says if she does not change soon, he will give up on her. And if that happens, Uncle Homer will have one of his Officers teach her, only his way.

What that way is, Margaret says she does not know, nor does she want to know, but she will either learn to drive, or she will never ever be able to get any drivers license in the state of Missouri, because Uncle Homer will make sure it will never happen.

CLEMENT

October 28th 1967

Peggy;

Well, now that we have decided to put all of our furniture and Bed and some other stuff in a storage place, we are now living in this travel trailer. You actually have taken to living with me very well and we seem to be much happier than we have been in several years. Your cooking of my meals is most importantly improved, and I never worry any more as to whether you will ever burn any of your meals that you fix for me.

You have also told me that you really like the extra storage that I have made available to you, because you can get to most everything that you need without even going outside of the trailer. That the only things that you need that is stored on the roof of this trailer, you will only need when I am with you. And all of those things are things that are fairly light, like Paper towels or toilet paper, and that I also have extra toilet paper stored in the floor storage.

You tell me that it is amazing how much extra storage I really had installed that can be gotten to from inside of this trailer. But some of the trailer parks that we have parked in have caused you to have some problems, because of which some of these persons appear to be.

Because you tell me that some of these male persons, come and knock on our door, and I ask you what you were wearing, and when you tell me, I ask if you were a man, would you not come calling, and she says I guess she would.

So I keep telling you that you cannot dress like you are in some tropical scene, when it is almost wintertime outside, just because it is warm inside of this trailer. And that I will most likely worry when it really gets warm outside, what will you then dress like. And who will then be going to bed with you in our trailer home.

You ask why don't I trust you, and I say because you just don't seem to give a damn who you bring inside of this trailer. I ask you, what would you do if I had my Daughters with me. Would you still invite strange men into this trailer and have sex with them, with my girls watching, so they can get some idea what having sex with another person other than your husband is really like. That will never happen while I am pulling this trailer.

My girls will remain with their grandmother until I say otherwise. And if I continue to hear that you are having sex with every man who comes to this door, then the next thing I will do is I will take you back to your parents, where I will leave you, and take my girls and leave and never come back, and I will Divorce you, and you will have to begin all over completely on your own. If you are not ready to do that then cease and desist from all of your extra activities or that is just what I will do.

Of course you will be able to live on your own now, because you are now receiving twenty thousand dollars every month from various magazines, so I am not obviously needed in your life any longer. So when we go to the St Louis area in a few days, which is what I will do. I will contact Margaret so she can alert my girls as to what I will be doing.

CLEMENT

October 29th 1967

On this day I have hooked up the trailer and we are now heading for the St Louis area. Where I will drop you off at your parents that is if they will accept you, and if they will not then you will have to find a different place to live. Because they will not allow you to bring strange men to their house, where you will have sex with them in their basement bedroom. We stopped in Jacksonville, Illinois to buy some gasoline for my vehicle, where you called a Cab and you left me. I know not where you have gone to and I really don't care. Since you also have your checkbook and all of your credit cards, you will not starve nor will you have trouble finding a place to live.

I actually called the local sheriff and gave him your description just in case you still might be in this area, and then I told him where I would be for the next two days, just in case he needed to contact me. He says he will call me in that area, before I will be leaving that area, as to whether they had any reports on your whereabouts.

When I got to the Ferguson area, I knew of a Trailer park where I parked my trailer, and where I locked it and left it for a while along with my Cats, who are still inside of this trailer.

This is a very good trailer parking area and I am not worried about anyone trying to get inside of my trailer. And since I am hooked up to Electricity and the Phone service and also the Sewer system, I am completely self-sufficient. After all I will be returning to this trailer when I am through talking with my daughters. And maybe they will be coming back with me also. That is still to be determined.

The next day, my phone rang, and it was you on the phone, and you asked me why you had left me in Jacksonville, Illinois by yourself. I told you that I had the restroom searched where I was having gas put in my vehicle and all of the other buildings on that property, and you were not to be found.

And besides I was told that you had called a Cab wherein you got inside of it, and you drove away from this gas station. So for you to tell me that I left you in that small town is just a figment of you imagination. I actually contacted the Law in that town and reported you missing, and if they found you, then that is the real reason you are now calling me.

You then tell me that you are in Jail in that town, and that I need to come and get you, because they will not let you leave on your own, unless I am the one who will take you away from their town.

That you are not wanted in this town, because any whores are not welcome anywhere in this town. So I got in my vehicle and went and got you and when we returned back to the St Louis area, I dropped you off at a Holiday Inn Motel, and I left you there. Telling you that you will have to now make your own way in life, that I am sick and tired of always hearing about all of your liaisons with other men, but never again.

CLEMENT

November 21st 1967

Dear Peg;

Why I keep writing these letters, I am uncertain, but it seems to allow me to keep my head cleared of all kinds of bad thoughts regarding you. I am sending these letters to your girlfriend Hazel, just in case you have let her know where you are now living, because your parents do not know where you are now living. Margaret tells me that you don't even call her or Joe, and they are worried that something may have happened to you.

Of course I tell them, that you are just punishing them along with me, to see if I will maybe do something about trying to get you to come back to me. But I tell them that, I will not make the first move, which it will have to come from you. And if you are so inclined, then you can let Hazel know and she will contact Margaret.

I have still left my daughters with Margaret and Joe, as I am still traveling a lot. Though lately I have had to go on some special assignments, where I had to travel for two and sometimes more days to even get to that assignment, because there is no one who can take care of my Cats, so I am now getting a lot of mileage on this vehicle and travel trailer.

Because some of these places, I have had to travel to in some mountainous areas, so getting to know what this vehicle is really capable of doing is making me feel that buying this travel trailer was a great idea.

I actually purchased a complete road atlas of the most modern highway system in this country, so just in case when I ask questions about any possible low bridges that may be in a particular area, I then will always get a local map that always shows where these places really are.

One time, when I was traveling to a particular town, I did come across a low bridge, wherein I had to back this trailer a quarter mile where I could back it into a driveway and get it turned around so I could take a completely different route.

So whenever I drive into a new town, I always stop and ask at the local Sheriffs office or at a local bank, which seem to really know all of the back roads everywhere. It's still a learning project.

Now as you know, this is the second time you and I have been separated. I still have not decided whether I will file for a Divorce from you. Mostly because of my girls, I suppose. Because they do need a Mother, but since you only have tried to make contact with Mary Beth, I think you probably may want to somehow try to influence her to do your bidding, and that is the one thing I do not want you to do to her, ever.

It is hard enough for me to keep her in a good mood, without you trying to get in touch with her and making her life more miserable also.

You will be very surprised with how little influence you will really have on her. What you will try to do to her now, will only show up in her when she becomes much older, and I am hoping when that happens she will also see through what you have always tried to do to her. And before that happens, I will Divorce you, and then you will never have any influence on what she does.

You see, I am not going to have this job all that long anyway, because I am thinking that I will probably resign within six months, and once that happens, I will leave this area and not come back until after my girls are all grown up and married and will have children of their own.

So if you want to go to some other location, or you want to go with me, forget it, because that will not happen, because with all of your extra activities with other men, I will not have you influencing my girls with those kinds of activities.

CLEMENT

January 11th 1968

Peg;

It has been about two months since I have written any letters to you that I ever wanted to send to you. My life has been good to me, as I have been from one coast to the opposite coast, and all in my trailer.

I already have put another eighteen thousand miles on my vehicle and my trailer. That moped that I purchased, I actually gave that to Mary Beth, and she has gone to a lot of places with it, and now that she is working part time after school, and since she does not have to have any kind of drivers license while using it, she is now realizing how valuable that drivers license really will be to her, because she now knows that what I and others have been trying to teach her to do, is more important than being such a stubborn person.

In fact last week, Uncle Homer told her that she will soon need to have a drivers license to even continue driving that Moped, beginning in 1969 but because it is more like a Motorcycle, she will actually need to get that kind of a license, so the officer that tried to teach her how to drive an automobile, will now also try to teach her all of the rules that a Motorcycle driver needs to know.

I fear she will be a big problem, but she may also surprise others and me. Because she actually did learn how to drive an automobile, but she actually failed her driving test, when she took it, and she has to wait six months before she can take the test again. She did pass the written test and actually got a hundred percent, but when she was taking the driving test she gets nervous and makes too many mistakes. So I have taken her out in the country and using a dune buggy that I borrowed from a friend of mine, I have given her every kind of driving test she will ever encounter while taking an official driving test, and I have pushed her so much that she says that if she can handle me then she can handle any highway patrolman who will actually give her that driving test. I also contacted Uncle Homer and he talked to the Highway Patrol Captain for that area, and he has gotten special permission from the Highway Patrol so Mary Beth can take whatever driving tests she needs to take.

So tomorrow I will drive her to where she will take the test, using my vehicle for an automobile drivers license, and then using the Moped, she will take that test also. The instructions for the Moped will be given to her before she gets on her Moped, and then a highway patrolman, by using a megaphone will give her additional instructions from his motorcycle when she takes that test. I have instructed her in that one also and she thinks she will pass with flying colors. Anyway after they returned, this Highway patrolman says she is the coolest person he has ever given any test to, and that she actually knows all of the moves and all of the answers. That whoever taught her how to drive that Moped, must know more than he knows.

Mary Beth tells this patrolman that her Dad taught her what she knows, and that is why she knows all of the answers on all of the written tests also.

Let me say, that I felt ten feet tall when she said that, and I now know that all of my teaching of her did not go unnoticed by her, and never has.

Mary Beth is still not all that sure about my knowledge regarding how I know so much about the human body, but Martha says she does not have to know, because of the fact that Martha and Mary Beth have the same size body, so whatever Dad makes for Martha, he can also make for Mary Beth.

Mary Beth says she did not know that her father made most of her clothes, because she thought that Margaret always made all of her clothes.

So now Mary Beth has a regular drivers license and also a license to drive either a motorcycle or a Moped. So I guess I will now have to buy her a vehicle. Mary Beth says when she needs an automobile, she will no longer need the Moped, but for now she will just use the Moped.

I think to myself that my oldest daughter is finally growing up.

CLEMENT

March 14th 1968

Dear Peg;

I am back in the St Louis area once again, after spending most of February of this year down in Florida, Auditing many different areas. That trailer sure came in very handy.

On this day I have decided to take Mary Beth and Martha out to Dinner at a well-known restaurant where they have live entertainment too. It should make them feel kind of grown up I think. I do not know what Margaret and Joe have lined up, but when I told them what I was going to do they did not seem surprised.

Actually when we got to where I took them, I did see Uncle Homer and some of his family also, even though they were in a very secluded area of this restaurant, so I am thinking that Joe is having me watched for some reason. Maybe they are planning some kind of surprise for Mary Beth.

Anyway after three hours we left that place and when we got back to Margaret and Joes place, and we came into the house, there was a surprise party and most of their friends were there, at least all that they could find from school.

Anyway it was a great success and Mary Beth got all kinds of presents and a lot of surprises. Uncle Homer and his family were there too. Uncle Homer says when he saw me in that restaurant he hoped that I would not say anything to my girls, and apparently I did not, so that made this surprise what it was supposed to be.

After I went to feed my Cats, I did go back and spend the night with my girls, because we sat up most of that night and talked about a lot of different things. Mary Beth asked if you and I were still married, and I told them that we are, but how long that will continue I am uncertain at that time. It all depended on what you wanted to do with the rest of your life.

That since you were now bringing in a lot of money, that you really did not really need me as your husband, and that it probably would be better if I just Divorced you, so I and my girls could get on with the rest of our lives.

That I figured that I needed to find a different woman who could be the Mother of my two girls, someone who I could love with the passion like I wanted to, especially someone who would always be true to me, and not someone like yourself.

Because I was getting real tired of always trying to make excuses for you, because you were never with me. That I will wait for one more month, and if I did not hear from you in that month, then I will file Divorce papers, and again try to have our marriage Annulled in the Catholic Church.

CLEMENT

March 28th 1968

Two more weeks has gone by and I have not heard from you, nor did I ever send this letter to you, so you never really knew that my ultimatum really existed. I actually write these letters, to only make notations in my life, rather than to let you know what I am really thinking. So when you eventually get this letter, you will also probably get the Divorce Documents along with it.

So if you feel I have not been letting you know what I have been thinking then you will just have to excuse my abruptness about my true feelings. Because I really don't have to send these letters to you any longer, since it is obvious to me that you no longer care about me in any way. I know that I no longer care much for you either.

But these letters are just a reminder of what I have been going through for all of these almost 13 years. They are a kind of record of what I have had to put up with regarding a delinquent wife.

It is hard to believe that I have put up with you for all of this time, because these years have not been very happy ones. So when you do get this letter, along with it you will also get Divorce documents, wherein I will state many reasons as to why I want this divorce.

And if you try to fight me, you will find that I will eat up most of the money you have so far earned in whatever ways you have earned it, because I will have this divorce, whether you want it or not. I will no longer put up with any more of your shenanigans...............

Clement

March 31st 1968

I still have not heard from you and since the Divorce papers I had served to you have not been returned to me, I am suggesting that you agree with all of my reasons why I want this divorce. I also filed documents with the St Louis Archdiocese, whereby I want this marriage annulled in the Catholic Church. They did contact me, wanting to know how my children will be educated, and when I told them they are going to Catholic schools, they seemed satisfied with my answer, so I may actually get that annulment.

Yesterday I was contacted by a Catholic Priest, who wanted me to sign documents guaranteeing that my girls will be educated in only catholic schools and I told him to get lost, because I will educate my girls however I see fit, since I am no longer a catholic, and that the catholic church has no control over where I actually educate my girls.

He seemed to think that I was still a catholic, so I told him to prove his statement, and after he called the Cardinal, he then backed away from his request and left. I am supposing that you probably told him that you were the mother of my girls, but I was waiting for the catholic church to bring forth any documents that would prove that statement, but they did not, so I guess you are fighting this divorce in whatever ways that you can. You will lose, whatever you are trying to do.

Clement

April 6th 1968

I finally heard from you, and you are trying to dispute this divorce, saying that you have not been treated fairly, because of my working position with the WWIB. And that my girls are not being treated fairly either because I am away from home a lot, and they do not get proper care while I am away from them.

To think that you would make such an accusation against your own mother makes me wonder what kind of a person you really are. And how desperate you really must be regarding how you may feel about your own mother and father.

It really does surprise me that you would stoop so low as to accuse them of not being good parents or grandparents to whomever. When they gave you so much of their lives, to you and your sister, and for what.

Because it is quite likely that you do not appreciate what your father and mother had to give up to give you two the kind of life they thought that you needed to have. All of the extra hours your Dad worked at the Wabash to put you through College and also through Pharmacist school, which you say you did not want to go to. What kind of fool do you think he is? He would not have sent you to that school if you had told him that you did not want to be a pharmacist. What a waste of time and money.

I wonder if your sister thinks the same way, that all of the money he spent sending her to college and Nursing school was a waste of time. I do not think so.

I venture to say that you really want to go to California with my girls and me but you are too proud to humble yourself and tell me…

Hazel told me that you told her, that you do want to go to California with my girls and me but you will never ask me if you can go along, or that you will never tell me that you still Love me, which is probably not mostly true. That if reality now came to the surface, that you no longer have liaisons with other men and in fact you have not even had a date with any man for over six months. That in reality, you have not slept with another man in over eight months. Hazel says that I should feel sorry for you, and relent and take you back.

I told Hazel, that the only way I would take you back would be if you signed a Special Contract, that if you violated it in any way, that every dollar you have earned with your Crossword Puzzles or whatever money you will earn from those puzzles will all go to me. And that I will have Total control over all of your finances.

When I conveyed this last suggestion to Hazel, after a few days went by, Hazel again contacted me, and told me to write that contract, because Peggy will sign it.

In fact Hazel suggested that I also put in that contract how much of whatever monies that I may get from Peg, will go to educate my two girls. Hazel says it sounds like she expects to violate that contract.

I told Hazel at that time, that the main reason she has not had any liaisons with other men, is because she has been living with you and Bob. Will she continue her Liaisons in California; only time will tell that story.

But I suspect she will find a way to continue with that practice. So if she fully expects to violate this contract that I will write, then she can also fully expect that I will not allow her to have any control over any money she will make, no matter how she makes it, unless she keeps it in her panties or bra and not in any bank.

CLEMENT

April 8th 1968

So I wrote that contract, and it goes something like this.

This Contract is between Clement and Margaret Royal dealing with an agreement between these two parties, stating that Margaret will no longer have Liaisons with unknown male persons, for the purpose of having SEX with them, because that is what she wants to do, thereby violating her Marriage Vows and his Trust, and she is doing this without his knowledge, and is actually committing this offense against this Agreement. That if Clement does discover that Margaret is doing these acts, then this contract will take effect immediately.

What this Contract allows Clement to do, is, Whatever Money Margaret has made or will make regarding all of the Crossword Puzzles she has invented, any monies realized from the publication of these puzzles will be totally controlled by her husband, Clement.

Also if Margaret decides to go to work for a company in California, in whatever city that may happen, Clement will also have complete control over all of that money also.

In reality, whatever Salary's Margaret is paid, and by whomever, will all be totally controlled by her husband Clement, and any money that Margaret now has in any bank, in any State or City, whether it be in a Savings account or a Checking account or any other kinds of Savings, that too will be totally controlled by Clement Royal.

And lastly, Clement will cancel the Divorce proceedings. If Margaret dies when these two are still married, then Margaret will be buried in Calvary Cemetery in the family plot in St Louis, Missouri. And if Clement Dies before Margaret dies, then this Contract will be Null and Void.

This Contract will be signed by both Margaret and Clement and witnessed by two individuals that are not related to either of them, and they will include their present living addresses. Then it will be notarized.

Signed by ....Margaret Royal

Signed by ....Clement Royal

Witnessed by ....including their address
....
....
....
Witnessed by ....Including their address
....
....
....
....

Notary's Signature...
My appointment will not expire until.

So since I knew where Hazel and Bob live, after I consulted with a Lawyer as to the validity of this Contract that I wrote myself, and after he told me that no court would question it, I drove to where Hazel lives and since Peggy was living there, I presented it to her, and after she read it, she says she will sign it.

I then tell her that we need to go to my Bank in Black Jack, Missouri, where we will all sign all of the necessary copies and also where it will be Notarized, and then I will give you your copy and I will keep my copy. And then you will come back to live with me, until you either die or I will die, whichever happens first. And we will remain together through thick or thin, through rain or shine, through happy times or sad times, at any rate we will remain together from now on.

And that is what happens. After we left the bank, I took Peggy back to Hazel's place where Peggy packed her clothes, and then we drove to where her parents lived, in Ferguson, Missouri. Peggy's Mother did not speak to her.

Her Mother says that if her daughter was so low to question her about how Peggy was raised, then it will be a cold day in hell before she will speak to her again.

I showed the contract that Peggy and I had signed to Margaret, and she stated, when she saw her daughters signature on this contract, that she says she needs to tell me why Peggy is doing what she has been doing for all of these years against me.

She says she initially promised that she would never say anything about this to me, but now she feels I have a right to know.

Margaret says when Peggy was 18 she was going with Ken Jenkins. And one weekend he took her to a lake somewhere north of Florissant, or she thinks it was probably Portage De Sioux, which

is a kind of lower class community, where a number of families rent cabins, that are near the Mississippi River. Anyway Ken raped her several times for that entire weekend. He kept her a prisoner all during that time. She finally got away from him, after he had drank himself into unconsciousness. She was barefoot, and after several hours she finally got someone to stop and pick her up. And that person was a man who apparently lived somewhere in the Florissant area.

Anyway this person who picked her up, took her to a secluded area and he raped her again. Until someone came along and caught them while this was happening, and this other person was also a man, but this time he was a good man, because he was a Catholic priest dressed in civilian clothes, and he grabbed Peggy from this other man, and in fact he had to knock him out to get Peggy away from this other man.

Anyway, this priest wrote down this mans license number and then brought her home to Joe and I, but Joe was not home at that time, so he does not know anything about any of this.

Anyway, from the house here, this priest called the county police and also Uncle Homer and they did catch this second man and arrested him, and they put out an arrest warrant against Ken Jenkins. Ken moved to some place in Illinois, southwest of Chicago somewhere. The arrest warrant was only for when Ken returned to Missouri.

Anyway, after that Peggy did not date anyone for several months. And then she met some smooth man, who got her drunk, and he took her to some place that she cannot remember, because she was out cold. And she was raped several times again.

The guy left her along side of a road in the country near Bridgeton. He just dumped her into a ditch. Where some farmer found her a few hours later, and took her to his own farm where his wife was, and they called the county police, and they brought her home again.

But the sad thing is, that she somehow relates whatever man she married as being the real culprit, and she did fine when she first married you, but now she has misconstrued all of her fears, into getting back at you, who in reality is the gentlest person she has ever known. And the one thing that Peggy fears, she seems to need to do the most often, which is have SEX with whomever, just so she can get revenge against you.

She really needs Psychiatric help, but that person really needs to be someone who totally understands her situation. Margaret says she thinks I am that person, because she knows that I have degrees in both Sociology and Psychology and if anyone can actually help her, it will be you.

So treat her gently and try to make her as well as you can, because without you, she is totally lost. She cannot function without you.

If you Divorce her, she would kill herself, and she would know that she would end up in Hell. Which she also fears? Because she fears GOD more than she fears everything that has happened to her. So keep her close to GOD and try to help her to Love your girls.

She is really not a bad person, but has just had bad things happen to her, that she did not have control over, but she is too naïve to realize where she went wrong. She is still like a little girl, who is actually a brilliant person. She is very intelligent, but she does not know how and where to use that intelligence. With proper guidance she will one day make a real great wife for you. So be patient with her and most of all, Love her like you obviously Love your Daughters and your Cats and other creatures.

Clement

April 10th 1968

For the past two days, I left Peg with her Parents while I went to feed my Cats every day, twice a day. But they are just fine, and I have told them that Peggy will be coming back with me on this day, so be prepared to welcome her with Love. So on this day Peg and I drove to where I have my trailer parked, and when we were both inside of this trailer, Tai and Tak and Tiger came to Peg and got on her lap, and kissed her twice. I had not said a word to them after we arrived at that trailer, so this was something that Tai had apparently suggested that they do. Tiger was a little reluctant, but she too kissed Peg. Peg took tiger in her arms and said, that she knew that was difficult for her to do, but she would be grateful if she would show her more love from now on.

Tiger is a Cat who has difficulty showing any kind of love to any human persons, even me. So I know what it took to get her to do that to Peg. I told everyone that we have to leave tomorrow, because I need to drive to New Orleans, Louisiana, where I will be working for the next two weeks. And it will probably take at least two days to get there and get settled in a trailer park. So now I need to make us a meal and I need to get some of my reports ready to send back to my home office. I have been on a kind of self imposed vacation, wherein I have not done any Auditing during that time, but I still need to write reports on what I have accomplished while I was in this area anyway, and since I did do some special tasks for Jack Perkins, I need to report these back to him. I will not be sending any reports to my home office about what I have been doing for Jack, but I do have some other things I can report on to my home office. If they have any questions, I will tell them to just contact Jack Perkins in Chicago.

This is another Special Assignment that I have to go to. More Wharfage problems I guess, as I have also been instructed to contact the FBI office when I get there. They have already been alerted of my coming.

You may have noticed, that the license plate on this trailer is a Missouri plate, and I also registered my vehicle to be registered in Missouri. I use your Parents home as my residence, which it is when I am in this area.

Now if anyone were to check on this fact, like you actually questioned in your query against the Divorce that I filed, you would have run into a brick wall. And your case would have been laughed out of Court.

So when you decided to sign the contract that I wrote, you saved yourself a lot of money and troubles, because you would have lost your case, because that Divorce would have been granted.

CLEMENT

April 13th 1968

Since these letters only come to you, I will not address them to you any longer. Whether you actually read them, I do not know. But I am hopeful that you will read them, because you might learn something about yourself, and about me, and my actual capabilities in being able to really help you. Of which you have never acknowledged that I really could.

I think I can help you with all of your problems, but you have to be willing to work with me also, and to try to not break your contract with me. If you would be willing to do that, then there is help, and as close as just little ole me. I will wait for an answer from you, after you have read this letter.

And the funny thing is, I have always been here, but you have never even tried to communicate with me verbally. If you do not do this, then I will try to get you some additional help, but in California, not in Missouri or Illinois or Wisconsin. The choice is yours.

Clement

TWO WEEKS LATER

I know we could have stayed in our trailer, but I figured that sleeping in your parent's house would be interesting, especially since I told you to not wake up your parents when you went inside of their house. And wouldn't they be surprised in the morning when they got up. Actually when Joe and Margaret got up, Joe asked Margaret, did you hear someone come into this house late last night, and Martha says it was just Dad. But when Peg and I came out of the basement, there was much surprise in that house.

Then I told them what I could tell them, including how we came back from New Orleans. Joe says you sure live a very interesting life. And this kind of service, doesn't it cost you anything, and I said no, the U S Government paid for it, and in fact it is probably your tax dollars that probably paid for this return trip.

Clement

April 24th 1968

So after I called Jack Perkins on this day, to find out what my next assignment would be, he says for me to do whatever my own schedule dictates for me to do. He says my report on the New Orleans assignment sure is interesting. He says he also has a report from the ICC Auditor, but he cannot tell me what it says. I told him I could imagine what it says.

Remember I was there and I have worked with him before, and the main problem was to get me out of that area safely, and that is what they did. But I was told by Dick Tracy himself to not even tell you how that was done, so I will not, but it sure was fascinating and interesting.

Jack says there has never been an Auditor that has ever been like you before and there probably never will be again. You are a wonder and you have done such a wonderful job in this position.

I asked Jack if my vacation of four months has been set yet, and he says that vacation will begin on June 23rd, 1968, which is a Monday and it will end on October 31st 1968. I say thank you very much. He says you have earned it.

You are the only Auditor who has accomplished what you have done, which is, on all of the Special Assignments you have gone on, on every one of them you have probably saved the tax payers of this country several millions of dollars by what you have accomplished on every one of those special assignments.

Because you have been on 25 Special Assignments and on every one of those assignments you have found improprieties that has sent 75 persons to prison for at least 25 years each, even though the Federal Prisons will have to feed and house them for all of the time they will remain in prison, because of what they have done, you have still saved this government several million dollars each year, for as long as they all remain in those prisons.

But remember, and I sincerely hope that whatever else you do in your life, don't become a publicly well known individual in whatever you do, because some of these persons may still want your life taken away from you. Because of what you actually did to all of them. So whatever you do, do it quietly and don't make yourself to be well known in this world. Whatever you will do in this world, you will be a great success in whatever you do.

I say, Jack you sound like I will not be returning back to this area, and Jack says, you will not be returning back to this area, because you will ultimately remain in California, where you will make your millions.

I say, Jack it has been great knowing you also, because without your influence, I would not have been able to buy the trailer I use in this business, and because of this trailer, I now have the rest of my life back, meaning I and my wife are back together again and I thank you for helping me in that endeavor.

He says you deserved the best he could offer, and if what he did helped to cement that relationship in place, then he is very well pleased. I said I could not have done it without your help. He says you are most welcome. Then the call ended.

So since this day is Thursday, and where we have to go will

actually take me a day to get there, I have decided to remain in Ferguson until Sunday morning, and actually go to church on Saturday afternoon at the 5:00 PM Mass.

I called Jack Perkins again to give him some idea as to where I will be going next. And this is what I told him. The next place I will be going will be Davenport, Iowa, which is where the Mississippi River flows east and west for about two miles. There are also a number of other smaller cities near this town, like Rock Island, Illinois, and Bettendorf, Iowa, and Moline and East Moline, Illinois, and lastly Milan, Illinois. Six towns and villages in all, which will probably take us at least a month for me to finish all of them. And then from there I will go to Muscatine, Iowa and then to Burlington, Iowa and then to Fort Madison, Iowa and lastly to Keokuk, Iowa.

And when I get all of those done, it will be time to start on my four-month vacation to California. So this will be a two-month outing, and I will not be returning back to the Milwaukee, Wisconsin area.

Because I already will have gotten all of the travelers' checks that I plan to take with us. Jack says to let him know when I am within a week of finishing up with these assignments, and he will make sure I get my next Expense Advance check, including being paid for all four months of this vacation, because the extra month of vacation I am getting is also being paid for.

And if I decide that I will resign from this position, Jack says he will give me six months of Separation Allowance. So as you can see, I have made a lot of friends in very high places with this organization. Then this call ended.

Clement

April 27th 1968

Multiple Cities

So now we are parked in a trailer park just a little north of Davenport, Iowa. It is not a very clean park, and I think some of the persons here are actually ladies of the night, who are sleeping around with some of the men who work on the Island, that is now a munitions depot, which is in the middle of the Mississippi River where this river runs east and west for two miles.

This diversion was made to do this, when an Earthquake happened in 1811 and 1812 on the New Madrid Fault in southern Missouri.

This Island was also created when the river was in the process of being diverted. But just in case things get a bit dicey, then we will move to a different Trailer park in the state of Illinois. I will have to drive about twenty miles to get to work, but moving to this other park will most probably be much better.

Actually an unmarried friend of mine recommended this park where we now are parked, but we will not remain here, because it is in fact a place where Whores live.

As you told me, after that first day of me working in Davenport, and I came home around 4:00 PM, and you were outside in a pair of shorts and a Halter, and there were several men lounging nearby.

And as you know, I did not say anything, but I immediately began to load the collapsible tables and chairs and chaise lounges onto the trailer, and I unhooked everything, and then I hooked up my vehicle to the trailer.

Previous to arriving at home, I went by the office and paid for the time we had been there, and they told me that you had gathered a crowd of men to come to the trailer.

Later I talked to Tai and he told me that no men had been invited inside of the trailer yet, but you were getting close to doing just that. So it was lucky that I came home earlier than you expected me to do, because otherwise you would have violated the contract you have with me.

So now we are near Geneseo, Illinois in a much better trailer park, because according to the City Marshall it was just opened up this spring, and it is almost completely full already. Actually as you can see, persons who own Air Stream trailers are grouped together, and persons who own other kinds of trailers are grouped together. I think our neighbors will be a better class of individuals, at least I hope they will. I did not see any Zephyr trailers as ours is, but we were placed with all of the Air Stream trailers anyway.

I am usually a kind of person who goes and introduces myself to most of my neighbors that live within a hundred feet of where we are parked, and in doing this I discover what kinds of persons really live in these trailers.

Because I had decided to remain home the next day after we had got ourselves parked and completely hooked up, this is what I did. Some of the trailers were larger than ours is, but there were also some trailers that were the same size as ours is, and there are even three trailers that are only seventeen footers, with four persons living in them.

Persons who are on a vacation from California, who are interested in getting on a boat on the Mississippi and going down river to St Louis, Missouri and points south, even all the way to New Orleans, Louisiana.

Those persons I wanted to talk to, to see from what part of California they are from. And I found out they are from Santa Ana, California. They tell me that that is a great place to live, because it is one of the largest cities in Orange County.

That a number of Movie stars live either in that city and a lot of others live in surrounding cities. And John Wayne lives on Balboa Island, which is near Huntington Beach. He even has a Yacht near his back yard, because he lives right on the Pacific Ocean.

If I go to California, get to know that area, because they tell me I will like it. Anyway since we are going to be in this park for at least a month, I suggested that you get to know some more of the residents.

Every one of these other residents is all married, some with small children and some with no children at all. But with all kinds of pets, including birds.

This park has a three-hole golf course and tennis courts and a golf driving range and three separate small lakes where they tell me there are a lot of different kinds of fish.

Personally as you know, I do like to fish, so I will be going fishing when the weekend comes. I do also have some golf clubs, but I am still an amateur and I have never played tennis in my life. So there are a lot of things we can do while we will live here.

Since we are living in Illinois, I decided that I would Audit all of the towns that are nearest to where we are living. When I did go into Davenport, I was just casing every place I had to go to. In Illinois there is East Moline, and Moline, and Milan and Rock Island.

There are no less than three railroads in every town, with the exception of Rock Island, which has six railroads. And after I called Jack Perkins, he says I need to Audit the Munitions Depot on the Island itself also. But call them first to let them know that you are coming and approximately when you will arrive.

So I will have sixteen places to Audit. I know that some will only take a very short time to do, but others will take as long as three to four days to do. By allotting myself a month to do all of these was a good idea. And then in Bettendorf, Iowa there are five railroads and in Davenport there are seven railroads to Audit. So another twelve places to audit will most likely take me an additional three weeks.

Altogether there will be twenty-eight places to audit. That is a lot of work, and if I find no improprieties then that will make my job a lot easier in the long run of things.

Clement

May 1st 1968

In finishing out the month of April I ended up Auditing Six different railroads in those two days, and they were in East Moline and Moline, Illinois, so I now have ten more to go to in Illinois. They were all very small stations, and not too much business had gone on for the past year. Because each Agent told me that they had been audited a year back.

But you are a lot different then he was, because the way I go about auditing all of the records, says that you are more thorough than he was. But we do not do anything that is illegal, and wherever you go in this entire area, you will not find an impropriety in our methods. But if you do then we would all like to know about them, because we all have had a great reputation for many years now, and we do not want anyone in this area to give us a black mark in our methods.

They all told me that they know that each auditor is different in how they each do their jobs. We have heard that you are someone who is very good at what you do, so do your thing and we will see how we all will fare.

But now the weekend is here and I am going to go fishing tomorrow. Peg says you also promised the Cats that you would take them for a long walk. Peg also says she is sorry what happened at the other trailer park. She says it was such a nice day that she just wanted to enjoy the great weather, and before she knew it, a crowd had gathered.

She says she was writing some stories and she did not notice any of them at first, and then someone cleared his throat and a conversation started and it just grew all out of proportion.

I suggested that the next time we have a nice day like that one, to not go outside with almost no clothes on, because you have your natural beauty still, and you will always gather a crowd, no matter where it may be. Even though you do not have any teeth in your head now, you still have a natural kind of beauty.

Have you thought anything about getting teeth permanently implanted in your mouth? And you tell me that because it would take no less than three months to accomplish, that you would wait until we get to California. Then try to find the best Dentist surgeon that we can find and have it done some time in the future.

Now tomorrow, after I take all of my Cats that want to go for a walk, I will then put on some long pants and walk to where the closest fishing lake is located. And if I catch some good ones, I will then clean them and put them on my Barbeque and we will have a feast of whatever kind of fish I catch.

So try to think of something else that will go with some fish steaks. Actually in some places, on May 1st, it is a holiday, but in this country, it is just like any other day for my family and me.

Clement

Today is Saturday May 3rd 1968,

After breakfast I mentioned to all of my Cats that now is the time to go for a walk. Tribble who is a totally black semi-longhaired male cat immediately went and secured all of the Leashes from a hook, where they hang and brought them to me. As usual, Tiger did not want to go outside. Which is her choice to not do.

But Tai, who is a Chocolate Point Siamese, and Tak who is a Seal Point Siamese, and Tribble is always eager to take these walks. It appears that it will be a great day, and even though it is a little chilly this morning, these Cats always want to see what it is like to walk around and visit with other Creatures while they walk. None of them will ever run away from any other creature, even if that creature is larger than they are.

Tai is a very large cat, who weighs 18 pounds and he is solid muscle. Tak who is his sister is considerably smaller, but like her brother she will not back away from anyone. Tribble who is a little less than a year old, but with his semi-long hair appears to be much larger than he really is, and he like Tai will never back away from anyone. Tribble weighs almost 12 pounds, so he is going to be a very large Cat also.

Tribble and Tiger are mates. They have not mated yet, because Tiger is still too young to mate with a male cat. But soon that will happen, and then I will get Tribble fixed, and after Tiger has her Kittens, I will get her fixed. Both Tai and Tak are fixed. And that was done when they were both about four months old. Which is probably why Tai has grown to the size he is. Tak only weighs about 8 pounds.

Anyway as we walked among our neighbors, we encountered other cats and a lot of dogs. When these other creatures saw my three cats, they all backed away from them, which told me that whatever vibes my three were putting out, meant that together we are almost unbeatable. And I never take just one cat for a walk, because I would be asking for trouble.

Anyway we were gone for an hour and when we returned to our trailer, Tribble told Tiger what he saw, and she just got into her bed and went to sleep, meaning she was not impressed. So after they gave each other baths, they too got into their beds and went to sleep. Tai and Tak sleep together and Tribble and Tiger sleep together.

I then got out my fishing gear and put on some wading gear and I went to one of the fishing lakes. I was only using artificial lures, and at first I did not even get one bite.

Then a young man came by, and he says if I use worms, I will catch almost anything that is swimming in this lake. He says for two dollars he will go dig some for me, and I said fine, and that is what he did, and when he returned, I gave him the two dollars, and as soon as I cast my line out into the water, the Cork that I had about six feet from the end of my line, disappeared under the water, so I fought with that fish for twenty minutes before I could land it, and it weighed three pounds, because I had this young man weigh it, and he says it is a black bass.

So I put another worm on my hook and this time I removed

the cork and let my hook drift down to the bottom of this lake, and I reeled it in slowly and soon I hooked something else. This one really is a fighter, and when I finally landed it, it turned out to be a Cat fish, which weighed 8 pounds, and I caught it on an 8 pound test line. I fought with that fish for over 40 minutes.

This young man is visibly impressed. Anyway this young man went and got the two of us some lunch from a vender who comes through this trailer park on Saturdays and when he got back, I asked him if he wanted to fish, and he says no, because he likes to watch me fish and he will always help me land whatever I catch.

This went on all day. And when this day ended, I had caught fifteen fish. I asked this young man whether he would like to take some of these fish back to where he lived, and he says he would. I then asked where he lived, and he says he and his Mom live in a small trailer in the back of this trailer park. He says his Mom helps some of the other women clean their trailers every day. That is the way we live. And in doing this we do not have to pay any rent to park our trailer. Actually he says, he and his Mom were hitch hiking two years back, and the owner of this park came along and asked if we needed a ride, so we accepted.

Anyway they began discussing our situation, and it was then decided that we would live in this small trailer free of charge, if my Mom would help any of the women who needed help around their trailers. We don't pay any rent or other fees, because the owner of this park does that. I asked if he goes to school, and he says he does not, because his mother cannot afford to send him to a school. I asked if he can read and he says he cannot do that either.

So I asked, would you like to learn to read, and he says he would, but how. I said, I will teach you, and or my wife will teach you. We will teach you how to read and write. Don't tell your Mother just yet though, because I think you would like to surprise her with your talents. He smiles and I then tell him where I am parked, and I say come to my trailer tomorrow morning and we will begin these lessons.

Sunday Morning May 4th 1968. This young mans name is Tab Lock. He shows up at my trailer at 9:00 AM and we sit outside under my Awning at the Picnic table and I begin to teach him how to write the letters beginning with A − all the way to Z …By the end of this day he has written each of them down in his own hand writing. I say you have done very well this day. Now tomorrow, my wife will teach you how to use these letters, by teaching you how to make words out of them, and learning to pronounce each of them, and then learning what each word means.

When lunchtime came, Peg had made something for all of us to eat, and she asked how is he doing, and I tell her he is doing fine. That probably by the end of this week, if he learns from you like he has learned from me, he should be reading sentences. So when Monday came, Tab was waiting outside of our trailer when I went off to work. He seemed a bit disappointed at first, but then you came out side of the trailer and he seemed to change some. I could not put my finger on it, but something changed in him. Maybe it was the fact that you did not have any teeth in your mouth.

I called you at noon to see how Tab was doing, and you

told me he had gone home. That he felt intimidated with you teaching him. I told you to go to where he and his mother lived, and tell Tab to come to our trailer this evening, as I need him to help me do some things.

Don't tell his Mother that Tab is trying to learn to read and write, because he wants to surprise her with that talent. So that evening about 6:00 PM Tab came and we again sat at the picnic table. I asked him why he left and went home this morning after I left for my own work. He says my wife reminds him of his real mother, because she looks exactly like her. His real mother abused him in ways you don't want to know about.

That the mother he now has is gentle and nice to him. I asked is she related to you in any way, and he says no. I did not ask any further questions at that time, because I figured he would tell me when he felt more secure with me. But I had you come outside to help with teaching him, so he would see that you would not abuse him.

After about an hour, he relaxed a lot and he began to listen to you more and more, and by the end of this evening, he told you that he would return tomorrow morning and he now thinks he can learn what he needs to learn from someone who looks a lot like his real mother. But you are not like her, and after he saw that he was in no danger, then he decided that you are all right. So on Tuesday Tab returned to our trailer and when I called at noon, you told me that Tab is real smart and has already learned how to say fifteen words and knows what they all mean.

I told you to keep in mind the words you have taught him, because by the end of this week, I want to give him a test, to see how much of what he has supposedly learned, he still remembers.

All of the while we are in this trailer Park, we will teach Tab as much as he is able to learn. You see I remember when I was much younger, and how much I wanted to learn and when I was first taken to go to school, and my first grade teacher told my Father that I should be placed in the third grade, and how he prevented that from happening until I was ten years old, and then when I went to live with another man and went to the Catholic school, they put me in the 8th grade when I was ten years old, and when I eventually returned back to South Dakota, I was ready to begin my Senior year of high school and the school in Lily would not recognize a Private Catholic School's records, and again I was prevented from graduating from high school.

So because I purchased my own farm by that time, which was some distance from Lily, so at that new school, I presented my records, of which they accepted, and I ended up graduating from that school when I was fourteen years old.

So I think I know how this young man feels, and I just hope he is as smart as he thinks he is. So each day as I am just leaving to go to my own place of employment, Tab shows up at our trailer, and you teach him as much as he is able to absorb. When Friday comes, you and I have put together a test for Tab to take, and he has one hour to answer fifty questions.

Some of these questions need a bit of explanation, so he will need to write out those answers. When I come home on that Friday, you tell me that Tab got every question correct on that test.

And you had given him an A+, which meant to him that he

was retaining what he had learned for that week. You tell me that the more he learns, the more he needs to learn. Because that is what he has told you.

Let me tell you, I know how this young man feels, because that is the way I felt when I was even younger than he now is. By the way, Tab is 11 years old. He told me that he had not told you how old he is, but he felt that he needed to tell me because he now feels he may be able to some day to even go to a regular school. But for now, his mother cannot afford to send him.

I tell Tab that Peggy and I will probably be in this trailer park for another six weeks, and if you continue to learn as much as you have learned this week, then because both Peggy and I are qualified Teachers, I will try to get all of what you have learned from us, as accredited Grades and scores, which any school in this Nation will accept, and any School in this State will accept, so you will be able to get into High School. But let us not get too far ahead of ourselves.

Later that night I tell you that I am thinking of sending Tab to a private Boarding school, of which I will pay for, so he will be able to get into College if he continues to improve his grades. It will not be easy, but I know he will want to try Convincing his Mother, or at least the person who claims to be his mother now.

We need to find out some more information about her. And also about his real mother. So I will have a friend of mine investigate both of these women, to see how much we can find out about both of them. I suppose it will all depend on what we find out about both of them.

That evening I ask Tab about his real mother. What her real name is, at least what he knows about her. And what about the person you now live with. Tab is not stupid, because he asks will I investigate both of them and I say, is that what you want me to do. He says yes.

He is not certain what his real mothers name is, but he gives me what he knows about her just the same. And he tells me what he knows about this woman he is living with now.

I ask Tab, how many mothers have you had in the past six years, and he says four. I ask can you tell me about each of them, and he says he will tell me what he remembers. I say you are a very brave guy. He smiles and says maybe, but whatever I come up with will most likely help him get into a better situation than he now is in.

So later that evening I call a friend of mine in St Louis and give him all of the information about all of the women I know about and why I need this information. He asks, do I really know what I am doing, and I say that is what my wife asked of me. And my answer is, I don't know, but I think I am doing the correct thing, because some of this reminds me of my own childhood.

My friend says it will take him about a week, and he will come to where I am now located to give me his report. I ask, do you think Tab should be here to listen to that report, and he says because it will affect him, yes that is probably a good idea. I say I will ask Tab if he wants to be with Peg and I when you bring your report to me. The call then ends.

In the meantime, Tab continues to come to our trailer and he is learning faster and faster, because he is now reading more like a person who is in high school. Each test we give him, we establish on the back of that test paper at what level this person is now at.

Clement

May 24th 1968

Dear Peg

We have been teaching Tab for three complete weeks now, and he is already advanced into his junior year of High School. Because I teach him on weekends also, he has grown up a lot too. I see the woman he is living with every so often, because she sometimes is a few trailers away helping Midge Lewis clean her doublewide trailer, which also has an upstairs in it too.

After we taught Tab for two weeks, he finally told his mother what he was doing. She at first became kind of scared, so I asked her why she was scared, so she looked at Tab and said, because she has to tell me something that even Tab does not know about himself, at least she does not think he knows.

Tab then says, you mean that you really kidnapped me from one of my Mothers, and she says yes. Tab says he has known this from the very beginning. But before you he says he had had three mothers. But you will be my last mother, because his mother before you had done the same thing like all of the rest had done and that is they all molested me sexually, and you have never done that, and never will, because you are a good mother.

And Mr. Royal here is not going to have you arrested for being what all of the others should have been, which is a great Mother.

Tab then told this Mother, that he knows as much as anyone knows about anyone, but how that came about is not all that important. Because of Mr. Royal's influence, you are now my real Mother, and Tab says he has the document to prove it, and he hands this woman an Adoption document that has been signed by his Lawyer and Mr. Royal and by myself, stating that you are my real Mother. And no one can ever change that. Tab then goes and hugs his new Mom.

Because of names I will not tell the reader what Tab's real name was and now is, nor this woman, as to who she was and now is, because when this Adoption took place they took on totally different names, and that is what Tab wanted to tell this woman who is now to be considered his real Mother. I created the name of Tab, because writing this book may save some other young man out in this world from going though what Tab went through.

Tab says that Mr. Royal is sending me to a Private College, which is totally paid for by him, and I will live on Campus for however long it will take me to complete 60 Credits, so I can graduate at the top of my class. And when that happens, Mr. Royal and a Lawyer in St Louis, will come and get you, and take you to this graduating class, and then I will be able to get a position supporting you and me, and we can then live a better life than how we have been living. Because of Mr. Royal and the influence he has in various industries, he will help me find that position wherein we will be able to move into a real house wherever we want to live. I suppose it will all depend on where my position is located.

But Mr. Royal's Lawyer will help in that endeavor also. And I am now 12 years old. You see Mother, Mr. Royal had a childhood similar to my own, and he recognized that in me, and now because of him and his wife Peggy, of which you have already met, I am now ready to go to College and it only took me seven weeks to do all of this. So as they say, the Sky is the limit.

Tab then comes and hugs me. Tab says, it is a shame that Mr. Royal is married, because you and him would make a great set of parents. Mr. Royal has two daughters that he too adopted, and they live with their Grandmother in the St Louis area. One day I will meet them I think. At least I hope I will. I then leave the two of them and they walk back to their trailer. And I go to mine.

Because you and I were teaching Tab what he needed to know, instead of moving my trailer to a different location, I instead went to the other towns and stayed in a motel for a few days until I finished Auditing all of the railroad stations in each village, and when the weekend came I drove back to where I was parked. I felt this was a better idea than moving more often, and besides you kept right on teaching Tab what he needed to know so he could get into that college.

The College I got him enrolled into, he had to take an Entrance Exam, but like all of his other tests, he passed it with flying colors. This college is in the state of Illinois, but it is a private college outside of a great city. How far out I cannot say.

In all of the 28 stations I Audited including the Island of Rock Island, I did not find any improprieties. Not even one. When I sent my report to Jack Perkins he is well pleased with how I handled everything. Especially the Island in the middle of the Mississippi river. Because that is a Federal facility, that is considered a Special Assignment, and with any special assignments, I get extra money in even accepting them. And because I am only a few days away from beginning my vacation of four months, whereat we will end up going to California. I decided that I would bring my girls to this location, rather than take this trailer to where they live, because I wanted both of them to meet Tab.

Tab is a lot like me, because he stands 6 feet 1 inches tall, and he is as strong as any grown man. He reminded me of myself when I was his age. He like me grew up almost over night, because of being molested by three of his so-called Mothers. He was molested at a much earlier age, but it affects any person in the same way, because you are learning about things that you normally would not learn until you were at least sixteen years old, but when someone molests you at such an early age, you grow old overnight and it will affect you for the rest of your life.

Clement

June 23rd 1968

Dear Peg;

Beginning our Vacation of four months

Actually since I had finished my Auditing midweek of last week, I decided to go and get my Daughters and bring them to where I was parked near this small town in Illinois. Tab wanted to meet them, and he only had a week also, because he was going to go to Summer College, rather than wait until the fall schedule. And because this College was not all that far away from where we were now parked,

I decided that my girls and I would take him to this College and get him settled in his Dormitory room. I had already taken him to get him registered and the Dean of this College was very surprised at how young Tab really is, but I told this Dean, don't let his youth fool you, because he will go through the 60 courses in less than three years, and this Dean says if he can do that then he will be the youngest member of this college to ever do that.

I then told this Dean, consider this, nine weeks back, this young man could not even read or write his own name, and now since he passed your very difficult entrance exam, he is now going to be going to your college, so move over and watch out, because I want him to be allowed to progress as fast as he wants to progress.

If I find that you ever try to hold him back, I will have your job, because I myself have more education then you do. So let him progress as fast as he can absorb whatever he can absorb.

Mary Beth says you should never talk to any Dean of any college like you talked to him. I told her that if I wanted his Job, I could take it away from him. Or I could at least have him fired.

Mary Beth says you will not gain any favors in that way. I say I am not asking for any favors, but I am insisting that they let Tab advance as fast as he is able to advance. Tab says to not worry, because he will get through all of these courses in less than three years. He says one day I will pay you back all of the money you have or will spend on me. I say, just do what you want to do, and that is get through all of these courses and that will be thanks enough for me.

Tab says he will one day find a way to repay me. I tell him that you do not owe me a penny, because you know the best places to fish, more than any person I have ever known.

He says he just listened to what all of the other fishermen said about all of those lakes. And you seemed to need the information that I told you at that time. We sure did catch a lot of fish, didn't we, and we sure had some great meals.

Tab says his mother did not know how to cook these fish, so he ended up giving all of what I gave to him to all of the Cats in the Park.

After all of this time, you finally got around to telling me about what you did with all of the fish I gave you. I actually knew that, but I will not tell you how I found out, because you would not believe me.

Tab says you mean about you actually talking to your cats and all of the other cats in that park, he says he has always known that about me. Which is why you probably knew what I needed to do, because you actually read my own thoughts. Well, now we are getting somewhere. What else do you think you know about me? He says he will never tell anyone but me.

I said to Tab, you know that you are like a Son to me, and Tab says he does know that. I said that I have told you of the things I can tell you about myself. There are some things about Peggy that you don't need to know.

She appears that since you have come into our lives, she has changed a lot, and I welcome that change. You and her seem to get along great, even though she looks like one of the women you lived with for awhile. Tab says he was just a little scared at first, but Peggy has treated me like I have always wanted to be treated, and that is with respect and with Love.

Tab further says he is not certain whether Peggy really loves him, but he says he knows that she really likes me, because sometimes during the day, when we would break for lunch, she would explain to me what she was making.

Tab says none of his mothers could ever cook a decent meal, but your Peggy seems to know quite a lot about various meal preparations. I smile and say, she learned from me, and Tab says, that does not really surprise him. He asks what else can I do, and I tell him, you know all of those trousers you left with Peggy, for her to mend.

She did not mend them because I mended all of them. And I also made you some new trousers too, even though I let Peggy take credit for doing them for you. But that is enough knowledge from me for now.

You are now on your way to becoming anything you want to be, so keep up the good work here in college and when you graduate, I will be here when that happens.

If you need any additional money, you let me know and I will send you some. Tab says that probably won't happen, because he plans to work whenever he can find some time. I tell him you do not have to work while you are going to this college, and as far as paying me back, forget that also, because for you to graduate from this college will be enough gratitude from you to me.

I want you to have a good life, one that will be much better than how you initially began your life. You have done wonders since we have known each other, and I am not sorry that I helped you get your start in life. What you have done thus far is more than any man could hope would happen. Study hard and do what I did when I went to college, and that was to get through all of the courses in the shortest time that you can.

Otherwise learn as much as you can while here, and then go out and live your life with the same tenacity that I have done. Knowing you, you will probably go to more college's to gain more knowledge, so you will have something to fall back on. I asked Tab, do you know what you will Major in, and he says he is not certain yet. But he will let me know when he knows. I tell him, what ever it will be, you will do okay in it.

I then put my arms around him and held him close for about a half minute and then I said we have to go. By the way, what do you think of my girls? He says Mary Beth is not an easy person to get to know, but Martha, I like her and she likes me. I said it would pass. Tab says that Martha says she is going to write to me and keep me informed as to what is going on in her and your lives. Martha then hugged Tab, and Mary Beth just says goodbye, and then we left.

Thinking about him, I know he at first will have a bit of a hard time, but he has been alone for so long, that he will adjust quickly. Later that day when I had a few minutes, I wrote a short letter to his Mom, telling her that Tab will be okay, and he will try to get back to you every so often. Even though he really did not say that, I know that Tab will try to go and see his new Mom as often as he can, which most likely won't be too often.

Tab is in reality a lot like me, so thinking about home is something he will not dwell on. Mostly because his home is not all that great. It's interesting that I never once mentioned how he lived or what kind of a junky place his mother kept that small trailer in. She may have done housework for other women, but her own place looked like a pigsty.

But I never ever mentioned that to Tab and he never brought it up either. We just closed our eyes to how his Mom kept her place. So the likelihood of Tab returning back to that place, maybe once a year would be the most often he will do that.

Peg and I and the girls finally got on our way down to my sisters place in southern Missouri about ten am. It was probably about a six to seven hour drive, and pulling our trailer, I am quite sure it will take that long. But of course I have pulled this trailer all around this country anyway, and I usually can average about 55 miles per hour, no matter where I go.

So about 5:00 PM I pulled up in front of my oldest sisters

farmhouse. I really had not told her that we were coming, so it was a big surprise. I had written her telling her that sometime in June we would be dropping by, but I did not give her an exact date. It took me about seven hours to drive from somewhere in Illinois to where she lives.

I told everyone while we drove, that we came from a town near Chicago. I am not ashamed of what Peg and I did for Tab, it is just that they don't know anything about him. Because I never mentioned him to anyone, except my Lawyer in St Louis. And you all know the reason for that was, which was to get him adopted by the woman he has lived with for the last four years. Anyway we stayed overnight and all the next day and that night and then we got on our way again on June 26th 1968.

We drove back to within a few miles of Springfield, Missouri, where we picked up highway sixty, which was not an often-used highway, but it did avoid most of the large cities. And we did see a lot of very interesting country. We eventually did meet up with highway sixty-six though, which will take us almost straight west for many miles. That night we stopped in Amarillo, Texas. There are some things to see, but my girls said they were tired, so after we ate in a Restaurant; we went back to our trailer.

I fed my Cats their evening meal before we went to eat, so I knew they would be finished by the time we all returned. I just parked in one of the Public parks where there were Electrical hookups, but nothing else.

When we returned to our trailer, after I looked on every side, I did discover that one of the Jacks had been removed from one corner, but whoever did this left the jack. In any event, I do have extra jacks anyway. Probably just some Kids, trying to get into trouble.

I do have an alarm, but I did not think anyone would harm the trailer. So I then turned it on, so all of my outside lights would come on and if anyone else even came within ten feet of this trailer or my vehicle, an alarm would sound that will wake up everyone within two hundred feet of us.

I asked Tai who came by the trailer, and he told me two young male kids, and they loosened one of the corner jacks. They would have done more, but you all came back and they ran away. They came by about forty minutes after you all left.

Now since we were only gone for about 45 minutes, it was lucky we returned when we did. About a half hour before the sun came up, the alarms went off, and I would be willing to bet it scared the hell out of most everyone, including everyone inside of the trailer except myself.

I knew immediately what has happened, but I just went outside carrying one of my guns, and what I saw, was three young girls, who had come within ten feet of my vehicle and then the alarm went off and about a hundred feet away were three young fella's laughing as hard as they could, but when I raised my weapon, they all ran as fast as they could.

Of course these three girls were so scared they froze where they were standing. And in another minute, a Policeman arrived, and he thought I had maybe done something to these girls, but Peggy came out of the trailer and told this officer, that these three girls, had intended to do something to our trailer, because they had been baited by three young boys, probably on a Dare, but my husbands alarms scared them so much, they just froze.

This officer asked me if I had a license for that weapon, and when I showed him my identification, he apologized and took these three girls into custody, and off he drove.

The gun license that I have always carried, is a Federal License, because of when I went to school in Washington, DC for two months back in last year, and it was suggested that I apply for this kind of license, because of where I would sometimes be working, especially when I was working near the Docks, or in some other locations, that were near very terrible neighborhoods where the railroads seemed to always have their Depot's, or places of keeping all of their ledgers and other records, and because of my friendship with Dick Tracy and Perry Mason, who both carry similar weapons and license's, and they vouched for me when I applied for this license, and that is probably why I was granted this license.

So whenever any Police officer asks me, do I have a License for that Weapon, and I always show them that identification, they don't ask any other questions.

In reality, I am a special agent for the Association of Special Auditors, because in my field of Auditing, I have come across a lot of different kinds of Crooks, and an inside man in this Industry, or what is commonly called an Undercover person in any field is, it most often yields many truths in the field of Operating a large company. This was an idea of mine, and in fact when I was in Washington, DC, I not only trained with other Agents in similar fields, but in my field, it would mean that I would be coming in direct contact with more of the intermediate area's of Personnel which a lot of Executives don't even know about in any given company

Thereby solving many of the internal crimes in any given company. I would not get any medals for doing this work, but I would be able to know that me being there at any given time, meant a lot to many different persons, and especially the Interstate Commerce Commission and the Association of American Railroads and the FBI itself.

The other thing about me is that I am a man who cannot be bought by anyone. Which also means that no amount of threats or attempts to thwart my activities would cause me to stop investigating whomever I was investigating.

Why do you think I had so much influence with all of the FBI agents in all of the different cities that I went to? An auditor with a specific company or organization would not normally have that kind of influence with the FBI.

It makes sense that I was a Special Agent for some special organization. And in reality I was a special Agent for more than ten years, even including before I went to work for the Western Weighing and Inspection Bureau, but being in that position gave me opportunities wherein I could get chances to get inside of not only most railroad companies, but also inside of a lot of private companies, because of all of the graft I found while doing my auditing job.

I can now tell you this, because I do not plan to return back to Milwaukee, Wisconsin, because I will also resign from the Association of Special Auditors, effective on October 10, 1968.

Clement

June 28th 1968

Dear Wife;

We left Amarillo the next morning and continued to drive until we all got hungry, and then I found a place where I could pull off the highway, and I went back into the trailer and made ourselves a meal. And after we ate that meal, we then all got back into the automobile and off we went once again.

After that first day out of Texas, I made sure that I had made enough sandwiches to last us an entire day of driving. It actually took us two days to drive from Amarillo, Texas to the North Rim of the Grand Canyon. Every so often I had to stop, so my girls could use the commode in the bathroom, and every 300 to 400 miles I stopped at a gas station and topped off my vehicles gas tank.

And if we saw some place where we wanted to do some sight seeing, we took many side trips to do that also. One of those side trips was to go to the North Rim of the Grand Canyon, and another was to walk through an old Ghost Town.

On one of those walk through adventures we came upon a Rattle snake, but because I can talk to most any creature, and I did talk to it, it told me that it would not harm any of us, if we did not try to do anything to it.

I did have a weapon with me, but I did not have to use it. On another walk through at a Ghost town, while I was investigating one of the rooms in a Hotel, I came across a bag of what looked like Gold Dust, so I put it in my pocket and took it with me. It was not in any open area, but was attached to the underside of a Bureau Drawer.

Probably one of the last residents, who had stayed in that room, had either forgot it or had been killed for it. And Martha found some shells for what looked like an old 45 pistol. Mary Beth found some Jewelry on another walk through, of which she took with us. Whatever each of us found, we took it with us, and that person kept what they found.

At the Grand Canyon, I took a Donkey ride down to the bottom of the Canyon, which took most of one day, and then to get back to the Canyon Lodge, where we stayed for two days and nights, I had a Helicopter Pilot fly me back to the top of the north rim.

We actually flew around in the canyon for a while, but that was limited because it would soon be dark, and he wanted to return to where he lived on a Ranch at the bottom of the Canyon.

At the Lodge a singing group was performing, called The Sons of the Pioneers, and I had the opportunity to meet all of them, and in fact did sing a few songs with them, and that was a lot of fun for me.

Peggy asked me how can I always get myself so familiar with a particular group of singers, and I say I guess I have that kind of a personality or a way about myself. Anyway when we left the North Rim of the Grand Canyon, we had to backtrack for about a hundred miles, so since we were within fifty miles of what is called the Four Corners, which is where the states of

Colorado, New Mexico, Utah and Arizona come together, we did go there, and we took Photographs of each of us showing where we had put one of our feet, that touched all four corners of each of these states. I think that excited my girls more than anything, with the exception of being at the North Rim of the Grand Canyon.

My car was beginning to heat up some, and I wanted to get out of these mountains. Because I feared that probably because of the car had been overheated several times, that I might have burst a head gasket or something wherein it would cause my vehicle to heat up unnecessarily.

Clement

July 2nd 1968

Dear Wife;

So from the four corners, it was mostly downhill, we headed for Needles California. We left the four corners around midnight, so I could drive during the night time hours, which are much cooler than driving during the day time hours.

We pulled into Needles around 12:30 PM on this day and the temperature is according to a thermometer that is in a shady area, 119 degrees.

On the Northwest corner of that village, there is a Trailer Park, and after I got my trailer parked in the space that I had rented, and had plugged into AC Electricity, my big air conditioner came on and even though I do have a smaller air conditioner that runs from battery power while we drive, the temperature had gotten up to 87 degrees inside of the trailer.

And probably the real reason it did that was because the back window had been opened, but the blind had been mostly closed, so I did not spot it when I checked the trailer at the north rim of the Grand Canyon, and Mary Beth figured this is what would happen when she opened this window.

So when the small Air conditioner came on, it was like making the outside colder, rather then making the inside colder. What I will do to her for doing this, I am still uncertain, but I will do something. I fear she is going to be further problematic in my future.

My girls and Peg got into their bathing suits and went swimming at the park pool. Where they remained until after it had gotten dark outside. I did not go to that pool, because I wanted to make sure that my cats are okay. They had been panting for some time, and I worried about them doing that, but they seemed to handle the heat better than any of us did. We remained in Needles California for that night and another day, and then on that night we left Needles and drove towards Escolon, California, where another of my sisters lived with her husband and a couple of his children and two of her own children.

We arrived at her house about 4:00 PM that same afternoon, and again my vehicle was heating up more than I wanted it to, so I had to make several stops every so often so I could let the engine cool down, and then I could refill the radiator with water again. It was pointless to put any anti-freeze fluid in the radiator, because it would just boil out eventually.

Anti-freeze boils at a higher temperature than plain water, but I figured when we eventually reached our destination of Huntington Beach, I would take it to a Ford Dealership, and because my vehicle is still under warrantee that they may just fix it for nothing. Anyway we left her house shortly after 7:00 PM.

I told her I wanted to go over the Grapevine when it was dark outside, because my vehicle is heating up too much and I want to get into Northwest Los Angeles County by the time the sun is beginning to come up in the east.

I will probably have to stop at every water stop going over the Grapevine anyway. I drove to a Standard Stations Gas

Station in Fresno, and I asked if I could park to one side of your lot until about 10:00 PM, and the attendant says okay.

We all got into the trailer and went to sleep for three hours. When we all woke up, I pulled my car to a gas pump, and topped of my gas tank once again. I made sure all of my extra water containers were full and then we began our journey once again.

As I had predicted, I stopped at every water stop going over the grapevine and about 6:00 AM on July 4th, we stopped at the first Gas station after coming off of the mountain from the grapevine and when I stopped, my car was humming like it was tuning up an Orchestra.

The attendant told me to not shut off my engine, but just let it idle for a while. I raised the hood of my vehicle, and the attendant sprayed water on the radiator and the engine for ten minutes. Then with leather gloves on, I loosened the Radiator Cap one notch and let it boil and steam some more while I again sprayed water on that radiator and engine. When it finally stopped steaming, I then shut the motor down, and it only steamed for about two minutes. I let it set that way for about an hour. In the meantime, I allowed everyone to get out of the car and walk around some.

There was a Denny's Restaurant about a block away, and the attendant says to go have something to eat, and he will keep an eye on my rig. Of course I locked the door to my trailer, because my Cats are still inside of it.

We went and had some breakfast and an hour later we returned. I then filled up the Radiator with water again, and got into the car and turned the key and the engine started immediately.

I then drove to where I could put some more gasoline in my gas tank and filled up all of my water containers, and then after I got everyone back inside of my vehicle, after I paid the attendant what I owed him plus ten dollars extra, of which he did not want to take, but I insisted that he do so, we then got under way once again.

By that time the traffic had subsided considerably and once I got on the San Diego Freeway, which is the 405 freeway, it only took us about an hour to get to our ultimate destination, which is Huntington Beach, where the trailer park that I was scheduled to arrive at on this day.

The space that had been assigned to me was actually a doublewide space, meaning I had a place where I could park my vehicle beside the trailer, rather then in front of it. On the east side of that space are two Weeping Willow trees, of which are not native to southern California, and on the west side was a place where I could park my automobile. And on that side also was a Mountain Ash tree, which had been trimmed high so I could park my vehicle under the tree's branches. I must admit, that we had been very lucky to get such a double space for the price of just one space.

The reason was, because the space west of ours did not have a hookup for waste disposal or hookups for water or electricity. It was just a space where someone could only park a trailer, but without any of the niceties. I told everyone that this park has its own swimming pool, so if that is where you all would like to go, then get into your swimming gear and do so.

Here is a map of where it is located. It also tells you some information about the rules around that pool, and in an emergency, how to get some outside help to get them to come to where you are.

I will come there also after I check on how much mail has arrived from wherever. And ladies, try to stay out of trouble. After that I fed my cats and waited with them for a while. I checked the outside Phone line and hooked it up to my trailer.

I made sure all of the connections were tightly in place and my waste tank had been emptied and then I made sure that we were hooked up to the public waste receptacle.

The temperature was just about right inside of the trailer, but the one thing that disturbed me was, all of the windows were open. I do have screens on every window, and they are fastened in two ways. They are fastened on the inside and also on the outside too.

The screws on the outside are of a special kind where not any kind of regular screwdriver could be used to loosen these screws. It took a special tool, that only Martha and I knew where it was located. And the screen was a special steel screen, which I had invented, for situations such as these, and no person could break out this screen from the inside of this trailer, using their hands, because it would tear their hands to shreds.

I knew that Martha would not open any windows because the small air conditioner always kept the inside fairly cool, but Mary Beth would open these windows, because she always seems to do what I don't want her to do. You see, she hates any kind of Authority.

She always has. Margaret always had problems with her taking orders from her. And Mary Beth always completely ignored Joe. It always made him furiously angry.

She seemed to always get a laugh out of doing that. Martha says that one day that stubbornness will get her in serious trouble. Anyway I decided I would ask her when she returned this evening, whenever that would be. I then went to the park office and got all of my mail, and there was an entire box of it.

This box was the standard size box of being 12 inches by 16 inches. And it was full to the top with all kinds of mail. I also put down a deposit and got some change of address cards, and the phone number that had been assigned to me.

I took everything back to the trailer and placed this box in a cabinet of which I had the only key. I placed that key in the secret compartment that was above the Stove, and then I got into my swimming trunks and after I locked the trailer door, I walked to where the swimming pool is located.

Around this pool is a high fence, which is about 12 feet high. This fence is about thirty feet from any part of this pool, and there are chaises lounges placed in various places whereon anyone can lay on them. The owners of this park provide them.

There is a Barbeque that is permanently built on one end of this large lot, and there are some separate small buildings that probably are places where persons can change into their bathing suits or into street clothes.

If you need to use one of these small buildings, you have to rent it, and you have the only key, other that the one the owner has, just in case it might be used for something other than what it is designed for.

There is a public shower where you can shower yourself

with your bathing suit on. No one is allowed to undress while outside of these small buildings.

The gate that surrounds this pool is closed and locked at Midnight, every night. No exceptions. And only residents can use this pool.

If any persons who do not live in this park ever use this pool, they are reported and escorted from the park. And if any resident who knows of such a person and does not report this or these persons, then that person and their entire family are ordered out of this park, and their name and vehicle license and trailer license numbers are reported to every Trailer Park in these United States, and if you got into any of these trailer parks and you are discovered, you will then be arrested, even if you have changed and do not create any more problems in any trailer parks anywhere in this country. The rules are very strict and if any person violates any of these rules, the entire family suffers.

The first thing I asked of Martha and Mary Beth, did you read all of the park rules. Martha said she did and so did Peg, but Mary Beth says she only glanced at them. I picked up those rules, and I placed them in front of her, and I told her to read all of them.

And if you break only one of them, then I will put you on the first plane I can get you on and send you back to Missouri totally alone and without any explanation to anyone. You will have to explain why you had to return back to Missouri alone.

Oh I will explain why you were returned alone, but that explanation will only cause you more problems than you are willing to accept. And you will be grounded for two months.

Meaning the only way you will be able to go anywhere, will be with Margaret and Joe. Not just one of them, but both of them.

Now I know what you think of Joe, and if you think you can handle both of them, forget it, because they have instructions that if you get to the point where you cannot be handled any longer then I will have you sent away to a kind of a Reform School, wherein you will either learn to obey orders or you will end up behind bars until you are 21 years old. The choice is yours. And you know that I do not lay out a bluff that I will not fulfill.

Mary Beth says she hates me. I say you will do as I tell you to do or, this vacation will end very quickly for you. Mary Beth begins to read these rules. As she reads further, I can see the wheels turning in her head, because these rules are giving her all kinds of ideas, and every so often she smiles, like she has just thought of something new to try to pull on me and or probably Martha. But I hope not any of my cats.

Mary Beth hates all of my cats. Martha loves all of them and in fact they all love her too.

So after Mary Beth has apparently read all of these park rules, she says okay, she has read them. I say, just keep them all in mind when you are at this pool. And if you leave this park for any reason, without any of us, then you will be returned back to Missouri alone.

If you did not want to come on this vacation, you should have told me back in Missouri, because I would have made other arrangements for you.

Mary Beth says she wants to go back to Missouri as soon as I can arrange it. Or else she will hitch hike back. I told her tomorrow I will take you up into the mountains where you will have a better chance of catching a ride with someone, and that will be the last time I will see you, until you either get married or some other occasion happens.

She says she will pack a bag tonight, so she will be ready to leave early in the morning. I told everyone that I am going back to the trailer, because I have a lot of mail to go through. I then leave.

Privately I have to make plans by making some phone calls to some friends of mine who live up in the Big Bear Mountains. I will teach Mary Beth a lesson she will never forget. She will end up probably hating me even more, but she will learn a lesson in this venture, at least I hope she does.

I end up making eight phone calls, and when Peg and the girls return around 7:30 PM that evening I am still sorting through all of the mail that was in that box.

In the beginning, I separate the good mail from the junk mail, and then separate the Magazines from the letters. I throw all of the Junk mail in a wastebasket, of which I will put through a Paper Shredder later. I then go through all of the letters and separate my mail from everyone else's, even for the Cats.

Martha has a pile and so does Mary Beth, though I cannot think who would want to write to Mary Beth, because I did not know she even had any friends.

Martha got a lot of mail from a lot of her friends, including a letter from Tab. I will want to know what he tells her. I only glanced at the mail for Mary Beth.

Peg got some mail also. Some from some men, I did not know she even knew any other men lately, or that she had corresponded with any other men. According to what Peg had told me before we left Illinois, she has not had any Liaisons with other men for at least eight months

There was a letter from Ken Jenkins, so I put that one aside, and I did not intend to tell her about it. At least for now. I would ask her about him though.

I might steam it open and read it myself; just to find out what has been going on between them. To think that she may have been having conversations with him, and he supposedly raped her at least three times in the past. It seems kind of incredible.

Clement

July 4th 1968

Dear Wife;

Mary Beth's threat to kill all of my cats

While I was sorting through the mail, I had put a Roast in the Oven, along with some vegetables and some potato's. Also inside of the refrigerator I had placed some Pudding, which was made without any sugar. I will not go into how I made this pudding, suffice to say it tasted great.

Everyone always liked Chocolate so that is the flavor I made it in. After Martha had changed into her street clothes, I asked her to break out the collapsible picnic table and all of the chairs, and place them under one of the weeping willow trees.

Mary Beth says she will eat inside, and I told her you would eat where I tell you to eat, or else you will not eat anything at all, but you will still be sitting outside of this trailer while the rest of us eat our evening meal. If necessary I will hand cuff you to the trailer bumper.

Peg asks how can you treat her the way you do? I ask Peg, how does Mary Beth treat you and or Martha or any of the Cats.

Mary Beth says she will kill all of my Cats. I came to my feet with such suddenness that it scared even Martha and especially Mary Beth.

I tell Mary Beth to pack your suitcases immediately,

because you are going back to Missouri tonight. But you will not hitchhike; you will be put on an airplane that will not make any other landings except at Lambert field in St Louis, Missouri.

Your Uncle Homer will meet you at that airport, and he will have his own instructions as to what to do with you. I got on the phone and called LAX and got a non-stop flight all the way to St Louis, Missouri. I had to get a first class ticket, which cost me about three hundred dollars. I also got another first class ticket, but mine was a round trip ticket. Because if I sent her by herself, she may try something desperate while she is traveling on that plane. I did not see any other way to do this. Anyway after she had packed her two bags and a makeup case, I told her to open all of them, because I want to make sure she has everything that she brought with her.

She refused to open them, so I got out from under the floor, a hammer and a large screwdriver. I asked her again and she refused again, so I took the hammer and placed the screwdriver on one of the locks and raised the hammer, and then she says she will open all of them.

I told Mary Beth to sit in the bathroom while I go through all of your suitcases. In the large one I found a thousand dollars in hundred dollar bills, and I put that aside. I also found some of Pegs Jewelry and a pair of Martha's decorated blue jeans.

In the small suitcase, I found five one hundred dollar bills, so I put them aside, and I also found a watch that belonged to Martha. In the makeup case I found three one hundred-dollar bill's, and I put them aside. I then found in that case two complete books of Travelers checks of mine, each containing a thousand dollars.

Then I asked Mary Beth what were you thinking when you took all of these things, that obviously do not belong to you.

She says you seem to always have more than enough money, and she says she wanted to take some of it back with her.

I then told her that I could have you arrested for stealing not just cash money, but these Travelers checks are Federal Travelers checks, which makes it automatically a Federal crime, meaning if you were arrested, you would end up going to a Federal prison, if you were convicted.

I have always treated you with as much respect as you deserve, and even when you did not deserve to be treated with as much respect, as you should have been, I never once caused you any kind of personal physical harm.

You have broken every rule I have ever laid down, and all of my rules were easy to follow, and all you do is laugh at me and at others.

Well, young lady, your laughing days are now completely over. Because what will now happen to you is completely out of my hands, but what will now happen to you will depend totally on what you now do.

You see I will give a personally signed Report to Uncle Homer, and whatever he decides to do with you, will totally depend on how you handle yourself. You will not get any help from me or any other member of this family and you will not get any help from anyone back in Missouri either.

What Homer does with the evidence I provide to him, will depend totally on him and no one else. And as you well know, you have never been able to pull any wool over his eyes.

Now we will load these suitcases in my vehicle and we will leave. I will see all of the rest of you in three days. Martha, I expect you to take care of the Cats while I am gone. Peg I fully expect you to handle yourself like the wife you are supposed to be. If I find out that any other things have happened, well there will be hell to pay. Just as I was about to drive away, I told Peg that she got a letter from Ken Jenkins, but I have not read it yet, and until I do read it, you will not.

I then drove away and in five minutes we were on the San Diego freeway, headed for the airport. I drove my car to the area where someone else parks my car.

A young man with a golf cart was waiting for us and he loaded all of the Luggage onto this cart and Mary Beth and I got on board with her sitting between the driver of this cart and myself, and we were taken to the TWA Terminal, where all of her luggage was checked on board flight 333 to St Louis, Missouri.

We all then went inside and at the TWA ticket counter I paid for all of our tickets and the Red Cap guy tagged Mary Beth's luggage and then the guy with the golf cart took us to Gate # 17, where we immediately boarded our plane.

It had in fact had been waiting for us to get on board, because within two minutes it was being taken out onto the tarmac where it would taxi to where it would then take off. I asked for the head stewardess and when she came to me, I whispered in her ear about Mary Beth.

Mary Beth asked what I had told this stewardess and I said I told her what you had tried to do, so if you try anything on board this plane, the pilot will announce whom you are and what you tried to do. She said, you wouldn't. And I said I would.

Now just sit there and if and when you have to go to the bathroom, an Air Marshall, even into the bathroom itself, will escort you. So either don't drink anything or pee in your pants, because you will not do anything while we are enroute to St Louis.

This will be a four-hour flight, so just relax and go to sleep, because after what you have been through, you must now be kind of sleepy.

For a long time now, I have been wearing a new kind of underpants whereon if necessary, if I need to pee, I can just pee in them. And after all of what has happened, once I begin to calm down some, that is what happened. The absorbent underpants will hold three loads of pee, so if I remain fairly calm and not drink any further liquid, I should be able to get to St Louis without any problems. I had with me, an overnight bag that I just put under my seat, which had some more of these pants and another pair of Jeans in it.

This was a Supper flight, and in two hours they came and asked what we wanted, and I gave them what I wanted and Mary Beth did not say anything. I told them just a Beef Sandwich for my daughter. But nothing to drink. Not even water.

All of the rest of the money I was carrying was in a money belt around my waist. And my wallet I always carried in one of my shirt pockets which had two buttons on it. In the other shirt pocket was my return ticket back to LAX. I knew I could not sleep, even though I was tired, because as soon as I fell asleep, Mary Beth would try to get away from me. Or steal my return ticket.

So since we were in First Class, and I could watch a movie, and I did see a good movie that I could watch, that is what I did. When supper arrived, I placed the Beef Sandwich down beside me in my seat, because Mary Beth appeared to still be asleep. Of course I also knew that she was faking. So I had to remain completely alert, just in case she tried something desperate.

By the time supper was over with, we were still about thirty minutes away from St Louis. I knew that anytime now that Mary Beth would most likely try something desperate. What I am not sure. But something.

Ten minutes later she appeared to wake up and she began yelling at the top of her voice, that she was being kidnapped by me, who I was she did not know, but she was being forced to do terrible things with me, Sexually. Well she really got everyone's attention. The head stewardess came to where we were sitting and soon an Air Marshall arrived and he got Mary Beth quieted down so he could try to make some sense of all of this.

I showed this Marshall my identification and especially the Federal Identification that I always carried. Not the Gun license, but a different identity card, and when he saw that, he just went away and did not ask any more questions.

Mary Beth was totally confused; because she had thought she had made such a ruckus that most anyone would have arrested me by this time. She again began to yell and this time this same Marshall came to where we were sitting, and he told Mary Beth that if she did not be quiet, he would have to take her down where the Baggage is carried and lock her up until we arrived in St Louis. That blew her away.

We were now about ten minutes out of St Louis, and I suggested that she just be quiet, because whatever you do, you will not get the attention that you think you deserve.

You will in fact be taken below where the entire Luggage is stored, where it will be much colder than where we now are located. And you do not have any kind of Jacket with you that you can wear to keep out that cold. You won't die down there, but you will be completely alone. There may be a few dogs or cats down there. But no persons.

She just shrugged her shoulders and appeared to go back to sleep. It was pointless at this juncture, because about two minutes later we began to lose altitude and in a few more minutes, I could see St Louis off to the east about forty miles. We were now passing over probably Wentzville, Missouri, which was about forty miles away from the airport.

Anyway soon I heard the wheels come down and then we were touching down on the runway. Mary Beth did not stir. But I still knew that she was faking sleep, so I just waited until we had completely stopped and then other persons began to get up and because of my predicament, we would be escorted from this plane by the Air Marshall or even Uncle Homer. Mary Beth still did not stir. I did not want to touch her, because she would accuse me of needing to touch her sexually.

After everyone in first class had gone off of the plane, the Air Marshall came and reached out and touched Mary Beth, and then she came completely alive, and accused him of touching her in one of her private places. I just shook my head; because what you are trying to do will not work, so give it up.

Then Uncle Homer was beside us and he showed this

Marshall his identification and I got up and Homer reached out and put handcuffs on Mary Beth's wrists.

I bent down and kissed her on her forehead and then turned my back to her, but before Uncle Homer led Mary Beth away I handed him my report on her. Then Homer led her from this Airplane.

Clement

July 7th 1968

Dear Wife;

I sat and thought what a waste of time and talent I had apparently wasted on Mary Beth. Because she was just as stubborn and aggressively obstinate as she had ever been. What Uncle Homer would do with her, I am not sure. I knew he had taken in other young persons and had somehow made them realize the error of their ways, but I did not have the particulars of any of these cases. His brother Joe, who is my Father in law says he has been very successful in these endeavors, so whatever he will do to Mary Beth, I sincerely hope he succeeds in her case.

I really won't realize how much he succeeded until years later, when I will again see Mary Beth. I went to see Joe and Margaret to fill them in on what had happened, and what I had done in retaliation, because I knew that neither of you would be able to handle her in any successful way, so my only out was to turn her over to Uncle Homer.

I actually stayed with them for a couple of days catching up on what was happening with them. I tried to convince them that what happened was not any of their faults, but Margaret says that maybe she also failed Mary Beth, like she failed Peggy. I told Margaret that you did not fail Peggy, because she failed herself.

What you failed to do was to tell me in the very beginning, because if you had done that then I would not have married her in the Catholic Church and we would now not even be married, because even though I have a signed contract with her, she has still been violating that contract. Will I ever divorce her, I really do not know at this time.

Without me in her life, she would not even have a life, because even though she has threatened you with her possible suicide, she will never do that, because she does not have the guts. She knows how to kill herself, but that will never happen, so forget about that ever happening.

No she will die in her own bed one day and at home with me. I will not kill her because I will not go to jail for any person, not even my own wife. Later that night I caught my flight back to LAX.

On my return flight, it was in the early morning hours when we landed back in Los Angeles. I caught a golf cart ride to where my car was parked. I paid the attendant on duty and then I drove out of that parking lot and home to Huntington Beach and the trailer park. A great weight had been lifted from my shoulders, because I had actually failed with Mary Beth.

Adopting her was a good idea, but she never once applied herself, in the direction of trying to bond with me or anyone else. Martha and I had bonded when she was much younger, because I had really known her real mother and father when they were still alive.

Whether Mary Beth would even turn into a responsible person is still unknown to me or anyone else. I sure wish I knew what Uncle Homer did to make young persons change to the betterment of themselves. I will ask him, but whether he will ever tell me what I am seeking, I do not know. All I knew was that I could not handle Mary Beth any longer, and I knew if I had tried to get beyond the Anger that I felt in her case, whether I could even come to grips with the way she was.

And I still have Peg to deal with. What will she do, now that I know that she and Ken Jenkins have been corresponding with each other?

Because when I opened that letter from him, it plainly said that he has been real glad that she has chosen to write to him, even though he is now married to some other woman. And he actually lives in Plano, Illinois

That he still travels for a living and he even came to see Peg in the trailer for a few hours. I am surprised that Tai had not mentioned anything about him. My girls were not with us at that time yet and that was great, but what did he do to frighten my Cats with. I will find out one way or the other some time in the future.

When I tell Peg that I actually read his letter, she will be very mad but if she fully expects to further this relationship, then something drastic will happen between her and I.

Which will most likely be me threatening to divorce her. Now if she cannot handle that then hopefully she will stop corresponding with him or any other man. I fear that I have not heard the last of all of this, Contract or no contract.

I think the only thing that will scare Peg from continuing to correspond with this man will be if I take all of her money from her, and leave her penniless and completely alone.

Because I will take Martha and the Cats and we will move

to some other location where we can start all over again with a different life, while I look for another woman to love.

The thoughts that flowed through my head on my return trip from LAX to Huntington Beach were many and a little disturbing.

My vehicle was now beginning to miss, and it sounded like it was only hitting on four spark plugs, so I must take it to a Ford Dealer and have it looked at very soon. Maybe tomorrow. By the time I got to where my trailer was parked, Martha was the only one that was up at this early hour of this morning.

She had already fed the Cats. I asked her if she would take a walk with me, and that is what we did. I asked her if she knew anything about Peg meeting with some other man, and she says she does, but that person had threatened all of the Cats, and Peg told her to not say anything to me about it.

She was not with Peg and I at that time, but Tai had actually told her. She says she had not promised Peg that she would not tell me, but that she would not mention it until we were somewhere in California.

Well, we are now somewhere in southern California and she is now telling me that Tai told her that this man who's name is Ken something, told Tai and his brood that if there was any way to tell me that he had even been with Peg and he had actually had sex with her on the day he was there, that he would come back and shoot all of them.

Martha says it was when you were in Keokuk for that one day. It was apparently on the day that Tab could not come to the trailer, of which Martha says was instigated by Peg, so she could have sex with this man.

Tab was near the end of his studies anyway so it was not a

problem for him. But Tab says he passed by our trailer that day and he did see this man and his vehicle, and in fact he wrote down his license number and here it is, and Martha handed me a piece of paper. I tell Martha that I will pass this on to her uncle Homer in St Louis who will put out the word to watch out for this vehicle, and if he shows up in that city, he will be picked up and charged with Rape, by me. It will just be another criminal for Homer to watch out for.

It seems that I am furnishing him with a lot of leads for possible arrests. I will also let Peg know what I have done. Which may slow her down a little.

Anyway thanks for finally telling me about this, but if there are any next times, I want to know as soon as you can tell me, even if Peg threatens you with bodily harm, because we will just move away from her, and let her fend for herself, in whatever way that she can.

Because I now have complete control over all of her money that she has made and whatever money she will make in her future, while I am still married to her. Because if she continues to send in those crossword puzzles, I will have complete control over what ever she brings in to this household.

Be ready to move away from here, because I will be looking for an apartment in two more days, in fact I will have my Lawyer find one for you and I, where we can move to, and we will leave her in this out of the way place with no money and no way to make it, other than in the way she has been making it.

Now if she wants to try to fight this contract I have with her, then that will also deplete any additional funds she may accumulate. Of course she could try to find a job somewhere, but without any vehicle, how will she get there, and with no funds, how will she live.

I am not concerned whether she will live, because she does not have the nerve to kill herself. Even though she is an Accountant, she is not all that smart regarding business affairs, and I doubt that she would be able to figure out how to purchase an automobile.

It in fact is a simple thing to do, because all she would have to do is look in any newspaper and find what she may want to buy, and have the Salesman drive the vehicle she wanted to buy to where she lives, wherein she could accompany that person back where he works, where she could write that person a check for the total amount of the price of that vehicle. Then drive it back to where she is now living.

Since I actually rented the space where this trailer is parked, that means that I am the responsible person who would have to pay for that space and since all of the hook-ups are also in my name, makes me responsible for that also. Peg has always had a lot of trouble getting around, even though she did find her way from St Louis to Little Rock, Arkansas to Kansas City, Missouri to South Dakota. So if she really puts her mind to finding her way around Southern California, she could do it, but it would scare the wits out of her. And she would probably get lost, but she knows enough to ask various persons so as to find her way back to where she lives.

Clement

July 8th 1968

Dear Wife;

Getting my car fixed

On this day I took my car to Wilson Ford Dealership, on Beach Boulevard in Anaheim, and I got there about 7:00 AM. I had not called to make any kind of appointment, but just arrived there as early in the morning when I knew they would probably open their doors. And I was correct in my assumption. Martha actually went with me.

We left a note for Peg, just in case she might worry to see that Martha was not in the trailer. Anyway when I told them what had been happening with my vehicle, they drove it into their shop and said for me to either go home or I could possibly wait for it, but it would likely be later this afternoon before it would be fixed. I told them that when they found out what was wrong with it, to just fix it.

I gave them the documents I had on the Guarantee on that vehicle. Then Martha and myself walked to a Denny's Restaurant, which was a block away from this dealership, where we ordered breakfast. I was really very hungry, because I ordered three pancakes and six pieces of bacon and an order of hash brown potatoes and a pot of decaffeinated coffee. Martha says make that two orders, and I thought to myself, that she is just like me. I smiled and she smiled too.

I asked how are you doing with communicating with various other creatures. I told her since she was about two years old, when you kept telling me that you had talked to a Robin and it was telling you how it was able to hear the worms in the ground, so it could pull them out of the ground.

She says she remembers when she told me this, but she did not realize that I had really heard her. I then told her that I have always listened to you, even when your real parents told me to not listen to what you sometimes talked about.

Because you remind me of myself, when I was that same age and no one would listen to me, until one day when Sister Maryann was listening to me talk to all of these other creatures and they were doing what I asked them to do, she then realized that I really could communicate with most any creature.

It was a turning point in my life, because I had never been a lonely child, because of that ability to talk to any creature. So having the abilities that we do have is something that is not very common with all of the other persons in this world.

You see, I believe that you and I were meant to be with each other. And how it came about, we had no control in those events.

God did not cause that accident to happen. A drunk driver caused that accident to happen, and God just did not stop it, because he knew that you would be well taken care of, just like all of your brothers would be well taken care of by all of the other folks that came forward to adopt them.

You are where you were supposed to be, which is with me as your father. Peg will never be your mother though, so forget about that ever happening. She is not the Motherly type, and she never will be. No matter what she may try to convince you that she could become. She is too cold to be any kind of parent.

She only loves herself. She has never even loved me. Saying that you love someone does not make it to be true. It just means that is a way to possibly to try to control that someone, but I don't believe that she loves me and she never really did either.

When she came in contact with me, she saw a way to get away from the kind of life she was beginning to lead, and she may have even figured that I would be the kind of person who would forgive her for all of her strange ways, and maybe I would even be able to cure her of the insecurities that she has always felt. And I still may be able to do that, but it will take a lot more time.

Whether she will continue seeing strange men is anybody's guess. But for now I have stopped that movement into her life. I told Martha that after we finish eating breakfast, we could go to a movie, because there is a theatre about three blocks north of where we are now sitting. And they do show movies from 10:00 AM until 2:00 AM of the next day. Or else we can just walk around and window shop. Martha says she would just like to walk around and window shop, and maybe buy a few things if she sees something she would like to buy.

I asked Martha, what and where would you like to see, now that we are in southern California. She says whatever you think she would like to see is fine with her, because she never thought she would ever get to California this early in her life.

Martha says it is a shame that Mary Beth did all of those

things against all of us. She wonders whatever got into her mind to steal money and jewelry and clothing from any of the rest of her family.

One of the things I have never told you or Peg is, is when Mary Beth was in that Orphanage she stole all kinds of things from other children. But I thought I could educate her to the point where she might find that need to be ridiculous when she got older, but I guess I was wrong.

I really don't know how long she had been planning what she did, but I am willing to believe that she planned it a long time back, probably even before I even mentioned to the two of you that we were going to go to California for four months.

And I do not know if she stole any jewelry from Margaret, because Margaret has never mentioned it to me. Or whether she has ever stolen things from you before, and if she did, you never felt it necessary to mention it or she most probably threatened you with bodily harm if you ever did tell me. Martha then says, that Mary Beth had stolen a lot of things from her, and yes she did threaten me with bodily harm if I ever told you.

I then said, you see, she has never stopped stealing from persons around her, even her own family. I don't think what you did was necessarily wrong, but was just your own kind of way of protecting yourself, and I cannot attach any blame onto you for doing that.

I had heard from Granddad Joe that his brother Homer has started a kind of Reform Camp, where he takes troubled young persons, and puts them in a kind of a Military situation.

Around this Camp is a high fence that is twenty feet high, with Electricity running through the barbed wire that runs all the way around this Enclosure.

Males are put with other males, and females with other females. And some of the supposed inmates are actually undercover policemen and policewomen who because they look like they are much younger than they really are, who at various times do cause problems amongst the rest of their kind.

If any one person does something wrong, then everyone suffers, so even though all of the rules are laid out right up front, obeying those rules becomes the most uppermost thought in everyone's mind.

And because the implants are the ones who most often cause most of the problems, someone like Mary Beth may think that doing the wrong thing is a good idea so as to satisfy her, not really thinking that anyone else will really suffer the consequences.

She has got to be made to think that there are other persons out there who must also be included in her thoughts. How long this will take is still to be determined. Martha says that seems to be the kind of place that hopefully will cure Mary Beth of whatever problems she has been having, to a point wherein she might just turn out to be a much better person.

I then say that Mary Beth when she was still with her real parents did have serious problems with them, because she was molested by both of them. You see, she was an only child, and when her parents found out they could not have any more children, they kind of went bonkers, and began to molest Mary Beth.

That is probably why she is such a cold fish, and she cannot seem to love anyone that could get close to her. She has never even gotten to where she trusts me, like you do.

I have told her many times, that I have made all of her clothes, because she is the same size as you are, except her breast size is one size smaller than you are. But if I ever touched even one of her breasts, she would yell real loud, where you know that I would never touch one of your breasts unless I was measuring you for some kind of garment.

Martha says that you have always given her a bath since she was a little girl, so if you touch me in any of my private places, means nothing sexually to her, but is just something that happens every so often, not because you do it purposely, but it happens because you are usually helping her in some way.

You are just being the fatherly kind of person you have always been to me. Martha says, do you know that Henry never helped give her a bath. It was only her Mother or yourself.

Martha says that her father always told her that she was more like Mr. Royal, then like him, because she says I even resemble your features, and my mother always told me that I look like your father, but not Henry.

Now what was I to assume by that statement. I have always thought that you were my real father. I always thought that you apparently had sexual relations with my mother, and I was the result of that sex. Since I was the first child born to Elizabeth and Henry, and my mom got pregnant shortly after Henry and her got married, it was assumed that I was Henry's child, until I began to get older, and then my mom always told me that Henry was not your real father.

He is the father of all of my brothers, but not of me. Now what was I to think? Are you my real father? I looked at Martha directly into her eyes and told her that I am your real father. You were never the daughter of Henry.

I had actually met your Mom when I was going to St Louis University, and she was also attending that college, and one night in a moment of passion, we had sex, and that was just a month before she married Henry.

And after they were married, and she ended up getting pregnant, it was always thought that Henry was the father of that baby. When in fact, Henry and your mother only had sex one time, and that was on the same night they had gotten married, but Henry found out that he needed to be given Hormonal shots because his sperm was too weak to produce any children.

I too had a weak sperm, but that was discovered after I had gotten married to Peggy. When I was with Elizabeth, which was two years before I even met Peggy. And because I had been sexually active for those two years prior to meeting her, I guess my sperm had gotten weaker by that time.

That is why it was almost four years later when your first brother was finally born, because it took that long to get Henry built up to where his sperm was strong enough to even produce a child. And also because your Mom began taking certain drugs so she could get pregnant even if Henry's sperm was weak. And because she was on these drugs, when she did get pregnant by Henry, she got pregnant with Twins.

So knowing this, Henry knew he was not the father of you, but he did not know who the father really was. Then when Peg and I got married and we came to St Louis and I saw your Mom on the street one day in downtown St Louis, and she brought me to where Henry worked, which was Country Set Clothing

Manufacturing Company.

And then a few years later Peg went to work for Country Set eventually, and your father was Peg's immediate supervisor.

But before that even happened, Elizabeth asked me to take care of you when she and Henry needed to go to a Convention somewhere in New York City, which I did and you were then about two years old. And they brought you to where Peg and I were living.

And now as Phil Evans would say; you now know the rest of the story. Martha asks, does Peg know, and I said, I don't think so, she may suspect, but she does not know for sure.

I think your mom told her one time that I was the father of you, but since Peg was sleeping around herself, she did not make a big thing of that statement. For fear that I would Divorce her. But of course I still might divorce her. Martha says you would be much better off if you did divorce her, because she has never been a good wife for you and she never will.

One of the things I am going to do, I am going to call my lawyer Moses Lighthouse and tell him we want him to find you and I an apartment. I will also probably mention that I may want him to begin Divorce procedures against Peg, but first the apartment. He knows Los Angeles real well, and he knows the best places to live at this time, so I will leave it completely up to him. The divorce business may come later, after we get moved.

We had finally finished eating our breakfast, and since there was a public telephone inside of Denny's, I placed a call to Moses. After I told my story, he says he will get back to me probably sometime tomorrow afternoon, around 5:00 PM. I told him I would make a point of being in my trailer at that time. I then said to tell Lucy that I still Love her and you too, my brother, and we will see you soon. I then told Martha that he is my Blood Brother, meaning when I was nine years old and he was nineteen, we cut ourselves and let our blood mingle together, and because I am also considered to be a Holy Man, as far as any Indian is concerned, and he is a Lakota Sioux Indian, we are now Blood Brothers.

In fact I was going to suggest that you and Mary Beth do the same thing, which would make you to be Blood Sisters. Martha says she would do it but would Mary Beth. I then said we would have to see how her situation comes out before I can answer that question.

We had actually spent a little over two hours inside of that Denny's Restaurant talking about various things. It's always interesting how time passes quickly when the conversation is most interesting.

Martha then tells me that she is so very happy to finally find out that I am her real Father. She has wondered about that for many years and now that she knows for sure, she says a great load has been lifted from her shoulders. Because whenever Peg and you would argue, it always seemed she was in the thick of that argument. And she knew she always was, but she did not know how to quell the pain it always caused her.

She says she totally understands how children can assume responsibilities that are not there's to take on, because of how she has always felt regarding herself and me.

I tell Martha that no further arguments will happen regarding you and me, because if the subject ever comes up again, I will tell her the truth about you and me. It will just make her rant and rave even more.

You see all of this happened before I even met Peg, so if she tries to make something out of that, then I will know that she is grabbing at straws so she can blame me for whatever happened to her.

Actually I really loved your mother, but I am not the kind of person who would break up any marriage. And knowing that I was only going to be in St Louis for a certain length of time, and I also knew that Elizabeth needed someone who had his feet planted squarely on the ground, so I did not see her after she told me that she was pregnant with my baby.

Why do you think that your middle name is Philippa? Because that is a reminder that you belonged to me. Henry has never liked that name and he so stated his objection, but you know how your Mother was, when she wanted something from Henry, she always got it.

Martha says everything now makes complete sense. Others have questioned her about her middle name, and she always told her teachers and her friends that her Mother's relatives came from Spain, and that name was really her Grandmothers first name.

My Mom always told me that story, but now I know the real story. Martha says she knows that her Mother is looking down from heaven, and smiling, because she now knows that we as Father and Daughter are finally together, forever.

Clement

July 8th 1968

Dear Wife;

There are a lot of small shops on most of the six blocks where Martha and I walked on this day, and even though I saw a lot of things I would like to buy, I always wondered where I would keep it, so I passed them by. Martha saw some things she wanted to buy also, but she only settled on two things, which was some unusual stationery that she says she wanted to write to her friends with. And in one store some special stationery that she says is perfect to write to Tab with.

On that subject, she says she is glad that I helped him, because he is very smart, and if she went back to that part of this country, she and him might even end up getting married, because they really like each other a lot. Martha says that Tab already told her that when she is old enough, that he wants to marry her. I smile but do not say anything in rebuttal. Martha says she knows that is a premature statement, but she cannot help but have good feelings about Tab. He turned out to be a perfect gentleman. He only kissed me twice, but he never tried to do anything else with me. Like touching my breasts or any other place. He says there will be plenty of time to explore me at a later time.

By the time we had done all of our walking and shopping, it was getting close to 4:00 PM, so we walked back to Wilson

Ford, and when we walked in, and the man on duty in the front waiting area, he says my vehicle has been fixed and there is no charge for fixing it. But the one thing he would like to know is, what have I been pulling with this vehicle.

I smiled and then told him that I have pulled a 24-foot Zephyr Travel trailer 24,677 miles all over this country, and I have only owned this trailer for 13 months. This guy says that is amazing. I told him that wherever I went in this trailer, I wrote down every mile, because you see, it was a way for me to spend more time at any location while doing my job. And I have been from Seattle, Washington to New York City, to Houston, Texas to Miami, Florida and everywhere in between.

But now I am giving all of that up, and I am finally going to settle down and live in only one place, but not in that trailer, but either in a house or an apartment. I was then given my car keys, which I reattached onto my key ring, and Martha and I went out and got into my vehicle, and drove away from that place.

On the way home we stopped at a Safeway Grocery store and purchased some more supplies, as I was getting low on whole milk and Yuban Coffee. And a number of other things that are too numerous to mention here. When we got home, Peg was not there, so I figured she was at the pool. After Martha and I put all of the groceries away, I walked over to the office to gather up any mail that may have been delivered today. And again there was quite a lot. I took a paper shopping bag with me so I could put it all in that bag. When I got back to the trailer, Peg had returned and she was livid with anger.

She says that Uncle Homer had called and told her that Mary Beth has escaped from his custody. But a warrant has been issued against her, and she will be found, but it may take a few days. I smiled but said nothing in retaliation to what she had told me.

Peg asks, can he really help her, and I say I do not know. It really depends on Mary Beth. You see her personality was already formed when I adopted her, and with all of your plodding her and you trying to influence her in your direction of doing most anything, I am quite sure your influence has caused her to have second thoughts of even remaining on this earth.

Peg says she would never kill herself, because she is too set in what she wants out of life. I say, she could have had the world, if she would have wanted it, but she has been torn in so many directions, that she now does not know what or where she wants to go.

And you did not help one bit, by doing what you did to her. You were not a good influence on her. I tried but I failed her also. Now she knows that I am still her only Father, but will she ever learn to trust me, and because of you telling her that I am not a man to be trusted, I am afraid that she is now lost, until she can find her own way in life, because I do not know what else I could have done with her.

As for Martha, today I told her that I am her real Father, which is the honest truth. I know you have always suspected that I was her real father, but you did not know why. And I will not tell you the whole story at this time, except to say that because you have killed whatever babies you have been pregnant with, even Harry Hack's baby and mine also, that for me to ever get you pregnant again, will never happen, because I will as I have told you several times, will never have sex with you ever again.

And according to Tai you have had sex with Ken Jenkins, then according to the Contract I have with you, you are history in my and Martha' s life.

Because I will not have a wife that is sleeping with every Tom. Dick and Harry, and Ken Jenkins every time he or others comes into the town you happen to be living in just because it suits your whimsy.

And if you plan to continue to keep doing this, then you and I are finished as a married couple, because I am having my lawyer file Divorce papers as soon as he can prepare them. So if you do not want to remain in California, then you had better say so, so I can make arrangements to send you either back to Cudahy, Wisconsin or wherever you may want to now live.

I do plan to sell this trailer so Martha and I and the Cats can either move into a house that I will buy or into an apartment, somewhere in Los Angeles County. I do not plan to return back to Wisconsin either, and Jack Perkins knows this about me. Because I have already talked to him about it before I went on this extended vacation, and he is willing to give me six months Severance pay, because of the great job I did while I have been with the WWIB.

So if you want to own that house in Cudahy, then I will sign it over to you, plus your fifty percent of whatever else I now own.

But not including any money that I have put away for Mary Beth's and Martha's College time. Where either of them will go to college is still to be determined.

Both of my girls are smart enough to earn or be awarded Scholarship's from most any college in this country. What that college will be is still not known at this time. And wherever Tab Lewis wants to begin a business is still uncertain too, but I have set aside fifty thousand dollars for him, so he can do whatever he wants to do after he graduates from that college he is now studying at. Martha is writing to him and she will keep me informed about him as much as she can. I am also having the Dean of that college send me quarterly reports about his progress also.

Martha, I do not want you to tell Tab about those reports from the Dean of that college, just in case you had that in mind to tell him.

So Peggy dear, what is your answer? She says she wants to remain in California and remain married to me. That she will not have any more Liaisons with strange men, and if that ever does happen again, then she will move away from Martha and I and the Cats. I ask, will you sign a statement to that affect, and she says she will not. Signing contracts with me never gets her anything, because your contracts are too binding and cannot be broken, even just a little bit. I say that is the reason for any contract, so that whatever it says between two persons, causes them both to adhere to it as it dictates. I tell Peggy that I will agree to what you want on three conditions.

One = all of the correspondence and phone numbers including every name of every man from any of these Liaisons is given to me, and if any of them continue to correspond with you in the form of letters or phone calls, that you will not talk to any of these men ever again for as long as you live. I will keep all of this information as a reminder of the kind of woman you have been for these past thirteen years.

Two = you will go out and get yourself a job with an employer, so as to keep yourself busy and you will not bring any persons you work with home with you, even if they do not have any place to live, because they can always seek help with Social Services in the city of Los Angeles or where ever they are working.

Since they are obviously working with you, they too are making enough money to house themselves. The last time you did that, bringing home Susan Glitch, I went crazy for three months while she lived with us, when she was making more than enough money for her to rent herself her own apartment, and the only way I got rid of her was to have her arrested because she stole most of your Jewelry and some of our Silverware, so she was arrested for stealing from us, in the amount of about fifteen thousand dollars of merchandise and getting Uncle Homer and some of his men to come by our apartment, wherein they packed all of her clothes and other things and they picked her up bodily and carried her out to the street, then off to jail.

Where she spent the next three months awaiting her trial, and in the end, she actually stole fifteen thousand dollars from me and most of your jewelry that you had accumulated up to that time.

Three = if you get the urge to have any strange men to wherever we end up living, as your guest for whatever reason, forget it, because I will assume that is a violation of this agreement and you will most certainly end up either getting yourself killed or hurt or both, because you had probably scheduled more that one male person to come and visit you at the same time.

Because before that will happen, Martha and I and the Cats will be long gone, because I will always keep a place in mind where we can move to on a moments notice. And I will leave you penniless, until you can figure out how you will survive in a city that you really do not even want to be living in.

And if you ever have any of these men into wherever we are living when I am not there and Martha is there, and if any of these men try to harm her, I will make sure she knows how to use a weapon and she will end up shooting that male person, and I will accuse you of causing that male person of doing bodily harm to Martha, so as to get back at me.

And if Martha is harmed in any way, I will make sure you are carted off to jail, where I will never have a thing to do with you ever again.

Now if you cannot or will not agree to all of these demands, then I will request that you pack all of whatever you have in this trailer, and I will ship you back to Wisconsin or Missouri, and we will never see each other ever again, in fact I should probably do that anyway.

So what is it going to be? Because all of what I have said regarding these three demands will be written down as a kind of Contract, but it will only be between you and I, and not Martha and it will not be Notarized and witnessed by anyone else, with the exception of Martha, who will act as the only witness.

Peg says go ahead and write it up and she will sign it along with me doing the same thing and Martha will be the witness to both of our signatures. You will have the Copy and I will keep the Original.

So the next day after this agreement has been signed by both Clement and Peggy and witnessed by Martha Royal, and Clement contacts Moses Lighthouse and tells him of his new plans, Moses tells Clement that he has found an apartment that will be great for them.

So after being in California for about fifteen days, I take that trailer to where this apartment is located and for the rest of the day we move into this apartment. We all unload whatever is on and inside of this trailer and transfer it all into this apartment or into a storage place on the premises or onto a roof patio that is only privy to the residences of that apartment complex.

So Clement advises the Park office to make up his bill, because he is moving on for a while. He still has several weeks of vacation remaining, and they plan to go to northern California and Oregon and Washington before they eventually will return back to southern California where they will take up residence.

Clement

July 15th 1968

Dear Wife;

So another chapter in the life and times of Peggy or MAC and Clement nicknamed DOC or Father or Dad or Daddy has begun another version in their unending struggle of survival.

And as Clements real daughter Martha Philippa Royal and Clements four Cats - they rent themselves an apartment on west 8th street in the city of Los Angeles, California.

When Clement and Martha rented this apartment, the Manager says she has enough furniture in a storage place that will fill up this apartment, so Clement purchased all of whatever this manager had to sell and all of this stuff was placed or installed by the managers helpers, and when Clement brought his trailer to this complex and parked it outside on the street, where everything that could be moved into this apartment or onto a roof patio or into a separate storage area was done, then Clement had to take this trailer some place where he could store it until he sold it.

So Clement and Martha took this trailer to a place that rented spaces for trailers such as his, where it could be stored until he could sell it.

Then because they were pretty tired, they returned to 5708 West 8th street, Apt 11, and when they walked into their new apartment, they discovered that Peggy had prepared Supper for all of them.

So as to keep the Cats busy, Clement fed all of them, so they would not beg for food while all of the humans ate their supper. Clement had had a small television in the trailer, and he had set it up in the living room of this apartment.

Clement planned to buy a used TV at a store he knew about, but that could wait until a few days from now. He also did not have any dining table to eat from, but he did have several TV tables so that is what they used this evening.

He did have some steel chairs they could use for now, but he also will buy some chairs, which he hoped would match the dining table he will also buy.

The Kitchen in this apartment is kind of compact, because it is 8 feet long, and it has cabinets on both sides of this kitchen from floor to ceiling, with lots of counter top space for many things to be placed. It also has a Dishwasher, a Stove with an oven, and a place for what is just recently coming on the market, something called a Microwave. Clement planned to look into that also. It also has a double stainless steel sink with a Disposal attached to one side of this sink.

All of us will have to learn how to use this Disposal, because Clement figured it would save all of them a lot of problems when it came to disposing of food that had gotten moldy or had gone bad in some fashion. So it is decided that only Clement will use it for now. He will have to teach everyone else how to use it, before they could use it.

On one end of this Kitchen there is an area that can be used for a dining area, where about a four foot in diameter dining table could be placed, with at least four chairs placed around it permanently, even though Clement hopes there might be eight chairs that will come with this dining table.

Actually as you enter this apartment, you enter into the living room, with a four foot area that is not carpeted, but has linoleum on the floor, where you can stand while you remove your outer garments like coats and hats and such.

Anyway Clement has placed a kind of Coat Rack device near one corner of that area, where any person entering that apartment can hang their coats and hats and a place where they can place their umbrellas and other places to hang other things.

Then the rest of the living room goes clear across that wall for a distance of sixteen feet, where it ends at a doorway that is a hall that leads to other rooms, like bedrooms and a bathroom.

The door across from the living room door is the bathroom door, and I will describe the dimensions of that bathroom shortly. You turn right and go down a hall that leads to two separate bedrooms. But before I tell you about that I must tell you that where the dining area is located, there is a window which is six foot square, and it goes down to within a foot of the floor. And it has a widow sill that is five inches depth, so it is a great place for all of the cats to sit and look outside into the courtyard. .

Our apartment is on the second floor. There is a walkway that goes all the way around these upper floors and the corner apartments are large like ours is. Mostly because that is where some older persons live who have nurses who live with them.

Actually our apartment is a corner apartment, but it does not have an outside patio like all of the others do. Anyway getting back to our apartment, as you go down the hall from the main bathroom, you go sixteen feet and the first door on your left, is considered the Master bedroom.

In this bedroom there is a bathroom, which has only a shower and a commode and a sink with a countertop in it. On the wall where the bath is located, all the way to the entrance door is a large closet that has glass-mirrored doors on it. This bedroom is fourteen feet by sixteen feet, not including the bathroom and the closet. Which would add on another four feet. Which would make this room to be including the closet and the bathroom to be 14 X 20 feet.

At the end of the hall is another bedroom, which also has a closet completely across one wall, that wall being 14 feet long. That bedroom is 14 feet by 16 feet, because it does not have its own bathroom. But it is surely a large bedroom too. I think Martha may want to have an easy chair in her bedroom. And a dresser with a mirror and every four feet in this whole apartment is a double plug on every wall, even in the bathrooms, except where there is a shower and or a tub.

I figured I would keep my shaving stuff in the bathroom near the living room, because I always shave while Martha is taking a shower and I see no reason to change that schedule. Peg will not like it, but I don't care what she may want as far as when Martha and me are in the bathroom together.

She will think dirty thoughts about the two of us anyway, no matter what we do together. Anyway in the Master bedroom there is a window, which is six feet square and the same in Martha's bedroom, and these windows face north, so neither one will get any direct sun through these windows.

And because there are trees that are at least sixty feet tall on the north side of this complex, no one will be able to see into either bedroom, because the trees block the view. But since they are deciduous trees that means in the winter time they will have lost all of their leaves, so that will be the time when others could see in those windows.

So I will have some almost sheer curtains that will be double thick and have them placed across these windows, even though there are drapes already placed across them, but so as to have natural light come in these windows, these double sheer curtains will be installed too. And I only pay 75 dollars per month for this apartment.

The manager says for us to not advertise that price to any other resident. I figured we got a good deal because I also purchased a lot of extra furniture that this manager had in storage, that was probably costing her more money than she wanted to spend in keeping it, so because we probably saved her at least a hundred dollars a month, she probably only charged us half of what this apartment is actually worth.

All of the furniture that we bought from her was probably left by one of her former residents, because that person either died or moved away or whatever.

I will most likely find out what happened, because I can usually find things like that out from a woman Manager, because they usually want to talk a while when I go and sign whatever papers I need to sign. This manager says there will be no Lease either. She says leases just cost her extra money that is not necessary to spend if a resident does not have a lease.

Besides if she ever wanted to kick a particular resident out of an apartment, even though there are certain rules and regulations when any resident has a lease, the owner – Manager ends up spending more that it is worth to get rid of these residents, especially when she physically has to have them removed.

As the reader might suspect, all of the Cats end up going into Martha's bedroom and sleeping on her bed with her. Martha will sleep on one side of her bed and the cats on the other side.

And if any kind of excitement happens, they all immediately go under her bed and wait until either Martha or I tell them to come out.

If Peg tells them, they completely ignore her. I am not saying that Peg does not love them, but they love Martha and me more than anyone else in this family.

Mary Beth actually hated them, and if she could have, she would have kicked them all out of the trailer a long time back, but whenever she tried to do that, and she did try several times, they did go outside, but just climbed up on the chaise lounge and went to sleep.

One time she even tried to shoo them off of that lounge and then Tai and Tribble hissed at her and bared their fangs at her and then she backed away, and tried to tell me that they actually attacked her.

I told her that she had tried to shoo them from the chaise lounge they were sitting on, when they should not have even been outside of this trailer.

So take heed young lady, the next time you try to kick them out of this trailer, I have given all of them instructions they are to attack you and run you out of this trailer.

Mary Beth never tried to kick them out of that trailer again after that. But she still hated all of them. Probably just like she hated all of the rest of us, especially Martha and myself. If it hadn't been for me, she would still be in that Orphanage in Northern Missouri. And she would have remained there until she reached the age of 21. Because of how these children were treated, I was afraid they all would end up in Prison somewhere, and I still think that.

The only Orphanages where any child is treated as well as they can be treated are, in an orphanage that is run by the Catholic Church, where all of the children are Indians. And the only place where such an Orphanage is located is, in Chamberlain, South Dakota, and all of the children in this Orphanage are Indians of various kinds, or children who have Indian blood in them.

I have supported this orphanage for many years now, and will probably support it for the rest of my life. Occasionally they do take in white children, because these children have some kind of psychological problems, and this place seems to be able to cure these children of those problems.

Mary Beth always told me that she was part Indian so perhaps I should have sent Mary Beth to this place, where she would remain until she turned 21. And that may still happen, if Uncle Homer cannot help her. Since I have given them several thousand dollars through the years, getting Mary Beth installed in this place would not be a problem. And because a Catholic Priest runs it, she may respond more to him and his staff, than any other place.

We had a call from Uncle Homer today, which informs me

that he found Mary Beth and now has installed her in his Reform Camp. She told him she did not realize there were places like this camp anywhere in this country, especially in the state of Missouri, and it is so close to St Louis too.

Homer says the first thing she tried to do was to climb over the fence, and she ended up in the Infirmary, because she burned both hands pretty badly, but she will heal and survive. She says she will not do that again.

Even though every fence is posted; saying that the top two feet of wiring has 32 volts of electricity running through it. She just thought that was a way to keep anyone from trying to climb over that fence. Homer says she will not be able to use either hand for any kind of heavy work for about a month, so her duties will be fairly easy during that time. She can feed herself, but it hurts her quite a lot.

She also says that she hates you, but don't pay any attention to what she now says, because as time goes by, she will change her attitude about you. Because she knows that if you had not rescued her from that Orphanage she would now probably be dead.

She has a lot of spunk and Homer says over the next five years he will be able to help her. Because when she leaves this place when she is 21 years old, she will have a totally different attitude. She may even become one of our internal instructors, if she responds well.

I tell Homer to be careful, because she can make you think she has learned her lesson and as soon as you let your guard down, she will try to escape again.

Homer says that will never happen, because no member of

this place is ever allowed into the outer ring area where they could possibly climb over the outer fence, which is not electrified.

Homer says he has been thinking that it should also be electrified too. But he is just one member who can only suggest doing that. There are five members on the board of directors and he is only one of those members. In fact the Warden lives in the outer ring area, and he has children in his family, and he has to think of them also.

It is not that his children will try to climb this fence; because they can go anywhere anyway, but it will take a lot of money to just electrify the top two feet. I ask how much money and he says about 200 thousand dollars. I ask how large is this Camp, and he says it covers 1280 acres.

Homer tells me; so that all of these children have something to do, we have 580 acres that is farmed. And 80 acres is for the separate quarters, because the males are kept completely separate from the females for whatever length of time any of them are in this Reform Camp.

We plant almost every kind of vegetable one can plant. And when we sell these vegetables it goes to buy supplies for the children and helps to support the school.

Some of this farm is into Pastureland, whereon the Milk cows graze on, and there are also about 50 horses that graze on all of this pastureland too. We have Sheep and Goats too. Then there is the area where we raise 1500 chickens, which are mostly laying hens, with a few Roosters too.

So we not only raise chickens so as to get the eggs they lay, but also for the meat that some are raised strictly for that purpose. All of these children get a full education in how to actually run this large farm. Then there is the area where we raise Turkey's, and we have 500 of them.

Then where what little water is located, which is a 20 acre slough, we raise tame Ducks and a few Geese, but they are mostly just for show or some times our children want to raise a tame duck just for themselves, which in reality tames these wild children down a lot. We mostly let them do this for Therapeutic reasons, and it usually works very well. When some of these children become civilized once again, we reward them with their own small house, of which they first have to build by themselves. We will help them with the plumbing and electrical work, but they mostly do most of the carpentry work themselves. It gives them a feeling of having their first real home in their life.

I am real glad that Clement suggested that we do this for any troubled child, and we also thank him for giving us the money that he received from his farm near Watertown, South Dakota. That is that entire farm that he sold, which was for only 600 acres of it. The other 40 acres he still owns, because that is where his Lava rock mine is located.

Anything like electrifying this outer fence at the top two feet is a costly move. I tell Homer I will let you know what I can come up with. If I can send you that much money can you have that done, and Homer says that will make the difference.

I tell Homer to keep that in mind. Soon I will be coming into some extra money and now I have just found a way to invest that money. Homer says it will make you a definite member of the Staff here. I say I don't want to be a member of the staff there.

I tell him I will donate this money in Mary Beth's name, even though I do not want her or anyone else to know about it until she is released from that place, and at that time you or some member of your Board of Directors will tell her.

What effect that will have on her, may cause some strange reaction. I will not venture a guess as to how that will affect her. But if she is a cured person, then she may want something else from all of you, so be prepared for the worse.

Clement

July 25th 1968

My Dear Wife;

In the past ten days, we have been to many places, like Disneyland, and Knott's Berry Farm, and several Dinner Theaters, and Wild Animal Country in Irvine, and another one down north of San Diego. I have not tried to get involved with any of the many creatures, but it seems wherever I go, that kind of stuff seems to always find me, but I dispensed with all of them with as much swiftness as I could.

I think Martha enjoyed these adventures more than I did. Of course even though Peg was with us also, she never seemed to be as impressed with my abilities as Martha is, but Martha also got involved with each of these creatures. So that made it more interesting for her too.

We also went to the Los Angeles Zoo where we had an incident regarding an Ocelot Cat, which I solved when I contacted the San Diego Zoo where they had an Ocelot Cat of the opposite sex and in fact were looking for another Zoo where it could be placed. So when I contacted this other Ocelot when I was at the Los Angeles Zoo and also the head of the San Diego Zoo, I turned a good situation into a wonderful ending. The details I will not go into here, but in another book.

We also drove up to Big Sur and toured the Hearst Castle and grounds. It is a very interesting place. On our way back, a

Forest fire had started and we could only get to the city of Santa Barbara, where we had to stay in a Motel for a few hours until it was safe to continue our drive back to Los Angeles.

We finally got home around 10:00 PM that evening. My cats were kind of hungry, but as they usually always do, they save a little of their food, so they can eat it later, and Tai says that is what they did on this day also. In fact he says he had a feeling that today was going to be different, so he instructed his family to not eat as much as they normally do, which allowed all of them to have something to eat at a later time when we were late getting back home. Cat's abilities still sometimes amaze me.

I tell Tai that I want him and his family to think about eating some dry food. I will buy small portions of all kinds of dry food, and when you find the kinds that you all like, I want to be told.

That way I will only buy those brands and that way when we may be gone for a longer time than we had anticipated, you will have food to eat. Because I will also buy Feeders that will dispense these dry foods to all of you, and I will place all of these different brands of food in that dispenser, so you all will have a variety of food that you all like.

And besides, dry food is good for your teeth, because it helps remove Tarter that always seems to collect on your teeth.

Tai asks what is tarter, and I tell him, you remember all of the times I have to have your teeth cleaned. Tai says they always put him to sleep when they do that. I say dry food removes all of that stuff from your teeth as you eat this dry food. He asks, won't it hurt, and I say it will only hurt if you have bad teeth to begin with. And if that is so, then I will have those teeth removed, and Tai says they will again put him to sleep. I say you don't want to be awake when these teeth are pulled out, because it will hurt too much. Tai says he will do as I ask him and his family to do.

So the next day when I go to the Safeway store on Western and Beverly streets, I do buy the smallest bags of sixteen different kinds of dry cat foods. I also buy a food dispenser, and a water dispenser, which holds a gallon of water.

When I get home, I open up one of these bags of food and place it in a bowl. After every member of Tai's family eats some of it, I get a report from him. I tell him that I will give you the entire day to decide about this one, and over the next sixteen days, you will eat a different brand every day. At the end of each day, I want to know if you like or not like this food, and if some like it and some don't then I want to know that also. I think to myself that this is going to be interesting.

Anyway after sixteen days have gone by, and I have gotten reports on each kind and brand of dry cat food, it is discovered that they like only four kinds of food. So I take the brands that my cats do not like, and I place them outside my front door with a sign on each bag, that this cat food is free to whoever wants to use it.

By the end of that day, every bag had been carted away from in front of my door. We were gone most of that day, so I do not know who took any of it. And besides buying dry cat food is cheaper than buying canned cat food.

My Cats ended up selecting their favorite brands; Purina, IAMS, and Science Diet brands. All of them being the top brands of all of the cat foods. They surely knew what they were getting.

There was another brand, but it was more of a treat, which was called Kitty treats, which was a semi-soft food, and I will only give that brand to them to help any of them when they are having some kind of tooth problem. And these three brands are the most expensive on the market. As it is said many times, Aristocratic Cats know Quality from their breeding. That sure is the truth.

Clement

August 11th 1968

My Dear Wife;

On this day I asked Martha if she wanted to go Ice Skating, and she says no. That would be something that Mary Beth would want to do, but Martha says she never was very good on ice skates. But if we can go Roller-skating sometime, she would definitely like to do that.

She says that she even brought her own shoe type of skates with her, just in case. I told her that Peg and I also have our own shoe type of roller skates.

To the reader of this book, you have to remember that Martha and I have not been together very much since I adopted her, mostly because of my Traveling Auditor's position. So the likelihood of her knowing that I even have roller skates was not something she would have even known about.

I also want to remind the reader of this book, that you, when you were still in St Louis, when we were separated, had found a different Dentist who finally got to take impressions of the inside of your mouth, and you had false teeth made for yourself. But due to the fact that the upper teeth go back on the upper part of your mouth, actually makes you Gag, so this Dentist ground these Upper teeth back so you are able to wear your teeth for upwards of four hours at a time. So on this day you had both of your false teeth in your mouth. But there are still a lot of places that I want to show to Martha, because I know so many other persons in various fields.

Like in the entertainment fields, like Movie stars and Managers of Amusement parks, for example Universal Studio's Theme park and even a few places up further north in the Angeles Mountains. Or persons who live on Catalina Island, who have businesses on that island, who actually want me to go into business with them and even live on that island. But that I will still have to think about for a while.

There is one person in particular that I want to call on, that being Maggie Kettle, who owns the only Gun shop on the island. Her late husband did own his own gun shop, which was located near the Ball park Stadium, but since he has died, instead of Maggie being given that shop, it was instead left to his assistant.

Maggie sued the Estate and won her case, and forced this man to sell that original shop, wherein Maggie used the money from that Sale, to buy some land and a vacant store on Catalina Island, and she opened her own Gun Shop.

And because her oldest Son Peter was already living on the island, and he is a Contract House builder, he helped her get herself established also.

What kind of clientele she caters to, I do not know, but knowing Maggie, she would make sure she does not do business with any kind of Crooks, like her late husband always did do.

But it is rumored that Law enforcement persons from all over Los Angeles and Orange and San Bernardino Counties come to her shop to buy whatever is needed by their organizations.

I would like to spend at least a week on the island, because there is a lot to see and experience there. I have heard there may be some Wild Horses on that Island, and I have also heard that they may be in some kind of danger, so I need to see if there is anything that I can do to remedy their situation.

I have made inquiries with Moses Lighthouse, as to where they might be transported, in order to save their lives. And he tells me he is working on the problem. You remember Maggie, because I introduced her to you back in 1956, when I was transferred to Los Angeles to that off line agent's position.

But she was still married to her husband then. I suspected there was something in that marriage that I was not seeing, and now I think Maggie will finally tell me what that problem really was. I had heard that George was a wife beater, but that was only a story someone told me.

On one of our open days from sightseeing, I suggested that we go to the Brown Derby Restaurant to eat a noon meal. And while we are sitting in our corner booth, whom do you think came into that restaurant, Jimmy Perce and his wife walked in.

I had met him back in 1948, but I had not seen him in about two years, because that was the last time I was in Los Angeles on one of my special assignments as an auditor. He spotted me, and he came to our booth. I asked him and his wife to sit down and they did. Then a few minutes later who should walk in, yup it was Barbara Stanwyck and Jimmy spotted her and he asked her to come to our booth and I suggested she sit with us also, and order herself a meal, which she did.

And while we all were waiting for our meals to arrive, we all seemed to want to talk about a lot of different subjects. But right away Jimmy says to me, he says your wife and Barbara look like they are sisters. Martha, who was sitting on one end of all of us, got up and went out to my car and got a Brownie box camera, and brought it back and she took several photos of us all.

Of course they are all in black and white, but good photos nonetheless. It just so happened that you and Barbara were sitting next to each other, so after these pictures were developed, it was amazing to see another person who is actually a little older than you are by probably ten years, but the two of you really do look like you are definitely related.

Anyway, Jimmy asked me how we came to be back in California and when I told him, he asked, have I sold my trailer yet? I told him I had not, then he asked how much would I take for it, and when I told him, he looked at his wife for a moment, and then he tells me he will buy it for the price I quoted, which is $8,000.00. I tell him that I feel it is definitely worth that amount, because I have added several of my new Inventions to it, of which eventually will probably make me a fortune. Then our meals arrived and all of the conversations stopped for a while, while we ate our meals.

Jimmy needed to talk to Barbara about something, but he asked me to wait for a while, so we could talk more about my trailer, and when we finally did, we made arrangements to meet in a week at the address where the trailer was in storage.

Jimmy has also put forth an open invitation for all of us to come to his house in the Hollywood Hills. But to give him at least an hours notice before we came.

Personally, I don't like to give any persons such short notice that I am coming to see them. I like to have at least two days notice, just in case I need to get some things from the grocery store. I told Jimmy this, and he says he is not unlike that either, but told me what he did, because he had been talking to John Wayne and the Duke told him to watch for me. And to suggest that I go see his oldest son, who is an Agent for a lot of new Actors. That with my ability to act in the way that I do and can, that as an Extra, I may be able to actually get into some better parts with all of the other actors that I know. That if I get a few speaking parts, I will most likely excel in that field, and in that way get some much better parts in movies.

Anyway Jimmy and I made arrangements to meet on the following Wednesday, whereof I showed him all of my Inventions on this travel trailer, and I also showed him how to back up to this trailer, using one of those inventions. Jimmy's vehicle was not equipped like my vehicle was, and that would still have to be done, so using my vehicle I had him back up to that trailer using the device I invented, and it worked perfectly.

I also told him that I will even deliver that trailer to his home, and he said that would be great, so since I was connected to that trailer, I also showed him what had to be done to make that trailer to be the kind of vehicle that it ended up being when it was connected to my or anyone's vehicle. I also showed him all of the things inside of this trailer, especially the secret compartment, where I always kept the title to this trailer. And anything else that had been added to this trailer and when and where this had been done.

Then I showed him all of the extra storage places and how

to get to all of this storage. And all of the specialized equipment I had on board of this trailer, so as to make things much easier for him or whomever owned this trailer. And all of the special hookups, and how easy it was to operate everything. I even had a special antenna whereof a television could be connected to it, and also another antenna whereat you could connect a ham radio and how to deploy the extension to this antenna that would bring in stations from as far away as Australia.

I then attached the special rear view mirrors to my front fenders, and made sure that all of the other connections were in place. Then I told Jimmy to get in my vehicle and I will drive his vehicle, and we will now go to his house. He was not certain at first, but there is nothing like the present to get used to pulling this trailer.

I told him, all he has to remember is that he is pulling that trailer behind you, so don't turn corners as if you are not pulling that trailer behind you. I will follow you. But before I let him drive my vehicle off of that storage lot, I at first drove my vehicle so as to show him how he was to use the brakes on the trailer and when.

I had a duel hookup to the trailer brakes. But most of the time I used the automatic brakes, because when I applied my vehicle brakes, the brakes on the trailer, of which are electric, are always applied a mini-second before the brakes on my automobile are applied. When you are traveling on dirt roads or gravel roads, or in mountainous areas, then switch to manual, so you can have the brakes on the trailer applied much quicker than when it is in automatic.

To cause the changeover, just flip this switch, which is done electrically, and whenever you do whatever is done, this dial on your steering wheel will tell you in what mode this device is now in.

One thing I made sure of, and that is, there are no fuses between this switch and this dial, in fact there are no fuses anywhere on this entire hookup. In fact there are no fuses between this automobile and that trailer behind you. Everything is a direct hookup.

The plug that connects this vehicle to that trailer has a locking device on it, wherein it will never disconnect accidentally. If the trailer should somehow become disconnected, those chains that go between the vehicle and the trailer will prevent the trailer from careening off of the highway. That is also why the electrical hookup has enough play in that line, so you can still apply the trailer brakes before you apply the vehicle brakes, and if the trailer does come unhooked from this vehicle, the trailer brakes will automatically be applied, which will slow this vehicle down considerably, because that trailer, even when it is considered empty, still weighs seven thousand pounds.

Most automobiles do not weigh more than three thousand pounds, and a lot of them only weigh around fifteen hundred pounds. But a lighter vehicle could never pull this trailer. Since your station wagon probably weighs around 3500 pounds, then when it is connected to this trailer when it is considered empty, it will only weigh around 10,500 pounds. And fully loaded it will probably weigh around twelve thousand pounds. Now most bridges say they will handle ten thousand pounds, but in reality they will actually handle fifteen thousand pounds.

If you have doubts, stop and go to this bridge, and look at the sign that states how much it will really handle, which is usually in small print, too small for anyone to read while driving in your vehicle.

So after I showed Jimmy everything there was to show him, I then got out of my vehicle and he got in, and we began out trek to his house. It actually took only a little over an hour and when we did this, it was around 1:00 PM, which is when the traffic begins to get heavier on the California freeways.

Once we were off of the freeways, I went around Jimmy, and I kind of ran interference for him. And when we were getting close to some of the bridges on some of the streets where I knew they existed, I made sure that every one of them allowed at least fifteen thousand pounds to travel across them.

Once we got into the Hollywood hills, every street stated that no vehicle that weighed more than twelve thousand pounds could travel on it. I knew that Jimmy knew this also, but he apparently totally ignored what it said, because since I had not prevented him from getting to his own house, and when he pulled onto his driveway and parked and got out, I went to him and told him what I had discovered on all of the bridges that he traveled across.

Jimmy then told me that he was a bit worried when he got on to some of the streets in the Hollywood hills, but since I had not put up any barriers, he kept on moving, just like we had arranged before we left that storage lot. He says most of the time he really did not realize how easy it was to pull a trailer with a vehicle like a Ford Falcon. He says his station wagon is a Chevrolet Estate Special, which he says he had specially made for him, because they like to go camping a lot. But now they will be able to do it with more comfort.

I mentioned that if you go camping to some places where I have gone camping, you would not take this trailer to those places, unless you are pulling it with a full ton truck. He smiles, and says I am correct. But he says, some of the places where he has to go on location, there are hardly even any roads, and how they actually get to some of these places, they have to build their own roads.

And if some of those big heavy trucks can make it, then he figures he too can make it too. He says he has Chains for his tires, just in case he may have to travel in areas where there is snow sometimes.

I then tell Jimmy that I still have to teach you how to park this trailer, especially if you have to park it in a specified place. Where you will have to back this trailer into that space. But using those mirrors on my vehicle it will be fairly easy. But before I can even go any further in showing you a lot of other things, you need to take your vehicle to a place where they will attach a special hookup device to your vehicle. In fact I will take you to that place myself, so I can bring you home. For now, wherever you want this trailer parked, I will do it.

Then when you get your own vehicle back, and after I attach whatever needs to be attached to it, then we will hook your vehicle up to your new trailer, and I will teach you how to park this outfit, like you have been doing it all of your life. So that is what I do.

Then after I show Jimmy how to place Jacks under each corner of the trailer, and get it hooked up to his own houses electricity and even get a phone hooked up to it, and show him how the awning is unrolled and a few other things, we then get into our vehicles and we go to where he will leave his vehicle for three days, where the personnel there will install the special hook up to his vehicle, which in fact becomes a permanent part of his vehicle as long as he owns it. Then I bring him back to his own residence in the Hollywood Hills, and I then go back to my apartment.

While I have been gone, Martha has been arranging everything in her bedroom that she wants to have available to her. The cats all have mostly been lying on her bed watching her. Peg has rearranged a few things in other parts of the apartment, but she has mostly been working on another one of her Crossword Puzzles that she invents.

She says she now has fifteen of them created, that she has to send off to various Magazines to see if they will accept them to perhaps publish them. If a particular Puzzle is not accepted, she says she sets them aside, and later will send all of them off to just one specific Magazine Editor. Which will be the Dell Puzzle Magazine Editor.

They have told her that if she can come up with 25 Puzzles all at the same time, where none of them have been published before, they will give her two cents for each puzzle that is published. I have checked out as to how large their normal monthly publishing figure is, and it is around a million copies of Magazines.

And each magazine normally has a hundred puzzles in it. So if 25 of her puzzles were published all at the same time that would mean you would make 500 thousand dollars in one month's time. And since each magazine sells for $10.98 each, that means the Dell Company takes in ten million nine hundred eighty thousand dollars in that one months time. Not counting all of the advertising they sell space for in these magazines. Now if there are additional publications of this same magazine, because of public demand for this magazine, then she will continue to get additional Royalties until that publication finally ends. So how much money she will actually make from this one publication is still not known at this time.

With all other publications, she is also getting a penny each for every one of her puzzles that are published, in whatever magazine. So she has been getting no less than ten thousand dollars every month and upwards of fifty thousand dollars every month. I have been putting that money away in Trust funds for Martha and Mary Beth, for when they will eventually go to whatever College they decide they will go to.

Peg says since what she has been telling Mary Beth has not done much good for her, the next best thing she can do is to make sure she can go to whatever college she wants to go to.

And since she really does not have much influence on Martha, she also figures she can do more for her if she has me create a Trust fund for her, that she can access when she eventually goes to college.

Peg says she has not told Mary Beth about this trust fund and she never will. Because she fears that if Mary Beth knows about it, she will try to get a hold of some of this money, but knowing how I operate, Peg says that will never happen, because either I will write the contract or Moses Lighthouse will, and neither one of our contracts have ever been broken by anyone who has tried. Not even herself.

Peg says she knows that I want her to look for some different kind of employment, but she figures just as long as she is continuing to create more crossword puzzles, she will continue to bring in more money that way. She says after awhile she does kind of get burned out for a while, so at those times she may look for some other kind of employment. But just as long as we all are on this vacation, she will stay at home and create more new crossword puzzles. Peg says sometimes she can create as many as five new crossword puzzles in one days time.

Clement

August 18th 1968

Getting Jimmy Perce squared away

Dear Peg;

On this day Jimmy calls me and Martha and I go to where he lives. I look over his new hookup, and it has been installed as it was supposed to be installed. The plug they installed that is normally used to hook up the trailer is not the same as the one that I have on my vehicle, but it does not matter and I will explain that in a moment.

I get to work installing everything to Jimmy's vehicle that needs to be installed. I actually had my invention that I created that helps any person who pulls any kind of trailer manufactured by an electronics company in Santa Monica, California, and they now have the sole rights to manufacture this device.

The Contract that I have with this Company says they will create five hundred thousand each year. These rights are for only five years, and it will only be renegotiated if they create as many as the Contract says to create.

I did not write the contract. Moses Lighthouse did it. He says for everyone of these devices that are sold to anybody, I will make two dollars, and this company who has the only rights to manufacture this device, is supposed to according to their contract with me, are supposed to manufacture five hundred thousand each year.

And to buy this device, it will cost anyone who needs it, a hundred dollars each. No manufacturer of trailers will sell these devices. Anyone who buys them will have to buy them directly from the manufacturer.

Which means the manufacturer will have to package and ship this device to whomever buys it from them. The manufacturer of trailers will advertise these devices to buyers of trailers. And the trailer manufacturers will furnish documents to all of these buyers of trailers, who if they want to make their life a lot easier in connecting their trailers to their vehicle Hitches, will hopefully buy this device. Considering what I can do for them, they would be a lot better trailer owners if they did this.

I then give Jimmy a special small key. I tell him that this key opens up every lock on every door or drawer, with the exception of the front door. So guard it at all times. I will make you two extra copies, but it cannot be duplicated by any other means or methods. And I will not show you how I make them. I will show you where to put one of them, which is on the outside of this trailer, where it will never be seen, even when it is in plain sight.

The other one you will give to your wife, and you will tell her what I just told you. Now I will show you why it is so important to always have this key with you.

Using that key, I unlock the door to a box where there are all kinds of adapters for hooking up trailers to vehicles. Knowing what I am looking for, I find that adapter and using it I hook up the trailer to Jimmy's vehicle.

On each adapter there is a flexible steel cable, which I hook to a place on the underside of the hitch. I have Jimmy lay down on the ground so he can see it, but actually attaching it to this area of the hitch, it is not necessary to lay down on the ground.

Since you will most likely be only pulling this trailer with this adapter, you will leave that adapter in place all of the time. And if anyone tries to remove it, it will not come loose, no matter how hard they pull on it. I will show you how easy it is to remove it at this time. Because while we are lying on our backs, I just reach up and by doing this, it comes unattached very easily. Now I will reattach it and now I will just pull on this cable and as you can see, it does not come loose.

I let Jimmy do it a few times until he is comfortable that he can remove it when he wants to. If you know you will not be around for some time and leaving it attached to your vehicle would cause your wife some problems, I suggest that you remove it and put it back into the box where it came from.

No I do not recommend showing your wife how to remove it. And as far as anyone else, just tell them it came with the hitch.

It is best if you do not tell many persons about it. Maybe someone like the Duke or another one of your very close friends.

Since Duke is thinking about creating his own Production company, which will be called BATJAC, then he would need to know about this special hookup and all of these different adapters. If that happens, please tell me and I will make sure he is kept well informed about everything that I have invented, because there are still some things that I have not installed on this trailer, but would come in real handy for someone who has much larger equipment, like Semi trucks and very large trailers...

The hookup device will work on any kind of vehicle, just as long as your rear view mirror has a direct line to the rear window. There needs to be a window whereupon the remainder of this device can be attached or placed. If there is none then it will not work.

At least I have not invented it yet to work in any way other than how it does work. It is based in part on the Bomb Site device that was in some of the B-29 Aircraft.

Jimmy says most of those Bomb Sites were all totally destroyed after the second world war ended, or when all of those bombers were made into scrap. How did you ever get a hold of one of those Sites?

I tell Jimmy, I never have seen that Site, but I know how it was built. At least I think I know how it was built. But all I can say is that I have come up with this device and it works every time.

Trying to discover anything else about it has become a trade secret. And if anyone tries to copy it, I will make additional Millions of dollars from anyone else's design. Anyway, since I have a Patent on this design, no one has ever come up with this kind of design and since I have created several other designs that do not work, just in case someone else tries to design something similar to this one, no other patent will ever be issued for this one or any similar devices that I have created.

Because I even have patents on the ones that do not work. Any inventor, who does not protect himself when creating different inventions, takes a big chance that someone may invent something similar to his invention, but it will not work in the same way. But it might work just the same.

Now if it has any similar designs in his invention, just like you have in your invention, then you can petition the patent board, that that other invention was patterned after your invention, thereby preventing that other Inventor from getting a patent issued for his invention.

But he or she can still manufacture their invention, and state that his patent is pending, whether it really is or not. And if you have enough money, you can sue that other inventor, and if you win your case, that other inventor will not get very much money from that invention, and that other inventor will have to pay all of the court costs for that law suit that you filed against that person or persons for their similar invention. It is a dog eat dog world out there when it comes to inventions.

I show Jimmy everything about my inventions that I have installed on this trailer, and what each one does to better his ability to be fully up to date regarding all of them. I know that he did not fully expect to get what he did get when he purchased this trailer.

There were also a number of inventions inside of this trailer that would benefit his wife also. And when I got to all of those, I had her come to this trailer, so I could show her how everything worked. I also showed both of them where all of the storage places are and how you are able to get to various areas of each storage area. Some from inside of the trailer, and some from the outside. And especially the extra water storage and extra waste storage, and how easy it is to either fill or empty these containers. I also showed both of them the furnace that heated the entire trailer, and how that same heater heated whatever hot water that was used in that trailer.

This trailer did not come from the factory this way. These are devices I had installed by Zephyr factory mechanics when I was near the factory that originally built this trailer, which was Madison, Wisconsin. There is another factory in Fresno, California.

Then I tell Jimmy that I have to show him how he is to park this trailer. First I got into his vehicle and using all of the mirrors on his vehicle, I parked that trailer exactly where he wanted it parked, and I did it the very first time.

He says he will not be able to do it with the same ease that I did. I pulled this trailer forward and parked it in a catawampus way, so he would have to jockey it a bit so as to line it up just so. I then got out in front of his vehicle, and I told him to turn the steering wheel exactly in the direction that I indicated him to do.

At first he did not, then he realized that I knew exactly what I was doing, and when he did as I instructed him to do, he parked it perfectly. Then I had him pull the trailer forward and park it in the same way that I had parked it, and then I disappeared totally and after three tries, he parked it correctly again. He did it three more times, just to make sure he knew what he was doing.

The final time he parked that trailer, he came to where I was sitting on his front porch of his house, and he says he now totally understands how important those mirrors are on both front fenders really are.

He says when he trusted what I had told him regarding those mirrors; he did not have any more problems parking that trailer. He asks, does he have to remove those mirrors from his front fenders when he is not pulling this trailer. I tell him that he does not, but you will have to make sure that you never get close enough to any other vehicle, whereon you might scratch that vehicle.

They can be folded backwards, and can be held in that position by using another device that I invented, but in heavy traffic, if they remain in the position they are now in, will come in very handy, especially when there are large trucks near you.

He says he will remove them when this trailer is parked here at home. But he will leave them attached when he goes on location, no matter how long they will be at that location.

Clement

August 22nd 1968

An Extreme Emergency In my Family

Dear Peg;

When Martha and I came home on this day, you were not at home. I inquired with the Manager and she told me you left in a Cab.

She did not say when you would come back and Eve says she did not ask where you were going, because you are an adult and it really is not any of her business anyway.

It was about 3:00 PM and I wanted to bake a couple of pies and a cake, and that is what I got busy doing. I also removed a Rump Roast from the freezer, and when all of the pies and cakes had been baked, I then prepared this roast so I could put it in the oven. I added various vegetables to the baking pan, so all of these veggies would be sitting in the juice when this roast was done. I also put in some peeled potatoes and a cup of water and then placed it in the oven and set the timer for 2 ½ hours at 385 degrees. It is a small roast.

I then wrote out some checks that paid all of the bills that needed paying. Of which are all of the Utility bills for this apartment.

I then called Moses Lighthouse and asked him for the name of the In home school teacher that came to his house and taught all of his school age children their studies.

He says to come to his house on Friday afternoon about 5:00 PM, because she will be there also. Be prepared to stay for supper.

At 6:30 PM you returned home. I asked you where you had gone, and you told me that you went shopping for some new clothes, but you did not have any packages with you.

You told me that whatever you had purchased would be delivered in a few days. I then told you that supper would be on the table in a half hour. I also told you about all of us going to Moses Lighthouse's house on Friday and be prepared to stay for supper.

You did not say anything regarding that day, but just went into our bedroom. When that half hour went by, I then called both you and Martha to come to supper, and you told me that you were not hungry. That you were not feeling all that well, and you would be in bed. So Martha and I ate supper without you. But before we sat down to eat, I fed the cats first, and cleaned their cat john. Then I washed my hands and went and ate with Martha.

After supper was over and I had put all of the dirty dishes in the Dishwasher and the left over food in the refrigerator; I then went and checked on you.

You appeared to be asleep, but I sensed that something was wrong, so I lifted the blanket that was placed over you, and the Bed sheet was soaked with blood. I yelled to Martha to call the Police and tell them that my wife is bleeding considerably. You stirred a little and I told you to remain where you are.

You looked down where most of the blood had accumulated

on the bed and you then began to cry and you kept saying that you are sorry, over and over again.

Within five minutes the police and an ambulance arrived and Martha escorted them to our bedroom, and the two attendants after seeing what I showed them, picked you up and placed you on the Gurney and immediately took you from the apartment. I asked if I could come with them and they told me no, but they would be taking her to the UCLA medical center, which is closer than the County Hospital.

Two Policemen remained behind in our apartment to talk to Martha and me. When they asked about you, I told them about our day, and that I had not said more than ten words to you regarding much of anything. Martha confirmed what I had said, because she has been with me all day.

Even when we were with Jimmy Perce. They questioned us considerably about that, but we did not change our story, so after about thirty minutes they finally said that I could go to the UCLA Medical center. They then both left. I asked Martha if she wanted to go with me, but she says no, so I went and got into my vehicle and drove out to the UCLA Medical center.

When I arrived I went to admissions and told the personnel who I was and about whom I was inquiring about, and they told me that I have to place on file whatever Medical information that I have about my wife before I could see her.

Privately I believe it is a delaying tactic to allow the Emergency Personnel to get a handle on what could be wrong with you. Because I did not know at that time.

I was taken by a Blue stripper, who is a young woman who is in reality is a Gopher type of individual, who escorts persons to possible patients, who do not know where anything is located in that hospital. After going through many doors and down long halls, I am finally taken into a room, where I am told that you will be brought to when all of the Doctors are finished diagnosing your problem.

There are two metal chairs in this room, which have no padding on either of them, so sitting any length of time on either of them is something that I do not want to experience. I inquire about my wife at a nurses station, and this woman tells me, when she can be seen, my wife will be brought to that room. I tell this Nurse that both of the chairs in that room are not for sitting any great length of time, so I will go back to the waiting room in the Emergency area, and you can come there when you know anything about my wife. There is a long Couch in the Emergency waiting area, and since there are only two other persons in this area, I lay down on this couch and I fell asleep.

When someone wakes me, it is dark outside, and when I look at my watch, I note it is 10:15 PM. This Blue stripper says my wife has been admitted into this Hospital and will have to remain at least three days. Her Doctor will come here and talk to you in about five minutes, just in case you may want to freshen yourself up a little before he arrives. I ask do I look that bad, and she says no, but a little water on your face may bring you more fully awake. I smile but do not say anything. I am directed to a small room, where there are a couple of sinks and a commode. I do splash some cold water on my face and then wipe it dry with some paper towels, I use the commode and urinate and then I wash my hands and go back to the waiting room. In another minute a Doctor comes to me.

He introduces himself as Doctor Dore, who is the resident Gynecologist, as it is stated on his identity badge he is wearing. He asked, did I know that my wife was pregnant? I tell him no, I did not know she was pregnant. He tells me that she has lost this child. He further tells me that she has been pregnant at least five times before this pregnancy. Did I know that too?

I then told this Doctor about my life with Peggy. How long we have been married, and the last time I had sex with her. Dr. Dore says he needs permission to do a Hysterectomy on my wife. He says my wife says to ask me for that permission. If I don't grant that permission, then the next pregnancy will most likely kill her. He further says that she has probably caused all of these pregnancies to end on purpose, but he cannot prove it.

For this last pregnancy she went to an illegal abortionist who did a very poor job in trying to get rid of this baby. But whoever did it for her, killed her baby, but the baby is still inside of her, and he says he will have to remove this baby when he does the other operation.

I tell Dr. Dore, I will give him permission to do the Hysterectomy. But I also need him to recommend a Psychiatrist who will come to our apartment for sessions with my wife.

Because she has a gigantic problem and even though I am personally a Sociologist and a Psychologist, she will not listen to me. I know she figures I will Divorce her, because I have threatened to do that, but I fear if I do divorce her she might try to do something more terrible, like try to kill herself, even though she has never tried to do that yet, but has just threatened to do herself in that way.

You see she is Catholic, and if she killed herself, she

figures she would go immediately to Hell. She really is living within herself her own kind of Hell, by doing what she has been doing for almost thirteen years. And that is having sex with as many men as she can find to do it with her.

Dr. Dore asks do I love my wife. I say I am not sure I do any longer. I did in the beginning of our marriage, but after I found out she is having sex with a lot of men, that Love has reduced down to just a glimmer of light.

But I guess I feel sorry for her, and I also think she could never survive without me. He says I am absolutely correct in my last assumption. Without you in her life, she is nothing, and she knows it. He says if you were not in her life, she would find a way to end her life.

I say maybe she would be better off if she did not live any longer, because then I could possibly find someone whom I could love with the passion that I know that I have inside of me. I never thought that married life was like this.

Dr. Dore says she is still not out of the woods, because she has lost at least two pints of blood, and because of this very serious operation he still has to perform, she could still lose another Pint of blood, and if I had not gotten her to this hospital when I did, she would have died. I say it would have been better if she had died. She would be out of her misery. He says for me to just go home. Because there is nothing more I can do for her by remaining here.

So after I signed whatever documents were necessary for Dr. Dore to operate on Peg, I got in my vehicle and drove home.

While driving, I thought to myself, that I should have waited another hour before I went to check on Peg, and perhaps at that time she might have died, which would completely end my problems with her.

When I walked into the apartment, Martha says I look like hell. I say I feel like hell. I also say that if I had waited another hour before I went to check on Peg, she would now be dead, which would have been much better for me and you. But of course she could still die, because the doctor at that hospital still has to do a Hysterectomy on her and because of her weakened condition, she could die on the table.

And privately I kind of hope she does, because whatever Love I had for her has diminished down to just a drop in a thimble.

Martha comes to me and puts her arms around me and hugs me for five minutes. I feel drained of energy at this time of my life. Am I thinking the wrong things about all of this?

I have always felt that I most often have put your interests before my own, but now that the possibility that you could die, why am I feeling so drained of anything regarding the two of us.

I need to get some sleep. Martha says she has already fed the cats. She further asks, am I hungry and I say I am just very tired, so I am going to bed. I go into Martha's bedroom. Martha says she has completely cleaned up the bed, because there are no remnants of there ever being any blood on that bed. I feel as if I cannot sleep on that bed yet.

Martha has followed me and she says there was a lot of blood in that bed, and the blood did go completely through the mattress, but because of the plastic covering on the Box Spring it did not permeate any further, but it did look like Peg had lost a lot of blood. I told her the doctor says she lost two pints of her blood and she may lose another pint when he does this other operation.

Martha says I will have to buy a new mattress because this one is completely soaked with Peg's blood. But for now she has placed a plastic cover around it, which will prevent any blood from soaking into anything else.

I say I think the next Garbage pickup is in two days, so we will remove this mattress tomorrow and go out and buy a new one to replace it. Martha says we can just leave the plastic covering on it and just carry it out and place it in the dumpster. But after we place it in that dumpster we will cut the plastic from this mattress, so no one else will try to use it. It will make the garbage men wonder what really happened, but let them wonder. And if they call the police, they have already been here, so nothing should come of any of this.

Anyway I go to sleep and when I wake up, it is now daytime outside. When I come into the kitchen, Martha is doing some cooking, and she says that I slept sixteen hours, because it is now 4:00 PM of the day after Peg went to the hospital.

Martha says she got a little concerned when I did not wake up at noon today, but when she checked on me, she says I was breathing okay, so she just let me sleep.

She says the UCLA medical center called and said that my wife came through the operation fairly well. But it was very grave for a while, because she has now gone into a Coma and how long she will remain that way, he is uncertain at this time. But she is still in a coma, so no one can see her yet, so just remain at home until Dr. Dore calls to let us know when we can come to see her, if that becomes possible, because she is still a very sick woman. He is not certain how long she will be in this coma. It all depends on her will to live. Martha says that Dr. Dore told her that he couldn't say whether she will live or die.

I tell Martha that after we eat something, we have to move that mattress out to the garbage dumpster. Then after we have done that, we both will get in my vehicle and go to a used furniture store, where I know where they sell mattresses and a lot of other kinds of furniture, even Television sets.

We arrive at this used furniture store, and Martha and I walk all around this store for over an hour. I make mental notes of what I want to buy. Since all of the beds in our apartment are queen size beds, I finally decide on the mattress I will buy.

We also decide on a Television set to buy for the living room, which are a 21-inch with a remote control and also a 14-inch with a remote control for Martha's bedroom. Both sets are in Color, so the set we are presently using in the living room, will now be placed in the Master bedroom. This is the set that I had in the trailer.

I also buy a padded lounge chair for Martha's bedroom, including an end table to go beside her bed that the TV will sit on. There is already an end table on one side of her bed, and one side of it is a scratching area for the cats to scratch on.

Since the cats rarely come into the Master bedroom, all of the scratching areas are either in Martha's bedroom or in the living room.

For the master bedroom I buy a low Cedar chest that will be placed at the foot of my bed, where extra blankets can be placed. I also buy several extra blankets that will cover all of our beds, and also three king size blankets that will be used to cover our couch in the living room.

I also buy three other small end tables, which will be used in the kitchen and dining room, and lastly I buy a dining table that is four feet across it that is round, including five chairs.

Included with that is also a round coffee table and a Bar with two stools with backs on them that are also padded. All five of the dining chairs are also padded. I am having all of this stuff delivered, and the cost for everything is five hundred dollars, including the delivery charge.

The manager of this store asks where will I sleep until all of this stuff is delivered, and I say I have a six and a half foot couch in the living room that even folds out into a queen sized bed, so never worry about whether I do have a place to sleep.

Besides, maybe I will just sleep on the box spring of my bed. It might be a good change. When we are driving home, Martha asks, will I really sleep on the couch, and I say no, I will sleep with you. Why should I give up comfort if I have a better place to sleep? She just smiles but does not say anything further. As usual she just sits close to me as we drive.

Clem

August 28th 1968

Dear Peg;

AN END TO A WAY OF LIFE

It has been two months and five days since we have left to go on this extended vacation. And to find out that you had an Abortion that failed to get rid of the Baby that was formed when Ken Jenkins and you had sex, when I was on my job in Keokuk, Iowa, and you and Ken threatened to kill all of my Cats makes me so very sick, and Angry that I think that I should have Moses Lighthouse make out Divorce papers and hand them to you some day in the near future.

And it has been six days since you have been operated on, and you are still in a Coma. How long you will remain in that Coma is anyone's guess.

Actually I had hoped that you would not survive that operation. I know you do not want to hear such talk, but I cannot feel any different at this time, because I have had it up to the very top of my head and out to the end of all of the hairs on my head. I have agonized and have forgiven you so many times, that in each case, would be like writing a separate book on that subject.

Even though I did have Divorce documents handed to you in our past and I did divorce you, but I in one of my many weak moments took you back into my life, I now feel that you are back to doing what you have always done, since we have been married again, and that is you have continued to have Liaisons with other men.

Well woman, that will either stop completely now or we are History as a married couple. And knowing that you are now fighting for your very life in the UCLA Medical center Hospital does not slow me down in my venture to ultimately getting rid of you. No, I will not feel sorry for you any longer.

You are where you are, because you have continued to violate whatever agreements you have made with me, with full knowledge that these Liaisons would some day get you in trouble with me. This has to stop and stop on this very day.

Now maybe you will not survive this operation that you have had. Which will forever prevent you from ever getting pregnant again. You have always used this condition at getting back at me, even though I never caused your initial problem. Why don't you ever blame Ken Jenkins for your problems? If you love that man, then why didn't you marry him? I'll tell you why you never married Ken Jenkins, because you only used him as a way to get to me.

Well, wife – those days are coming to a quick end. Because I have had it up to the very top of my head with all of your Liaisons with other men. As far as I am concerned, we are no longer a couple. Even if you die. Or even if you don't die.

I now want a Divorce from you. And if the Catholic Church will not give me an annulment from this marriage, well so be it. I no longer want to remain married to you. Something Revolutionary will have to happen if I am to continue to keep you as a wife.

I also have to think of Martha and how this will affect her. She is more grown up than you or I had realized, so don't sell her short. She is stronger than you ever were, and she knows everything about whatever she needs to know about persons and Sex.

I remind Martha that this afternoon, we have to go to Moses Lighthouse's house for Supper. Martha says she completely forgot about it, with everything that has been going on in this household. I say just wear your beaded jeans that Mary Beth tried to steal. I will say one thing, and that is that Mary Beth recognized quality in clothes.

Martha says that Mary Beth always wanted a pair of jeans like that pair. I then asked, could you place beads on another pair of your jeans just like the pair you will wear today. Martha says she can and she will, and then she will send them to Mary Beth. I say that is what I had in mind for you to do for your sister. I will have to find out where to send them, but on second thought, I will send them to Uncle Homers residence, with strict instructions for him to give them to Mary Beth, and we will also put a card inside of that box, along with a few other personal things that I will make for her this weekend.

Martha says a kind of support your local Sister package. And I say yeah. You see, I really don't want to forget her, and I know that you tried to get through to her on a number of occasions, but she just would not listen to you or me or Grandma.

I know how I felt when I was growing up on that farm in South Dakota, wearing hand me down clothes and trying to make headway into that family that I eventually did become a member of.

I am quite sure that she now feels like she is not a member of anybody's family, and especially ours. So I think this Care Package will hopefully began to pour a little slow curing cement in her life. At least I hope she sees it that way. I tried so hard to make her understand what kind of family I wanted her to believe in.

But with you doing what you kept right on doing, and you trying to influence Mary Beth in whatever ways you could, I am quite sure that Mary Beth became very confused as to who to believe.

So I think that Martha and I need to send Mary Beth occasional Care Packages, at least until we are told that we cannot. I also think that we need to make occasional trips back to Missouri, to visit her.

I don't know if that is allowed, because Uncle Homer has not really told me a whole lot about what kind of regulations that are allowed by the parent of any of those of whom are housed in that Camp.. I will write a letter to him this weekend also, that I will send before we send this package to Mary Beth, alerting him that this package is coming for her, and that I want everything given to her, without fail.

Now we had better get ready to go to Moses house. Do you need to take a shower? I think I do, and I head to the bathroom in the Master Bedroom. Just as I am stepping into the shower, I feel Martha behind me, and she steps in also. She washes my back and I do hers and I help her with her long hair and then we rinse ourselves off and step out of the shower. After drying myself off, I place some shaving cream on my face and I shave it off. I then get a short sleeve shirt out of my closet and a pair of blue street shorts and a pair of Moccasins, which I put on over a pair of silk stockings that goes up to my ankles.

Martha then walks in the Master bedroom and she is dressed almost like me, except for the beaded jeans I asked her to wear. She says she also has a pair of short beaded jeans she can wear, and I say wear them, so she removes those long legged jeans and gets out the other pair and puts them on.

I asked when did you do this pair, and she says yesterday when you were sleeping on her bed. Martha says we do look very much like we are from the same family don't we. I smile but do not say anything.

I then go to the closet where all of the cat food is stored and I ask, who is to pick what you will all eat on this day.

Tiger steps forward, even though she is very bashful, Tai apparently has instructed her, that she has to select every once in awhile. She really looks over all of the cans, and then I get a thought from her that states that what she wants is not here. I send her a thought, what does the can look like. I get another thought, and then I open up another closet a little ways away from this one, and I take out four cans, and show her and she touches these cans like they are her long lost friends. After my experiment of trying to get my Cats to eat dry foods; it is working slowly, but they still like to eat food out of cans.

Every third day I add some of the dry food to their wet food, and they have been eating every morsel of food. At least they might get used to eating hard food for some of the time.

So I pick up the morning dishes and get out four new dishes

and place a can of food on each plate, which I place on their eating platform, which is on one end of the bathroom off of the hall. On the other side of that bathroom is the Cat john, which is actually about six feet from their eating platform. This platform is about two feet above the floor. Very few persons ever use this bathroom, because we rarely have any kind of company.

Clement

PART THREE

August 28th 1968

A NEW LIFE WITH A NEW WOMAN

PHILADELPHIA ING

Dear Peggy;

Moses Lighthouse and his wife Lucy live on Bonnie Brea Street. They have six children. The oldest is a boy whose name is Dallas. They actually have three boys and three girls. Their youngest, Christie just turned six years of age this year. When Martha and myself drive up to his house, there is a place for guests to park that is separate from the driveway that leads to the garage. Which is a two-car garage.

There is already another vehicle parked in another parking space so I assume it belongs to Philadelphia Ing. Moses is sitting on his front porch, which has a roof over it. It is a porch that is an open porch, meaning there are no other walls surrounding this area.

In a porch swing that suspends from the ceiling of this porch, Philadelphia Ing is sitting. I had already been told about what she looks like by John Wayne, but seeing her in person, she is very striking and quite beautiful. But she does not have any make up on, but she is still beautiful. When she stands she is more striking, because she is so tall, and in fact is six feet six inches tall. On her head is a straw hat with a yellow scarf around the upper portion of the hat that goes around her head and hangs off of the brim down her back.

This hat has a very wide brim, which appears to be about ten inches out from her head. She is wearing black slacks with a blue stripe down each leg on the outside of each leg. She is wearing a white blouse, which has short sleeves and pockets above each of her breasts. I would say that her measurements are: chest with Breast size as being 44 D, waist 34, and hips being about 38.

She notes that I am sizing her up and the first words she says are that I am probably absolutely correct in my assumptions of her sizes.

She says you look at me like you are a Taylor. I say you are correct in that last assumption. Because I do make all of my own clothes and all of Martha's clothes. Even her under clothes and whatever she wears on her feet.

Moses introduces me to Philadelphia and then I introduce Martha to Moses and then to Philadelphia. Moses suggests that Martha go into the house and introduce herself to his wife and to all of his children, which is exactly what she does. But before she leaves me alone with Moses and Philadelphia, she bends down and kisses me on my mouth. I patted her on her butt and then she left us adults to ourselves.

Philadelphia says it is nice to see such love between a parent and his child. I say I do love her so very much. And it is also nice that you noted that we do love each other as much as we do.

Moses says he has to go help Lucy prepare our evening meal and he gets up and leaves also. I ask Philadelphia, are you looking for another husband? And she says she is. She also asks, am I available? I say not yet, and I really don't know whether I will be available in the near future. But I know that we have met before this time.

There is a pause for about a minute, and.

I then say, let me go back about twenty years, to South Dakota, when I was going to High School in a small town in northeastern part of that state. And your basketball team was playing the my basketball team. You lived in another town south of my town about thirty miles at that time. Your younger brother Peter was playing on your team, and you were a cheerleader for your team. In fact during half time, you were the top of a Pyramid, when you all performed, and you were able to even touch our gymnasium ceiling at that time which was thirty feet high. But as that display was ending, one of the sides of that pyramid began to collapse, and when you landed on the floor, you sprained your left ankle so badly that you could not walk or put any weight on that foot.

So my Father and I picked you up and placed you on the Stage, which is at one end of the gymnasium floor, where the school Nurse examined your ankle. Your team was playing our team in a kind of two day tournament to determine who would be the Conference Champions. And my team did win that evening game. So after the game was over, and your ankle was really swelled up so large that we were afraid that we might have to even take you to the hospital.

But Dad and another man carried you to the Royal house, which was less than a block away from the Gymnasium and my Mother put some green liquid on that very painful ankle, and in fact she rubbed very gently some of this green liquid on that ankle, until the swelling began to decrease considerably.

This liquid also killed the pain in this ankle, so you could stand the severe pain you were feeling when they first brought you to our house. And that green liquid is called Omega Oil.

We talked all that night, and that is when I first fell in Love with you. I also knew that you fell in Love with me, but neither of us said that we loved each other.

Now here it is twenty some years later and that same feeling is still between us, because when I first saw you, something inside of me came alive, and after thinking about that feeling for just a moment, I then knew where we had met before. Do you remember that time and that incident?

Philadelphia says your memory is impeccable and very exacting and very accurate. She also says that you are now married, so what are we to do about these feelings for each other. I say I really don't know.

I then say, my wife is in the UCLA Medical Center Hospital, and she is in a Coma. I don't know if she will Live or die, and no one can tell me whether she will or not.

I am on the verge of serving Divorce papers to her, if and when she ever wakes up. But what if she does wake up and she has a totally different attitude about me. Do I still Divorce her and send her on her way and out of my life. I don't know what I will do.

All I know is that I do Love you, and very much, and I know that you are the potential Mother for Martha. I walk over to Philadelphia and I kiss her on her mouth, and I hold it for a full two minutes.

In the meantime Martha has returned to the porch and is sitting in a wicker chair near the porch swing.

Martha then speaks and says that looks very serious, and I

say it is, because I know this woman and I have known her for twenty plus years and she is the woman that I should have married first. I then tell Martha the story I just told Philadelphia.

Martha says to Divorce Peg, and marry Philadelphia. It's just that simple. Martha then goes and hugs Philadelphia and in that instant a Bond is formed between them. They kiss each other and something far beyond what I can even describe happens between the two of them.

Philadelphia asks Martha, are you looking for a Mother, and Martha says she has just found her Mother, the mother she wants to spend the rest of her teen years with and in reality the rest of her life.

I say I cannot think about what I will really do about my present wife, because I do not really know whether she will continue to be my present wife. I know this and that is I don't want to be married to her any longer.

Because I have finally found the woman I want to spend the rest of my life with. And I have found the woman that will be the Mother of Martha. Then Moses and Lucy come out to the porch and say that Supper is ready, so we should all come inside of the house. Which is exactly what we do.

Philadelphia and Martha and myself walk into that house like we are a family unto ourselves, knowing that someday we really will be. How that will happen, I am not certain yet. But it will happen.

Moses asked once we were all seated and the evening prayer had been said, have Philadelphia and I discussed what Martha will be taking as far as subjects she needs to take in order to graduate next spring. I say we have not gotten that far yet.

Something of more importance has come to the fore, and we had to solve that problem first. Which in fact brings forth another problem, of which we will not discuss at this time.

Martha then says, she has written down on paper all of the subjects she wants to take, in her senior year. There are more than enough subjects for her to graduate from any High School.

Why do you think I am now a senior and I am only 15 years old? Because I have always taken more subjects than was required for me, and I have been allowed to progress at my own rate, and that is because I always went to a Catholic School. And I understand that Philadelphia is associated with a Catholic Girls school, so they will accept all of my other credits from the school's I have been attending, even though these schools have been in two different states. Is that not correct Philadelphia? Philadelphia says she is absolutely correct. And the conversation died at that moment at that table.

After supper was over, Philadelphia, Martha and myself went back to the front porch and Philadelphia and Martha sat in the porch swing and I sat in a chair that faced that swing and we sat and talked about a lot of subjects.

Martha gave Philadelphia her list of subjects that she wanted to take and after Philadelphia looked it over, says she can teach all of them. Which in my opinion closed that subject.

Philadelphia says, from now on we are to both call her Phia, because it is obvious that saying her full name is something that is not necessary, because very soon we will be a family.

Because Phia says Phil and I want to get married but this marriage will only be a civil ceremony.

I looked at Phia and said, you have hit the nail on the head, because that is exactly what I was thinking. You must have read my thoughts. Martha says, is she going to be another person in this family that can do as we two can do? Phia asks what can she do that you two can do.

So we tell her what our special abilities are, and Phia says, I don't think so, but wouldn't that be something. Phia also asks can that ability be passed on to another child? She may have been adopted by me, but she is really my blood daughter, meaning that I had sex with her real Mother before she was married to the guy she married, and when I met her Mothers husband years later when Martha was about two years old, I discovered at that time that Martha was really my natural daughter.

Actually I say, this is a gift from GOD, and there is no other way anyone can get these abilities except in this way, so if GOD instills these same abilities in the rest of our children, than so be it.

And Phia says she will adopt Martha as her natural daughter after we are married. Martha asks can she do that, and I say she can and she will. Martha turns and hugs Phia again and she places her head on Phia's shoulder and cries awhile.

Phia asks why are you crying and Martha says because she is so very happy. Martha says she did not figure she would be going anywhere anytime soon, because she will be studying her lessons. Phia says school does not begin until September 10th, but because I will be becoming your real Mother, she says I guess you could start a bit earlier, if that is your wish.

Phia says any Home schooled child can really begin their classes whenever this child feels they are ready to begin them. So if you are ready to begin those studies, then she will return tomorrow morning to our apartment and bring all of those books back with her.

I tell Phia to park next to my vehicle in the underground parking, that you enter from the alley on the west side of the apartment complex. Phia says she knows that complex, because she still has a key to an apartment there. Phia asks what apartment do we live in and when I tell her, she says if the Manager did not change the locks on that apartment door, then she will be able to get into that apartment. I show Phia my apartment key and we compare her key with my key and they are identical, so that problem is solved. Apartment 11.

Then Martha gets up and goes back into the house and Phia and I are alone. I get out of my chair that I am sitting in and go sit with her in the swing and I turn to her and I take her in my arms and I kiss her with as much passion as I can come forward with, which is more than I had expected, because Phia asks, is there a place where we can go and have sex with each other. I say we can go to my apartment unless your house is closer. Phia says she lives in Santa Monica, about a mile from UCLA College Campus. I say let us go to my apartment. But first I need to tell Martha that we will be back in a little while. And I go and do that. I tell Moses that Phia and I are going to take a ride together, but we will return in a couple of hours.

Moses says he will bring Martha who is his new Niece back to your apartment in about three hours. When I tell Phia that Moses will bring Martha back to my apartment, she goes into the house and when she returns, she says she gave Lucy her car keys, so when Moses brings Martha back, she can drive Phia's car to my apartment, so she doesn't have to go back to Moses house to get it. And then we leave and go to my apartment.

When we go inside, I introduce Phia to all of my Cats, and Tai comes and sits with Phia while I am making some changes to Martha's bed a little.

When I come back into my living room, Phia is talking to Tai, just as if he totally understands her, which in fact he does, but Phia does not realize it. But whatever Phia is saying to Tai, he in like kind is responding, as she wants him to, which makes a believer out of Phia. I smile at Phia, and she says, do you know that he totally understands what I am saying, and I say, yes he does. I say to Tai, do you like Phia, and he stands up on his hind legs and reaches up and kisses Phia on her right cheek. Phia cries when he does that, and I just let them sit on that couch and spend some additional time together.

In a few minutes I hear Phia and she first walks into the Master Bedroom and when she does not find me in that room, she then comes into Martha's bedroom and she is still carrying Tai.

She places him on the bed and because I am lying on that bed, she lays down with me. Tai goes under that bed, because that is where the rest of his Pride is sleeping at this time.

But in time, they too would come and lay on this same bed with Phia and me. Phia says she has to tell me something important, before we go any further with this Sex that she wants to have with me. Phia says that you also know that after we met on that special day back in South Dakota. She says she thought about me for a very long time.

And then as you know, two years later when my brother Peter was coming home from his Senior Prom, a Drunk driver hit him and Peter was killed instantly. You even came to his funeral, and I thank you very much for doing that. In fact the entire Basketball Team of your town came to his funeral and Phia says she was so broken up over Peters death and all of his friends who came to that funeral, which she did not realize that we all knew him as well as we did. I broke in there for a moment. I tell Phia that when a Basketball player or a Coach of which I was, competes with other teams, we all get to know the other players on those other teams, so we all knew Peter very well. That is why we all came to his funeral.

Phia says it explains a lot about you and all of the others about who and what they really are. Or what they would eventually become. At least that is what she hopes will happen when they all got older.

Phia says she will continue with her story: Anyway Phia says she still thought about me for a long time after that, and even though she wanted to talk to me at that time, her father told her no, because it may not help you in my grief. But looking back on all of that, she wished she had come to me and talked to me, because she now thinks that we would have begun to date and we would have eventually gotten married after a short courtship.

Anyway after that I went to Brookings College after I graduated from my high school, and while I was at that college, one of my instructors began to date me, and he fell in love with me, but I was not sure I loved him, but he was kind of intimidating, and I finally agreed to marry him. And then two years later after I had graduated with a BA degree in General Education, he was secured as an instructor by UCLA in the general Los Angeles area of California.

So because I was going after my Masters in General

Education, I enrolled with that university. And while I was going to that college, one night a bunch of my so called friends and fellow students got me drunk and they all took me to someone's private residence, where they all Raped me, including all of the women.

Then they took me out onto Rodeo Drive, striped me of all of my clothes, and turned me loose to try to find my way back to UCLA. I apparently passed out and ended up in the gutter, where a Police officer found me and took me to the County Hospital in East Los Angeles, where I remained for the next four months, because I got a Bacterial infection from the wooden devices that were used on me. She says I think it is called a Dildoo

While I was there, my husband filed for a Divorce from me, which he eventually received. He claimed that I flaunted my Natural Beauty, which is what got me raped. .

Then I decided to go to the UC Irvine, even though it was a very long drive for me. So I rented a small apartment in Irvine because I did not want to live in the Campus Dormitory with other students who were all so much younger than I was.

I did get my Masters Degree in General Education, so then I came back to the Los Angeles area and moved back into my house in Santa Monica, of which my father had built initially.

But before I enrolled in UC Irvine, I turned in all of the names of all of these other students who had raped me, and every one of them got kicked out of UCLA. They all were eventually sent off to various prisons where some of them still are. Because of how it was all planned out, they all got the Maximum that the Law would allow.

Then after a few years had gone by, I began to date a few

persons again, because I got to know a lot of the Los Angeles policemen. Some of these Policemen were single, so I began to date a few of these men.

Then after 12 years had gone by, I began to date just one of them. And we eventually got married. He always was a perfect gentleman while we were dating. I remained married to that person for two years.

Every time something happened in his career, whether it was good or bad, he would always drink and when anything bad ever happened he always got drunk, and when he got drunk, he would come home and Beat me, until I got fed up with it, and I went over to Catalina Island and purchased a gun, because when I tried to purchase one in Los Angeles county, I was always refused.

I interrupted Phia here and said that you went to see Maggie Kettle. Phia did not blink an eye but she noted the name that I mentioned.

Phia says she purchased a Special gun which she could wear as rings on her fingers or as part of a necklace, that will fire three bullets, and it only takes her 90 seconds to put it together, because whenever she even mentioned buying a gun, her husband would search her personal body by insisting that she remove all of clothes and all of her closets and drawers to make sure she did not have one, because he was fearful that she was going to shoot him one day.

Phia says that is what she did when he came home about six months back, drunk as usual, and before he could lay a hand on her, she had assembled her weapon and when he came towards her she shot him, using all three bullets. She said that he had such a surprised look on his face, like how in hell did she get that gun into his house.

Phia says actually they were living in her house and he wanted her to put his name of the Deed of that house, but she never did.

Phia says he got within two steps of her before he fell to the floor. She says she waited for five minutes, to make sure he was not going to get up anytime soon, and then she called the police, and when they came, they took him away.

But before she called the Police, she dismantled her weapon and placed the pieces on her fingers and around her neck, and when the two policemen who initially came to the house had remained behind to ask her all kinds of questions, she says she took her husbands gun which he had hung on a chair and said she made it appear that she had shot him with his own gun.

During those five minutes that she waited before calling the police, she says she took his own gun and went outside and placed it in a barrel of water and fired three times.

She says she picked up the three casings and threw them on her living room floor, so that the bullets they took from him would match what they took from his own gun.

The casings from the bullets she shot into him she still has in a special place in her house. Because she used the same kind of shells that her husband uses.

He was in the Los Angeles county hospital for five months, because of complications with his Heart, and he finally died of blood poisoning because he fell out of bed and fell on some glass objects which apparently had gotten some foreign materials on this glass into his body, so his death was ruled accidental.

Because he did not die of his wounds from being shot by herself. She says isn't that amazing. I say that is a terrific story. One day I will write a book and I will include all of that in that book.

Phia asks how did I know I purchased my weapon from Maggie Kettle. And I told her because I have known Maggie since 1948. I knew her husband when he owned his gun shop out near the Los Angeles Zoo.

When he died of a heart attack, he left his shop to his helper, so Maggie sued his estate and won her case, because Moses Lighthouse handled her case.

And using some of that money she bought some land on Catalina Island where her youngest son lives, who is a Contract house builder over there, and she purchased an empty store and made it into her own gun shop and he also built her a house. He lives on the island also. Phia says, if she is a friend of yours, you have a very good friend for the rest of your life.

So I understand that you have some concerns about this Bacterial infection returning to you, huh? Phia says you are very correct. I tell Phia that I need to tell you some history about my wife, and myself because I believe you need to know everything about me that there is.

So I tell my story about myself, at least up to the time when Peg and I met and got married. Then I try to summarize our thirteen years of married life, up to this very day. I conclude by saying; that is why I am not sure that I can divorce her in the next few weeks, if not months.

But I do know that I want to marry you, and as soon as we can arrange it. Whether we go to Mexico and do this is still to be determined.

Because like you, I want the two of us to have children by the two of us and I want them to have a father they know is their real father. Because even though I lived with my real father, I really never knew him. Phia asks how soon can we go to Mexico and get married.

I say as soon as I can make some phone calls to some airlines to get some reservations and get to LAX. We can always leave a note for Martha, or we can wait until Lucy brings your car to this complex, because you can park it next to my vehicle. Then we can tell Martha personally instead of having sex now; we can wait until we get to Mexico. And while we are waiting, let me show you something. As you surmised over at Moses place, I am a Taylor and I can make all of your clothes from now on.

Someone with your measurements and height must have a lot of problems buying any kind of clothes, so looking at what you have on, which was probably made by a seamstress, which probably cost you a lot of money.

Think how much money you will now save by having me make all of your clothes. Come with me into the Master Bedroom where I will show you some of the outfits I have made for Peggy. She never wears any of them. Why I don't know for sure, except because I rarely take her any place now because of the way she has been treating me for all of these years, and I no longer want to make her any more new clothes. I then show Phia what I use to measure any persons body with. Phia asks can you measure her now, and I say I can and will if you will remove all of your clothes, including your shoes. I get a light blanket from the cedar chest at the foot of that bed, and I tell Phia to lie down after I measure her in every way that is necessary, including her feet, because just as I was doing the latter, I could hear Moses and Lucy and Martha come into the apartment. I further say; there is a robe in the closet that is mine, which will fit you very well because it is extra long, just in case you want to go out to the living room to visit. But I also suggest that you put on a pair of my under shorts and a pair of my street shorts, just in case.

Martha comes into my bedroom and when she sees Phia lying on my bed, she surmises something that has not yet happened. I note her thoughts, so I send an answer back to her telling her that no we did not have sex yet. She is this way, because she had to remove all of her clothes so I could measure her.

Now all of these thoughts took place within about 20 seconds. Martha asks Phia, what kind of outfit is Dad going to make for you, and she says we never got that far yet. Telling our stories about ourselves has taken up a lot of time. Mostly mine but still we have accomplished quite a bit. Martha asks Phia, when are you two going to Mexico to get married. Phia asks why do you think we will be going to Mexico soon to get married.

Martha says why else would Dad make you a special outfit, except for you to get married in. I smile at Martha and say, isn't she wonderful, to Phia. Phia says you two talk telepathically, which is much faster than spoken speech. Martha says it has taken her several years to get to this point where she can talk to her Dad this way. Phia says this is going to take some getting used to when we are all together. I say normally, when we would speak to each other in Pegs presence, it was easier to talk telepathically than in the spoken word.

But with you, we will not do that, because we will not have

any secrets from each other, ever. Unless you want to keep a few secrets from Martha, but never from me.

I hate Secrets between married couples. I ask Martha, did Moses and Lucy go home, or are they still in the living room. Martha says she sent them home, telling Moses that I will call him in a few days about something that I have to settle between Peg and I.

I have lived with a woman who has had nothing but secrets from me, but she really does not know that she can never keep her dirty secrets from me, because I can always read her mind.

But reading your mind may be a bit harder because you are a different kind of woman. All women are not alike, and hopefully that will remain that way.

Diversity is what I am seeking and diversity is what I have now found in you. For example: you did not tell me that you are Millionaires, and that you have at least six million dollars in various banks in Orange county. Money is not all that important to me. It's what a person does with all of their money. If they just put it in various Banks and savings institutions, and do not invest it in various businesses, then that money will never grow very fast.

But if that money is invested in businesses that will make a lot of other money then that makes a lot of difference to me. Whenever anyone wants anything, Money always does the talking.

Now for me, I am an inventor so I am always making money some place from all of my inventions. Some time in the future after we are married, we will go talk to Moses, because he gets three percent of whatever I make from all of my Inventions.

From his business, I get two percent of everything that he

makes from his business. I in fact have made him a multi-millionaire, and he has made me a multi-millionaire.

I don't really have to work at any job, but boredom would kill me faster than any other method. Because whatever I do, I always become the best there is in that profession.

Whenever I go to work, I am always happy and smiling and other persons think there is something wrong with me, and they often ask me, how can I be so happy when things are going so wrong?

I tell them when things go wrong, then my mind is working a mile a minute, because it is then that I will come up with an Invention to solve all of the problems we are having, thereby making me a lot of money. So why should I not be happy.

Phia and I do not have any problems yet, but I am sure we will have a few in the coming years. Because Divorces take no less than six months for them to become final.

I am going to have to live a different kind of life. How long that will continue, is anybody's guess. But however long it will go on, I will always be happy. I have been so very unhappy for so many years that it is a wonder that I am still standing and still functioning like I do. One of the things that Peg told me and lots of others, is that I rarely get very angry, because anger is only a letter away from Danger. That thought has always been with me, since I can remember anything.

But with Phia and me and Martha and whatever other children we have or will adopt, we will be always happy. What I am really thankful for, is when I Adopted Martha, I did it alone, and not with Peg, because I have always known that she would never produce me any natural children.

Martha is my natural daughter. I have known her for quite a

few years now, and I wished I had known her from when she was born. But that was not to be. But we are now finally together as father and Daughter and now she will have a Mother, who will Love her like she is supposed to be loved.

There is no person like Martha, and there never will be another like her. Phia and I will have other children, but none will be like Martha. Maybe similar, but not identical. Even if some of them are twins and triplets. But first we will try for just one child at a time, and if we get more than one than that will even be better.

CLEMENT

August 29th 1968

Peg

MARRIAGE TO PHILADELPHIA

Phia and I have decided that I and Martha and the Cats will move in with her in her house in Santa Monica, where we will live until the Divorce from Peg is final. I will also move all of the Cats to Phia's house along with all of their toys and food and scratching places that are on some of Martha's side tables.

Moses says that moving in with Philadelphia will complicate the Divorce that he has filed in Court, so I am to still keep my residence to be at the apartment until this divorce is final, which will be in about six months if everything goes alright.

That I will have to live in that apartment during the daytime hours, but at night I can go live with Philadelphia and Martha.

I will keep the apartment for however long it is needed. I still did not know whether Peg will regain consciousness, and I really do not care whether she does or not.

I think a great weight has been removed from my shoulders when I decided to go live with Philadelphia. Even though some persons will look down their noses at me if they knew that I was filing for a divorce from Peggy while she is still in a coma in the UCLA medical center in Santa Monica, California.

I also packed all of my sewing materials including all of the extra piece goods, that I had already cut out of bolts of material, for clothes I was in the process of making for Phia.

Martha says she has never seen me so happy before. And I know she feels this same way, now that she has a real Mother that she can talk to about anything and everything. I never thought that true happiness could be so wonderful.

Martha decided that she would take her television out of her bedroom to Phia's house and place it in her bedroom there. All of Martha's clothes also were packed and will be taken to Phia's house. But except for my own clothes, of which I will take some of them to Phia's house, the rest will remain in this apartment.

I know there will be times when I will not be able to be with Phia because of undetermined circumstances in Peg's and my life. But I will try to spend as much time with Phia as I can, because it is not just because of Phia, but also because of our children.

It is now September 3rd of 1968, and this is the day that Phia says if there will be any Bacterial infection, it will show up in her Vagina, this will be that day. So when we first wake up on this day that is the first thing that I check after Phia goes to the bathroom to urinate.

She says she does not itch in that area, so that is a good sign, because she says the first thing she noticed back when she got this problem, was that her vagina itched severely.

Which is all of the Sperm eggs that both of us have put forth while having intercourse, and since some of those eggs will combine with each other to form a nuclei to form a baby or babies. All of the rest of the eggs just congregate in a specific area of her womb where they will sometimes cause this

Bacterial infection.

Because I am a Veterinarian, I have certain instruments whereby I can see inside of certain areas of any creature's body, so using these special instruments, I look inside of Phia's womb, and there is no infection anywhere. Phia asked is she pregnant and with conviction I tell her that she probably is. But let us wait an additional ten days before I take you to your Gynecologist.

Because I am not a Gynecologist, even though in my veterinarian practice that I will eventually have, I will be checking various creatures for those kinds of signs, and I have studied the human body, for emergencies, so I will acquiesce to your own Gynecologist.

Phia is ecstatic with happiness, and as soon as she dresses, she goes out to the kitchen where Martha is finishing preparing breakfast, and before Phia can say a word, Martha turns around and says that her new Mom is pregnant.

Phia looks at her and asks, how do you know that is what I came here to tell you, and Martha says it is written all over your face.

They hug each other and cry together, and then Phia says; do you know that this is the very first time I have ever been pregnant with anyone's baby or babies.

Martha holds up two fingers, and Phia asks how do you know, and Martha says that Dad knows, and he is rarely wrong. Phia asks how can he know at such an early stage, and Martha says that Dad has abilities that even she does not know about yet, but she is learning. But Dad always seems to know about these things.

I remember when my first mother got pregnant with my first brother, and Elizabeth kept telling Henry that she was pregnant with twins. But when Dad examined her by just placing his hands over her lower abdomen area, he says, there is only one baby in there and it is a boy.

Phia asks, can Clem tell me whether these two babies will be boys or girls, and Martha says when you are two months pregnant, then let him place his hands on the area of where those babies are and he will be able to tell you.

Now remember that since Philadelphia and I have both been Divorced and have re-married again, then in the eyes of the Catholic Church, we don't exist in their world, But I also remember that everyone on this earth lives under the auspices in GOD'S UNIVERSE. So in anyone's Church we are only violating GOD'S LAWS.

Now if this means the happiness of three persons that are most important to me, which are myself, Martha and Philadelphia, and of course the Cats, then I am hoping that GOD will look with kindness on the two persons who are committing this sin, but with our happiness comes also other children, that I believe should have really happened twenty years back anyway. And the marriage that I have with Margaret would never have taken place.

And if for some reason, Margaret does not survive her time in the Medical center, then Phia and I can get married after the divorce is final.

Now these letters that I write to Margaret, are written to her because she has chosen to not communicate with me using the spoken word. And since one day, if she survives, she will hopefully read what I have written here, and she will realize that since I have gotten Phia pregnant on our Honeymoon, then all of the problems that my wife Peggy has been having for all of the years that we have been married, are totally her own instigation's, because of what happened to her long before I ever knew her initially.

And since I have been so very unhappy for all of these years I have been married to Peggy, that now is the time for me to have as much happiness as I can make happen.

So when Peggy said to her parents back some years ago, that I was the main problem that she never got pregnant, she was lying to them just like she has always done. And I believe that the initial problem that she stated back so many years ago, about her getting Raped, probably did happen, but with her total approval and that all of what has happened since that time has been from her own sick imagination of what she thinks she needs or what she thinks she can get from me.

So from now on, it is my happiness that I will concentrate on, and never Peggy's any longer. Because in my own life, I have had so much unhappiness that, I wonder how much does a man such as myself have to endure in this life.

It has been said that enduring a lot of grief, strengthens ones character. Perhaps the person who made that statement never has gone through what I have gone through for all of the years that I have put up with the ranting and ravings of a psychologically sick wife, who only thinks of herself, and never of her husband, or anyone else.

So this will be the last letter to Peggy for a long time, or until she regains consciousness and begins once again to make my life a LIVING HELL.

Clement

PART FOUR

THE INGFAMILYNAME

Peg

I must go back several years when Grandfather Ing was working for the ruling Family in Spain, where he was one of the Palace Guards. Guarding the King of that Country. His name at that time was not Ing, but was actually ATLAQUEST.

Abel Atlaquest, when he was 65 years old he requested that he be allowed to migrate to the United States, because he says that he cannot do what he is supposed to do any longer as one of the guards and the Editor of the Palace Newspaper for the King of that country.

So the Ambassador of that country to the United States secured all of the necessary documents that Abel would need to get into the United States, and he and his family, after they had gotten all of the necessary shots for all of the diseases that the United States were always trying to prevent any Aliens from bringing into this country, they were placed on a ship, which took several days to reach this country.

They came into New York Harbor and actually saw the Statue of Liberty, and they entered into the United States through Ellis Island.

They were checked for all kinds of different diseases, but they did not have any problems. Abel's first cousin met them, when they stepped onto the soil of the United States, who came to New York from Philadelphia.

After he and his wife and Son arrived in this country, and after Abel looked around for some kind of employment, where he could continue to exist on what he would make at that job, he discovered that his name was causing him to not to be able to secure the kind of position he was seeking.

So since he had this Cousin in Philadelphia, where he and his family had traveled to, who was a Lawyer, his cousin said that changing his last name would probably make a lot of difference in allowing him to secure a pretty good position.

So after considerable thought on that subject, he decided he would go with the name of ING. His cousin asked him why that name, and Abel says that everybody keeps telling him that with a very short name, he would have a better chance of getting whatever position he was seeking, and since, after studying the English language, he says Ing sounds good to him.

Abel asks his family what they thought and his Son, whose name is Reed, says it has a nice ring to it when he says his first name and his last name, and he says Reed Ing. Abel's wife, whose name is Paige says she likes her total name too and it now sounds thusly Paige Ing. Then Abel says his name Abel Ing, and he says he likes the sound also. Abel says our new name kind of sings.

So when they were going to become Citizens of the United States a few years later, and the Judge asked each family by what name would they be called in this country, they all at the same time said ING.

So each person had to say his or her entire name when called upon to do so. And it sounded like this. Abel Anthony Ing,

Paige Sarah Ing, Reed Myron Ing. And that is how the ING family name was born.

And Abel Ing did get a good position, with a Newspaper running printing presses, because he had some experience in that field, when he printed the Palace Newspaper in Spain.

Now Reed Ing met and married Irma Louise Stoddard, when he met her when he was in the U S Army, and he was stationed near Alexandria, Virginia.

After he was discharged from that branch of service, he ended up moving to Brookings, South Dakota, because he says that part of the country reminds him of where he was raised in Spain for the short time he was there as a young man.

He also likes to hunt Pheasants and Ducks, which he says they are plentiful around this area. And since he had gotten a Bachelor of Arts Degree in General Education in the Army, he now wanted to get his Masters Degree in the same subject. So he had decided he would do that on the GI Bill, so him and his wife could live reasonably comfortable while he attended the University in that small city.

And then after five years had gone by, Irma got pregnant, and after nine months had a Daughter, who they named Philadelphia, because of where his father had really gotten his first good position in the United States, because it was in that city. And the date is April 6th, 1930.

And then two years later, in 1932, Irma had a Son, which they called Peter, who was the heaviest baby that had been born in the Clark, SD Hospital. Because he weighed 13 pounds 5 ounces. The doctor, who delivered him via C-section surgery, says he is already half grown.

Phia says no one in their immediate families are tall, but it did not matter, because Philadelphia kept right on growing, even after she reached the age of sixteen. Peter was a whole lot different, because even though he was half grown when he was born, he did not grow hardly another inch until he reached the age of one year of age. Then he too began to grow, and at first his parents thought he might become as tall as Philadelphia, but when Peter reached the height of six feet three inches, he stopped and did not grow any more.

When Philadelphia was two years old, Reed got a position Teaching in this town of Clark, South Dakota, where he was one of the teachers in their High School and because he had taken as a minor subject in Brookings, he had taken up the Sport of Basketball and a few other related sports that usually effect most high schools. So when I first saw Philadelphia, at that Clark and Lily Basketball game in Lily, I thought she was the prettiest girl I had ever seen.

I did notice that the Coach and her and one of the players looked a lot alike, but I did not put it together at that time.

Only after Philadelphia had gotten hurt, did these other two persons make sense to me, because when she got hurt, her father who was the Basketball Coach came to where she was laying on the floor of that gymnasium and he looked real worried. Peter also came to where his sister was laying. I was an assistant Coach at that time, even though I was only 14 years of age. Because I have a bad foot, due to Polio when I was very young, whereon I cannot play any sport that I have to run extensively and aggressively a lot, so I just became an assistant coach.

Now I must tell you a little about Peter Ing. He was born on March 23, 1932. If the reader of this book, notes these birthday dates, you will see significant dates that coincide with these same dates for other persons in this book. In my story about the Ing family I did mention when Peter was born, and how he progressed when he was growing older.

After this basketball game that had been played on that eventful night where Philadelphia had gotten hurt, and she was eventually taken to the Royal Residence, where she was catered to in helping to relieve the pain in that ankle. And where she remained for the rest of that night, and where Philadelphia and I had first fallen in Love.

Two years later, when Peter was driving home from the Senior Prom he and some of his friends had attended. He after dropping off all of his friends and their girl friends, was about six blocks from his parents home, when a Drunk Driver went through a Stop sign and hit his vehicle on the drivers side, when this other driver was estimated to be going close to sixty miles per hour even while driving in the town of Clark, South Dakota.

Peter was killed instantly, because of the impact of that other vehicle. That other vehicle pinned Peter inside of his vehicle so securely that it took the Firemen three hours to extract his body from his vehicle. It was determined that Peter Ing was killed instantly.

He was not wearing any kind of seat belt, mostly because seat belts had not been installed in earlier model vehicles of which he was driving, by that time of the 20th century. It was an accident that could have been prevented, but folks in South

Dakota were not up to speed about some of the more modern restraints that were coming to the fore during that time.

In my own vehicle that I was driving at that time, which was a 1939 Oldsmobile, club coupe, Royal Blue, I had installed my own seat belts that were fastened to the floor of my vehicle. I did not have a chest belt, but one time when I had to drive into a deep ditch, and it appeared that I might roll over, that seat belt kept me from being thrown around inside of my vehicle.

My passenger, who did not believe in seat belts, had not fastened her seat belt around herself, hit her head on the dashboard and she needed twelve stitches to close up that wound. Several years later, she had plastic surgery on that scar to get rid of it.

After that night, she says she will never ride in any vehicle that does not have seat belts in them, because she says she probably would not have gotten injured if she had had her seat belt fastened around her. I did not get hurt at all. It was indicated by the local Police that Peter was only driving thirty miles per hour, which was the speed limit on the street he was driving on, on that fateful early morning.

Now forward to September 4th of 1968.

Because Phia had already had beds in all of the bedrooms of her house, I did not have to move any beds from my apartment on Eighth Street. Phia's house was a one story Ranch style house with a three car garage that was attached to her house via a breezeway, which is a covered portion of the house that is screened on two sides, that connects to her two-car garage.

This house had originally belonged to her Father, because he had initially built it, and then to her, and because her first husband wanted his name put on the Deed to this house, of which she did not do.

On the east side of her house there is a Porch, which has Screens all the way around it on three sides. On the north end is a door, which leads to an equipment shed made out of Tin, where there is a Riding Lawn Mower and a Push Lawn mower and several other kinds of tools and all kinds of boxes where several kinds of seeds are located.

About twenty feet further north of that shed there is another larger wooden shed that is used as a drying shed where Grapes and other vegetables and fruits are stored, because it is a Refrigerated building.

Phia says that is where her Father used to make all of his Wines from the Grapes that grow on this property. Phia says her Father built this place.

Phia says she believes that her EX convinced all of these UCLA Students to take her to a house away from the University and Rape her and almost kill her, because she thinks that her husband wanted to own that house and grounds totally.

She says she could never prove it, but while she was in that east Los Angeles Hospital, she had a lot of time to think about what her husband at that time really wanted from her.

When he was dating her, he indicated that he wanted a lot of children, but after they had been married for six months, and they had only had intercourse twice in all of that time, and he was very aggressive in his methods, and was not very gentle, she finally asked him about having children, and he told her he never wanted to have any children, because he does not like young children, but only after they get around 18 to 20 years old.

She says she knew at that time, that she had made a most egregious mistake when she married him. So when what happened to her, made her stop and think even deeper thoughts and that is why she thinks that he only wanted her Money, and not her body, because she thinks he was Gay and or was a Queer, because he seemed to like boys most of all.

Now she says that she finds that I am an Inventor and that I probably have more money that she does. I tell Phia that I really don't know how much money I really have. Only Moses knows. Most of my money goes to support all kinds of Foundations that support Cat Retirement Centers, and Dog retirement centers, and some of it goes to support Private Zoos in just about every state in this country. I am no doubt worth multi millions of dollars, but because all of this is done without using my own name, but a name of another foundation as the Originator of all of these funds,

I only know about some of these places because Moses sometimes mentions a new place to me and wonders if I might be interested in supporting that one also. Like I said earlier, how much money a person has, does not excite me, but what your money can do out there to help others is what really interests me.

But with a lot of money, it is too complicated for me to keep it all straight in my own mind, so I hire others like Moses and some of his Lawyers to handle it all. If I want to channel money from one of my many inventions, I just tell Moses and it gets done. He tells me where this money is located and when I need it, I can go and get it, and I have all of the necessary documents to withdraw whatever I need.

I figure that I will have Moses open a Trust fund for every child that I raise, whether that child is natural born or adopted, in the amount of one hundred thousand dollars, which will be an interest bearing account, and when the amount gets too large to support by the FDIC, then another account will be opened in that child's name, that they can access when they reach the age of lets say 18 or 21 or whatever, Phia interrupts and says 25.

Okay, when they reach age 25, wherein they can use it to buy whatever they think they may need, like for some clothes or whatever. Phia says we will talk about all of this with Moses. I say you and I will talk about all of this before we go see Moses.

Anyway the idea is, that when any of my children graduate from College or get married, whichever comes first, they will have a minimum of a hundred thousand dollars to get a good start in life.

The money is already out there; I just don't know where it all is. Only Moses knows. I have already created a Trust fund for Martha and Mary Beth, even though Mary Beth will not be able to have access to any of her money until she reaches age 25, because she doesn't know a damn thing about money.

She is now in a kind Reform School Camp kind of place. Maybe you and I can go and see her to see how she would respond to you. Phia says not for at least four years. Phia says let that camp straighten her out first.

If she is as belligerent as you have indicated, she says she does not want anything to do with her, because she fears that she would be just like all of those students that Raped her all those years back. I say whatever you want is yours for the asking. And whatever you don't want is also within your power.

One thing I want to make absolutely clear, and that is, you will have no contact with Peg or any of whatever friends she might make while living in this area. I will show you a picture of her when you want to see what she looks like, and then whatever you want to do about that picture, is totally up to you.

You will make the rules of this household only. It is not that I cannot make rules, and I do have strict rules for my Cats and for Martha, but ask her what I want from her. She is older than she appears to be, meaning that she had to grow up real early in her life, because she in effect became the Mother of her own Brothers. I had to grow up very fast also.

When my Sister molested me when I was ten years old, I went from being ten years old to being eighteen years old. I don't want any of my future children to have to do what Martha and I had to do.

Clement

PEG

CHANGING THINGS AT PHIA'S HOUSE

It was decided that the Porch at Phia's house would become the place where I will put the Cat John, mostly because it is screened in.

The door on the north side of that porch was permanently bolted shut, because we did not want anyone to get onto that porch from outside of the house. I discussed with Phia, that how about installing all kinds of shelving on the three sides that is screened in, where we could place all kinds of house plants and even some midget Orange trees. Just to experiment a little in trying to get them to grow that way, or whatever.

Once I had installed all of this shelving, my cats mostly slept on them all day long, even when a little of the south sun shown on a few of them.

I also installed a ceiling fan, because in the winter time, when I would lower all of the storm windows that I also installed, to keep whatever rain might fall off of the Porch floor, that I also carpeted with indoor--outdoor carpeting, and these storm windows will also prevent any water from landing on that porch floor when the Lawn was watered with the automatic sprinklers that came on every morning at 6:00 AM, so every evening these storm windows will always be lowered so no water will ever get on that carpeting.

Phia had an old Couch that she put on that Porch, and on that couch I placed one of my many old blankets, and the cats always slept on that couch when the Sun became too hot for any of them on the shelving.

Or if they tired of it for whatever reasons. Once I began putting houseplants on all of that shelving, curiosity got the better of most of them, but they never tried to eat any of them. Tai knew what was good for any of them so I guess he told all of his Pride what not to do.

I really love Phia's place. She has a total of four acres around her house, which is loaded with all kinds of fruit trees, including two different kinds of Apple trees, that she says bear fruit every year. There is two of Grapefruit trees, Two of Orange trees, and two of six other kinds of fruit trees. Her Father planned it all.

There are even two different kinds of green grapes and dark grapes. Phia says the dark grapes were always used for making wine, but we ate some of those grapes also, and they are always kept in the Refrigerated building. She says there are some of those grapes in there right now. I had not been in that building yet, but soon my curiosity will get the best of me.

Phia says the only thing that her Dad did not do was, he did not dig a basement under this house, like a lot of other houses on this cul-de-sac. In fact she says he only built this house on Rocks that he embedded in the ground six inches. She says if a major Earthquake happens, it will most likely be moved completely off of those rocks. Thereby probably doing a lot of damage to the house.

She says Los Angeles wants to Annex this land, because it

juts out into a kind of needle towards Los Angeles, and a large company who wants to build a manufacturing plant that they have already started building, that you can see when you look out the kitchen window, but they have not offered her what she wants for this land yet.

She says she wants four hundred thousand dollars an acre, and they have only offered me half that amount so far. She says all of the other homeowners have already sold their properties to this concern, but she is the hold out in the Pot.

I ask is Moses handling this deal, or are you doing it yourself, and Phia says she is handling it herself. I say let Moses handle it and you will get what you want for it. She says she will call him right now, and that is what she does. In ten minutes she comes to where I am sitting at a desk I am using to pay some of my bills from back in Wisconsin that did not get paid, because I have not officially sold my house back in Wisconsin yet. She says give him six months and he will have this land sold.

Phia asks why did we not get together back twenty years ago, and I say because your father was a very strict person, and he had his own ideas about young farm kids like me. I think he was wrong, but who can actually go against ones father when their minds are so set in concrete that hardened back around the turn of the century.

I really had money even back then, but I never let the rest of my family know about, especially my father. If he had known how much money I had at that time, he would have tried to take it away from me, but even back then, Moses was my Lawyer, and he controlled most of my money.

He allowed me to have whatever I wanted whenever I wanted it, because he knew that I had a business head on my shoulders, because of all of the great deals I had made in buying other farms, that my father did not know about.

By the time I was fourteen I owned a 640-acre farm that was located fifty miles from my home town. About ten miles southeast of another town that was southeast of my home town. I purchased that farm after I returned from harvesting Kansas Gold. Which is Wheat. I made 28 thousand dollars in that year alone from that adventure. Some day I will write a book about it.

I never really understood my own father, and we rarely agreed about anything. One time he hit me with his fist and knocked me down on the ground.

When I got up, I told him that my mind has not been changed, and when he drew his fist back to hit me again, I stopped that fist halfway to my jaw, and I told him if he ever wanted to try that again, you will be picking yourself off of this ground, of which I own completely, no matter what you say about it. I have the Deed to prove it.

I purchased another farm for five thousand dollars when I was fifteen years old. My father knew about this deal, because he was partially instrumental in making the deal, but because it was my money that closed the deal, it totally belonged to me.

But my father says that because I was under the age of 21, he thought that my oldest brothers name should also be put on the Deed, and it was, but after mine. He left me where I stood, and never came back to my farm.

Many years later when my oldest brother came back from spending 20 years in the Air Force, told me personally that he was going back to South Dakota to farm the land that Dad had purchased for him, and I asked him what farm, and when he told me, I told him that farm totally belongs to me and me only, and I have the Deed to prove it. I have paid the Taxes on that land for the past fifteen years.

Three months later I heard from his lawyer, but I sold it to my most mortal enemy, just so my oldest brother could not get his hands on it.

He told me he was going to give it to a Church he belonged to, that was based in Pasadena, California. I told him that you couldn't buy your way into Heaven. That church eventually went bankrupt.

Of course my oldest brother always wondered how I had accumulated so much land, even while I lived in different parts of this country. I never told him how I had accomplished that. He wouldn't have believed me anyway, because my whole family has always thought that I would never amount to a hill of beans. When in fact even before I was 21 years old, I was most probably worth more than five million dollars.

As I have said before, I don't like Secrets in anybody's family, and in this family there will be no secrets. That is why I want you to talk to Moses Lighthouse, so he can tell you how much money all of my inventions have made since I have been 14 years of age. Because that is when I created my first Invention. I will let Moses tell you what it was.

It made me fifty thousand dollars in the first six months that it was put on the market. And since that time, it has made me several million dollars, because some persons still like to have interesting things on their desks. Moses has one of them on his desk, just as a reminder of how any person can make millions of dollars in any given year. If you have been in his home office, you probably have noticed it, and have even picked it up, saying what a unique object this is. Phia says the only thing she has noticed on his desk, is a round rock that is the prettiest rock she has ever seen.

I asked do you know what that rock is made from; Phia says she thinks it is a Lava rock, which looks like it might be made from some kind of colored glass.

I tell Phia that was my first invention. I really did not make it, but I just dug it up one day, and when I dug deeper where I found it, I found several thousand of them all in one pile.

You have to remember, that most parts of this country were at various times covered by Tons and tons of Ice that came from other places. Because these kinds of rocks are not native to any area of South Dakota.

Where I found them was actually located on my 640-acre farm down near Watertown, SD. I still am having them dug out of the ground on that farm, even though I only now own forty acres of that once section of ground, and they seem to be unlimited in quantity, and the quality gets better and better, the deeper they go. And they are all about the same size, which is, as you know about 2 ½ inches in diameter.

Because that invention alone actually got Moses started in his Lawyer's Firm. Remember three percent of whatever that invention brought in, helped create Moses Law firm.

And then I discovered, wherever there is a problem, at that time and place, AN INVENTOR IS BORN. Because in solving various problems, I create an invention so as to keep right on solving that problem. No one does anything to get rid of that problem, but they just keep right on dealing with it, and getting beyond it by using my invention. That's why wherever there is a problem, there I go, to solve that problem by creating another Invention.

People just don't seem to see the handwriting on the wall. If this invention solves their problem, why change it. It's very simple Logistics. Creating the Invention most often takes a lot of Intelligence, and a lot of know how. That's why I have always been considered a problem solver.

Phia asks, how many Inventions do I have, that have Patent numbers assigned to them. I tell her I have 77 so far, with another one pending. Of course I will still create many more inventions before I leave this world, depending on how long that may be. I am hoping that I will live to at least 105 years of age, and if I get that far, I will go for 20 more.

And will continue until I am at least 150 years old, because more persons are living longer these days, then in years past, and as progress keeps going forward, because of Space travel and other elements that are being discovered, thereby causing the study of Medicine to be able to create more cures for diseases that have plagued mankind for centuries, and when most sicknesses have been totally eliminated from this earth, then people will be living much longer.

Phia says she has always considered herself to be very intelligent, but you seem to be so much farther ahead of where she even wants to be, even after she gets her Doctorate degree in place. She says our children will most likely be very smart, and she is willing to bet, that GOD with give some of them the same abilities that their father has. Martha was listening to all of this conversation between Phia and myself, so at this juncture, she says at least three of the thirteen she is going have are going to have the same abilities that her Father and herself now have.

Phia asks, why thirteen, and Martha says because that is her lucky number, because that is the number that was assigned to her when she first started first grade. Because even in this modern age, persons are still given numbers for certain reasons, and whenever her number was called, she always stood up and answered every question that was asked of her.

She supposed that every one of her teachers had a list of every student in any particular classroom, wherein that student was called upon to answer any questions when that person's number was spoken. I say this is a Mad world isn't it. I did not know that about Martha and her School and her teachers.

Phia then says, that is one of the real reasons she began teaching in people's homes, because she did not like it when she was instructed to call each student by using a number.

It was like she had heard it had been back during the second world war over in Germany, because there each student that attended school was given a number, of which they were instructed to always answer to. And she felt that if this country was adopting procedures introduced by the Nazi's, then she had to try to change things for the better.

She says she does not think it is like that in any of the Colleges in this country. Because when she was in College, all of her instructors called her by her last name.

Phia says after her last husband died, she went back to

using her Maiden name of Ing. But now it is Royal; Philadelphia Royal. Phia says she does not have a middle name, and never had one.

She wondered about it, but her mother always told her that using Philadelphia was more than enough to make any person take notice of her. I tell Phia and Martha, because I did not cancel the Los Angeles Times Newspaper, and I noticed that you already get it, what do you think I should do about it. Phia says cancel it, until your other wife comes back to that apartment.

I say, you mention her as my other wife, of which she is, but you seem to be kind of angry when you say it. While I am living with you, I probably will never mention her at all. And if she does wake up from that Coma, I will still try to spend more time with you than with her.

And it should be obvious as to why. The hardest part of my life is yet to come. But it will also be my happiest part of my life, because I am now married to you.

And with Martha and the children we will also have between us, will make that time with you even happier. You see, the story you told about yourself, when you got raped, and your husband divorced you.

Do you really expect that I will divorce Peg at this time. Most likely, because it is going to be very hard for her to get back to some semblance of a life, even if she never cheats on me again.

It is true that I don't love her any longer, but things being what they are, why would I want to make it more difficult for her if she becomes a normal person, with no ambition to do anything but to try to make me a little happier.

That does not mean that I will want to go back to be with her more than with you, because that is not going to happen. My fear is that if I divorce her and she committed suicide, I would have to live with that guilt for the rest of my life, and I don't want to do that.

Now if that happened, it is true that I would not have to feel guilty, but let me ask you, would you feel guilty if you did something that would cause me to do something drastic, that might totally destroy my way of life.

Phia says yes and no. She says she just feels a little jealous of Peg, because she is your first wife, and not the second wife. She says she knows that she is living in Sin, and that does not make her feel very good about a lot of things, but if this is the only way that she can have me, then that is the way that she will keep me in her life, even if she has to share me with that other person in my life.

She says she will rarely call her my other wife, but she will call her a lot of other names, whatever they might be. She then says let us not talk about her any longer. While she is in that Hospital in a Coma, she should never be mentioned again as long as she remains in that Coma.

CLEMENT

SQUARING THINGS WITH PEG
THROUGH MOSES LIGHTHOUSE

Since everything that was required to be at Phia's house, had been moved there, I called Moses to make an appointment with him to talk to him. Which became September fifth at thirteen hundred hours, which is 1:00 PM. When I was ready to leave to go see him, Martha asked if she could come along with me, and I asked did you ask your Mom first, and she said she did, and she even encouraged me to go with you. Martha says this is kind of strange, asking her new Mom if she can go places with me, but I guess I will get used to it in time.

She says I really never figured this would ever happen, so just give me a little time to get used to Phia as Mom. Martha says I really do love her, and so very much, and she loves me the same, because she has told me many times so far.

I say you are easy to love, and then we get in my car and we leave Phia's house. As we are driving to Moses house I ask Martha, what should we call Phia's house and she says HOME. Nothing else is said all the way there. When we arrive and we knock on their front door, over a speaker comes Moses voice, saying the door is unlocked, so come inside and come to my office, where we can talk privately. That is what I do, and Martha goes upstairs to be with the Lighthouse children.

Moses asked am I living with Phia now and I tell him what we did, and he asks, can you live with that idea and all of those facts. I say I can and I will. No matter how long it keeps going on, and Phia feels the same way.

And we are pregnant already, at least that is what I have told her, and I rarely tell the woman that I love an untruth. As you know I have abilities where I can see inside of persons, being able to sense a specific thing about that person.

Ask Lucy how many times I told her that she was pregnant when even she did not know it herself, and I was never wrong. And as you know, I wasn't even in California when I told her, because you were on the extension when I told her and you thought I was just pacifying her, but I was not.

Now first I am going to tell you about Philadelphia and myself and when we first met and fell in Love with each other. After I finished my story, I said, now don't you suppose that I am doing the correct thing?

Moses says if he had known all of this before about the two of us, he would have encouraged me to divorce Peggy a long time back, when you all lived in Missouri.

He asks did I ever get that marriage annulled, and I say I did not, because my Father in law prevented it from happening. But he doesn't know a thing about what Peggy has been doing while I was away from home. Even in the Trailer Home.

He is her father, but he does not know what his wife knows about their oldest daughter. Because the reason she is in that Hospital now, is because she got pregnant by the guy that supposedly Raped her way back when, long before I ever met her. Because he came to the Trailer when I was in Keokuk, Iowa back in the early part of June of this year.

I don't doubt that this guy never raped her because he is

that kind of guy, but I think she encouraged him to rape her, because why else wouldn't she have turned him in back then. I'll tell you why, because she did not want to get married to this guy, but she wanted to have sex with him and as often as she could convince him to do it with her.

There is something else you do not know about Peggy, which is, since we have been married back on October 1st 1955, she has slept with and has had sex with over a hundred fifty six different men, and some of them were married when they did this, and I have each and every name and addresses of these men, because I picked these names from Peggy's mind.

I had to do some additional searching for their addresses, but I am absolutely positive about all of those addresses.

So if and when she comes out of this Coma, and when I or you tell her what I have done, and if she decides to turn me in, then I will send to several Newspapers in this country, all of the names and places where all of these Liaisons happened and took place, because I have all of that information with me at this time, just in case you might want to know who these so called men are.

And at that time I hand Moses a thick envelope, which he puts aside for now. I tell him that is just a copy of the original. And I have several other copies just in case, but not in the Apartment, but in lock boxes in several banks. I did not come here to talk about what Phia and I have done and what we will continue to do for as long as we live.

I came here to talk about Peg and what I can and should do

for her, to help her get back on her feet if she survives all of this. I will not be able to spend a lot of time with her while she may be doing that, because I want to be with Phia most of the time.

And I need your advice on how I should treat her and how much time should I spend with a woman and a wife, of whom I do not love any more. What I need from you is how much of what money she has earned, should I give back to her, if and when she does come back to consciousness. And should I do it personally or should I have you do it.

Without thinking Moses says he should handle everything, without me being in that apartment when he contacts her or does anything with her. I say that is fine with me.

Because I really do not love her anymore, because of what she has been doing for almost thirteen years. My problem is that I am a nice guy and I hate to do anything that hurts anyone else.

I am not saying that if someone was trying to hurt me or kill me, that I would not try to stop that person from doing all of that, because I would, and I have.

While I was on that traveling Auditors job, I kept Journal's of all of my adventures, including all of my Special Assignments and I will leave those with you also, so you can see what I have been doing for the last three and half years. It is very interesting reading.

Someday I will write a book and all of what is in these Journals and many others will be in that book. The other thing about all of this is this, Phia does not want me to even talk about Peg, and I totally agree with her, so whatever you can do to help relieve all of this extra stress on both of us, will be a great advantage for me.

Here are all of the records of where all of Peggy's money is located in whatever banks I have put it in. I also have two separate contracts that she signed, and one of them was even witnessed by two others and that one was notarized, and the other one was just witnessed by Martha.

If she has her copies, which I do not know if she does or where they are located. Then that might make this a little easier.

I ran that first contract that I wrote by a Lawyer back in Wisconsin and he said it was written perfectly, but the other one I just wrote and using carbon paper so each of us would have a copy and we both signed it and Martha witnessed it.

Moses says as usual, you always keep impeccable records about everything that happens in your life. He wishes everyone did that, because it would make his part a lot easier.

He says leave all of this stuff with him and let him study it, and then he will do some other things and talk to some other members of his Law Firm about all of this.

He says he is not sure what he will do about my possible reporting of all of those names of all of those men who spent time with Peggy, but after he discusses all of this with other members of his Law Firm, he will have some answers for me. It should take about a week or probably two weeks. There is a lot to know here.

As info, Martha is upstairs with your children or somebody, because that is where she went when I came in here. Moses says five of his children are at a Camp up in the Angeles National Forest, and Lucy and Christie are the only persons who are upstairs, so maybe they are just talking.

I tell Moses that I think she wanted to talk to Lucy, to try to find out what she needs to do to make her new Mom like her even more than she already does. It's just a feeling I have.

Moses then flips a switch on an intercom, and asks if Martha is with you, and Lucy answers yes and we are talking about something important right now and she will be down in about ten or fifteen minutes.

I say that is what I need to do, is get an intercom installed in Phia's house. Moses says there are some Monitoring devices that all you have to do is plug them into any electrical socket in your home, and then place one of these devices in every room and you should be able to communicate with anyone in that entire building. Now if you need to actually Monitor the sounds in a Baby's room, then it can be programmed to do just that. They have about three different buttons on each of these devices, which will allow you to do different things. Each device costs about ten dollars.

So Moses and I go sit on his front porch and watch the birds and other things that always seem to go on in his neighborhood. Some people walk by and wave and others yell hello. Since I still smoke a pipe, I light the one I brought with me, and Moses says he has always liked the tobacco that I have always smoked. Moses says he doesn't smoke himself any longer but he says it is all right to smoke outside of his house. But never inside of it.

I say Phia will not let me smoke inside of her house either, so I go outside and sit under the Weeping Willow trees where no bugs seem to ever come to and I just relax and think about so many things.

In about fifteen minutes Martha, Christie and Lucy join

Moses and I on the porch. Martha asks did you get everything done that you wanted to get done? I nodded my head yes. I asked, did you get all of your feminine questions answered like you needed, and Martha says Yep.

We get up to leave, but first I go to Lucy and Hug her and tell her that I Love You and then I start for the car. Martha hugs Moses and tells him she Loves him and then she hugs Lucy and says I love you too, and then she comes to my car and gets inside and after we both fasten our seats belts, we drive away. I ask as we drive back home, can you tell me what you needed to talk to Lucy about, and Martha says not at this time, but after she talks to Mom, then we three will get together and I will tell you everything that Lucy and I discussed.

I asked are you comfortable with the answers that Lucy gave you, and she looks at me and says, are you reading my mind, and I say no, because I have already kind of figured out what you were having problems with.

You and I are very close, and I usually am able to sense when something is troubling you. I think I know what it is, but I won't venture what I think it is at this time. I will let you tell me later.

What I have done is I have written down the problem you are having, and I did this last evening at 2300 hours, which is 11:00 PM and dated it, and place it in that very small Safe that I purchased at that Furniture Store about ten days back. So when you tell us your problem, then I will give you the Combination to that Safe and I will let you open it yourself, and let you look at and read what I wrote down, last evening.

At that time I will also give Phia the same combination to

that safe, so we all will have access to what is inside of it, no matter what those items may be. What I am saying here is, I expect between the three of us to have TOTAL TRUST between all of us. I don't know if she already has a Safe in the house, and this one I was able to move it by myself, using a hand truck. It really does not hold all that much, but if there is something that any of us think we need to place in that safe, then it is guaranteed that only the persons who have the combination will be able to open that safe.

This safe is about eighteen inch square and it does weigh about 250 pounds, and it does have wheels under it, but to move it from an apartment down fourteen steps and place it inside of my station wagon vehicle is not an easy feat.

Luckily I do have a hand operated hoist that is attached to the inside of my vehicle, that in fact has become a permanent part of my vehicle whereon which I rigged a lifting device so I could get it inside of my vehicle. When it is not in use it just folds to one side, where the Spare tire is located, that has it's own cover, so you never see it, even if you look directly where it would be if it was out in the open.

It takes Martha and me about a half hour to get home, because the Los Angeles traffic started to become a bit heavy by the time we did head for Home.

When we arrived Phia had her head inside of the kitchen stove oven, because she was cleaning it. When she stood up, I asked her, did you have to do that today? Phia says the next stove she gets will be self-cleaning. She says she made the mistake of baking something about two weeks back, by not putting a cover over it, and it splattered juices all over inside of that oven. She says she will never do that again when she cooks the same item again.

I say I need to go out to the garage and see what tools you have there, and Phia says there are all kinds of tools, but they all belonged to her Father.

She says her former husband did not know one end of a hammer from the other. He even had trouble cleaning his own weapons.

She also says she always used to clean the gun he used in his police work. He never allowed me to have access to more than one gun at a time. For fear that I would keep one of them and use it on him. But I fooled him.

At least with you, I won't have to ever consider using my three-shell weapon against you. Then I say maybe I will just take a short nap and let you girl's talk to each other. And with that comment, I go into Phia's bedroom and lay down on the bed and in two minutes I am asleep.

CLEMENT

DEAR PEG

FINDING OUT WHAT WAS ON MARTHA'S MIND

When I wake up, Phia is lying beside me, but is not sleeping, but is just lying looking up at the ceiling. I say, a penny for your thoughts. She says what she has to say is worth a lot more than just a penny. She says Martha and her had a long conversation this afternoon, and she says she really loves that girl more than she ever thought that she would Love a young girl, because that girl is so very thoughtful when it comes to you and I.

She says from the time that she began to realize that you may possibly be her real father, she began to treat her real mothers husband like he was some kind of stranger.

Because when she was probably about three years of age, and you were baby sitting her, because her parents at that time, went to some gathering having to do with her mothers Teaching position. She thinks it was probably something to do with the Parent Teachers Association.

Anyway when it came time for her to take a bath, it seemed to be second nature for her suspected father to help in that endeavor. He ran my bath water, and made sure it was the correct temperature, he let me play with some bath toys that he brought me, and he washed me everywhere, and it seemed so natural for him and me to be together.

Then when my parents came home, and they had obviously been discussing something to do with my suspected father and me.

Because my mother lashed out at Henry, and says Martha is not your daughter, but I will not tell you who her real Father is.

At that time Clem was just a person that Henry had gotten to know through Peggy. Peggy introduced Henry and Clem, because Henry was Peggy's Boss. Peggy did not want to come and baby sit like Clem agreed to. She remained at home.

Now I knew, even back then that Peggy was sleeping with other men, but never her husband. I did not know this at that time, but I realized it much later when I used to come to stay with Clem and his wife, when my parents were off on a vacation together. This is all I am going to say about Clem's 1st wife.

We also discussed what subjects she wants to take in her final year of high school. Which will begin officially on September 10th. But because Martha wants to get a head start on everyone else she will begin tomorrow morning. And she will be taking on six extra subjects, so when she graduates next spring, she fully expects to be Valedictorian of her graduating class. Of which I will determine when she takes her final exams

She says one of the reasons she wanted to go with me was because she has never had a Married Aunt and Uncle before, and she figured that she could consult with at least Lucy for now, to get some answers to some questions she had been forming in her mind.

She says that you suspected what those questions are, and that you wrote down those problems on a piece of paper and put it in that Safe that you brought with you last evening and placed it in the office. And that before we go to bed tonight you will give her the combination to that Safe and she will have to open that safe herself, and at that time you will give me that combination so I can open it also.

And the last thing he told is He does not want to have any secrets between the three of us, and whatever is in that Safe, we will all have access to it.

I ask Phia, what did she ask Lucy. And Phia says, now it gets kind of complicated. First Martha says she will not try to eves drop on any of her thoughts when you and I are making love or talking about things that only we should know about at that time. Martha says that she is always connected to me Telepathically, and she has to purposely Block my thoughts from her mind. She knows that you can block your thoughts from her mind, but in the past that was never necessary, but she figures now I will have to block some of my thoughts from her mind, so be very conscious of that ability in Dad, because he may forget to do that when he should, so you may have to remind him once in awhile.

Phia says she loves you so very much that she really beams all over when she talks about you. I hope I never get jealous of you two, with all of your abilities to communicate in the way that you do sometimes, because I know that thoughts pass between you two with so much more rapidity that just knowing that, kind of scares me sometimes.

And the other thing that Martha wanted to talk to Lucy about, was how can she make herself to be more likable and loved by me, because she has never had a Mother who she has ever cried with before, and when she told me that, I cried again and so did Martha.

I told her that she is easy to Love, because of how thoughtful she always seems to be about not only her Father, but also now her new Mother.

You know we sat and cried together for ten minutes, because of what you and I have done, has created such a wonderful family, that I could never have asked for anything better to ever happen to me in my entire life.

I think back to when we first met, and if we had dated and would have eventually gotten married. Would you have met Elizabeth and had gotten her pregnant and created Martha, or would we have had a child that turned out almost like Martha.

I tell Phia, knowing how I am regarding children, if we had gotten married back lets say in 1954 when I was 20 years old, and we began having children within two years, we by this time would have at least a dozen children. And most likely one of them would have been just like Martha and maybe would have been called Martha. We will never know. Or will we?

I asked Phia, how many children do you want us to have, and she says five natural and three Adopted. Phia says if we can select how many of each gender, then she would like to have four Girls and four Boys. What we will name them will be determined at that time.

Phia says Martha wants one of our children to be named Martha. She will be Big Martha and our child with be little Martha. Martha also says she will baby-sit for us when she is needed. And that she will live real close to me after she gets married, just in case you cannot get to me, because of unforeseen things in your other life.

And lastly, Martha says that Dad says that she is easy to love, just like you told me. She says I believe that you and Dad were definitely meant to be together, because you two think very much alike.

Because she says she Prayed for a long time last night before she went to sleep, and she had a dream about the two of us, and in that dream, GOD actually married you. Actually she says it was Jesus who married you two, and the next scene was when she was being born, coming out of her new Mother.

Phia says she cried again for another five minutes, and Martha held me. It's like she grew up overnight because she really understands about what true love can do to two persons who should have been together when they first met each other.

Then I put my arms around Phia and she cried again while I held her. But these tears are happy tears, and I am hoping that I will never cause Phia to cry unhappy tears. I could not think of anything else to say about anything after that.

We stayed together for at least an hour, until Martha knocked on the bedroom door and asked if she could come in a moment, and without asking Phia and without even moving, I said come in, and when Martha walked in, we were still in each others arms.

Martha asks are you two going to eat tonight? I say I completely forgot all about Supper. Phia has kept me totally mesmerized for the past two hours or more, and when one is enjoying ones self, time flits by so rapidly.

I smile while Phia goes into the bathroom to make herself presentable. Martha comes to me and asks is anything wrong and I say definitely not. Everything is Rosy and coming up roses. I reach out and grab Martha and pull her down on me and I kiss her on her mouth and she says, we should not do that any longer, and I ask why not, and then Phia asks why not.

You two are Father and daughter, so what is wrong with kissing your daughter on her lips. Martha gets up and says okay, and then leaves, and we follow her to the dining room.

Martha says she would like to say the prayer tonight, and it goes like this: Since Phia and I have been Catholic and Martha is catholic, we all crossed ourselves and then Martha began praying thusly =

" Heavenly Father – that dream that I dreamed last evening, I am hoping and praying that it really does take place, because as you know, Mom is pregnant, and since you also know that she is going to have twins, allow one of them to be a girl, just like me. And GOD please bless this food that you provided to us and guide us in your heavenly direction. I pray this in Jesus' name, Amen."

I had tears in my eyes and so did Phia, but I did not say anything, but just smiled at Martha and reached out and touched her shoulder. We waited until Phia had wiped her tears from her eyes, and after another few seconds, I said, please pass the potatoes.

Martha says, since we are now a family, we should lay out some rules regarding saying prayers at meals, and who should say them. Just a thought!!! Because when your children get old enough to say a meal prayer, then they should be taught how to say that prayer.

She says I remember when I came to stay with my suspected Father, and he told me that when you say a prayer, whether it be before you eat or before you go to sleep, or for whatever reason, say that prayer just like you are talking to one of your close friends.

Meaning speak clearly and enunciate your words so everyone will totally understand your meaning of every word, and talk like this is something that is second nature to you. That is the way Dad taught me and whenever I was allowed to say the Meal prayer at my other home, they always marveled how it was so easy for me.

Elizabeth always asked me, aren't you afraid of GOD. I told her that GOD is my friend because I can talk to him anytime of any day. Dad taught me to think this way, and I still totally believe what he told me.

Phia says, one of the things that amazed me about Clem is how easy it was for him to say a prayer, at anytime of the day or for whatever reason. She says she has always had a problem saying any prayer out loud, off of the cuff as they say, meaning just making it up as you go along. And when you or Martha say prayers, it does appear as if you have rehearsed it several times before you have said it. She says further, I guess it is because you both are so familiar with GOD that talking to him is like talking to a friend.

She says this will take some getting used to, but she really likes the way we feel and talk when it comes to GOD. Phia also says that there is a Catholic church about a mile away from here, which she used to go to until about a year back when she was criticized by one of the Priests when she went to Confession one time, and he ridiculed me so harshly that she says she just quit going to that church.

I say I will check with the Los Angeles Archdiocese, to see what Church we really belong to and then I will check it out. Phia says because this church was only a mile away, she assumed it was where she was supposed to go, but you may be right in your thinking and wherever we belong, and it may be some different church, then if that is so, then we will go wherever you say we should go.

I say actually we can go to any church, whether it be catholic or some other denomination. But because Martha has always gone to a Catholic school and a catholic church that is why I am suggesting that we go to a catholic church.

Phia says because she is affiliated with the Holy Cross Catholic Girls School, everyone figures that she is a Catholic of good standing.

She says in reality she has been excommunicated from ever being a catholic ever again, but that does not mean that she does not believe like how she was raised, which was in the Catholic Faith.

And of course, Clem has been excommunicated from the Catholic Church because of your divorce from your other wife sometime during that earlier marriage.

Phia says I guess we two parents are a couple of defrocked Catholic's who can only decide to educate our children in the Catholic faith, even though the Catholic Church cannot demand that we do. So does that make us better Catholics? I wonder.

I say let us not worry about what we should or should not do on this subject, because I will make that determination when I do what I said I would do.

So our lives began to come together like they are supposed to do, and because I had not heard anything from the UCLA medical center regarding Peg, I actually put her out of my mind.

When Phia had been pregnant for ten days, she went to see her Gynecologist, and she told Phia that she definitely is pregnant, but it is too early to know whether she will have twins, even though Phia told her that I said she would. Phia says the next time she comes to see her GYN she will bring her husband.

So our lives began to kind of level off for a while, because Martha is always busy studying her lessons most of every day. And Phia has other homes to visit because she still has other clients to take care of. So in any given day I do not see Phia very much. I have decided I will look for another position, so I went to see the Personnel Manager of the Santa Fe Railroad and after extensive testing and finally a Physical that is required of me to take, on September 18th of 1968 I began working for that railroad company. Even though my seniority began on September 12, 1968, because that is the day I made out my application to work for the Santa Fe Railroad Company.

Previous to doing that I wrote out my Resignation and sent it to Jack Perkins in Chicago, and the day after I began working for the Santa Fe railroad, I received a letter in the mail from Jack with a letter of Recommendation and several letters of Accommodations about all of the great things that I had done while working for the Western Weighing and Inspection Bureau, and including several checks for different things; for example – a separate check for all of my Vacation pay, and a separate check for my Regular Salary, and a separate check for my Special Assignment pay which included all of my travel pay for all of the traveling I had done during my three and a half years of traveling, and a separate check for my Severance pay, and a separate check for my final month for all of my other Expenses. All of these checks totaled $ 53, 925.00, and because I had done such a great job after I purchased that Travel trailer, they decided to pay off that trailer, so when Jimmy Perce gave me eight thousand dollars for it, I decided that I would add that amount to this other amount, so the grand total of money I actually received will be $61,925.00.

Because I had not deposited that check from Jimmy Perce into any Bank yet, but was holding on to it until I received what I was hoping I would get from the WWIB. And from all of this money I had received from the WWIB all of the Taxes had been deducted all ready, so knowing this, in reality the total amount will be much greater than what I received. I will have to wait until they send me my W-2 at the end of this year, to really know how much money I really earned in 1968.

CLEMENT

DEAR PEG

GOING TO WORK FOR
THE SANTA FE RAILROAD

The starting wage I will be getting from the Santa Fe railroad will be $ 25.47 per hour, and because I am beginning on second shift, I will get an additional $1.78 per hour, so my daily hourly rate is $27.25 per hour times 8 hours equals $218.00 per day times five days equals $1090 per week times four weeks equals $4360 per month times twelve months equals $ 53,320 per year gross. Then after they take out for Federal and State taxes and a payment for Medicare and a Payment for Union dues and FICA,

I will take home about $38,394. Because all of what is deducted comes to about 28 percent of my gross amount. Of course I was also being paid for being a Special Investigating Auditor with another company while I was working for the WWIB.

So this is a reduction of what I was making as a traveling auditor, but the nice thing is that I am home every day, even though I will get home when everyone else is in bed and asleep.

Because my hours are from 3:30 PM to 12 midnight, and even though it will only take me about a half hour to get home, no one is going to ever be up and awake when I get home. And because I will always have a bite to eat after I arrive back home, it is likely that I will never get to bed until after 2:00 AM. So if I am to ever get to see Phia and or Martha, I will have to wait until sometime later that same day.

Also my days off will not be Saturday and Sunday, but will be Wednesday and Thursday. And the likely hood of me working any overtime for the first six months is never going to happen.

What do I do at my job, I am a Less than carload (LCL) Billing clerk, and I am the best and fastest they have ever seen, because when I took the typing test I typed 98 words per minute without any mistakes. And I would have gotten a better score if the typewriter had been an Underwood, which is what my own typewriter is. And the typewriter is a manual typewriter.

Now these Billing machines, because when I type a Waybill, this is an electric billing machine, and I am making five additional copies, so there are Four carbon copies whereon everything has to be readable, and if you make a mistake, then you have to begin all over again for that one waybill.

Because I can type so fast, and the machine cannot keep up with the speed that I can type, sometimes I have to wait for a full thirty seconds for the machine to catch up with the amount of words I have typed. It does have the capability to store and remember what I have typed, so it is always interesting to watch me as I type these waybills, because of my overall speed. I usually type three times more waybills than all of the other Clerk's combined.

And there are three other Clerks. Persons always come and watch me type these waybills, and that does not bother me at all, in fact I probably do even better. The other three clerks always get nervous and make mistakes when these other persons watch me, but I completely ignore them all.

After working in that position for two months, one evening the Manager of the entire Department asked if I would work two extra hours overtime, and I told him only if you Sign my Overtime slip before you go home, and he says he will not do that, so then I say I will not work the overtime that you want me to work. You will either trust me totally or I will not work that overtime.

A few days later, the General Manager of this entire building asked me to come into his office, of which I did and he asked me, did I refuse to work overtime for Lloyd Martin who is the Manager of several departments, including the billing department, and I told this General Manager whose name is Harry Epp, that I asked Lloyd if he would sign my overtime slip before he went home that day, and he told me he would not, so I refused to work the overtime he asked me to work.

I say Harry, I have heard of others who had been asked to work overtime, and when they brought their overtime slip to Lloyd the next day, he would not sign these slips. Now what was I supposed to do?

I will not work and not get paid for it, and if Lloyd is that kind of Manager, then maybe he should be replaced with someone who is totally honest. I said I did not just fall off of the Turnip Truck.

If you want me to work, then before you go home you come and ask me and sign my overtime slip yourself before you go home, even though there will not be any time written on that slip yet. It's all a matter of Total Trust.

Now I know I am the Best Billing Clerk any of you have ever seen, and I will not change my way of doing things just because you are having trouble controlling one of your Managers, but don't think that I will work for nothing while I continue to do something that no one else can do.

Which is type over four hundred waybills in an eight hour period, and yet I am expected to work overtime because the other three clerks cannot hold up their end of their billing responsibilities. They are required to type no less then 150 waybills if it is required of them to do, and if they cannot do the work, then maybe they too need to be replaced with someone who can do the work. I type five hundred waybills in eight hours and all of them cannot type 450 waybills in the same length of time. I think I have made my case.

Harry says go back to work and let me think about your proposal, and if I decide to do as you have requested, then I will have an entire pad of overtime slips printed up just for you with my signature on every one of them, which everyone in the Payroll department will honor, without fail. I then go back to work. It took about a week, but one day when I walked into that building, Harry met me outside of his office, and handed me what he said he would do. I checked each and everyone of those overtime slips and they all had his signature on them. I say I will never cheat you or this company.

Harry says he called the Main office of the WWIB today, and says he talked to Jack Perkins. He says he will not repeat what he told me about you, because it is obvious that I have his total respect and confidence. Jack told me that you are the Best he has ever seen as a Traveling Auditor and you know more about Railroad accounting then even himself.

He told me a lot of other things, which I am quite sure you know what those things are. He says if you do not trust Mr. Royal totally then you are a damn fool. Harry says whenever you need more of these, just leave a note with my secretary and she will make sure you get what you want.

After that day, I only turned my overtime slips in directly to the Payroll Manager. And I always got paid for all of the overtime I worked, for all of the time that Harry Epp was my General Manager.

Around that same time, before I went to work one Saturday, Martha asked if I would place my hands on Phia's abdomen to see if I could determine what gender her babies will be.

I did as Martha asked, and after several minutes I told both Martha and Phia that you are carrying a boy and a girl and the boy will weigh 7 pounds 4 ounces when he is born, and the girl will weigh 6 pounds and 7 ounces when she is born. The girl will be born first and five minutes later the boy will be born. Martha smiles and Phia cries.

Martha wrote down what I just stated, so Phia can give this information to her GYN, so they will know how exacting I can be when doing this forecasting. I tell Martha to place your hands on this spot and then feel the movements of each of them and tell me where the boy is and where the girl is located in her womb. Martha does what I instruct her to do, and after another five minutes goes by, she says the boy is here, and the girl is here, which means that the girl will be first. I say you are absolutely correct.

She says she always wondered how I was able to know

where each child was located in the womb, and now she knows, but she will have to do this each time Phia gets pregnant and also each time when she herself gets pregnant so she can be sure of what she feels. I say when you are sure of your predictions you will always be sure of who will be born first.

I say I have even done this same thing with Cats and Dogs and Horses and Cows and several other kinds of creatures and I have yet to be wrong. Martha says that Tiger is pregnant also, so you should check her too.

So I find Tiger and I lay her down on a level surface, I note that Martha is writing all of this down, and I place my hands on her area where her kittens should be located.

After about five minutes, I say one of her kittens will be born dead. Because it is not fully formed. It is still alive in her womb, but when it begins to be born it will die.

She has two other kittens and one will be a multiple sexed kitten because externally it will be male, but internally it will be female. So it will be bisexual. And the other one will be male. He will most probably be an introverted Cat, meaning he will be afraid of his own tail when he is sometimes surprised by it. Now you may ask, how do I know the specific particulars of these three kittens, I cannot tell you how I know, but I know I am correct. Only time will tell whether this is all true.

CLEMENT

PEG

LIFE AT THE SANTA FE RR

Life at the Santa Fe railroad did not always go along with ease, because of my relationship with Harry Epps, other persons who did not want me to become successful anywhere with that company, were always putting roadblocks in my way, and because I could always go to Harry Epp, but I never did, these persons only went just so far.

I remained always cool to everyone around me and who worked with me. And I was always checking the Bid board, to see if there were any new positions that I may want to bid on.

I had heard through my own grapevine that these LCL billing jobs would soon be abolished, because the Santa Fe was no longer going to accept LCL shipments of this kind of merchandise any longer. All of this is now going to be handled by trucking companies.

So after working this position for eight months, I put in a bid for another position, which was a Corrections Clerk position. And I got it.

There was no real Manager for the Correction department, but because George Eastman was the Manager of the Car Accounts department and the corrections department was a new department, they made George the head of this department.

Now George had inquired and received a copy of my Employment application and when he realized what my qualifications were for this position, he requested of Harry Epps that I be made the Supervisor of this new Corrections Department, even though I was the only clerk in this department, of which I became.

I advised Harry Epps that I needed four more Corrections Clerks, and after a lot of discussion with the Union, that request was granted.

So not long after I became the Supervisor of the Corrections Department, I now also had four clerks who are under me, that I could train in doing their new duties. And I worked very hard and had them all trained within three days time. In this correction department, there were sixteen boxes stuffed full of several thousand pieces of paper and each piece of paper was a correction. After another month we had these sixteen boxes of corrections down to eight boxes, and after another two weeks had them down to four boxes.

What we had to do was to determine what all of these documents pertained to. Once we determined what duplicates we could glean out, it became much easier. Then we had to determine which are inbound and which are outbound.

Once we made that determination, we then determined which documents were just switching documents and what kind of switching. Were they interchange switching, or intra terminal switching or whatever? Once we made that next determination we had to match up with whatever shipments they pertained to. It was a very big job.

After three months, we all had it down to just inbound and

outbound corrections. Being just three boxes. Now how to organize them so as to create another document we could send back to whomever it regarded.

I first determined that for all outbound corrections a number would be stamped on the front page, which would be any number over 100,000. And for any correction that is on an inbound shipment the Numbers from 70,000 through 99,999 will be placed on each of these documents.

Any number under 69,999 belonged to Freight Bill documents. And once we reached the top number, then we would start back on number seventy thousand again and go forward to 99,999.

Actually there are more corrections on outbound shipments then there are on inbound shipments, so my system worked fine and as far as I know it is still in operation at this time. If there are more than one document, then that same number that was placed on the top document has to be placed on the attached documents, thereby keeping each number totally together, and if for some reason a document ever became dislodged or unattached from the original document, it would still eventually get found and reattached to the number it belonged to.

Once all of these numbers are placed on all of these documents, then they are all sent to the Keypunch Department and all of these documents are tied together once they are all created onto and into punched cards because for each shipment the Car number determined how all of these cards would fall into place for each correction number.

Once it had all happened, lists are printed and freight bills are created and sent to whomever it pertained to and " WHAM " then suddenly things began to happen.

All uncollected items are covered under what is called Item 17. Of which are all Uncollected Monies Owed to the Santa Fe Railroad, and all of these Corrections are considered to be in Item 17. That is until whomever needed to get bills for all of these Shipments, did get them, and then the money began to roll in.

After the first bills went out to all of these customers, within two weeks, checks began to arrive and in another four months, all of these corrections dwindled down to not more than fifty in any given day.

And they are all handled just like all of the previous ones were handled. And Item 17 went from 37 million dollars down to a little over 50 thousand dollars.

Can you imagine what all of higher officials thought, when they began to see how much of the uncollected monies are now being collected. I am sure they wondered how this all has taken place.

What I did in that department actually eliminated five additional positions, because once most of the money had been collected from all of these corrections and all of those corrections dwindled down to only 50 for any given day, it also totally eliminated the four clerical positions I initially requested, and it also eliminated the Item 17 Clerks position.

Because that Item 17 position could now be handled by any cashier position, so I helped create additional duties for some Cashier position. In the end I was not all that well liked by my fellow clerks in any department. I knew how to make things happen.

Persons like Harry Epp knew that I knew how these things happened. I was mostly liked by all of the Managers of all of the departments. So I saw the handwriting on the wall, so I Bid another position in the Revising department and got it.

And it was a job rating every shipment dealing with any kind of Livestock shipments. And like any position I had worked before this one, I excelled in it and made it look easy. The person who worked it before me, who was Jim Barrows says I must be doing something wrong, because he says that job was very hard for him to do, because he had that position before I took it over. I told him he made it hard for himself, because when he did that he figured he had a job for as long as he wanted it. He was correct in his thinking, but he also was a Job Padder, meaning he made it look like it was complicated, even though it was not.

Then after I worked that position for a year, like the LCL position, that position too was abolished, allowing me to bump another position. Wherein with whatever my Seniority is, I could bump the person on that position. Then I began to really make some enemies.

So over the next two years I went from one position to another and finally ended up Bumping a position back in the Revising Department.

As part of that position, I had to keep all of the Rate Tariffs up to date for the In house Tariff files. Including passing out Tariffs to all of the other Revisers including the Supervisors and the Manager of the Revising Department who is Milton Paulson. He is a very serious kind of guy but he is also very smart and could be very funny. I got to know him very well. I worked in his department for about three years, and then one day he did not come to work, because he had a stroke and it incapacitated him, so he was only able to mostly remain in his home with his wife, and then after suffering for about a year, he died.

I went to see him several times when he was homebound, and he told me that I was the only person from the Santa Fe railroad who came to see him at home. It is a sad thing when that happens, and I hoped if that ever happens to me, that I am not treated in the same way.

CLEM

Peg;

Meanwhile getting back to my life with Phia and Martha.

As usual Martha excelled in every subject she took in her final year of High School, and in the spring of 1969 she graduated Valedictorian of her overall class. The speech she gave was about what her overall life had been like up to the date she graduated from this school. This speech lasted about forty minutes and the entire audience gave her a standing Ovation. I personally felt ten feet high and so did Phia. We are so very proud of our daughter.

But before Martha graduated from high school, Phia gave birth to Twins on May 29th 1969, exactly nine months to the day after inception, a girl first and five minutes later a boy.

We named the girl Martha Toosom, and the boy we named Philip Arthur, and of course their last name is Royal. What I predicted each would weigh is absolutely accurate in every way.

Also back in November of 1968, Tiger gave birth to three kittens, the first kitten born is the one who is bisexual, which we named Trinket, and the second kitten born is a male cat, which we named Topanga, I will explain their names in a moment, and the last kitten born was born dead, because it was not completely formed.

The name Trinket, because she is a girl psychologically, and Topanga because of water raging down the canyons of

Topanga Canyon. Because of all of the Rain we had received late that November day.

The third kitten, I named her Hope, because I hoped that GOD would take this real Female kitten into his personal house where she would be completely whole once again, to live the kind of life I would have given her if she had been born alive and completely whole. .

That last kitten, I placed in a Special box I had prepared earlier in that same week, and I buried it under the three Weeping Willow trees on Phia's property. It was the least I could do. We all said some prayers over her grave and cried a lot, and I put up a marker with all of the pertinent information on it. It is likely that it would not remain for a long period of time, but one never really knows do we?

When Martha graduated, Phia did not bring the twins, and Martha did not remain very long after everyone had received their Diploma's. I took a day off so I could attend Martha's graduation.

Martha invited some of her other friends she has made to our house and we had to get home to be there when they all began to arrive. And Phia wanted to Nurse the twins, soon after we arrived at home.

The party was well received and every person who is invited came and they all had a good time up to a certain time. Phia and I remained mostly in the background and only came into where Martha and all of her friends were in the Rumpus Room, mostly talking and laughing and being silly. We did not think any shenanigans would happen.

After about two hours went by, Martha came to me and told

me that there are some girls who are smoking dope. So I went into the Rumpus room and told all of them to leave. That no female will ever smoke Marijuana in this house again. And if your own parents allow you to do that, then I surely do not want to know any of them any longer.

They did all leave, with some of them saying they will never return. But Martha says to not worry about those girls; because she only invited them because they were some of the students that Phia had introduced her to.

Phia is surprised and says she will inform the parents about all of the girls who were carrying this Marijuana on their persons. And that is what Phia did, because she immediately got on the phone and called each and every parent of each of these girls who had Marijuana on their person.

I felt there would be hell to pay regarding some of these girls, because I too knew all of their parents. They all pooh-poohed the idea that any of their girls even smoked Marijuana, and that she must have been mistaken. Phia told each of them, that if they wanted her to teach any of their children this fall and into next year, they had better do something about preventing their offspring from continuing to smoke this terrible drug. And then she just hung up the phone.

I told her there are a lot of other parents out there who will want you to teach their children whatever is required of you. But it obviously did upset her quite a lot. I tried to quell her concerns, but she says it will take her a few days to get over her anger about this.

I say you have to think about your own children, because if you continue to have these feelings, it will effect how you give milk to your twins. She asks how do I know so much about what a mothers milk will or will not do in any given situation. I say because this will happen with any Mammal, whether it is human or otherwise.

She says okay, she will try to calm down. Martha then comes to Phia and says, Mom, I will always be here for you, whenever you need me, even when I am going to College.

Phia says you will not go to UCLA alone, because she says for the next three years, she is going to take a Sabbatical, so she can try to get her Doctorate in General Education, which will bring her much more money when she teaches other peoples children.

After Martha gets through talking to Phia, I go to Martha and say thank you very much for taking her mind away from that incident on this day. What you did will make a lot of difference in how she thinks about any other person's children. In fact if she does go back to College, she will not think about any other persons child for those three years, and that is great.

Martha says she knew that I was very concerned about Mom, so she had to do something and what she did was out of great Love for her new Mom.

I then tell her that I Love you more than I can show and or tell you. Martha says you show her every day how much you love her, by how you treat her and how many times you tell me how much you love me.

I then tell Martha, that I have made a vow to myself, that every day that I am with you, I will tell both of you how much I love you and Mom and the twins, as often as I can, just how much you all mean to me. The twins do not understand me, but they hear the sound in my voice and the inflection in it, so they too know how I feel about them. What effect this will have on them will only come forth as they get older.

I never had that opportunity to do this when you were their age, so we will see how that all develops over time. Martha says you are the best Father she has ever known, and any child who does not Love you, is either deaf and dumb, but even those kinds of children seem to know when their father is telling them something very personal.

CLEM

PEG

BACK AT UCLA MEDICAL CENTER

Meanwhile back at the UCLA Medical center, Peggy continues to survive in a Coma. She is no longer in the ICU unit, but has been placed in an area, that is part of their Nursing Home, where there are Doctors and Nurses and Helpers who can cater to her every need.

Of course this is all costing me a Fortune, because when I went to work for the Santa Fe railroad, she was already in that center, so I did not even try to get her on my insurance. Actually I never even mentioned that I had a different wife other than Phia, because Phia is on my Santa Fe Health insurance program.

Phia really does not work for any real concern, so she has to carry her own health insurance. But now that she is on my health insurance, when our twins were born, my insurance actually paid the bills, because as far as the SFE is concerned, I only have one wife.

I in fact wrote Jack Perkins and told him what I did, just in case the SFE might inquire. And they did. Jack told the SFE that he had never met Mr. Royal's wife or his children.

Peggy is holding her own, but there is no indication of when she may wake up from this Coma. Of course I have not mentioned her name since Phia and I first spoke of her and I never will.

I continue to keep the apartment on 8th street, even though there are no persons living there. I have special devices whereat they turn on specific lights every evening and in the morning turn them off again. And if any mail comes to that apartment, the Manager always checks in my mailbox and intercepts whatever may be important for me to know about, because she calls me and I come by the complex once a week to get whatever has accumulated there. I did send the Post office change of address cards, just for Martha, and me but not for Peg.

Every once in awhile I get a card from the Post Office, asking what has happened to Peggy, and I tell them that she is visiting other relatives, but that all of her mail still is to be sent to this address.

That I have her Power of Attorney, which gives me the authority to make whatever changes regarding her, and I do really have her P of A, because I have had to come forth with that document to give to the Post Office Authority.

So life continues, just as if I was still living there. It has also been surmised that Peggy and I are separated and that is why my mail does not any longer come to that address.

Of course the U S Postal Authority cannot, under penalty of Law, tell anyone what kind of documents I have put forth, to cover whatever happens, regarding either of us.

CLEM

PEG

MARTHA AND PHILADELPHIA
GOING TO COLLEGE

In the fall of 1969, Martha begins her first year at UCLA, and Phia begins her first year studying for her Doctorate Degree in General Education. Martha needs a total of 60 credits so as to get a Bachelor of Science Degree in Biology with a Minor in History. She decided to take the exact same path I took when I first went to College.

Phia's Degree is much more complicated, so I will not try to inform you how she gets what she is going for. Phia drives to that Campus every morning, and because they both have classes until 2:00 PM, at which time they come home to the twins.

The twins are being taken care of by a Lakota Sioux Indian woman who also has a young child, of which she is also nursing on her own Breasts, so the twins also get some of her Breast Milk. They need less then they needed when they were first being breast fed, and because they have reached the age where they can now eat some baby food from Gerber's baby food jars, they become much easier to take care of.

Moses Lighthouse recommended this woman and she is great, and there are times when I am sleeping, and then I wake up and Mona has already made me a Bag lunch for me to take to work

She is very capable and it will be difficult to ever let her go, when that day comes, if it ever does come. Because Mona says this is a wonderful family, and she hopes she can stay for the rest of her life.

Mona lost her husband after the Korean War ended, because he had gotten hooked on Drugs while in that country and he got in with some bad persons after he returned back to the States, and one night someone put a knife in his back and he died of that wound. What a waste of time and trouble.

The baby she had recently was born out of wedlock, because someone Raped her, and because the person who raped her is really a distant relative, that she cannot ever go home again, because she would be a disgrace to her family.

Because she was working for another family in the Los Angeles area when this Rape happened, she says she did not want to go back to them either, so because Moses is a Lakota Sioux, of which she says every Lakota Sioux who lives in the general Los Angeles vicinity knows about him, that he was the only person she could go to.

Moses placed her in a Women's only Hotel and paid her way while she was there, and so she can work off her debt to Moses, she says that is why he got her this Job with us. Phia says she is invaluable to all of us, because she even makes all of us laugh a lot with some of her strange stories.

Her own baby is obviously a full-blooded Indian, and he really is a quiet baby. I look at him and I ask Mona, when was the last time you saw a Doctor, and she says when she lived in that women's only Hotel shortly after her baby was born. He is now almost five months old.

I say I think we should take this baby to see Phia's Gynecologist. . Mona does not think that is necessary, so I call Moses from work, and tell him my suspicions. He says he will look into the problem and the call ends.

The next day Phia and Martha do not have any classes, so since I also called Phia and told her my suspicions about Mona's baby, she loads up everyone including Mona and her baby and takes her to her Gynecologist.

After several tests, my suspicions are confirmed about Mona's baby. He has a very rare disease that only shows up with babies of Pedigree origins. Like with Black persons and or American Indians or even Chinese.

To mention it here, the reader would not be able to pronounce the word, nor know what it meant, so I will not say what it is. But this child will not live to be more than two years old if he is kept at home with his mother.

This disease cannot be passed on to other children in any way, so our twins are not in danger if Mona decides to keep this baby until it dies. But watching this child die will be very difficult for any Mother and especially Mona and possibly Phia.

I tell Mona that there is a Hospital in this area where you can take your baby, and it is called Cedar Sinai Children's Hospital. They will not charge you any money to keep this child, because this hospital survives totally by private donations. I myself give to this hospital.

And I have Foundations who give great amounts of money to this Hospital. It will be better for everyone concerned. When he does die, and he will, even though they are studying this disease in all of their many experimental Laboratories, I will pay for his funeral and the Plot where he will be buried. If you want him buried here in the Los Angeles area, I will pay for that also.

If you want, I will bury him in the Royal Family Plot Burial site, which means you can give him my name as his last name.

And that Plot is in Irvine, California, which is where we will eventually move. You see before you came to work for us, I investigated you and your family, so I probably know more about you then you know about yourself, so you have nothing to worry about.

I will let you talk to Moses and whomever else and when you decide then please tell me and I will make all of the arrangements for you. And you can still remain with us for as long as we need you and or you need us, which most likely will be for many years yet. Because Phia and I will still have many more children, so you can raise our children. And if you find a boy friend, I want to meet him before you go too far with him. And we still need you to take care of our twins, so you will not be without any child for many years.

Mona is in reality 33 years old. She is a plain looking woman. She does not wear any makeup, but she does have a beauty that is only found in Native American women. Her face is round, and her hair is black as coal or like a dark night in a hole in the ground. She is five feet seven inches tall and weighs about 140 pounds (estimated weight) she does not wear any kind of Bra, because I accidentally saw her without any clothes on one day as she stepped out of the shower after one of our twins had thrown up all over her.

She just smiled, and I told her I would not say anything to

anyone else in this family. She asked do I like what I see, and I told her I only see a younger sister. She says you are a wise brother, and she loves me as such.

She then tells me that she has decided to send her baby to that Hospital that I had mentioned some days back. She asks how did I know what was wrong with her baby, and I tell her that I have special abilities to be able to sense these things in certain persons. I did not know for sure, but just suspected what was wrong with him, and I do not want you to suffer for endless weeks and months about him.

I need to tell you about me, when I was born onto this earth. When I was two months old, the family Doctor told my Mother that I may have Polio, and then when I was six months old, that sickness was definitely confirmed. It was a severe case of Polio. So it was decided that my parents would send me away to the Mayo Clinic until I either died, or I did not die. But I did not die, because they gave me many experimental drugs and I continued to survive.

I am not telling you this to give you hope, but just to let you know that there are things that no one can know why they do happen. Anyway when I was around two and a half years old, one of the Catholic Nuns discovered something about me that actually made her think that I was being watched over by GOD himself. I will not go into what she discovered about me yet, but it was an amazing thing, and I continued to survive. This Catholic Nun, whose name is Sister Maryann, told me some years later that I was being watched over by GOD, because any person with the talent that I had, would always be taken care of by God almighty.

So here I am, and not with any Polio left inside of me, but I am a much wiser person for having gone through all of those experiences. After sister Maryann brought me back to South Dakota, and she stayed with me for six weeks, and when she left, I knew I would never see her again, and I never did.

So throughout my life, I have used that talent that God gave me, which is to speak for all of the different creatures in this world, that in every case cannot speak for themselves, but with the ability that I have, I can and do speak for whomever cannot speak for themselves. I am considered an expert in this field, and there are only about fifty of us on this entire earth.

Because it is a gift from GOD, I do not charge any kind of fee for what I do for whomever. That is just my rule, but not others who have this same ability in other parts of this world. And I can speak to any creature that walks on this earth, or swims in any of the Oceans and or Lakes, or flies above this earth, or even Crawls on this earth.

In most Indian communities I am known as a Holy Man, and wherever you go in any of these communities, just ask the leaders of these communities about my abilities and me and they all will tell you who and what I am.

Mona says she has heard of Holy Men who can do as I have just stated, but she never thought she would ever meet one of them, nor ever work for one. I say you just treat me like an older brother and we will get along just great. I do admit there is many things you do not know about me, and I will not tell you if I do not have to.

Phia knows everything about me, but she will not tell you anything except what you need to know regarding raising our children.

CLEM

PEG

MARY BETH

I need to write a few words about my other daughter Mary Beth. She is living in a Reformation Camp near St Louis, Missouri, where she will remain until she is 21 years old. She was ordered to stay in this camp, by me, because I am her father, suggested that she go there so she could be taught about Authority, because that is her main problem, because she does not like anyone ordering her to do anything, and since this place is famous for helping young children with that kind of problem, that is where I sent her. No Court ordered her to go there.

Even though that could have happened if she had been arrested, but with my influence with a man I call Uncle Homer, who is in fact my Father in Laws younger Brother. And he is actually your real Uncle.

And it is run by five individuals, one of them being Uncle Homer, who are from all walks of life, but are all connected with young persons in one form or another. And both male and females live in this Camp. Anyway back in early September of 1968, Martha and myself made up what we call a CARE PACKAGE for Mary Beth.

And in this care package we packed some new Jeans that Martha had decorated with several dozen beads, and I made her three complete outfits, including underclothes and slippers. Martha made her some jewelry and I did also. We each have our own specialties of what and how we make such jewelry. We sent the care package to Uncle Homer.

He called me soon after he received it and told me that this will be much appreciated by her, and all of this will reaffirm her faith in her Father and Sister.

Anyway when Homer gave this care package to her, she at first thought that it had came from him, but because I had also sent along two letters, one from Martha and one from myself, she then finally accepted this care package with a lot of happiness, and Homer said she even cried for awhile.

Homer gave this package to Mary Beth in private, and it was received with much gratitude. Homer says she is in reality real smart and in her schoolwork, she is doing real well, but he says he will wait for another six months before he recommends anything else for her. I am glad he is heeding my warnings about her.

We have not forgotten her and Martha and I will never forget her, and when she is ready to return back to California to live with us or near us if she wants to have her own apartment, she can also do that, but she has to Graduate from this place first. Or maybe she might remain as one of the instructors for this place. Only time will tell that story.

It has been suggested that we not mention anything about returning back to California in any of our correspondence with her. And we have not.

Most of these children are from broken homes and are from homes where these children have been molested by their parents, just like Mary Beth was before she ended up in the Orphanage where I found her. It is a terrible world out there, when parents treat their children like adults, ten years or more before they become adults.

But what it does to children is they come to think of themselves as being an adult, with no additional consequences, Authority being one of the main problems with that advanced life they are forced to lead. I thought that since I grew up this way, I could help her, but I guess I could not.

It is a very harsh realization when you discover that what you know about life, you cannot help others who are going through that kind of life themselves. It is something that has to be experienced, rather than taught.

Teaching has always been my strong subject, but with problem children, I am helpless I guess. The reason I could not help Mary Beth was because I remembered all of the anger I felt while it was happening to me, and I could not get beyond it, to help Mary Beth. Because whenever she defied my authority, she always made me very angry.

I taught her that the word Anger is only one letter away from Danger, but she used that against me, and I did not know how to counter act it.

Now Martha and I have made a kind of pact between us, that we will every three months send Mary Beth another one of our Care Packages. So here it is, the next to the last week of May of 1970 and we are getting ready to send her another care package.

We so far have sent her six care packages. The one thing that Homer says we are not to send is any kind of Money. It is kind of difficult to not send any money, but we have desisted from doing thusly. This time Martha says she will send her several kinds of cookies and even a carrot cake, without any frosting.

I decided to send her a Fruitcake, without any kind Liquor in it, because that is strictly forbidden. So I have had to use a little bit of extra imagination in making it, and I had Mona and Phia eat some of it and they like it very much, so I made another one for Mary Beth. I will not say what I put in it but, I did cheat a little, because the one thing I did use was some of my homemade beer.

But you cannot taste it so I think I will get away with it. The one problem with Fruit Cakes is after the cake becomes about a week old, you can usually smell any liquor that may be in it. But not this one, because I waited nine days before I gave any of it to Mona or Phia. I kept it in the refrigerator all of this time.

So maybe I need to not keep it under any kind of refrigeration for the same length of time. To see if it ever smells like it may have some kind of liquor in it. So maybe I will send it about a week later than the other care package. Martha says we will wait until I am ready to send it all, at the same time.

Now here it is a week after we sent the care package to Mary Beth, and everything got through, and Homer says every one of Mary Beth's friends loved that Fruit Cake. He wondered if there was any Liquor in it. He says he could not smell any in it so he let it go through to her. He even had a piece and he says, there was something familiar about it, but he couldn't put his finger on it.

CLEM

PEG

THE FIRST BIRTHDAY OF OUR TWINS

The one thing I noted that I had to remember about the twin's birthday is I had to make sure that I let Mona know so she could make two Birthday cakes. Mona not only takes care of our twins, but she is also our housekeeper and our cook, mostly because she lives with us also. She even does most of the grocery shopping.

I try to do some of it, and sometimes we shop together. I think some people think we are married, because when we go shopping we take the twins with us. Mona has her own car, even though it is an older model, but it runs good and it looks okay, so when anything goes wrong with it, I take it to my mechanic and he fixes it, just as if it belonged to me, because I am the one who usually takes it to him. And then Mona picks me up with my car. Of course we always do this on one of my days off. In fact my days off have changed recently because I bid a different position.

So now I finally have Saturday and Sunday off, so we can all go to church together. How long this will remain is uncertain at this time. Anyway when parents ever have children, and if their first children are a set of twins, then do you invite other children to a birthday party when they are just one year old? I don't think so because they won't remember it, unless they are some kind of geniuses, so we just had a birthday party and only invited Moses Lighthouse and his family, and because May 29th 1970 fell on Saturday, it was ideal for everyone concerned. And everyone had a great time.

All of us adults, except Mona played softball. We did not have enough persons for two complete teams, but we made due with what we had. It was a tie game, and no we did not play any extra innings, because it got dark.

We started playing too late in the afternoon. We also sat around and sung songs and I read some funny jokes that I had accumulated through my years of traveling all around the United States.

And all of my Cats through all of this either watched from the porch or went into Martha's bedroom and when necessary hid under her bed.

Moses and Lucy and the children went home about 9:00 PM. Phia and Martha had some studying to do and I made up a shopping list for Mona for the coming week. It's interesting that now that I am home on weekends, I somehow was appointed to be the provider for this family, meaning that I not only brought home a paycheck every two weeks, but I also planned most everything including making up shopping lists to cover future weeks of meals that had to be planned.

Phia did not have anything like a freezer, and when I mentioned I could bring the one from the apartment, she says no, so I went to my favorite used furniture store and I purchased one just for her, which was an upright freezer, which is a 15 cubit feet size, which means I can put a half of a steer and a half of a hog inside of it, and also two turkeys and three ducks and three pheasants and a host of other things, like bread and Angel food cakes.

The pheasants I got from some friends who had gone back to South Dakota and shot them themselves. The ducks were tame ducks. The beef and the hog were from a farmer in Orange County, southeast of Los Angeles, who I got to know through another farmer I know. I had it butchered and prepared by the persons who killed each beast in Orange, California. The ducks and turkeys I purchased from the local Safeway grocery store. And the freezer I put inside of the Garage.

As part of Phia's house there is a breezeway between the house and the garage that is enclosed with screen on two sides, and it has a solid roof on that breezeway. It is about fifteen feet from the house. About two feet from the floor there are flower boxes on both sides of the screen on both sides of the walkway so when it rains, most of the rain rarely comes in to where the walkway is under this roof.

But if there is a north-- south wind during any rain storm then water will get under the roof area. So in the wintertime when most winds come from the north, I have placed some clear plastic on the north side of this breezeway. Winds only blow from the south in the summer time, and sometimes they will blow from the northeast, which are called Santana winds, which are usually very hot and strong winds. Because most of them blow around seventy miles per hour. The entry to her house is on the south side and the same for the garage.

She has automatic garage door openers for all the two bays. One side of the garage is considered a workshop, even though there is room to drive an automobile into that same bay area.

Martha still does not have her own vehicle yet, but she is thinking that she should have one, just in case something happens to Phia's vehicle. So I have been checking the newspaper adds and there are a lot of used cars that I can buy whenever that event needs to happen. Martha first needs to get her California drivers license.

So I did stop by the place where she will take her drivers test, and they gave me a book for her to read and study, and then she will take the written test first and then if she is ready, she can take the drivers test soon thereafter. When she does that she can use my vehicle.

Martha still has her Missouri Drivers license, so she may only have to take the written test. So if that is what she has to do, then Phia can take her after they get away from UCLA, and in fact can get it done on their way home. I usually am not home during the daytime hours, because my hours are now from 7:30 AM to 4:30 PM with an hour for lunch.

CLEM

PEG

July 4th 1970

Declaration day, of which July 4th is, fell on Sunday, and that is perfect for all of our family. I am not one to buy any Firecrackers and or Rockets, because I saw one of my friends lose an entire hand when he mishandled one of the big rockets some years back.

But I do enjoy watching professionals fire some of these things off. Phia lives in a neighborhood, which is mostly commercial now, because there are many Factories going up all around her property, and most of them do fire off many rockets on this day, so we saw some beautiful displays that evening.

There have been some inquiries about Los Angeles Annexing her four acres, because it juts out like a finger towards the rest of Los Angeles on two sides of her property. She says she will sell if she gets what she wants for it, which is four hundred thousand dollars per acre, but so far they have only offered her two hundred thousand for it. At an earlier date I told Phia to let Moses handle that Sale and he will get you what you want and maybe even more.

Because he knows more persons in this city than any other person that I know of. You see Moses knows all about her property. And I would be willing to bet that there are other parties who want her property also, so they can build a new factory on it, or perhaps use it to make a parking lot for one of their factories out of it, because it is located in an area where there are many other factories, and if the city of Los Angeles could annex it, then they could commercialize that land, which would cause that land to go up appreciably.

I explained this to Phia, and then she now knows why I wanted Moses to handle the sale of her property, because he also knows what I just told you, and he will probably jack up the price per acre to 600 thousand dollars per acre. And maybe ever more than that.

Don't push him for any kind of answer, because when he gets what he wants, he will inform you in plenty of time for you to make a decision about it.

Phia is not stupid when it comes to selling property, but sometimes not seeing what is right in front of you can sometimes divert any person's thoughts.

So time passes on, and we are all working hard to get ahead in one form or another. Martha is doing great in college and she says she is handling eight credits a Semester, so she is way ahead of her schedule, which she made out before she even began attending this university. Now since there are three Semesters in any given year, if she continues this same regimen, in two and a half years she will have enough credits so she can graduate. And since she has already gone to college for eleven months, she only has a year and a half to finish.

Phia says she too is doing great, because she says in about year and a half she will have her Doctorate Degree in General Education. Now if my two women do finish all of their studies in that period of time, then what other college will Martha go to?

Probably most likely will be in Orange County, because a new University will be opening up in Irvine soon, which will be called the University of California – Irvine. And to abbreviate it, it will look like this: UCI.

It is said that everything is better organized, even though it is a smaller university, so far, but there are plans to expand it, and in fact I will have something to do with that expansion, but that is in my future yet about five years away.

CLEM

PEG

Meanwhile back at the SFE;

Thanksgiving and Christmas come and go in 1970, and I have progressed up the ladder at the Santa Fe another notch. It's always interesting about persons that I sometimes meet and associate with. When I bid in to a Revising Position, I met a guy whose name is James Hamilton.

He is very smart and he does his job very well, and in fact he and I are the two most knowledgeable persons who know about Transit Rates. He is about ten years younger than I am, but we still get along very well. So we get all of those files and whatever problems they entail. And when one of us has a problem with something we often confer with each other, which makes us both even smarter still. It is a great relationship.

Sometimes during our lunch period, since I have brought to work several Frisbee's, we go out in the parking lot and toss it back and forth to each other.

It really helps to calm our nerves I guess. Because it gives each of us a chance to think about some particular problem we both are having, and when one of us solves that problem, one of us will yell to the other, I'VE GOT THE ANSWER. Then we stop and discuss the answer and if we both agree, we take it to Milton Paulson and if he agrees with us, we go back to solving more problems.

This relationship is very unique and Milton says when we have a problem, then we should just go outside and do what we do that helps solve that problem. And if other employees have similar problems in that department, then they can tell the two of us about them and we can solve their problems also.

I am not sure what nationality he is. He does speak Spanish fluently and he does have a Mexican wife, whose name is Dorothy, and I like her too. They do not have any children yet, but they are trying. I say when you least expect a child, which is when they will come forth. At times we talk about various persons in Politics also, and whatever answers we come up with always happens.

I must go back to December of 1968, because it is important to know that Tiger, who is the Mother of Trinket and Topanga, had something wrong with her, so I took her to see a Veterinarian and he says she still has some after birth inside of her, but since she is now here, he will Operate on her and remove it and when she again goes home she will never get pregnant again.

Something happened during that operation, because three days later she died. I did not think she was as sick as he made her out to be, and because he would remove whatever organs needed to be removed when he operated on her, he should have removed what ever was causing her to feel very uncomfortable. That Doctor said I had waited too long, and she was sicker than he had suspected

I told Moses about this Doctor and he told me that this doctor was one that should never have been allowed to continue with his practice, because he has killed other Cats before this one.

I asked Moses is there any chance that I can sue him for any kind of damages and he says, probably not, but we can put him completely out of business in California for good, so that is what Moses did.

It did cost me some bucks but it was worth it. Anyway Tiger is buried under those weeping willow trees. So Tai and Tak and Tribble took over raising Trinket and Topanga after that time.

I cried every so often for a week, because I really loved Tiger, and she had gotten to totally trust me by that time. So she will be missed a lot.

Sometimes during the night time hours, I can hear Martha talking to Tai and the others and she sometimes cried for her also. Phia never knew her all that well, but she too cried for her. So we had to all comfort each other during these times.

CLEM

PEG

THE SYLMAR EARTHQUAKE

FEBRUARY 1971

On this February morning about 5:50 AM the ground began to shake aggressively and it seemed like it would never stop. It did in fact go on for a minute and 56 seconds. The first thing I did after the shaking stopped, I went out side and turned off the Natural Gas.

I checked the Garage too and it looked like the Roof would fall in any moment so I went back and got all of the keys to the cars and drove them out into the driveway in front of the garage.

I could not do anything about the Upright freezer, but it was next to a wall anyhow, so it was not likely to get damaged if the roof did collapse downward.

A few minutes before all of this happened the Cats all huddled under Martha's bed and would not come out even when I called them, so I knew that something menacing was soon to happen, and I so stated my fears to everyone.

Most often Martha was the first to get up every morning, which is 5:00 AM. It is not that she has programmed herself to get up at that hour, she just tells Tai and he wakes her whenever she wants to get up, no matter what time of the day or night it may be.

I used to use him in the same way when I was traveling alone in that travel trailer. Martha then gets me up and then I wake Phia up. We were all sitting on our couch drinking a cup of coffee, and our coffee table has sides all the way around it, just in case something like this might happen.

Anyway our coffee cups began to migrate towards the edge of this coffee table and the shaking got worse and worse.

It actually felt like something was under the house and it was running a very rough roller that had long knobs on that roller.

I tried to stand and had to grab onto a sofa chair to stabilize myself. The first thought was to run outside, but Phia says to just remain where I was, but I could not.

I smelled Gas so I was concerned about the Gas furnace blowing up and starting a fire. The things that go through a persons mind when something like this is happening is something I don't want to experience any time soon.

But of course there are always aftershocks, so I was going to have to endure what ever happened. But Phia remains completely cool all through all of this. I have always prided myself in remaining cool under fire, but this really rattled me.

Probably because I have not experienced something this drastic before. Knowing that I could not do anything about it. Which made me feel completely helpless.

In anticipation of my twins crawling all around on the floor, I had placed latches on all of the doors at floor level and once I got started, I even put these latches on every drawer and door on every cabinet (no matter where they are located,) in our kitchen and also in every bedroom.

It is a bit cumbersome until you get used to them, but in this case, these latches saved countless dishes from falling out and on to the floor and breaking all of them, because I never lost a thing because of all of these latches kept everything inside of every cabinet.

CLEM

PEG AND THE EARTHQUAKE

After all of the time that Peggy has been in a Coma, Lord and behold she wakes up just minutes before this Earthquake happens.

And when it does happen, the Medical center of UCLA takes a kind of a direct hit, even though it is about fifteen miles from the actual Epicenter of where the Earthquake is centered.

But because of how and on what the Medical center is built on, it began to shake an awful lot, and since she is in the Nursing Home section of this Hospital, it is on the ground floor, but it too was built on a Rock solid foundation. So everything began to shake terribly.

I guess she thought she had died and gone to Hell or something, because things are rolling across the floor of her room and things are falling to the floor, but I guess the Hospital thought they would get as much money from me as they could, so they loaded up her room with as much equipment as they could muster.

Anyway in the beginning no one came to her room, and because she had not used her voice for several months, she did not even know if she had a voice. But when things did not stop shaking, she then screamed with everything that was in her.

And then in a moment someone was at her bedside and they told her they just had a very strong Earthquake. There is a lot of damage to the Hospital but this building is still pretty well intact.

In a few more moments some men came to her room and picked up everything that had fallen on to the floor and they rearranged all of the furniture that had become catawampus to the room itself.

Peggy at this time had all kinds of tubes in her arms and legs and other parts of her body, so a Nurse came into her room and began to remove most of them.

This nurse says that the Doctor will be in later this morning, and at that time he will decide what else to remove from her body. Peggy asked this Nurse, has her husband been to see her recently and she says she has never seen your husband, and did not know that you even had a husband.

Because whatever rings she had on when she entered the Hospital, were all taken away so no one would steal them, including her wristwatch. Peg then said that she never really felt like she was ever married, but was just living with this specific man, who happened to be her husband.

When Doctor Dore came to see how she was doing, he was very surprised that she was awake and was eating on her own. Not much but a little Jell-O.

Peg then tells Doctor Dore that she does not want her husband to know that she is awake. Doctor Dore says your husband has not come to see you since you were put in this Nursing Home, and that has been thirty months since he has come to see you.

Peg says he probably now has another wife to support and live with, who will probably make Martha, one of his daughters a great mother, because she says she could never be a mother for any child, whether it was hers or his. So don't tell him that I am now awake and will most likely be getting out of this Nursing Home when I get well enough to function on my own.

Do you know if he is still living in the apartment? And Dr. Dore says he will have to check on that, and when he knows he will have someone come and tell you what you need to know about your husband.

CLEM

PEG

THE CONDITION OF PHILADELPHIA'S HOUSE

Meanwhile back with Phia and me and Martha. The city of Santa Monica came to our house on that same afternoon and after they looked at the house and grounds, told us it was not fit for anyone to live in it. That we had three days to move out of it.

All of the trees had been laid down on the ground including the three weeping willow trees. And all of the Grape vines had been knocked down onto the ground. There are some trees that are just leaning, like some of the Cottonwoods and Poplars, but all of the other fruit trees are all flat on the ground.

Later that day I went with the garden tractor and a wagon and I picked up as many of the fruits I can find and I picked up as many of the Grapes that I had not already picked earlier last month.

I also went to a garden store and purchased several Plastic Pots, wherein which I could place as many of the Grape vines as I could dig up, knowing that for some of them I did not have enough of their roots, but they can sometimes surprise a person.

We did not know at that time where we would now live, and I knew that it would not be in Los Angeles County, but most likely would be somewhere in Orange County.

Phia and Martha called UCLA and they are told that a lot of the buildings have completely collapsed so there will not be any further teaching for at least a month, because some of the buildings will have to be torn completely down. So Phia says to give her the front office, and the person says the front office has completely collapsed. She then says to give her the Records section and she did get through to them and Phia says that her and her daughter and she gave them their names and when she had the correct person, she told them that she and Martha want to transfer to the new University in Irvine, and as soon as it can be arranged.

Apparently that person had had other requests of the same kind, so Phia was told that in a week, you two could begin continuing your classes at UCI. But call them there and make sure you are registered with them. And the first day you begin your classes with them, go an hour early so you can get your parking arranged.

Martha says she needs to buy a bicycle, just in case her classrooms are some distance from where Phia will be going to classes. Which most likely will be close to where she will park her vehicle.

I then get on the Phone and call the Santa Fe and they tell me that a lot of files are on the floor in the backroom, but all of the Tariff files are all right, because I always locked all of the doors and drawers before I came home. If anyone needed any of the Tariffs in the cabinets they will have to see either you or Milton Paulson, because you are the only two who have keys.

As to coming to work, don't even think about it. Take care of your family first and if you need to find another place to live, then do that too, then you can come back to work. I was actually talking to Harry Epp, so that is written in concrete. I did not question whether I would be paid for the days I will take off, but it did not really matter anyway.

I then got on the phone and called several moving places and they told me that renting any kind of truck will not happen for more than two months, because every truck has been rented until that time. What about trailers and he says the same for them also.

So the next thing I did was, I phoned Cal Worthington who is a used car dealer, and I asked him if he had any two-ton trucks he could sell to me. Especially one with Motorized lifts and tail gate. He says he has two left. He tells me what they are, so I tell him I want the 1966 Chevrolet truck, and I will give you six thousand dollars Cash for it, and Cal asks when do you want to come and get it, and I say I will be there in two hours.

It was already almost 4:00 PM in the afternoon, but Phia and I got into my vehicle and I drove to his used car lot, and an hour later I was driving off of his lot with that 1966 Chevrolet Two ton truck, and on that truck it had an enclosed bed and another part of it had places where I could just place a kind of open kind of racks, with tailgates also. And it also has a motorized tailgate lift on it, which is what I was looking for.

Phia says you really know how to make things happen. Did you see the original price tag on that truck? He wanted nine thousand dollars for it, but I said I gave him six thousand in Travelers checks, which is just like cash to him. Because any bank will honor them. I made a great deal, but I am a person who usually gets what he wants when I want it, when it comes to doing business with anyone.

When we got back home, Phia asked do we move everything ourselves or do we ask for help. Mona says she knows three men who might be willing to help us move, so I told her to call them, only have them come tomorrow morning, because we will remain here tonight still. After a half hour went by, Mona came back to me and told me that the three men she had told me about will be here around 7 :00 AM tomorrow morning.

Martha asks how did you get a truck with a motorized tailgate on it, so I said I purchased it for six thousand dollars. They wanted nine thousand, but I paid cash for it, so it was a good deal for all parties.

At that time I checked to make sure it had enough oil in the crankcase and everything else that needed checking. I say I will fill up the gas tank on our way to wherever we are moving to tomorrow, just in case there may be persons in or around this neighborhood that may think they can get some cheap gas for their own vehicles.

Phia asks do you think there are persons like that in this neighborhood, I say no, but since this quake happened, I have seen some persons driving by this house who may think they can get something for nothing. So I will sleep while all of you watch and then when I get up I will watch while all of you sleep.

But first I have to find us a place to live in, so I get out the Phone book and in a few minutes I am making some phone calls. After twenty minutes I tell Phia that I have found us a place where we can rent for 200 dollars a month, and it has three bedrooms and it is a Townhouse in Garden Grove, California. It is called Bixby Green.

When things like this happen, some persons become criminals overnight or in an instant. I will also use the birds of the air to help me in this endeavor. I then went and lay down on our bed and in a little while I felt Phia lying next to me.

Eight hours later I woke up and Phia had already awakened but not much before, because she was still in just her panties and bra. I asked are you in a hurry to go out side of this room and she says no, so she made sure the door was locked and we made love for the next two hours. Before that night we had only petted each other and cuddled with each other, but never made serious love. Phia asked do you want to get me pregnant and I tell her that is my intention. If not tonight then some time in the near future.

Phia says can we wait until our twins are at least two years old first. I say that is fine, but I will probably have to use rubbers if we continue to do this fairly often. She says you'll get over it. I kiss her and pat her butt, and then I get up and go into the bathroom to take a shower and the next thing I feel is Phia behind me, but she is feeling around in front of me for Junior.

I will not go into any further detail as to what happened after that, but it sure is enjoyable. Anyway, in a little while we both got dressed and went out to the kitchen and made something for us to eat, and when we showed up, Martha and Mona disappeared and probably went to bed. It was then a little after midnight so I know I needed to go outside to watch for persons who should not be anywhere near our residence.

I did not have long to wait, because three men showed up about 2:00 AM and when they got to within twenty feet of my truck, I turned on the Security lights and I had my weapon drawn, the one that was still pending for a Patent, so I was well equipped with a lot of fire power.

When I did this Phia called the police and in five minutes they showed up and by that time I had switched weapons because I did not want to have to explain an un-patented weapon to the police that they even might take away from me. I did this in front of these three potential burglars, but I was not worried.

The police asked why they are in this man's yard and so close to his truck that he obviously just purchased, because it still had the dealers license on it. They did not answer, but one of them said that I had a weapon that he has never seen before and it looked like it may have been made overseas like in Russia.

These two policemen asked if I have such a weapon, and I told them I don't know what he is talking about. He must be trying to get out of going to jail or something. Nothing else was done or said, and they put these three burglars in another vehicle that had been summoned and everyone left the yard. These policemen didn't even look very hard for any other weapon.

They did ask if I had a license for the weapon that I had in my hand, so I showed them my Federal license, and that was it. I am quite sure these three men wondered how powerful a person I really am.

I left the security lights on after that episode, and no other persons came anywhere near the house and or grounds. I think the three men who did come were probably from some other neighborhood, and did not know what kind security lighting I really had on all of this property, because every place where someone might try to steal anything, there were security lights, even near the fruit trees and the grape vines. Even though most of the grape vines had been dug up and put in separate pots.

When 6:00 AM arrived, Martha called Phia and I to come inside to have breakfast, which we did, and by seven AM four men showed up and they began to load all of the furniture onto the truck.

One of them asked where I had gotten such a truck, because he says he could not rent any kind of moving vehicle for at least two months, so he will have to remain where he lives, even though part of his house is falling down. But luckily he has enough grown children still living at home, who can watch everything while he is doing this job. He says he is not a rich man, but he is wondering if he could rent this truck so he can move to where his brother is living in Santa Ana. I said, lets just get us moved and then we will concentrate on getting all of the rest of you moved. And you will even get paid for helping us get moved. The man who first spoke up says that is not necessary, but I say I insist so lets just do what we have to do, and then we will see what else can be done with all of you.

Martha then came to where they are loading our couch and she asks have all of you eaten breakfast, and all of them say they have not, so she then says to come into the house and have some good food.

It is at that time that Mona appears, and this man who first spoke up says he did not know that she also lived at this address, and Mona did not say anything, but just went to doing something with the twins.

Mona came to where I was and told me that this first man is the father of her baby, and he is a fourth cousin and she did like him at one time, but he is no longer a friend of hers, but is a friend of the man who is called Tony, who is that man at the end of the table. The other two men are Tony's brothers, and they are good persons, but don't trust this fourth cousin.

If they use your truck, you had better drive it yourself and be sure to carry your weapon on your person, and make that fourth cousin aware that you know how to use it expertly.

If you thought about renting it to someone, then rent it to Tony, but to no one else. But she suggests that I just drive it myself, and don't let her fourth cousin to ride inside of the cab, because he may try to do something violent against you.

As far as she is concerned, she wished he had not come to this house, or with these other three men. He was not any of the men that she had called. She says she only talked to Tony. You have probably noticed that he does not lift much weight, but just carries the light items.

So tell him to not show up for the next load that you take away from this house. Mona says she knows how to use any kind of small weapon and she will shoot him if he comes onto this property again.

When you take this load to wherever we are moving to, leave her and Martha and Phia here at the this house and we will all protect it, because she knows that Phia also has her own weapon, and she really knows how to use it, because she knows about her former husband, and how he got shot by Phia.

But he did not die from those bullets but by another method. So since Mona's fourth cousin was the actual person who actually brought the other three men to this address, I told him to not return back to this address, because I will make sure that these other three men are returned back to their homes after they finish helping me get moved to my new address. I handed him ten dollars at that time and told him because he only carried small and light items, that is all you are worth.

I told him to just get into his automobile and get the hell off of this property. And if you decide to return after we leave, then I will have you arrested by the Police as soon as you step on the first inch of this property. He asked what did Mona do with his baby. I ask him can you afford to take care of that baby, and he says it doesn't matter whether he can afford to take care of, because it is his, and he will take her to court to get it. I tell this man I will break you financially, so forget that baby. Because you will never see it ever again, for as long as you remain alive.

And if you try to steal any baby's from this house, I will see to it that you never see the light of day ever again, because every person, including Mona belongs to and in this family totally, because you see she is my younger sister, so completely forget about Mona and that baby and any other child in this house.

If you have other ideas, forget them, because if you step foot on this property again, you will go to jail and you will never get out of jail for the rest of your life. The choice is yours, when I tell you something; you had better heed that warning.

Because if you don't then you are history. Now get out of my sight and never return to this property or even try to get close to any member of this family.

Because the next time I see you I will kill you. And I won't even think about doing anything different. So this man got into his car and drove off of my property. I never saw him again until many years later, but that is another part of this story. It took a total of three loads in that truck that I had purchased. The final load included all of the Cats things, and along with this final load, we drove all of our vehicles to our new home.

Of course all of the Cats are in their own carriers, of which have a place for food and water, but since I had fed them two hours before this last load, they had all pooped and peed so putting any food or water in their carriers was unnecessary. When we left Santa Monica on that final trip to Garden Grove, this house and garage was completely empty. The only thing that remained is the buildings.

I asked Phia, is there anything in the attic in that house, and Phia says she does not know, so I got the Ladder off of the truck and looked in the attic, and the only item in that attic was a kind of Antenna. Probably for a Television.

Phia says to leave it, because we now will have Cable. So we left. We never saw that place again while that house was still on it. Once we were completely moved, I no longer had any use of that truck, but I somehow could not sell it. We did use it to get two of the men that helped us to get moved also. Henry remained where he lived in Whittier. So I took that truck to a place where I could park it, and I covered it with several pieces of Tarpaulin that I had sewed together using some very strong String. I did this by hand, because my sewing machine could not handle the Canvas tarpaulin material.

CLEM

THE RETURN OF PEGGY

I called Eve Wilson, who is the Apartment Manager where the apartment is located, two months after this quake had hit, and she says my wife is now living in that apartment. I asked why did you not call me, and she says because your wife asked me not to. I don't know where you live, because your telephone number, when I called the Phone company, told me that it is a Portable Telephone, so they cannot tell where I live, because the bill for that Phone Number is sent to Moses Lighthouse's address and when I called him, he says he cannot and will not tell me where Mr. Royal now lives. Or even where he used to live. So what was I to do?

I then asked how long has she lived there and Eve says two weeks. Eve says that she woke up just minutes before the Sylmar Earthquake happened, and she was finally able to get out of the Nursing Home that the Hospital had put her into.

Eve says that Peggy was discharged from that Nursing Home two weeks back, and she came directly here. Then the call ended.

I had not even checked with Moses about her condition and apparently he did not know that she had awakened from that Coma either. So I called him and told him what I knew about her. He says he will check her out.

He did tell me that there are sufficient funds in her checking account, wherein she can live however long she wants to live without even working for the next forty years, even if you never go back to live with her ever again. You have provided very well for her. Then the call ended.

So Peg has been awake for two months now, and she apparently did not want to see me. That is fine with me. Because I did not want to see her either. It's funny, because I still felt responsible for her.

I would suppose that if she hired a private detective, that person could find out all there was to know about me and Martha and Phia and even our twins. But I refuse to worry about it, mostly because Moses will handle her.

CLEMENT

PEG

BACK TO WORK AT SANTA FE

In the meantime, I had gone back to work and I was back to my normal grind of duties at the Santa Fe railroad. James Hamilton says he had a lot of damage to his house, but they did not have to move, but did have to bolster up one side of his house. He says he does not have a garage. He drives a black Chevrolet pickup truck, half-ton size. He had helped a number of his neighbors to move to different locations, because their houses were completely wrecked. So he feels he is very lucky.

I was off an entire week, and I did not get paid for any of it, but I really never expected to get paid for any of it. Some persons were off for two weeks; because of how much damage they had on their houses.

One guy I know, who lived in Van Nuys, which is west of Pasadena about fifteen miles told me that his house literally fell completely apart and they were lucky that no one in his family was hurt.

That he lost everything because the house collapsed on everything and he and his family, when they first felt the first shudder, ran outside and they just sat in the middle of the street and watched their house collapse on everything.

He says their cat survived because he crawled under one of the beds which was extra strong because it had drawers built into the base of that bed, because ten minutes later he came running out of that house and that is when they caught him.

He was real scared and whenever he hears any kind of sharp noise now he panics and always wants to run away from everyone.

I say it will take a lot of time, so just be patient with him and he will calm down in about six months. But if he doesn't then let me know and I will try to do something different with him.

What you might do is get him a female kitten to play with, which will divert his attention to someone he can love in a more personal way, and when she gets to be four months old, have her spayed, so she can never get pregnant, and she will take care of the rest. He says he can and will do that.

I say if you wait longer than four months he will try to mate with her when she is too young to mate with him, so be sure you have her spayed when she is four months old. In fact let me know when you get this kitten, and how old she is when you get her, and I will take care of the rest. At the end of this day, I make a note in my journal about this guy, so I won't forget him and his cat.

CLEM

PEG

UCI IRVINE AND MARTHA AND PHIA

When Phia and Martha first go to UCI, they arrived about an hour and a half earlier than was required. Martha was correct in her thinking about where her classrooms might be, because they are at least a quarter mile away from where Phia will be having her classes, so purchasing that bicycle was a great idea.

Martha says it will also give her some extra exercise anyway. They both tell me that the students at UCI are a more upper class kind of persons and they also tell me that they like all of their professors.

Martha says this is a better University than UCLA, not just with all of the students, but with much better professors too. And the Campus itself is beautiful.

Martha says you will not even find a piece of paper anywhere on this entire campus on any of the many lawns. She says there are even places where students can gather together and have jam sessions, kind of impromptu like, which makes for better relations with other students. Martha says Dallas Lighthouse is going here also; only he drives everyday from Los Angeles to this university.

He too is studying the exact same courses that she is taking, and he says he wants to become a Veterinarian like Mr. Royal is. And when Mr. Royal begins his own Hospital he wants to be part of it, so he can be close to Martha, because he knows she will also work for her father.

Dallas says that his father wanted him to go to Pepperdine University and become a lawyer like his father, but he says his other brothers can become Lawyers and they can eventually take over Dads business. He says he and Martha will take over Mr. Royal's business when he decides to retire from the medical field.

Martha says it is quite apparent what he intends to do. She says she does not disagree with him, but she thinks he is kind of ahead of himself. I ask Martha, are you also interested in Dallas, and she says she is, but they cannot even think about marriage until after she gets her Doctorate degree. I say ask him what his intentions are, and maybe he does not want to get married until after he gets his Doctorate degree either.

I personally won't let you get married until you at least reach the age of 25, which is probably when you will get your Doctorate Degree in Veterinary Medicine. When you are 23 you will get your PH'D in Creature Communication. Now since I already have all of the degrees dealing with Veterinary Medicine, I will help you write a Curriculum for UCI involving Creature Communication, which will be a Battery of tests that can be given to other students, of which they will have to get no less than 77 percent of the answers correct, to even be considered for that program of learning how to use that ability; which will give UCI something else to also consider you for employment with that University.

Because you can work at the university and also at the hospital. When the time comes, I will give you and Dallas that hospital, and then I will teach you how to operate it and keep all of the books also. Now since you and Dallas are around the same age, you will have to cease and desist or he will have to use many Rubbers so as to keep you from getting pregnant before you graduate with all of the necessary Degrees that you will need to even run this Hospital. I must insist on you two doing that.

Of course if you get pregnant before that time, you will just bring that baby to my house and we will take care of him or her, as if Phia and I had this baby ourselves. Do we totally understand each other? Martha says she understands, but will Dallas.

I say you bring Dallas to me and I will make him understand. It's either my way or no way. This family has functioned very well since I have married Phia, and I do not want that to change anytime soon.

CLEM

MEANWHILE BACK TO PEGGY

I have not heard from her or from Moses Lighthouse regarding her, and I am wondering why. Not that I am in any hurry to go back to her for any reasons. But I do call Moses, and Lucy says he is over talking to Peggy at this time. I tell Lucy to have him call me, and then the call ends. Since I always seem to have a number of things to do around our town house, I get to work doing those things.

Phia is at UCI with Martha on this day, and since I have been trying to keep all of the Grape plants alive that I brought along with us, it is sometimes an iffy thing to do. But so far I have been completely successful in doing that very thing.

Since living at this address, there have been various Cats that have shown up on our doormat, and today another feline did just that. This one is a male cat, probably about two years old. I have not had a chance to talk to him yet to know where he may have came from, but that is always one of the first things I always do, when a feline shows up on our doormat. This cat is black and white, with most of the white on his stomach area. All of his feet are white with white on the tip of his tail also. I check him out thoroughly to make sure he does not have any fleas on him and there are none, so I ask him if he would like to come inside my residence.

He is greatly surprised that I can actually communicate with him in the usual way that he talks to other cats. But he does accept my invite, and the first cat he meets is Tai, who asks where he came from. I tell Tai that we both will inquire of that story after we give him something to eat. What happens in any Cat Pride, (which is a Cat family) is if the head of that Pride accepts another addition to a family, then the rest of that Pride accept this new cat also, so no cat fights happen.

Tribble gives this new cat an interesting look, but nothing else happens at this time. After he eats some food, and he does seems to be very hungry, and then Tai shows him where to go to the bathroom, he then is escorted to where I am sitting on the couch in the living room. All of the other cats are with me. After this cat finishes with his bath, he sits on the floor in front of me, with Tai sitting near him.

I ask him if he has a name and he says his name is Buttons. He says the human who had him before me did not call him that, but he heard some other humans saying to other humans about him, that he is as cute as a Button, so he has decided to adopt that as his name.

I say it fits, because you are as cute as a Button. I then introduce him to all of the other cats, and once that has happened, I then tell Tai to show him around this Townhouse.

So everyone takes Buttons to the upstairs portion of this residence, and the next time I see him is when Trinket and Topanga are chasing him. And then he is chasing them. And the next thing I see is when he is at the very top of the Scratching post I made for my brood of felines, which is actually fifteen feet high. And he is lying at the top most ledge sleeping. I make a comment to Tribble that it is quite apparent that you have totally accepted Buttons as another member of this family.

Then the telephone rings and it is Moses. He says he has talked to Peggy, and she wants me to stay away from her for one year at least, because she wants to see if she can survive on her own. She will take over supporting herself also, and he says he has agreed to what she wants to do.

She wanted to know where you now live, but I did not tell her, nor do I intend to ever tell her. I did not tell her that you are married again either, because I figured that kind of shock might push her over the edge. Nor did I tell her that you did not divorce her yet.

I did allude to the fact that you may want to Divorce her, and she says she has expected me to do that for several years, just like he did once before. But that is on hold for the time being. Moses says if she can survive on her own, then that is the time to Divorce her.

She intends to see a Psychiatrist, hoping that that person can help her with her former problem, but I am to not worry or even think about her any longer. I say how can I not think about her, and Moses says to just put her out of your mind, because he says he will be the one who will keep an eye on her.

Actually Moses says he won't keep an eye on her, but one of the other Lawyers who works for him will keep an eye on her. I tell Moses, make sure this other lawyer does not get personally involved with her.

He says he never thought about that, because this lawyer he has in mind is in reality a single man. But he has been married before. I then say that is the worse kind of watchdog to put in charge of a wife who is suffering from things that even she does not fully understand. I say you might reconsider assigning a different Lawyer to her case. Moses says he will think about it. Then the call ends.

So aside from knowing that she does not want to see me for at least a year, basically not much else has changed. I don't think I will tell Phia anything about this phone call, but I may tell Martha. Giving her strict instructions to never mention anything about it to Phia. I am quite sure that Phia will possibly ask about her in the future, but I will try to never mention her name again while I am married to Phia.

Another item I am considering is from this place where we are now living, where will our next residence be located. Because this place is not large enough for all of use to live. So I have asked Moses for yet another thing for him to do, which is to send me to someone here in Orange County who can either help me find another house or find someone who I can buy a piece of land from, where I can have a house built on it. And what is involved in getting a great General Contractor who will be in charge in getting my new house built.

So eventually I do buy an acre of land in the middle of a bean field in the city of Santa Ana. And one of the things I like to do in my spare times is I design houses, meaning I design them in every way, by designing every room in these houses, down to the very last piece of lumber that will be used in actually building them. And so far I have seven designs laid out on paper. In order to have any of these houses built, I would have to take these designs to a Blue Printer and have several copies made up. The General Contractor I finally select seems to really know his business and after a lot of thought and discussion, Phia and I decide on a particular design to have built.

Then this General Contractor takes that design to a Person who will make up no less than twenty Blue Prints and then after several building Permits have been acquired, the building of this house is begun. And that day is August 7, 1971. I am hoping to be able to move into this house on April 6th, 1972, which is my and Phia's Birthday's.

One of the things I have to do is I have to have some Streets built to where this house will be located. Before I can do that, I have to consult with the street engineer of this city to see if there are any idea's that may have been submitted about this area. If none have, then it is totally up to me as to where these streets will be located and what each one will be called.

I also have to study all of the surrounding streets, so if I decide that some of the streets that the city of Santa Ana may have to build at some later date, when some additional houses are built in and around my own house will be built. So being a simple act of doing is not something that can ever be considered.

The street my house will be on will be called Sierra Avenue. This street will be a brand new street, so if the city decides to extend that street or pick it up further east or west is totally up to the Street Engineer of this city. Only time will tell that story.

My house number will be 209 West Sierra Ave, because this street will be west of Main Street, which is one of the Main streets in this city. This house will have ten rooms in it. It will have a three car Garage and it will be a two-story house. I am just considering how large I expect my family to become.

In the meantime, Peg's father in March of 1970 has died of a massive heart attack, when Peg was still in a Coma, and I asked Moses if he told her about his death, and he says he did, and she took it badly, but she will survive that tragedy someway. She says she did not get a chance to tell him how sorry she was, when she made an issue of how he and his wife had been accused of how badly they had taken care of her and her sister. That she was just lashing out at her husband at that time, and since she wanted to go to California with him, she did the only thing she could think of to do when she was fighting his Divorce of her at that time.

Now since it has been almost two years since his death, Margaret is now asking if she can come to live with Clement and Peg in their new house. This was conveyed to Peg in a letter, So Peg asked Moses, was Clement building a new house somewhere?

Margaret Chapman not knowing that Clement has another wife that he is actually living with. So because of this new Revelation, Clement again asks Moses to find him another piece of ground where he can build yet another house for Phia and his family, because Clem says he will let Peggy and her Mother move into the ten room house in Santa Ana. Phia gets on the phone and says she has already found the house she wants to move into, and it is located in the city of Irvine.

In fact she says she has already put a down payment on it to hold it for her and her family, until she can get to one of her Banks where she can get a Cashiers check for the balance of the House. Her and Martha have already been in it, and in fact she says they already have the keys for this house. I didn't know a thing about it.

So much for No Secrets. And I so stated my disappointment

in that matter. Phia says she did not have time to tell me, because with me working Second shift at the Santa Fe, has made our communicating kind of difficult. I say whatever happened to leaving a note for me.

But Phia did not venture into that trap, but just did not say anything else. I let it pass for now. It's interesting to note here that Phia has not put me on any of her Bank accounts, but has put Martha on all of them. I am not sure I like that but what can I do about it.

Phia is turning out to be more independent than I have hoped she would become. Is this a rift starting between Phia and I? I wonder.

PRIVATE THOUGHT: women in most instances do have minds of their own, and some of them can even completely function without a man in their life. Just like a man can function with out a woman in his life.

But I believe that the right man and right woman who are meant to be together for most of their lives should always remain together come what may.

I am not saying it will always be this way, but one can hope. And remembering what I have already gone through with one woman, should not reflect on this mans true Soul Mate, dealing with the rest of his life. Since I have been very forgiving with the woman that I really don't want to be with any longer, then it is only natural that I should also be forgiving of my Soul Mate.

In reality I don't need any of Phia's money for me to survive, because I probably have more money than she will ever see in her entire lifetime.

I have not put Phia on any of my Bank accounts either. Nor

have I put Peg on any of them, because I always created separate bank accounts for both of them. Martha is on all of my bank accounts, and I am now thinking that, that is the case with Phia also.

A Developer has contacted me, regarding the rest of my House designs and we have agreed on a price for each of them, which is eight thousand dollars for each one of them, and since I had six of them, I now have a Cashiers check for 48 thousand dollars, which I took immediately to my bank in Garden Grove to make sure that this check will clear his bank, of which it has done. So I have an additional 48 thousand dollars, which is now in that checking account. And in selling all of those designs I have now completely dislodged any holdings in the city of Santa Ana, except the ten-room house, of which I will continue to own. Even though it is unlikely I will ever live in that house.

In the meantime I took Buttons to a Veterinary Hospital and had him Castrated, before he got any ideas about peeing in anything but the Cat John. And he seems to have adjusted quite well to his new feelings. I think Tai is the influence in how each cat acts in any household.

Phia says she actually loves all of my cats, especially Tai and Buttons, but as for the rest of them, she says you can take them to the other house in Santa Ana, and let your other wife take care of them. I am concerned about how Phia says my other wife.

I think she is letting me know that she does not like being number two wife. But I let it pass for now. I have to walk a very fine line between these two women. Even though I want to be with Phia always.

She knows that about me, but I still am in a very iffy position. I say I will have to give all of that about the cats a lot of thought because of how Tai actually feels about all of them.

That's like saying that you only like certain children, so take the rest of them to some other house and let someone else raise them.

Phia says she did not think about it that way. I then say consider that all of these cats are just more of our children. Then tell me which ones you want to farm out to some other family. Phia says she is just lashing out at me, because she is tired of being wife number two.

I then say blame your father for that fact, because he kept us from seeing each other back twenty years ago, and knowing how lonely I was for you at that time, you would not have remained single very long if I had been courting you.

And then this subject would be moot. And consider what I feel also, because I too feel as if I have been left out of parts of your life, because you still have not learned to totally trust me, when it comes to money. Like I told you in the very beginning, money does not impress me, it is what any person does with the money they do have. If you don't invest it in any kind of business, but just put in a bank and let it lay there, what reasons are there for even having that money.

Phia says because I have my own money, she did not think that having access to her money also would make a difference in our lives, but she says she is totally wrong in that thinking, so on her first day that she can arrange it, she will have me put on all of her bank accounts.

But she says she does not want herself to be put on any of

my bank accounts, for fear that my other wife will try to get control of some of them, if not all of them.

I then tell her that my other wife will never get control of any of my bank accounts; no matter how hard she may try to do that. Because she has her own bank accounts, so why would she want any of my money. No she will never get any kind of control over any of my bank accounts.

CLEMENT

PEG

MOVING TO THE HOUSE IN IRVINE
WITHPHILADELPHIA

So on October 17th 1971, (big Martha's Birthday), I again took out of storage the Chevrolet two ton truck, after I made sure that the 12 volt battery had been charge up and everything worked on it properly, and using some of my friends from the Santa Fe railroad, it took four loads before we could get everything moved into this new house.

This new house actually has 24 rooms in it, but it is a ~~very~~ three story style house on a three acre size lot. How much money Phia actually paid for it, she never did tell me. But after we lived there for a year and seeing the Personal property Tax bill, I surmised that she probably paid about 250 thousand dollars for it. I figured if she wanted to tell me she would, but she never did.

The county had it appraised for 310 thousand dollars. I in reality complained to the county appraiser, and he lowered it to 250 thousand dollars, because of the kind of neighborhood this house is really in the middle of.

This house has a swimming pool on the grounds that is a fairly large pool, because it is 150 feet long and 50 feet wide and is 15 feet deep on the deep end and two feet deep on the shallow end, and it has two diving boards at two different levels.

It also has a Spa on one corner of it with that draining into the main pool whereat that drain creates a waterfall from that Spa area.

And all of the water is heated by Solar Panels that are all insulated that are on various Roofs of this house, where all of these Panels face South all of the time. These Panels are 5 by 10 feet size and four of them also heat the house water for this entire house, even though there is a Gas heater also inside of the Garage. The Gas water heater tank holds 52 gallons and the Solar Heater tank holds 82 gallons, and since the temperature is set at 140 degrees constant, there is 134 gallons of extremely hot water available most of the time for any kind of washing that may be done in this house.

Because all of the water comes from City water, I have also had installed a Water Softener tank inside of the Garage area. And then in the Kitchen I have had another Filtering system installed wherein any water that goes to the Ice Cube maker in the Refrigerator and any water that is used to make Coffee and Tea or Soft drinks comes from a separate faucet that is located on the sink in the kitchen.

There is a Cabana house located on one end of the Pool that is about thirty-six feet square, but has inside of it ten separate rooms where persons can change into their swimming trunks. Where there are chairs and a lounge in each cubicle.

On one side of this Cabana there is an outdoor shower where anyone can remove the chlorine water from their bodies before they change back into their street clothes.

Each room in this Cabana has its own key, which needs to always be given back to the owner of this house. And if that person tries to leave the pool area, and they still have that key in their pocket, then an alarm sounds which tells me or Phia or whomever that they still have that key in their pocket. It will embarrass a few persons until they realize why the alarm sounded.

There is also a Television hookup showing whom is at the front door, and an electronic lock, which can be controlled from certain rooms in that house. Like from the Master Bedroom or the Office and a few other places, which I will not mention here at this time. I also will not mention the Address of this house. I will not describe each room separately because it is not all that important to do so.

The garage is a six-car garage, with extra parking beyond the driveway area for guest vehicles. I will have plenty of room to plant all of the Grape vines, with plenty of space for other fruit trees also.

And like the place in Santa Monica, I will also have a building that is refrigerated where I can store all kinds of fruits if that is necessary. But I will not store any kind of meats in that building.

There will be a large freezer in the Garage that will do that. Every modern appliance that is available in these times will be installed in this kitchen.

CLEMENT

PEG MOVING INTO 209 W. SIERRA AVENUE

As for the other house in Santa Ana, when Peg moves into that house, I am quite sure that whatever furniture that is in that apartment she will have it all moved to that house.

And since her Mother also has her own furniture, of which she will move all of it to California, that house will most likely be filled almost full with all kinds of furniture. And like I was figuring initially she moved into that house on April 14th, 1972, and her Mother moved in with her on May 17th 1972.

Margaret asked where is Clement, and Peggy says her and him have been separated now for almost two years. He lives somewhere in Orange county, but she does not know where. She says she has called the Santa Fe railroad but they will not tell me where he really does live. And they did not even know I am his wife. She says they did tell her that he does have a wife, but they cannot tell her what her name is, because they do not give out that kind of information.

Peg says she even called her bank, and they can only tell her that he resides somewhere in California. Peg says he is no longer on her Bank Account, because he removed himself from it. Peg says it is quite apparent that he does not want to be found.

Peggy says she has made a deal with his Lawyer, wherein she wants to see if she can fully survive on her own, and if she can, then he will most likely Divorce her. It would be nice to know where he and Martha are living but it is not absolutely necessary.

As you know we have not had a very happy marriage and now since his oldest is somewhere in Missouri in a kind of Reform School Camp, which she says she has inquired about with Clem's Lawyer, but he will not tell me anything else about it, and no one else seems to know where she is located.

And when I asked you, you told me that I do not have to know where she is located, she figures that she has been completely cut off from any other members of her family.

Peggy says not even her sister Mary knows anything about Mary Beth. In fact Mary says she did not even know that Clem had adopted two daughters.

Margaret asks Peg, why do you need to know where Mary Beth is located, because you are not even her Mother, as Clement adopted her and Martha as a Single parent.

And even if he might be married again, maybe he got a Mexican Divorce from you, but you have not been informed of that yet. Peg says she thought of that, and she asked Clements Lawyer that same question, but he did not have an answer and did not know that answer, so apparently Clem has not even told his Lawyer everything about his life. Of course he cannot tell me anyway, because of Client – Lawyer Privilege Laws.

Peg says she needs to get herself her own lawyer, who might know this Moses Lighthouse, who is Clements Lawyer. Thinking that she could come in the back door, to find out information about Clement.

Margaret asks, why do you need to know whatever about Clement if you want to try to live on your own, because he probably does not want to know about you, except to know that you are now living in this house that he owns, so he has obviously thought about your well being, which is more than most men would have done for you, considering how you have treated him for all of the time he has been married to you.

As your Mother, let me tell you this, if Clement does not want to be with you any longer, then that is his right, because you have never treated him like he was ever your husband, except that you wanted to have his reputation as your own, because as far as anyone in the Ferguson, Missouri area, your own reputation is so far down in the gutter, that you will have to dig more than a thousand feet into the ground to find it.

Now that you are in California and supposedly on you own, why don't you turn yourself around and build a new reputation by yourself. A reputation that you can be proud of.

You only got married because he is a very responsible person, and his reputation preceded him even to Missouri. Margaret further says that when she and Mary came back to Missouri after they drove to South Dakota to see what kind of a husband you had gotten yourself, she says she was well pleased with your choice, but from the very beginning of that marriage, you blew everything she had hoped for you to have with Clement.

Margaret says when she returned back to Missouri, she contacted the University where he went to college, and they had nothing but praise and great hopes for him, because he was the only Student who ever got perfect grades for all of the time he went to that college. That he was the smartest student that has even attended that University.

And from the very beginning of your marriage, you just had to run around on him, when he did not give any reason for you to do that. Why in heavens name would you do that to such a nice person as Clement Royal is?

You have never really loved him, but you only wanted his Reputation for your own, but when that did not work, then you thought you could come to California and begin all over. But you just had to get yourself pregnant by Ken Jenkins again, and when you tried to get rid of that Baby like you got rid of all of the other babies before when you got pregnant by so many other men, but never Clement, because you feared childbirth, which almost killed you, and if Clement hadn't given his permission for you to have that latest Operation, you would now be Dead, so thank your lucky stars that you are even alive, because of him, but don't ever expect him to ever come back to you and live with you again.

Margaret says she would be very surprised if he ever did that. Margaret says she does not know where Clement is now living either, because he told me a few months back, that he will not, because he wants to now live a life completely apart from you.

This was probably about the time when you first woke up from your coma, which you thought that he did not know about you, but remember he is the one who paid your Hospital Bills and Doctor Bills, so he probably knows more about you then you obviously do not know about him.

He is very knowledgeable about most everything, but you have always sold him short, because you never thought he knew about all of your Liaisons, but he told me about how many men you have met and had relations with since you two have been married.

Margaret says she almost fell out of her chair when he told her that figure. And you wonder why he does not want to ever see you again, and you wonder why he never came to see you in that Hospital.

Margaret says if she were a man, she would have let you die, but that is not Clements way. Margaret says Clement is the gentlest man she has ever known, and that includes your father.

Margaret says she would like to know how she could contact Clement, and Peg says to just contact his Lawyer and if he thinks that Clement needs to be contacted, then he will do it. That is the only way either of us will be able to contact him for any reason.

So it is likely that he may be in this county, but Peg says she thinks he lives up near Sacramento, because he has a lot of friends near that city.

And he has always talked about starting a Grape Orchard, because as you may know he makes very good wine. And that is a great place to start a Grape Orchard. Margaret asks Peg, do you make any payments on this house, and Peg says that Clements Lawyer says this house is completely Paid for.

And Clements Lawyer has put it in my name, so I have to pay the Personal Property taxes and I have to secure Fire Insurance on it that is supposed to cover the house and all of the contents inside of it.

Margaret says she knows what that is all about, because she had to do the same in Missouri, so if you need some help in doing that, she will be glad to help.

Peg says she will appreciate whatever you can do to help for anything to do with Taxes and Insurance premiums. Peg says she has plenty of money, because apparently Clements Lawyer handles some of his bank accounts. Peg says she thought she could find out where he lives by checking with some of those banks, but Moses says whatever money you may think you need, has to go through himself and not through any bank.

Peg says she called the bank where Clement used to bank, but they referred me to Moses Lighthouse. She says she even pleaded with them but they still told her that she has to talk to Moses Lighthouse.

Margaret says Clement is very smart, which is why she wanted her daughter to get to know him better, but you had your own agenda, and you totally blew it with him.

And as far as having babies and experiencing childbirth, these days they put you out just enough so you rarely remember much of anything about the actual birth of your child. Most women want this kind of child birthing, and they most always get it. Now you will never be able to have any babies, because you will never ever get pregnant again, so you blew that one also.

Margaret says you are not a very loving daughter and you really never were. And when Clement tried to get his marriage with you annulled in the Catholic Church, she says she went along with her Husband when he fought it, but she says she was wrong in doing that too, and whether Clement will ever try again, she does not know, and that is the reason she needs to contact this Moses Lighthouse, so she can tell him that she will not appose it again.

But will in fact totally approve it, and will insist that the Catholic Church grant that annulment. Which will set up any Divorce to be approved without any fanfare.

That she actually needs and wants to apologize to Clement for ever apposing any annulment. Peg says it sounds like you are on Clements side now, and Margaret says she has always been on his side, but fighting your father and the Church was not something she was prepared to do at that time, but now she feels it is his right to have that annulment and a divorce from you.

Margaret says the one thing he did, that she never seemed she could ever do, was he taught you how to cook. Peg says if she had not written everything down in a book, she still would not know how to cook, but that is what she did, so now she can cook for herself and even others.

Clement

PEG

MEANWHILE BACK AT THE SANTA FE RAILROAD

One of the things that Management will sometimes do, is when two persons are knowledgeable in doing the same thing, like handling Transit Grain rates, is they will transfer one of those persons into doing something different. And that is what they did with me.

Having a Revising job is the same in anything that has to do with that position, with a few exceptions. Jim Willows before he was advanced into a supervisors position, handled some special accounts, like rating the Livestock shipments and some others also.

And those others are in reality all of the shipments of Automobiles from all of the Manufacturers of automobiles in Southern California.

But what is different about this position is, on occasion I have to go and inspect their Records at their plant. In effect I am to be an Outside Auditor for the Atchison Topeka and Santa Fe Railroad Company.

It is not a Supervisory position, but it has supervisory responsibilities, and it also has an Expense Account. When I first hired on with the Santa Fe railroad, Jim Jones, who was the General Agent for Los Angeles, tried on many occasions to try to convince me to take a Traveling Auditors position with the Transcontinental Freight Bureau, but I told him I did not want to travel any longer.

And then when he had a heart attack while at work, and Harry Epps took over his position, and that position was expanded into being the General Manager of the Car Accounts and Accounting Departments and the Same for the Revising Department, which in effect is part of the accounting department. So this new position was in effect made for me, because of all of my experience in railroad accounting.

So working with automobile rates became another easy job for me, and in fact like everything else I did, I made it look easy, and some of the immediate supervisors wondered if I was doing something wrong, but when Harry Epps personally investigated some of my files, he told the Manager of the Revising department and all of the Inspectors of that same department, that I knew exactly what I was doing, and whoever said otherwise is totally wrong.

In fact Jim Willows was the person who told the Manager of the Revising department that I must be doing something wrong and this manager told Harry Epps, so that is why Harry personally inspected some of my files for one entire day, and then told everyone that Clement Royal knows exactly what he is doing in his position.

Willows had Egg all over his face, so he went on Vacation and never came back because he got himself transferred to Topeka, Kansas.

How many different persons in my working careers have tried to have me removed from a particular position, but always failed in that endeavor. 57 varieties is a figure I first think of …

Anyway I got into my vehicle and drove back to the Santa Fe railroad and after getting permission to use the Conference room as my office, I begin studying all of my printed reports.

Harry Epps came to where I was doing this and he asked me what I was doing, and when I told him, he asks have I seen any improprieties yet, and I tell him that first, they are keeping double sets of books. One for any Auditor to see and another set for only their eyes to see. He asks how do I know this, and I tell him if I told you, you would not believe me. But I suggested he call my former Boss in Chicago with the WWIB again, and talk to him, and let him tell you how I solved all of his internal problems. I will talk to him first and then you can talk to him.

And when you get through hearing about my methods of securing some of the information that I can secure, then tell me that I am wrong. Harry says he needs to know what I am saying. So first I look at my watch and when I figure Jack Perkins will still be in his office, I make that call.

Jack answers on the second ring and when I tell him my reason for calling he says to put Warren on the phone. Harry talks to Jack for about ten minutes and then after he hangs up his phone, he says he fully understands now, and you were correct in suggesting that I talk to your former Boss in Chicago, because this is very important information.

When I leave the Santa Fe to go back home on this day, I note that someone is following me. So instead of driving to my home with Philadelphia, I instead drive to a Motel where I know other agencies use, when they are trying to hide federal witnesses. But instead of just checking into one motel room, I in fact rent three of them that are connected to each other through bathrooms in each of them.

As some of them are so large that they have two bathrooms in them. Of course the Motel records will only show that I have rented just one motel room. I also called Phia with my portable telephone, telling her that I will not be home this evening.

Luckily I always carry at least one weapon on my body and I have two others in my vehicle, so I will not be helpless, and one of the weapons I carry in my vehicle is the one I invented myself, of which I am still waiting to get the Patent approved on it.

So I watch Television for a while and then I go into the other room through the bathroom, leaving the lights on and the drapes completely closed in the room I just left. And from that other room, I can still go through another invisible door in a closet into another room, leaving the lights on and the drapes completely closed in the room I just left.

And when I get to the final room, I do not put on any lights nor do I cause any movements on any windows, nor do I run any water or flush any toilets in that final room, but I just lay down on the bed and go to sleep.

I have the kind of wrist watch that will wake me at whatever time I have it set for, when it extends a device from one side of this watch that does not make any noise, but it touches my wrist in a sensitive area, waking me up.

I then reverse my procedure and begin to go back to my original room, and when I get to the middle room, I hear someone in that room, so I go back to my final room and open the door and by going the back way to my vehicle, I get in, start it and drive away before they even know I am gone.

FBI persons sometimes use the combinations of rooms that I rented when they are hiding a Special witness in a particular trial, that they will testify at.

How did I know about this place? Well I cannot tell you. It's a secret. In every room except the final one, I left clues for persons to find, which would send them in a totally different direction than where I had been going initially.

Whoever was doing the searching would think that I was some kind of person from the Association of American Railroads, which would possibly slow them down a bit. At least it would make them stop and think for a few minutes... Anyway when I arrived at my office, only two persons were there at that time of the morning, and they did not seem surprised that I was there, because I have always maintained a decorum of getting to work at least an hour or more before I am supposed to be there.

Even though I am a member of the Transportation Communications Union, as long as I do not do any work, I can be at work as early as I want to be.

I sat down in a chair outside of Harry Epps office and played solitaire with a deck of cards I always carry with me. At 7:00 AM he showed up at this office and because I was sitting where he could not see me, when I suddenly said good morning, he jumped a foot off of the floor.

Which told me that he did not expect to see me this morning, which told me that he was the culprit who was keeping the powers with the auto manufacturing companies completely informed when there might be some trouble for them.

So I walked away from him and went into my office and closed my door and I called Bing Torpin, who is the Vice President and General Manager of the entire Santa Fe railroad, and told him of my suspicions.

He was at his office, so he says he will be there in ten minutes, but to call the Santa Fe police and have them restrain Harry Epps. I did that, but when they arrived Harry was not in his office. And his car was gone from the parking lot, so wherever he had gone, he probably went to inform someone at one or both of the auto manufacturing plants. And to probably totally destroy the second set of records or maybe all of them.

I also called the Representative of the Association of American Railroads, but he was not yet in his office, but I did talk to his secretary who told me that she would have him call me as soon as he arrived. Then the call ended. I did not want to tell the secretary what my call was all about. Too many ears may spoil the soup. I was again just doing my job, but looking back on all of this, I made it appear that there was still too much graft still going on at too many Railroads in this country.

I will not, nor can I in reality tell you the outcome of all of this, except to say that many persons went to jail at these two auto manufacturing companies and some personnel from the Santa Fe railroad. Who these persons were I cannot say.

What happened to key personnel at the Santa Fe railroad is all embedded in those now secret records that will not be allowed to be opened until 2050. Which means that all of the personnel with all of these companies will all be dead by that time. And probably myself also.

I was pulled from that position soon after I caused all of this to happen, and then that position was completely abolished. Thereby allowing me to be able to bump someone from their position, just as long as I had more seniority than they had.

When Milton Paulson passed away, another man was brought in from Amarillo, Texas, but he did not last long, because he tried to have me fired for something that he himself had initiated, which caused management to send him back to Amarillo, Texas, and back to becoming a Clerk, and after a short time he soon died because he could not face the humiliation that he forced upon himself. How he died, I cannot tell you, because I really do not know.

He did not die naturally. Then I was in the running for that position, but because I knew too many persons near the top of the Ladder of success, I again was gone around and it was given to another person with less seniority that I had, meaning also that he had less experience regarding anything to do with Revising, so I instead Bid a position in the city of Santa Ana as Chief Clerk of that station.

Which in reality is the second in command of that entire station. Who that agent is I will not say, but he is a very shy person. He was so shy that he had me go out to meet all of the Representatives of every company that the Santa Fe Serviced. Meaning that every industry that had cars switched to that industry, I was their only contact usually. So as to get to know where every industry was located along the Santa Fe railroad tracks, I walked every mile, which was 68 miles.

Sometimes I had to make out the Clicking sheets for the Train Crews, which take all of the cars that need to be switched to all of these industries, and they thanked me many times for my overall knowledge of where all of these industries are located, because when I did that for them, I rarely made any mistakes. Meaning once again I became the best there ever was at doing any job.

And because I also knew the Morse Code, and sometimes when the Telegrapher did not show up for work or was sometimes late for work, and something needed to be sent using this Morse Code, I would get on the telegraph key and send these messages, and the operators at the other end of where these messages were going, always told me to slow down some, because they could not print as fast as I was sending these messages.

A lot happened while I worked that position in Santa Ana, but for me to go into as much detail as I usually do, would take another twenty pages to write about, so suffice to say I got several Accommodations while working that position, and with some of them saving several hundreds of peoples lives, by preventing trains from colliding with each other and killing hundreds of persons, to saving an actual two mile long trestle by driving a Diesel engine pushing nine cars of what is called Chat, which is highly absorbent rock, and causing these nine cars of Chat to coast to almost dead center of this trestle where they all stopped, where there was more than two feet of water going over this trestle at that time, thereby keeping this trestle where it was and not washing it away.

Then after I worked that position for fourteen months, someone who had over forty years seniority bumped me out of it. So I bumped a position in the Freight office, which is in Los Angeles.

And it was at this time when my writing was getting so bad that I could not even read it myself, because I at that time was writing right handed, which is how I had been taught to write from the very beginning of my early life.

But because I had gone through the windshield of my automobile back in 1959, where I injured my right elbow, and at the time I bumped into that position in the freight office, I had to do something, so I practiced writing left handed, and I did this every day for six months, and slowly I learned to do something that most anyone else said was probably impossible to do.

And in doing this, I learned how to use the Right side of my brain also, and what happened is, that now that I could use both sides of my brain, my memory increased fifty times more than it had been previously.

It also did several other things, but if I mentioned them here, you probably would not believe me, so I will not. And then the Powers in charge of the Santa Fe railroad decided to introduce computers at all of the stations, and how to do that was the big question.

So they sent out questionnaires to every employee, asking who had any experience regarding anything regarding any kind of computers, and when they got through reading my qualifications, they all decided that the Programmers would teach me and another employee that I selected to help me, because she was the smartest person on all of the other shifts.

So two programmers came from Topeka, Kansas and over a six week period of time, taught Delores Garcia and myself everything there was to know about how to totally run the entire system, and probably more than we even needed to know, because I too knew how to program the two separate computer systems that the Santa Fe used.

Some of the Managers of some of the departments at this freight station objected to our being the only two persons who knew anything about how to run this entire system, but these Programmers asked these Managers, do you know how to program any of these computers and of course they all said no, so then these two programmers said, that Mr. Royal knows, so you will take all of your instructions from him. He will teach all of you Managers what you need to know about running each of your particular stations.

He knows all of the commands and if that is not enough, if he has to program any further instructions into these computers, he can do that also.

So don't give him any Static. So again I was making a lot of Enemies, and this time I was starting at the Managerial level. Delores asks, do you think you will ever get away from some of these managers, and I tell her, just watch and learn from me. So wherever I went after those times, Delores was close behind me. And I did make a lot of Enemies while doing all of that.

Or when I bid a position at what is called the Intermodal facility, which is in fact the yard where any Ocean going container that is placed on a chassis and Trailers are brought, where they are all loaded onto Flat cars and then are transported to other parts of this country.

And at this same facility these same kind of containers and trailers are brought to on flat cars from other cities, where they are unloaded and transported to wherever they are supposed to go, like to various Grocery stores or almost any kind of store. Where they are all unloaded.

And then there are all of these same kinds of vehicles which inside of some of them, there is loaded what is called Hazardous Materials, and since no one seemed to know all that much about any kind of Hazardous materials, I decided that I would become the Expert and the Authority regarding all of these hazardous materials. Including even Hazardous Waste.

There was an incident when I was coming to work early one morning, where I saw a light green cloud floating across this vast yard, and due to my very fast thinking, I had all of the buildings in the path of this cloud evacuated, and called the Fire Department so they could knock it down using Foam, thereby saving hundreds of other residents in the eventual path of this Chlorine cloud, which if you got just one whiff of any of this gas, would kill you instantly.

And another incident when all of the Clerks went on strike, but I remained on Santa Fe property, thereby never crossing any picket lines, and I wore many hats during that weeks time, from being the General Manager of that entire facility to being a Yardmaster, to even running a Diesel Engine switching cars within that yard, to being an operator of what is called a Straddle Buggy, which is the machine that is used to load trailers and or containers onto flat cars, and also unloading the same from other flat cars.

And when the Union that I belonged to took me and some others to Court, I handled all six cases and won them all, and when I counter sued the Union, I also won all of those cases too.

Enemies that would hound me for several years until I finally said, I want a transfer away from all of them. So I went to Bing Torpin once again and told him of my problems with some of the managers and he says, start packing, because in two weeks there will be a Moving Van driver knocking on your door, so be ready to leave, because you will be moving to Topeka, Kansas.

CLEMENT

PEG

MEANWHILE BACK WITH PHILADELPHIA
AND MY CHILDREN

Freedom at last from Peggy

In 1978, Moses met with Peg and Margaret and because of what Moses and I had previously discussed, it was decided to have an in ground pool installed. Moses had persons come to that now much smaller lot, because Moses had sold off everything except the lot where the house of 209 west Sierra Avenue was located, and Mosxes had a six-foot high redwood fence built all the way around that yard, with the exception of where the street was located.

Moses also had sidewalks built and Moses also had the original driveway removed and had a concrete one with inlaid bricks with my the Royal name blazoned across that driveway, and Moses also had a new sidewalk put in leading to the front door.

Moses also had built on the south side of this house off of the Living Room, a Solarium, which is like a covered patio, but it has a clear roof that is shaded with a plastic material, but because the Sun in California is much brighter than it is in other places, Moses also had installed inside of this Solarium, movable curtains that could be used to prevent the Sun from heating up this Solarium too much.

Moses also had built some planting beds out of brick and he also laid had down bricks along side the west side of the house, and also installing a drainage system that I had designed which was, by inventing a type of system, which would cause any water that was collected from the patio and the walkway along side the west side of that house, would shoot out into the street with such pressure, anyone would think that it was pressurized using some kind of forceful method, but instead by using various sized piping by going from a four inch pipe down to a two inch pipe and then back to a four inch pipe created the kind of pressure that this water was forced out twenty feet into the street.

Peg and I had still not gotten to where we felt comfortable to be with each other for any length of time. Margaret wanted to know where I was living, but I told her when the time was right, I would let her know

Peggy had proven to herself that she can survive without me in her life, and I firmly believe that it was because of her Mother living with her that has allowed that to happen.

Margaret says that there have been a few men who have asked her to go on dates, but she has refused every one of them and she is home every night from where she works, which she says is at Union Oil Company in downtown Los Angeles.

She is the Payroll Supervisor with them. As part of that position, she has to meet a Loomis Armored Truck out in front of the building every week, and she gets on board and it goes down to a specific Dock in Long Beach Harbor, where all of the Money that is inside of that Truck is transferred to a Motor launch, which takes her and these two guards and all of the money to a specific Tanker ship in the Harbor, and they have to climb on board this ship and the money is lifted on board of this ship, where all of this money is given to the Master or what is commonly called the Captain of this Tanker, who uses this money to pay whatever crew is on board of this ship, and sometimes they are treated to a meal on board this ship and then are transported back to the truck that is waiting back on dry land, and she usually has to do this at least once a week.

She even gets extra money for doing this. The driver brings her back to the Office building of Union Oil, until the next time. She especially loves that part of her job.

She drives her car to the Santa Ana Train Depot and because she has convinced the Santa Fe railroad that she is a relative of me, and I have affirmed that she is a relative to me, she then only has to pay a half fare rate for her train ticket to Los Angeles and back to Santa Ana. When she gets to Los Angeles, where she has another car that she keeps parked at Union Station, which she drives to where she works and parks it in their parking garage on the seventeenth floor, and then everything in reverse when it is time to return back home.

So she is functioning quite well without you, which I think is very good for her to do this, so in effect, since you have obviously found someone else to spend your life with, Margaret says she would like to meet my present wife.

Phia and I rarely talked about Peg. She knew I had done some improvement at that house on Sierra Avenue but I had also made improvements to Phia's house also. Probably even more.

My name had still never been put on the Deed to Phia's house and we never talked about getting it done. Martha's name has been put on that deed, and so had the Twins names, but never mine.

Margaret told me that she would support an Annulment from Peggy if I wanted to do that, so I did, and the Cardinal of the Los Angeles Arch Diocese asked why had I waited so long to do this, because when he read my report about Peggy, he told me that the Cardinal that was alive back when I filed in St Louis, died ten years back, and I told him that no one ever told me that had happened.

So I figured it was always my father in law who had prevented me from ever getting an annulment from his daughter.

I also mentioned Philadelphia Ing, about when her Husband had divorced her, and she had been excommunicated from the Catholic Church, which I thought was completely wrong of them, because she had not done anything wrong, but it was her husband's fault at that time. So that was reversed also.

So then I told this Cardinal what Philadelphia and I had done, so I could have a little bit of happiness in my life, and because you have now completely annulled my marriage to Peggy, I will now file for a Divorce from her also. Now what will that do to my marriage with Philadelphia? He says I will have to get remarried to her again, and he says he will do that as soon as my Divorce is final from Peggy.

So when I told Philadelphia all of this, she says having that Mexican Marriage is enough for her. That I am the father of her twins and any other children we may still have, and I am her only husband.

I then asked why can we not try to have a few more children, and then she told me that she is already pregnant, but with how many she is not certain, and she will wait for when her Gynecologist tells her of how many she will really have and she will have Martha tell her what they will be, because she now believes that she can tell her. But she will not have her do that for her yet for another three months.

Phia does tell me that she is glad that she is no longer considered excommunicated from the Catholic Church, because that makes a lot of difference in her life.

But she asks, won't you still be considered excommunicated from that church, because you still divorced your first wife before this last time. I say you are correct, but I think the Cardinal here in Los Angeles believes that I got a raw deal from the St Louis Archdiocese so he is reversing that order also. So we are both completely free of any excommunications from the Catholic Church. And that is why the Cardinal says he will personally marry us himself when we are ready to have it done.

I then tell Phia what Margaret has requested of me, and I really do not see any problem in doing what she wants me to do. But I will leave it totally up to you. I really think you would like her, because she is nothing like her daughter.

I know this, and that is if my former wife had died, she would have asked to come and live with the two of us instead.

Phia says it would be nice to have a Grandmother for her children and for any future children, so bring her to this house next Saturday afternoon, and maybe we can convince her to remain with us and go to church with all of us.

Phia says she will make sure that Dallas and Martha and all of their children are also included, because I am quite sure that Martha would like to see her Grandmother once again. I say I will call her while Peg is at work and suggest that she bring a change of good Sunday clothes also.

Phia says to just drive around for awhile, in case she may know some of the areas around where we live, and make sure you do not pass any signs that will tell her in what community we really live in.

I tell Phia that I will tell Margaret that we live in a place called Southern Hills, but since this is a new community, they have not gotten around to putting up a sign saying it is what it is.

I tell Phia that I know where to drive, coming to our house. But just in case Peg has decided to not go to work on this day, I do drive by the house at 209 W. Sierra Ave., and I notice that Pegs car is not in the driveway nor is it in the Garage, because the garage door is open when I drive by her house. I say it is her house, even though I do actually own it, but since she lives there, I feel it is fitting that I call it her house also.

The area where we live is a Gated community and my vehicle has a sticker stating this, as does Phia's and Martha's and Dallas's, but we could still be living in an area called Southern Hills. There are many Gated communities in southern California, and some of them have separate names and some do not. Ours in reality does not.

There is a Guard on duty 24 hours of every day of the year, and anyone who is trying to find someone, and wants to drive into this Gated community, cannot, because it is what it is, which is a Secured Gated community.

Once the main gate is closed and locked, the only way I can get to my house is to use my electronically secure pass card, which is a card about the size of any credit card, but no credit card will open the front gate. Many have tried, but have failed.

I just pass my special card in front of a special reader and if a constant sound happens, then the front gate will open just enough for me to drive inside, and once I am in side it immediately closes electronically behind my vehicle.

If there is another car immediately behind my car, lets say even touching my bumper, it will not get completely through the gate, because when this gate closes, it will push any vehicle into the steel girder which is on the opposite side of this driveway. Thereby trapping this vehicle, and if this vehicle tries to drive forward this gate will squeeze even harder against this vehicle.

A demonstration was put on for my benefit when we first moved in there, and it in reality almost cut a panel truck completely in half when this gate closed on it.

There are no signs that says what this community is called, so my story about it being called Southern Hills, will fly, because this community is located on some very interesting elevated land. Which could be called hills. It is in reality near some very close, very high mountains.

I then go to a store that is out of the neighborhood that Peg lives in and using a telephone that I can drive up to in my car, I then call Pegs phone number. Margaret answers the phone on the second ring. I ask is Peg at home and she says she is not, but is at work.

I say this is Clement Royal, your EX Son in law. I ask would you like to come to my house on Saturday afternoon, and bring your Sunday best clothes. She says yes she would. I will give you an address, which is a Restaurant in a Strip mall.

Get out of the Cab and go inside and ask for me, bringing your suitcase or however you transport your clothes with you. She verifies the Restaurant address and then the call ends. Today is Thursday.

I go home in a round about way. This is kind of a habit, since my days of when other persons had me followed who thought I was getting too close to finding out the truth regarding Chevrolet and Ford Motor companies, back when I was an Auditor for the Santa Fe Railroad. I no longer have that position, but it has led to better positions.

CLEMENT

PEG

MEANWHILE BACK AT THE SANTA FE RR

I am now in Special Collections, and I work for a man who is in charge of that Department. What I do is, when monies have been tried to be collected from a company, and this company has refused to pay that money to the Santa Fe. I take up this case, and I do a very special investigation regarding everything that is involved with it. When I present my Bill for all of the charges that are due from this company, and if they refuse once again to pay, I then take this company to court, in whatever jurisdiction that this company is located in, because I too am a Lawyer.

I am licensed to practice Law in several Western States, and I have yet to lose a case, so I am beginning to establish a Reputation wherein, most companies now just pay the Bills that I present to them. And so far I have collected more than ten million dollars.

Every check that is paid to the Santa Fe Railroad is also made out to the Santa Fe Railroad and me. But in doing this job, I have once again made many enemies, so I will not continue doing this very much longer.

I am just biding my time, waiting for just the right position to open up. Back about five years ago, the Administrative part of most of the Santa Fe Railroad, moved into what is called Santa Fe Plaza, which is a group of buildings that in reality represents a kind of Campus setting. Some buildings house one department and another building houses another department. And another building houses several departments.

In the main Complex, which is the Center building, it houses the Telephone Operators and the Teletype and Communications Departments.

And a Telephone Operators position and a Teletype position has opened up, which really sounds quite fascinating to me, so since my position in Special Collections has been Abolished, I now am in a position to Bump that position, which is what I do.

ALSO

The head telephone operator is retiring, and she thinks that I am not qualified enough to even handle her position, but I have three days to learn how to handle it. On the first day, she shows me all of what she does, and because of whom I am; I never make notes, but just rely on my excellent memory to do the job.

As part of that position, I also have to get on a Teletype machine for awhile and for another short period of time (about two hours) I have to copy messages from pieces of paper, that could be and usually are written on most any kind of paper, sometimes even hand written messages. On my second day, I am allowed to put on my headset or whatever gadgets I need to have on my head so I can do my job.

One of the first things that happens is that I am supposed to set up a Conference call between 12 different persons in six different cities, and the head Operator says it cannot be done.

So I told her to sit and be quiet and observe, and I will show you how it will be done. Within ten minutes, I have every person on the line that are supposed to be on that Conference Call line, and when I flip one lever, they are all tied together.

She listened in on this Conference Call, just to make sure that what I did was the real thing. This is the first time any Telephone Operator has set up this kind of call, and this is only my second Call on my second day on this position. So did I know how to handle this position? I would say that I do.

On the third day, I set up five different Conference calls, where 14 different persons from ten different cities were on this call all at the same time. There was no stopping me. This lady left the Santa Fe, knowing that all of these persons are in very capable hands. And when I would either use the Teletype or any other similar kind of machine, I was always ten to fifteen words ahead of the machine, because sometimes I had to wait as much as 20 to 30 seconds for the machine to catch up with my typing.

And I never made any mistakes. All of the time I did those jobs, I never made any mistakes. The Manager always watched me whenever I was on this Teletype machine. But like all of the other positions I have worked, this job did not last either.

Because from that position, I bumped into a position on second shift again, at the Intermodal facility, which is also called the Ramp. And I stayed there for the next ten years, working various jobs from Clerical to Management positions.

CLEMENT

PEG

DEALING WITH RAILBRIDGE COMPANIES

Because I am preparing lists of trains that will be traveling to different port cities, indirectly, because sometimes some of these trains also go to Chicago, Illinois and other large cities, where some of these cars are switched to other railroads whereupon they will then go on to port cities, there is a need for me to more fully understand the complexities of some of these Rail bridge Companies.

What is considered a Rail Bridge? A rail bridge is when a railroad company, like the Santa Fe railroad acts as a kind of bridge, but is considered what it really is, which is a Railroad, which is also considered a Rail Bridge concern.

Now a Container line, can be companies like K-LINE or HONG KONG ISLAND company or several other companies that ship Ocean Going Containers, which are loaded deep down into the Holds of these Container Ships, and these containers are also stacked ten containers high above the Decks of these ships. And these container carrying Ships are most often about nine hundred feet long.

So a lot of materials can be shipped on just one of these Container Ships. One of the things I wanted to do, was to go to one of these Container carrying companies, to see how they function.

So on several of my Days off, I went to the concern called K-LINE, which is near Long Beach Harbor. Now since no one from the Santa Fe railroad had ever done this before, I was treated like Royalty.

I was shown around several of their offices, and then I was taken on board one of their Container Ships, while it was being loaded with these Ocean going containers. And one of the things I wanted to see and do, was to get up inside of the device that is used to pick up these containers and load them deep down into the Holds of these ships. I had to climb up a ladder that is about eighty feet long, which took me to the entrance to where the Operator of this device was seated.

There is another seat where I can sit and observe how this operator manipulates this giant sized device that picks up containers from chassis's and transports them to where he deposits them on or into this ship. I asked how long did it take you to learn how to use this device and he tells me four months.

So I asked could I learn how to do what you do, and he says if you know how to use a Railroad Straddle Buggy, then learning how to use this device will be much easier. I tell him that I do know how to use and operate a Straddle Buggy. He says he will mention this to his Manager, and lets see what happens.

We do a lot of talking about what we two have done in both of our pasts regarding several places we both have worked. I tell this operator, that whatever I have learned to do, I became the Best there ever was, no matter what it was that I had to do to attain this level of competence.

He says he suspected I am that kind of a person, mostly because I seem to automatically know about a possible danger even before he knows it.

Anyone who can sense things of that magnitude must have some kind of inner sense or maybe even an extra sense in his makeup. And in this business, that is invaluable knowledge.

Anyway I don't tell anyone at the Santa Fe that I am spending my off days at this company. But when it comes time to get things done regarding that company, I know exactly whom to call and when.

And things always get done with smoothness when it comes to Land Bridge Shipments. After I have been on this position for about four months, I am told that every railroad container flat car will be loaded on the property of the K-line company yards.

Then several Railroad Engines will go and get these flat cars and will bring them to the Rail yard in Los Angeles. In the past this has never been done before. But because of my apparent expertise in these matters, It has been determined that this will become much more efficient and more speedily done, and it is.

Now how did I make this all happen. Well once I knew how a particular company operated and how their overall operation functioned, I went to Bing Torpin, who is the Vice President and General Manager of the entire Santa Fe Railroad and he instigated this procedure.

Like I have said before, if you want anything to get done in an expeditious way, begin at the top or as close to the top as you can and there will not be any problems.

CLEMENT

PEG

MEANWHILE BACK TO MY
OTHER DAUGHTER MARY BETH

This year is now early in 1979, which is a little over ten years since Mary Beth went into the Reform School Camp. Many things happened after she entered that place, and most of them for the betterment of her life.

Mary Beth did learn all about Responsibility, not only of herself, but of others as well. And after she spent five years in that facility, one of the Universities in St Louis, put forth some special instructors who went to this Reform School Camp and taught whomever wanted to learn particular subjects, which when they were ready to leave that facility would graduate with a Degree in their particular field, which Mary Beth graduated with a Bachelors of Science Degree in Sociology, with a minor in Biology.

And then she enrolled in St Louis University, where she studied to be a Nurse. And after that had happened, she went after her Credentials so she could become a Registered Nurse. And accomplished that level also.

Then she met a young man, and they fell in Love, and now they are married, and she is pregnant with her second child. Mary Beth and I are no longer enemies, but have become kind of good friends.

She has called me several times in the last two years, asking questions about her possibly going back to college and becoming a Doctor, and I have encouraged her to do just that.

She says it will be kind of difficult, because her Husband is in the Air Force and until he gets a more permanent Posting, she cannot go to any college where she can study for her Doctorate degree in Internal Medicine. But she is taking some Correspondence courses that will keep her mind active in that same field.

We don't talk about Peg or even how she felt about Peg in her past life. She says she is very happy that I found my Soul mate, and began having children, and someday she would like to meet Philadelphia. I have suggested that she come for a visit very soon, because Philadelphia is having all kinds of problems carrying the three babies that are inside of her, and I fear that something may happen to her when they are born.

Philadelphia is a very stubborn woman, and sometimes I have to over ride her decisions regarding her, and I fear I will have to make the same decision again when she has these three babies.

Remember Philadelphia will soon be 49 years old, and having three babies at this age will be very dangerous. Not only for her but for these babies as well. She wants to have all of them naturally, but I want all of them taken by Cesarean Surgery. I tell her that these three will be our final natural born children, and she agrees with me, but she still wants to have them in a natural way. So it is a never-ending battle as to what is the correct thing to do.

I do not want to lose Philadelphia, because without her in

my life, I would be completely lost. Martha says to just do what you want to do, no matter what Philadelphia wants to do.

Tell her doctor to just give her a shot and then take these babies out of her and when she wakes up, then after some time has gone by, she will forgive you, because she knows without you in her life, she would not have any kind of enjoyable life.

You two were made for each other, and if anything different happens with either of you, Martha says she will have to take over raising our children. It is hard to even think about my life without Philadelphia not being in it.

When I am alone, I cry for hours, just thinking what I might have to do, if something happens to her.

Getting her pregnant this last time, was a mistake, but Philadelphia wanted to have at least one more baby by me, but three of them, this is a bit much. But I will do what I have to do, whenever whatever happens, when these babies are being born.

So I no longer have to worry about Mary Beth any longer. She now has her own life to live. Martha says her and Mary Beth never have made peace with each other, mostly because she has been too busy giving birth to her own children to worry about whatever her Sister might be doing. Martha says she put Mary Beth out of her life, when she sent the final Do a Good job Package to her back six years ago.

She says her sister could have gotten more out of her life, than she did, but she thought doing everything in her own way would get her what she wants.

Martha says Mary Beth is still unhappy but there is nothing she can do about it, because now she has the responsibility of her own children, and now she will learn what it feels like to be really left out of a good family.

Of course Philadelphia and Mary Beth would never have gotten along, mostly because Mary Beth still thinks that I did the wrong thing against her. So forget about her, and lets get on with our lives.

CLEMENT

PEG

MONA AND HER WISH
TO HAVE ANOTHER BABY

My adopted sister Mona has been telling Philadelphia that she wants to have another baby, and she wants me to be the father of that baby. I tell Philadelphia that I have a friend of mine who is an Italian, who will be most happy to be the father of her baby. They may even fall in love and get married. But it will never be me. And that is final…

So I contacted my friend Tony Ferraloni, and put this idea to him and on the next weekend he is knocking on my door. Tony is rather dark skinned, and he could even pass for an Indian, any Indian. He has the type of nose that is prominent with most American Indians, and the same in the shape of his face and jaw.

The only thing that is different, is he has a mustache that really makes him very good looking. Mona agrees to date him, and after several weeks go by, she says she has even slept with him and she thinks she is now pregnant with his baby.

I say I think you had better tell him, just in case he may want to marry you. Mona says he has asked her to marry him several times, but she is not certain about going that far. I ask what more can you want from any man. You will have a good father for your child, of that I am quite sure

Martha and Dallas will hire him to be their Chauffeur and all around Handyman, because he knows how to do so many things around any house, and He can even build the two of you your own house on the same property that we all live on.

So get on the stick and get married, so he can build you two that house, and you can get on with the rest of your lives. So that is what happens.

Mona and Tony get married, and he is beginning to build their house on a plot of ground that is part of Philadelphia's property. In the meantime, it is now the second week of July of 1979, and Philadelphia was due to have her babies a week back.

I suggested to her Gynecologist that she should take them by C-section. Because the longer she waits the more dangerous all of this becomes.

Then on the first day of the third week of July, Philadelphia begins having labor pains, and they are real fierce this time. I say C-section Surgery can remove a lot of fear in Phia's eyes so I tell her GYN to just take these babies now, and give Phia a shot to put her under enough so these babies can be born.

Phia says she wants to have at least one of them first in a natural way, and then you can take the other two by C-section. But fifteen hours go by before that first child is born, and during that time. Phia has lost a lot of her energy.

I insist that C-section takes the other two, and I even get Phia to sign the order to have it done that way.

Ten minutes later I am the father of Triplets, but Philadelphia is very weak, and I am very worried about her surviving even through the next twelve hours.

She does survive, but she is very weak and she will not be coming home any time soon, because she cannot even hold up her head long enough to take a drink of water from a glass. So she is fitted with every kind of device that is necessary to keep her alive. And I just sit and hold her hand and talk endlessly about these three babies, and how they look.

The first child born is a boy, who is 23 inches long and weighs 8 pounds 7 ounces. The two that were taken by C-section are girls, and they each weigh 5 pounds 5 ounces and are 15 inches long.

It seems as though the boy took most of her energy, even when he was growing inside of her womb. We have not decided on any names yet. I have some in mind but I don't know what Phia may think yet.

One thing when I go see my children, one of the girls looks at me like she is reading my thoughts, and I do feel some kind of feeling in my brain when she holds one of my fingers. I think she will have the same gift that I have been given.

Even though Philadelphia is being given all kinds of nutrients that are supposed to make her get better, it is like they are all for naught, because she seems to be getting weaker and weaker as the days continue to go by.

So I figured that since she is still conscious I had better discuss the names of our triplets that I want to call each of them.

Philadelphia has always been partial to the Book of Mathew in the Bible, so that is what I want to name him. Then in memory of her Own Mother, I want to call the first of the two girls born after her Mother. But Phia says no. Mathew is fine for the boy, but Phia says she wants the girls named Molly and Mimi.

She says they brought both of these girls to see her this morning and they appear to be identical, and these are the names they are to be called. So we now have Mathew Edward, Molly Ann and Mimi Wright. And the twins are called Philip Arthur and Martha Toosom, and before that I had Mary Beth and Martha, so we now have seven children altogether. Her blood Mother had given my first Martha a middle name of Philippa. Philadelphia says she will not see her 8th and 9th children, because she says she will die soon. I say please do not talk that way. If you die, I do not know whether I can live without you not being in my life.

Philadelphia says go back to Peg, not right away, but maybe after about five years. You don't have to Love her, but just like her, just a little. Get married to her for the third time, because they say the third time is the charm in anyone's life. By that time the twins will be 15 years old and the triplets will be five years old, and if Peg will not take our children into her life, then let Mona and Tony raise them. They will still always be our children, and no one can ever take them away from you and I. And you can go see them and interact with them whenever you want to.

Philadelphia says that Margaret would, if she was much younger help you raise our children, but she is now too old to do that, so if you don't want to be alone, without another woman in your life, then go back to Peg. Because having any woman in your life at your age, is better than having no woman. At least you will have a warm body to sleep next to, even though she says she knows I will never have sex with Peggy ever again. She may need you now also, because since she no longer has any other men in her life, it is better to have a husband that she knows, rather than have a husband that only wants her body.

Maybe you can even cure her of whatever she has had for all of these many years. You don't have to forgive her for what she has done to you; all you have to do is be pleasant to her.

Her mother says that Peg now misses you, because she no longer has any other men in her life, because she cannot wear her false teeth and no other man will even look at her. But you could handle that problem.

I say I will think on your idea, but not now, not until I really have to. Phia says bring Margaret to her house as often as you can, because she really wants to enjoy what she considers to be her grandchildren, which are our children. She already has Martha and Mary Beth, and they have provided her with Great Grand children, but there is nothing like Grandchildren. Phia says she will not be here when our children begin having their own children. Phia says she is getting kind of tired, so she will now go to sleep for a while.

When I wake up you will not be here and in reality she says she will be with GOD. So Phia went to sleep, and slipped into a Coma, and she remained in that Coma for two months, and then she died on September 18th 1979. Me and all of my children, including Mary Beth were at her bedside when she did die.

Whether she really knew it, is anyone's guess. Philadelphia and Mary Beth never got a chance to talk to each other, which was probably better for both of them. I was holding her hand when she stopped breathing.

It took me by surprise, so that it probably took me a few seconds to even realize that she was no longer breathing. We had spent a little over Eleven years together. We never did get married in the Catholic Church, because it never seemed to be that important, even though we considered ourselves to be a married couple.

I did Divorce Peggy for a third time, but Phia never seemed all that eager to get married in the Catholic Church. But all of my children go to a Catholic School for some of their education. The rest of their education they get from me.

Philadelphia left the House to Martha and Dallas. And Martha gave Mona and Tony the lot where Tony built their house on. And Mona and Tony still work for Martha. Even to the date when this book was written.

I knew there would be hundreds of persons who would attend Philadelphia's Funeral so I delayed in having her buried for one week. Philadelphia died on a Wednesday, so I had her Funeral a week later on September 25, 1979.

Over 600 persons came to her funeral, and many persons gave Testimonials as to the kind of woman and Teacher she really was.

I kept all of those records of her funeral, but when Peg and I were moving from the house on Sierra Avenue, and the vehicle that I was driving was struck by an 18 wheeler Truck, and I was hospitalized for 49 days, I discovered that all of the Records that I was carrying in my vehicle, all were burned up when the Gas tank exploded and consumed everything that was in that vehicle.

Philadelphia is buried in our family burial plot in Irvine, California, and there is a place for me to also be buried there, but I am not certain yet where I will be buried.

That plot of ground that I purchased back in 1969, I made sure there would be enough places for twenty persons to be buried on that family plot, because it is not only in the Royal name, but it is in four other names, of which I will not mention here. The Headstone has all of our names on it.

I did eventually go back to Peggy and we got married for the third time. I waited for three years before this happened, because living without Philadelphia was like living without two arms, because it even got difficult to even do my job at the Santa Fe railroad sometimes.

It was like I was just going through the motions of getting up every morning and coming home every night, and trying to keep my mind clear enough so I could raise all of my children like they should be raised.

It took awhile, but Mourning someone who has become so very important in ones life, just takes time and understanding from the other persons around you. I had the moral and psychological support of my family, and eventually my mind began to get clearer and clearer, and I even had the same kind of support from some of my friends at the Santa Fe railroad, and also all of the Veterinarians and other persons at my Veterinary Hospital. With that kind of support, I knew I would be able to continue to survive, just like I have always done.

After I had gone back to be with Peggy, I adopted a Lakota Sioux Indian boy, called John Running Bear, who became my 8th child and then in the early part of 1989, I adopted another daughter who is called Eunice, who became my 9th child. John was 16 and Eunice was almost 18 when I adopted her.

When I got hit by that eighteen wheeler and ended up in the

UC Irvine Hospital for 49 days, and I had six separate operations on various parts of my body, and in doing this, I had been given six Blood Transfusions, and because more than half of the blood in my body had been replaced, it actually changed my chemical makeup of my body, because I no longer have a Y Chromosome that would allow me to reproduce myself, thereby causing me to become a Double XX Male person.

Which is a very rare condition. What this would do to my overall ability to fight off various diseases is anyone's guess. I asked another Doctor friend of mine about this, and he says I will most likely be able to keep most Virus's at bay, because with me being a Male person, with the Chemical makeup of a women, will make me a lot stronger when it comes to any kind of diseases and virus's.

In 1982 when Orange County and most of the surrounding counties got 23 inches of Rain, and the Los Angeles River was almost over it's banks and the Santa Ana River did go over it's banks, which flooded all of the area east of where that River was actually located, which was two miles west of where 209 W. Sierra Avenue is located.

But because of when I built that house, because where I planned to build that house, I instead had two hundred loads of Black Dirt, with each load consisting of twenty Cubic yards of this dirt, and I raised up the ground where this house was to be built by fifteen feet, but after it had all been packed down, this area where this house was built, was ten feet higher than any other house around it. So when the neighbor hood became flooded, this house was above all of the others around it, but because Water will gravitate upwards in any kind of situation, and especially when it is raining outside of this house, there was still two inches of water inside of this house, which came up through the ground and not through any broken windows.

When I filed a claim, the Insurance adjuster told me that I should have broken a window, where all of this water could have come in that way. But in the end, I had all of this damage written off of my Taxes as collateral uncollected damage when all of this happened.

I had gone back to Peg and we had gotten married in a Civil Ceremony by a Catholic Priest, but not in the Catholic Church, because just in case anything happened with Peg again regarding any other man, I did not want to go through another annulment with the Church.

All of my children remained with Martha and Dallas, but were all taken care of by Mona and Tony Ferraloni. All of my children all lived in the house that Philadelphia had purchased, where we had lived for almost nine years together, while we were married.

Peg said if I wanted to adopt a couple of more children, she would try to be a good mother for them, but don't expect her to Love them. I thought to myself, she is still the Cold person she has always been towards me and even her own Mother.

Actually Margaret and I would often go shopping together and everyone thought we could possibly even be married to each other.

It could have been that way, because if she would have approved of the two of us getting married, I would have married her instead of marrying Peg. Then Peg would have become my Daughter.

Stranger things could have happened. I broached this to Margaret one day, and she told me that she had entertained this very idea, before I had decided to come back to Peggy.

I told her I wish you had mentioned it to me, because I think it would have been a good idea. Actually I Loved Margaret. And she loved me. We never talked about that subject again, but I know we both thought about it many times after that time.

I never did Love Peg again. I am not even sure whether I even liked her, but I just tolerated her.

We slept in the same King sized bed together, but that is as close as I ever got to her for many years. In 1986 Peggy had a Heart Attack, and she was in the UC Irvine Hospital for eleven days, and recuperated at home for two months, before she decided she would go back to work for Union Oil company. Where she remained for only a month, when she was forced out of her job, because they decided they would computerize everything.

So she retired that year and came home and went back to creating more of her Crossword Puzzles to keep her mind active, at my encouragement, and made an additional quarter of a million dollars, which she spent mostly on improving things in that house, just because she did not want me to have any of that money.

Any previous contracts we had had together became null and void when I divorced her some years before that time. So she could totally handle all of her own money now.

I had no say in whatever she decided to do with that house. I told her she would never get any of whatever she spent on that house back, and she says she did not care whether she ever got any of it back. She just did not want me to ever get my hands of any of her money.

In the meantime, I was making all kinds of money with more of my inventions, but I personally did not receive any of this money, because all of it went to fund Several Foundations that were selected by Moses Lighthouse and his law firm.

Around that time, I decided that having all kinds of money in the bank would only create all kinds of problems when I would eventually died. So I had Moses set up Trust funds for all of my children and grand children, which would be given to each of them when they reached the age of 25 years of age.

Each child will get 100 hundred thousand dollars when they reached that magic age. I had Moses remove my name from any funds dealing with these Trust funds. Just in case Peg or any of her relatives or any other woman that I might marry, would try to get their hands on any of it. Knowing how most anyone thinks about a lot of money. Some of my children had already reached that magic age, so whatever monies were due them they had already gotten.

No other money would be forth coming to them from now on. If they wanted any additional money, they would have to ask Moses and his Law Firm, and not me. You see having all kinds of money is of no importance. It's what you do with all of your money, is of more importance.

I had invested a lot of my money in various businesses in various parts of California, but I did not know where all of these finances were located, because I let Moses and his Law Firm handle all of this. If anyone was getting rich from all of the monies I was bringing in, then I was happy for them all.

Moses would make sure no persons would steal from me. I trust him totally. I made him a Multi-millionaire, several times over, so he had no reason to steal from me. When I became fully disgusted with how things were happening at the Santa Fe Railroad, and I had actually heard that the Santa Fe was going to Contract out all of their services to another firm, thereby allowing themselves to get completely out of the Los Angeles Area, I went to my friend Quincy (Bing) Torpin and he secured a transfer for me to Topeka, Kansas. And in two weeks Peg and I and one Cat (Heycat) headed for that part of these United States.

We arrived on December 30th 1990, and that evening Peg had another Heart Attack, and she ended up in the St Francis Hospital. I in the meantime had to find us all a place to live. I asked some of my friends who had come to Topeka before me, and they suggested that I check a place called Montara, which is a community about five miles south of the city of Topeka.

When I got there, they showed me five different houses, and I picked the one that I thought that Peg would like. My Moving Van was three days behind me and Peg was due to get out of the Hospital two days after they arrived.

When I brought Peg home, and got her settled on the Couch in the Living room, she liked the house, because she says she likes all of the many trees that go completely around this yard and house.

There is a very large window on the south side of this living room, but since there are several trees south of that house, the hot sun was shaded by those tall trees.

I told her that I had planned to build a planter bed next

spring so I could plant all of the flowers she liked to see outside of that window.

It would be a planter that would be made out of wood, so when and if we eventually moved, unless I purchased this place, I could take it with me after I removed all of the dirt.

In the meantime I had two weeks to get everything unpacked and put where it was supposed to go, before I had to report to work. A week later our Television that we had had for 20 years decided to quit working, so I went out and purchased another brand new one. Which was delivered the next day.

In the meantime, Peg called her sister Mary, who decided to come for a visit, and because Margaret (their Mother) had broken both of her Legs at the knee, she was in a wheel chair, and I did not have a place for them to even sleep yet. I had rented a three-bedroom house, but I had not set up the bed in the guest room yet. It was mostly filled full of boxes filled with most of my books. So I had to remove these boxes of books to another bedroom, which I had intended to use for my office.

Then Mary called her oldest son Willie, who came with a two ton truck, and he began to load all of the furniture that Margaret had given to me, when I remarried Peg again for the third time.

I had been called to come to my new office, because there was a meeting of all of the Heads of all of the other departments, of which I was a Manager of one of them, and Mary took advantage of that day, and she had Willie move every stick of furniture that Margaret had given to me in California into this truck and he had already left by the time I had gotten back home that day.

Including all of the Dishes we had gotten for one of our Wedding Anniversaries. I ordered Mary out of that house, and told her to never come back, no matter what might happen to anyone in this house. I would hire other persons to take care of my wife if that became necessary.

Then in 1992 I had to have a quadruple Heart bypass operation, and I hired a neighbor to take care of my wife, but Peg called her Sister again, and she came to that house again, bringing her son Willie and his two ton truck also, and once again they loaded up everything that they figured they could legally take with them, and left Peg to take care of herself.

Mary actually stayed for ten days, but the damage had been done anyway. Peg even began to hate her sister after that episode.

I hated Mary after that, because she could have actually killed her sister by leaving her completely alone. I came home in a Cab just minutes after they had left, because I still could not drive my own car, and I called the Registered Nurses Association, who dispatched two registered nurses to my house. Because I was too weak to take care of her.

But because of my personal determination and Will power, these nurses only stayed two days and then I sent them home, because I told them that I would take care of my own wife by myself.

They objected but I told them I am paying your wages, so get out and go back to wherever you came from.

I had spent 12 days in the Hospital. Two days after I

dispensed with the Nurses, I was walking through the neighborhood in eleven inch of snow that had happened on the very day I sent those nurses home.

Two days after that time, I got into my vehicle, which is a 1973 Cadillac, and I pushed the Mailman up several hills with my vehicle, because he did not have any chains on any of his tires, and my vehicle did not have any chains on either, but because of how heavy my Cadillac is, it could travel anywhere.

From the time I left the office and the time I returned back to my office, 51 days had gone by. Most persons are gone no less than six months when they have the same kind of operation that I had done to me.

I was much respected at this office, and as time went by, I began to hear of other things that were going to happen within two years.

But I continued to do what I am most qualified to do, which is take care of all of the customers who shipped all kinds of Hazardous Materials, including every branch of the Military. Because of the Santa Fe having been fined severely on many occasions regarding Hazardous Materials, no one shipped anything that was very hazardous until they talked to me first.

Because I told them how to package everything and where in a trailer or boxcar to place it, and with what other kinds of non-hazardous materials they could ship this hazardous material with, and pretty soon not even competitive railroads were getting any fines levied against them.

Because I helped everyone, including other railroads. Once again I became the Best there ever was. During those times, a lot of the persons I had once worked for, came to me and asked me if I knew of any positions where they could work at, and I asked each of them, what had you ever done for me, and when they could not come up with any kind of answer, I told them that is my answer to your question.

I heard later that they all were either eventually asked to quit or they would be fired from the Santa Fe railroad. All of them retired.

Then there was some talk about offering some of the Managers some buyout money, and since I knew that my position would soon be completely computerized, I inquired as to whether my position is one of the Managers who will be offered this buyout, and they told me that they will pay me two years of my present salary. But I have to take all of it in this year, which is 1994. Since I was getting 75 thousand dollars a year, that would mean I would have to pay taxes on 150 thousand dollars in 1994.

So I offered to take only 112,500 dollars, and they will pay me over six months time. They counter offered to only give me 75 thousand and they would pay me over a 12 month period of time, effective December of 1994, but that I would also get paid for three additional months as a kind severance pay, if I retired in September of 1994.

In effect my Retirement would not take effect until December of 1995. Because of being paid every month in 1995, even though I was not physically working in any office. I took the latter offer, because it would mean that I would be getting my full salary, for the next fifteen months.

And because I would still be paying into my Railroad Retirement program, I would not be able to put in for my retirement money until three months after my official retirement date. Which would mean that I could apply for Railroad retirement in December of 1995, but my first check would not be deposited to my bank account until April 3rd 1996.

So since I would not be working anyplace, I would not have the expenses of paying for parking and gasoline costs and food costs while working. I could probably save more than a thousand dollars just remaining at home.

Of course I will still have to pay Federal taxes and State taxes to whatever state I lived in, but in the end I could save a lot of money.

I would have to have enough money to tide us over until April 3 of 1996, but that is just a matter of saving that money in a special account. So the next thing was to decide where we would remain after we retired.

Peg wanted to move to Missouri, and I told her you still want to be close to your Sister who has stolen everything we have ever gotten when we were married, even when we were not married, because she took presents from my house that I had received when I was married to Philadelphia.

Peg says if I mention her name again, she will kick me out of this house. I tell her you are in no position to bargain with me, because I can put you in a Nursing home and completely forget that I even knew you, so don't push me, because that is exactly what I will do. You will either do it my way or no way.

As information, dear wife, when I was married to that other woman, she gave me five children and eleven very happy years of the best years of my life.

All you have done is given me tons of Grief, with nothing to show for any of it. If I had it to do over again, I would have Divorced you just that one time and left you back in the St Louis area, where you could have killed yourself, and put yourself out of your misery and we could have all gotten on with our lives without you.

You never ever loved me, and you still don't love me. Of course I don't love you either. I only came back to you, because my other wife suggested that I do this, so you would have someone to blame for everything that you have done all by yourself.

But if I had it to do over again, I would have quit the Santa Fe, because I could have made many more millions in the Veterinary Business.

I'll tell you what we will do. I will make four straws of the same length, and one straw of a short length. Whomever gets the short straw gets to choose where we move to. But you have to pick it on the first try. Five straws, and all you have to do is pick the short one. I will let you pick first. I guess my luck had run out, because on her first pick, Peg picked the short straw, so I purchased a house before I had even seen it, in Ferguson, Missouri, and we moved on November 29th of 1994.

Our moving van would arrive two hours after we arrived, so there was no stopping anywhere except to get something to eat. We arrived at 1:00 PM, and the moving van arrived at 4:00 PM. By the time I thought they had everything unloaded, it was close to 9:00 PM on November 29th 1994.

This was a two-bedroom house and it was full of boxes everywhere. I moved boxes into every room except the living room, which is where the Couch was located, which was where

Peg would sleep that night. I had to sleep on the floor, because I had not put the bed together yet. And I had three cats to contend with, but they just went down in the basement and got into all kinds of trouble.

The next day I had to extract one of them out of between the ceiling and the floor above and keep them in another bedroom until I could fix everything in that basement so none of them could get into any kind of trouble.

There were inner walls that had not been finished, and the cats could get between these walls and the actual basement wall. This basement was supposed to have been completely closed in with some kind of boards, but it was only partially done, and what was left was in terrible shape.

And the porch was supposed to have been completely covered with screen, but that too was only partially done. So after having to go to a hardware store to get whatever supplies I needed to get everything done, it was almost the next day before I could even let the cats out of the small bedroom where I had put them. And I still had not gotten the porch completely screened in. I called the person who I had purchased the house from and he says he cannot come for another week.

I also told him that all of your tools that you left in this basement, if you do not come and get them, the garbage man would haul them away in the morning.

An hour later he was there, removing all of his tools and other junk. I told the original owner that you will meet us at such and such a bank in two days where all of the documents will be signed and all of the monies will be transferred to you and the bank at that time.

The bank that I have gone with tells me that you have a lien of 15 thousand dollars on this house, that you did not mention initially in the original deal, so that amount will be deducted from what I will actually pay you. And if you do not take the deal as I have just stated it, then I will have the movers come back and load up everything into their truck and I will leave this state, never to return ever again. What you do with my wife is totally up her sister. Because she is the one who made this deal with you, and Peg, but not with me.

Now since I am the one who will be paying all of the bills for this move, then whatever you do is whatever you do, but it will not include me. Take it or leave it.

Initially the deal that Peg had made with her sister Mary was that I would pay her Son in law 63 thousand dollars for this house, and it was stated at that time that the porch was completely enclosed with Screen and the basement was completely enclosed with inner walls, which also included an extra bathroom in that basement. When we got to this house, none of that had been done, only part of it.

Apparently he had floated a loan, which he used to buy all kinds of materials, which he supposedly had used to do all of what was mentioned to Peg.

Now since I would only pay him 48 thousand dollars, he would have to pay off his initial loan using that money, and whatever else he would most probably still own on this house.

He would also have to clear off this Lien before he could even pay off the initial loan on this house, so he was not going to come out ahead on any part of this deal.

Because my bank would not accept an IOU from this

original owner for any amount of money unless he paid off that lien first.

Probably he would borrow it from his Mother in law, so he could clear off everything regarding this house. But I did not care how he did it, just as long as he did it. Because if that did not happen, then I had according to the agreement that I signed with Peg's sister, if this deal fell through, I had two weeks to get out of this house.

This was a contract that I wrote myself, and I had it signed and notarized by my bank in Ferguson, Missouri. Earnest Fink (the original owner) says he may want a separate deal regarding the fifteen thousand, and I told him if you want a separate deal, I will write that contract, but only Peg will sign it, because I will not.

He says fine. Her signature is good enough for him. I tell him, be sure you read the entire contract before you sign it. He says go ahead and write it and he will sign it.

CLEMENT

So I wrote that contract, which goes like this.

This contract is for fifteen thousand dollars, which Margaret Royal will pay to ~~Earnest~~ Ford over a period of 120 months. There will not be any interest charged in addition to this fifteen thousand dollars. This is a simple Contract. If Margaret Royal dies before this Contract ends, then this Contract will be considered Null and Void. And no other monies will be due to ~~Earnest~~ Ford.

Two persons not related to by natural blood nor adopted by either party will witness this Contract nor have any monetary interest in either party.

And an uninterested party of both parties of this Contract will notarize it...

Signed by Margaret Royal...

Signed by Mathew Ford...

Witnessed by...

Current address..

Witnessed by...

Current address..

Notarized by ....

My Notary expires on ....

I wrote the Contract, and all parties signed it when the other house documents were signed at my bank. The witnesses were persons who were persons just working at that bank and The Notary who Notarized all of the other documents, also Notarized this Contract, and she said that how this contract was written, it could never be broken.

Whoever wrote it must be a Lawyer. I just smiled at her, but I did not say anything further. This was the First day of January of 1995, and Margaret Royal died on May 27th 1996, almost 18 months later.

Peg had gone into a Coma on May 25th 1996. Before that happened she wrote a check for one hundred twenty five dollars and she wrote a notation on that check, which said, " this will be my final check in the contract between Mathew Ford and myself. " After her Funeral was over and she was in the ground, Mathew Fords wife, Who is my Niece by marriage came to me and pleaded with me to give her another hundred twenty five dollars, but I told her that contract is Null and Void, so go away and don't come back.

But she kept hounding me for months after that, but I kept telling her that she would not get any money from me.

She says she will take me to court, and I asked her with

what. And I closed the door in her face. She called and threatened me several times, and finally I had to get an unlisted telephone number installed in my house.

Then other members of that same family kept coming by and tried to steal various items from my yard.

I called the Police several times, but after awhile they too never came. So all I could do was totally ignore all of them. I never did go see any of them at any time or place. I wanted to get out of Missouri, but until I could, I had to sell this house, and until that happened, that would not be possible.

I could have just given up and moved and left that house for whomever wanted to come and live in it, but I wanted to get at least most of what I had put into it, because I had made many changes to it, for the betterment of it.

After fifteen months had gone by, I called someone who I had known back in Kansas, and this call sparked a Romance. I did sell that house and I moved back to, Kansas. But that is another story, which will be written in a different book.

I remained with Peggy until she died on May 27th 1996. And she is buried in the family plot of ground at Calvary Cemetery in St Louis.

There is also another grave plot where I can be buried in the middle of Wisconsin on a high hill overlooking a vast valley. On a clear day you can see Madison, Wisconsin, which is 40 miles away, south of where this Cemetery is located.

I purchased my Veterinary Hospital in 1977, and in 1980 I expanded it ten times larger and made it into a Teaching Hospital. There is 4 acres under roof, not counting all of the outside cages that are under overhangs on three sides of this vast Hospital. There is a total of 300 acres surrounding this Hospital, which consists of a Runway where Airplanes can land, and this complex also has it's own Control Tower, which is manned 24 hours of every day by no less than two persons in that Control Tower, mostly because sometimes when a Pilot is seeking to find the John Wayne Airport, which is sometimes completely fogged in, where my Airport is located, which is up against some mountains, it is usually clear, so the runway can actually handle a small Jet Airplane, like a 727 or a 737 or any fixed wing airplanes.

In an emergency it could actually handle a 747 or an L-1011 Jet Liner. This Veterinary Hospital and grounds are located north of Saddle Back Mountain.

There are places where most of the Veterinarians who own their own airplanes can park them in a specified place and there are also places where Helicopters can be parked, and also places where other Mobile Hospital Vans can be parked.

When you drive by this vast complex, it appears to be some kind of Large Prison, because the fence that goes completely around this complex is 30 feet high, with the last three feet having 120 volts of electricity running through it, which is also Razor sharp wire that looks like some Barbed wire out of some outer Space movie.

Once the gates are closed and locked at Midnight every night, the only way onto this property is from the air. Or with a special card pass you can enter through these gates. Of course I no longer own nor operate this vast complex any longer, because of the fact that there are 20 veterinarians working at this complex, and they now totally own and operate it.

It is located in a place called Southern Hills, California. Also as part of this vast complex, I set aside twenty acres, which is a Pet Cemetery, and I contracted with a Company who makes Special Coffins for all kinds of small creatures, so persons who want to bury their pets in my cemetery, can do so, and have spiritual words read over their graves. It has become very popular. And many other Pet Cemeteries have sprung up in many places in California especially.

CLEMENT

PEG

There is so much more to all of my life, and there were many incidences that I did not write about, not that there was anything wrong with those parts of my life, but I think to write about every day of anyone's life, would make this book to be much too large.

I decided to write about a few of the things that happened between Peggy and myself during the Seventeen additional years we did spend together, after Philadelphia had died, I remained with Peg, but they were not all that happy either, because Peggy was just as bitter as she had always been, but just in different ways.

Peggy and I had been married to each other for a total of 30 years 8 months and 27 days, which in any persons life is a fairly long time, but most of them were not happy years.

Once I had cured her of all of her ills from most of her previous life, we had about five years of mostly happy times. By that time she was mostly bed ridden or was confined to whatever house we were living in. I took her outside every so often, so she could enjoy all of the flower gardens I had planted for her.

It is not easy to watch any person die of diseases that cannot be operated on, and watching Peggy die for the final two years of her life was the most difficult thing I have ever witnessed.

Watching someone die is not for the faint hearted, because in the final six months she was alive, I had to carry her wherever she wanted to go, and that included taking her to the bathroom and cleaning her up after she did what Mother Nature required her to do.

And when she took a bath, I had to carry her to the bathtub and carefully lower her down into the water. Then I had to wash her, everywhere, because she was too weak to do it herself.

Finally when she was three months from the day she died, she refused to let me carry her into the bathroom any longer, so whatever needed to be done, I had to do it while she was laying in her bed.

Which meant that if she accidentally messed up the bed in any way, I had to move her to the other side of that bed while I changed her side of the bed. We had a bed that had two separate sections to it, but once both sections were put together, it became a King sized bed.

But when Peg was totally bedridden for those final three months, it made cleaning up her side of the bed a lot easier for me. I never complained while this was going on, and I am still not complaining.

It was the least I could do for her. Writing about our times during all of the sessions that we had, will most likely become a totally separate book some time in the future.

But it will be very difficult to even write about it, because we both cried a lot during those times. I felt so very sorry for her, and I knew she did not want my sympathy and I tried not to give it to her in the way I just stated it.

But it is not easy to fix a very serious problem that had

been created many years before I even knew her. Writing about our life before I knew about all of her problems was a very difficult thing for me to do, and I tried not to let it spill over in how I wrote that part of my and her life.

In the final three months of her life, because the pain in her stomach became so terrible, I had her on a Morphine Pump, which pumped specific amounts of morphine into the area where she had her worst pain.

If that Pump had not been there, she would have most likely gone into a Coma much sooner, because the Pain was too terrible for her to stand, and she had a very high pain level.

I had Last rites read over her on May 24th 1996 by the local priest of the church we belonged to. She ate solid food up until the final three days of her life. She went into a Coma on Saturday Morning May 25th 1996, and she never woke up, because she died on Monday morning on May 27th 1996 at 6:50 AM.

She weighed only 80 pounds when she died. She once weighed close to 180 pounds when we still lived in California. But most everyone who came to her wake said she looked pretty good, for someone who had died of Cancer of the Stomach.

It's amazing what can be done to any human body to make them look almost like they are just asleep in their Casket.

THE END

E P I L O G U E

Bringing this book to a close has been very difficult, but it must be done. I had a life beyond this book, but that is still another Novel.

Not knowing how to handle various situations during my life, but learning as I did has made me to be a much wiser person. Most of the situations that I encountered during my life thus far have made me to be not only a wiser man but a stronger man also. What is interesting is that there are no books written about how to handle whatever happens in anyone's life. Many have tried, but until you live a certain kind of life, no one can really know how to handle each situation as it comes along.

Writing books has become my last love in life. It allows me to use my brain and imagination like I have never used it before. Creating different scenarios when writing these books is very stimulating, which will cause me to live a much longer life. And maybe make someone else's life more interesting. So enjoy all of the books I have written and all of the books I still will write.

Dr. Philip Corbin

ABOUT THE AUTHOR

P. Arden Corbin was born on the family farm in northeastern South Dakota. When he was in High School, he was the Editor of the School Paper. He pursued higher education throughout his working years, earning Degrees in various fields. Mr. Corbin was instrumental in establishing a Veterinary Hospital in Southern California in 1977.

Mr. Corbin's mystery novels, *The Puzzle* and *Somewhere County, Kansas* as well as his science fiction novel, *The Lake That Wasn't There*, are available in both eBook and print.

Future writing efforts will include a novel called "Pioneer Breed" and "Unanswered Letters" just to name a couple. Mr. Corbin is also writing some stories about all of the Creatures he has encountered during his lifetime, only from their Perspective. Which is the Central theme in his stories in his books called "TRAILS". He has plans to write at least 6 books in this Series.

After Mr. Corbin retired in 1995, he also taught school in a particular school District as a Substitute teacher, wherever he was needed. He was also a Special Olympics Coach for a Topeka, Kansas Chapter for three years, and a Para-professional teacher for two years. Teaching Handicapped children how to survive and function in life today.

He makes his home in Topeka, Kansas and is a member of the Kansas Authors Club – District one.